BOHEMIAN
LOS ANGELES

The publisher gratefully acknowledges the generous contribution to this book provided by the Lisa See Fund in Southern California History.

BOHEMIAN
LOS ANGELES
and the Making of Modern Politics

Daniel Hurewitz

To Piper —

Thanks so much for your
support!

UNIVERSITY OF CALIFORNIA PRESS

BERKELEY   LOS ANGELES   LONDON

University of California Press, one of the most distinguished university presses in the United States, enriches lives around the world by advancing scholarship in the humanities, social sciences, and natural sciences. Its activities are supported by the UC Press Foundation and by philanthropic contributions from individuals and institutions. For more information, visit www.ucpress.edu.

Chapter 3 was published as "Goody-Goodies, Sissies, and Long-Hairs: The Dangerous Figures in 1930s Los Angeles," *Journal of Urban History* 33, no. 1 (November 2006): 1–25, and is reprinted here courtesy of Sage Publishers.

University of California Press
Berkeley and Los Angeles, California

University of California Press, Ltd.
London, England

Library of Congress Cataloging-in-Publication Data
Hurewitz, Daniel.
 Bohemian Los Angeles : and the making of modern politics / Daniel Hurewitz.
  p. cm.
 Includes bibliographical references and index.
 ISBN-13: 978-0-520-24925-7 (cloth : alk. paper)
 ISBN-10: 0-520-24925-9 (cloth : alk. paper)
 1. Edendale (Los Angeles, Calif.)—Politics and government—20th century. 2. Edendale (Los Angeles, Calif.)—Intellectual life—20th century. 3. Edendale (Los Angeles, Calif.)—Social conditions—20th century. 4. Pluralism (Social sciences)—California—Los Angeles—History—20th century. 5. Artists—California—Los Angeles—History—20th century. 6. Political activists—California—Los Angeles—History—20th century. 7. Community life—California—Los Angeles—History—20th century. 8. Los Angeles (Calif.)—Politics and government—20th century. 9. Los Angeles (Calif.)—Intellectual life—20th century. 10. Los Angeles (Calif.)—Social conditions—20th century. I. Title.
F869.L86E24 2007
979.4'94053—dc22   2006017928

Manufactured in the United States of America
16 15 14 13 12 11 10 09 08 07
10 9 8 7 6 5 4 3 2 1
This book is printed on New Leaf EcoBook 50, a 100% recycled fiber of which 50% is de-inked post-consumer waste, processed chlorine-free. EcoBook 50 is acid-free and meets the minimum requirements of ANSI/ASTM D5634–01 *(Permanence of Paper).* ♾

*For
Michael
and
our girls*

CONTENTS

ILLUSTRATIONS

IMAGES

Looking east across Edendale and the Silver Lake Reservoir in the late 1930s.
(Photograph by Walter Reagh;
SECURITY PACIFIC COLLECTION/Los Angeles Public Library.)

Introduction

Traversing the Hills of Edendale

HIGH ON A HILLSIDE OVERLOOKING Los Angeles' Silver Lake Reservoir stands the Villa Capistrano, the former home of film and vaudeville sensation Julian Eltinge. Built in the late 1910s with a typically Angeleno combination of Spanish, Moorish, and Italian elements, Eltinge's villa once commanded the surrounding area like a baron's manor. At the time, the neighborhood bore the poetic name of Edendale, and it bustled with the comings and goings of the early film industry. The topography undulated with little hills and valleys, and its roads twisted and bent, following the curve of the reservoir or the slope of an incline. At some points the streets billowed out into vistas, offering brilliant views across the plains of Los Angeles and out to the Pacific Ocean. At other points, where the hills were too steep, the streets simply stopped, replaced by stairwells that continued their climb.

Few homes sat near the gardens of Eltinge's villa. The tower and terraces and the estate's high perch on the hill spoke loudly of wealth and security, and they exuded a sense of unprecedented celebrity at a moment when movie stars were first coming into existence. According to one local chronicler, Eltinge "was one of the first actors to establish a palatial home in Los Angeles," and the press was captivated by its construction, tracking even the building materials that were being used. One film buff claimed that around the house there "gathered the scent of scandal," but even that was an exotic and alluring scent: local realtors promoted their developments by their proximity to the villa, and in the 1920s you could purchase a postcard with a picture of Eltinge's manor to impress the folks back home.[1]

Today, though, Eltinge's villa hardly dominates the landscape. It sits crowded in with homes beside and beneath it on the hill. The neighborhood it overlooks, now called Silver Lake and Echo Park, beats with the seemingly new pulse of a vibrant creative multicultural scene. There is a steady line for bands playing on Santa Monica Boulevard. The Silver Lake Film Festival, launched in 2000, attracts larger and larger audiences with its music, video, and film presentations. The gay bars on Sunset—like the Mexican restaurants and dance halls down the way—fill regularly with men and women out on the town. And the houses and apartments are teeming, it seems, with screenwriters, painters, architects, and performers struggling to craft and create. In such a context, Eltinge's home—let alone his life—seems insignificant, unrelated to the hip bohemia that surrounds it: just another time-worn house on a hill.

Much the same could be said on the opposite side of the country, in the heart of New York City's new 42nd Street, where Eltinge's presence remains as another forgotten shadow. There on the corner of 8th Avenue, the AMC movie chain operates a twenty-five-screen multiplex out of a beautiful vaudeville theater that Eltinge built in 1912 with two business partners. In fact, in 1997, AMC lifted and moved the Eltinge Theater 168 feet so that its broad terra-cotta façade, triumphal arch window, and domed auditorium could serve as the lobby for their new multiscreen extravaganza. Now as moviegoers ascend the escalator to their screen of choice, they ride beneath three portraits of Eltinge painted onto what was once the proscenium arch of his stage. But Eltinge floats there unnamed and little noticed.[2]

That Eltinge lingers, standing watch over Los Angeles' contemporary bohemia—and hovering in the heart of New York's theater district— makes a certain sense. In the world of vaudeville, Eltinge was as successful as they come. According to some estimates, his weekly income in 1912 exceeded even that of President Taft. Indeed, the theater that was moved down the block had been financed in large part by the income he generated during his four-year run starring in *The Fascinating Widow,* a show written specifically for him. And Eltinge's success was hardly only local. His vaudeville shows toured the country and the world, garnering him fame and fans. He was invited both to perform for the king of England and to star in several early Hollywood films. Eltinge's success certainly warrants his standing guard at the center of the nation's cultural and performance centers.

Nevertheless, Eltinge is not a vaudeville or film star who is well remembered at the start of the twenty-first century: neither his home nor his theater is celebrated as a vestige of his life. Unlike figures such as Al Jolson, Fatty Arbuckle, and Louise Brooks—whose stage stardom and brief film careers burned them into the national consciousness—Eltinge's name and career have been lost to popular memory.[3] And they were not lost by accident. Eltinge's career is not remembered sixty years after his death because Eltinge was a particular kind of performer—a kind that made him a star in the 1910s but whose mode of performance was scorned by mid-century and largely forgotten at century's end: Eltinge was a spectacular female impersonator. A tremendously talented performer, he brought laughter to his audiences by portraying young men in straits so dire that they could be solved only by his disguising himself as a woman, and once in that guise, he astonished them with the beauty, style, and glamour he revealed. He was hardly the only female impersonator pounding the boards at the turn of the century: such performers were a much-enjoyed staple of the vaudeville world. But he was at the top of their class: the best paid, the best known, and the best regarded, even by those who normally had little patience for such performers. And the three figures floating in the 42nd Street theater are portraits of Eltinge at work, at the height of the career that was to be forgotten, Eltinge in costume as three beautiful women. Those figures open a window onto a lost world.

I did not set out to find Julian Eltinge. Instead, I stumbled across him while on a search for another man. That man, Harry Hay, had, like Eltinge, immigrated to Los Angeles in the 1910s and also became involved in the world of performance. But from there his life spun in an entirely different direction. Indeed, in 1950 Hay helped to found the Mattachine Society, the first long-lasting American homosexual rights organization. He was a key figure in shaping the social and political movement around sexual identity and was emblematic, fundamentally, of the birth of identity politics. As I began this project, I was curious about exploring the history of Hay and Mattachine as a way to understand the formation of late-twentieth-century American identity politics. Yet just as I set out to find Hay, I discovered Eltinge.

Hay and Eltinge lived in the same neighborhood in Los Angeles. Ten years ago, I interviewed a longtime resident of that neighborhood, hoping he would tell me something about Hay and gay politics in the 1950s; instead he told me about Eltinge, who had built his palatial home just down the street. He pulled out an old newspaper clipping. It showed Eltinge in full stunning attire, and I was intrigued. What do you mean that a female impersonator was an international star, let alone a movie star, one hundred years ago? How could such a fact have been so well buried? The man hinted at rumors that Eltinge had sexual relationships with other men. Well, was he, in fact, homosexually active? And why did he come to live in this neighborhood? Was the neighborhood some sort of homosexual retreat? And was there some connection between Eltinge and Hay and his Mattachine organization? Those questions, tying the identity politics of the later twentieth century to the sexual and cultural world of the early century, began to race around in my head and ultimately gave birth to this book.[4]

Julian Eltinge and Harry Hay did not know each other. Eltinge became a star before Hay was born, and Hay reached his greatest influence after Eltinge had died. Yet Eltinge and Hay had a fair amount in common. These two tall white men loved to perform: one strode the boards of vaudeville stages around the globe; the other played small theaters in Los Angeles but performed even more dramatically as a public speaker, educator, and activist. One man married, the other did not, but both pursued sexual relationships with other men. And both men lived for several years in the hilly Los Angeles neighborhood once known as Edendale. In fact, both of their homes sat on the same hill rising along the eastern bank of Silver Lake Reservoir. Eltinge's home was built on the southern crest of the hill and faced west, across the lake; Hay's sat farther north, at the peak of the hill but with a more eastern orientation, toward the city's downtown. If you left the home of the first man and forged a path up and across the ridge of the hill, within minutes you would arrive at the second's home, facing out across a very different urban valley.

Perhaps you could throw a stone across the face of that ridge today; their homes were just that physically close. But in historical terms, the distance between the cultural world of 1918 that brought Eltinge to Edendale and the world of Hay when he moved into the neighborhood in 1942—let alone when he left in the 1950s—was enormous. The story at the heart of this book is the story of that cultural distance between them and how it was crossed. It is the story of how Eltinge's world was undone and remade into a world that we might recognize—of how a place like Edendale became a place like Silver Lake.

Of course, the ways that Los Angeles in the 1910s differed from the 1950s are myriad. But the path across that Edendale ridge which lies at the heart of this book is the changing way in which people understood themselves—indeed, understood what their "selves" were. At one end of that path was a world of Victorian values where exterior character, public behavior, and performance were the very measures of selfhood. At the other end lay a profound emphasis on an interior realm of personality, essence, and identity. Indeed, the very possibility of identity politics, which so marked late-twentieth-century United States political life, lay in the transformation that intervened.

Americans today think a fair amount about identity, and they do so in ways that are the results of multiple historical trajectories. On the one hand, contemporary Americans typically live some portion of their lives searching for themselves, taking to heart that countercultural imperative and believing that there is a "self" for them to "find." That interior self, we believe, stands as the irreducible core of our uniqueness: it is our essence, our persona, the very particular expression of our psychic DNA. According to philosopher Charles Taylor, Americans have embraced the imperative that "there is a certain way of being human that is *my* way. I am called upon to live my life in this way, and not in imitation of anyone else's life. . . . [T]his notion gives a new importance to being true to myself. If I am not, I miss the point of my life; I miss what being human is for *me*." This ethic of unique self-fulfillment has yielded a "search for authenticity" that, according to historian Doug Rossinow, has become a "pervasive yearning in the United States." As Jeffrey Weeks explained in the 1990s, we now "need a sense of the essential self to provide a grounding for our actions, to ward off existential fear and anxiety and to provide a springboard for action."[5]

For many Americans, particularly gay men and women, sexuality has been raised up as the epitome of that authentic self. Weeks claimed that in the search for "self-identity" the ultimate goal was "sexual identity"—meaning a consistent pattern of choosing sexual and romantic partners based on their sex. In making such an assertion, Weeks echoed French scholar Michel Foucault, who charged that modernity cast sexuality as "the truth of our being." While that claim may be too broad, it is clear that in our age a sexual identity has become accepted as one of a handful of essential private truths about who we are.[6]

These private truths are treated so naturally in our lives as to seem eternal, as if people have always everywhere gone on searches to find themselves. And yet far from being natural, the very notion of a self or an identity—let alone an interior self that you can find—are the products of a distinct cultural and intellectual history. As Taylor pointed out, only a few centuries ago, "being in touch with . . . God, or the Idea of the Good—was considered essential to full being. But now the source we have to connect with is deep within us. This fact is part of the massive subjective turn of modern culture, a new form of inwardness, in which we come to think of ourselves as beings with inner depths."[7] That modern turn toward a valorization of subjectivity developed slowly, over the last two or three centuries, and had far-reaching consequences. It was one of the historical currents that pushed Americans over the course of the twentieth century toward a growing fascination with their inner selves.

At the same time, beyond the personal imperative to find ourselves, individual identity in the United States has also taken on a powerful public and political significance. In the last few decades, Americans have been asked repeatedly to consider the political and social implications of a defined set of personal identities. They have joined organizations to fight for equal pay for women and marched in Washington, D.C., demanding equal rights for gay men and lesbians. They have engaged in debates to argue whether race-based affirmative action violated fundamental American principles or whether a single-sex golf club or military academy had the right to stay that way. Concerns about discrimination based on race, gender, and sexuality have become prevailing themes in American political life.

To some degree, these public battles over identity are a contemporary expression of a long-standing preoccupation within American political history. Americans have been fighting about the meaning and power accorded to group memberships since the nation began. During the debates over the drafting of the Constitution, James Madison wrote compellingly about the need to structure the government in a way that protected minority political factions. One hundred years later, activists and reformers built organizations and strategies to safeguard industrial workers. And in the intervening years, abolition and women's suffrage advocates constructed arguments that served as foundations for the claims about racial and sexual discrimination put forward by the black civil rights and women's liberation movements late in the twentieth century.[8]

Nonetheless, identity politics battles about race, gender, and sexuality in the late twentieth century carried a new emphasis and a new language that distinguished them clearly from their earlier predecessors. As L. A. Kauffman explained, nineteenth- and early-twentieth-century social movements were "firmly rooted in the public sphere tradition of emphasizing public institutions as the crucial loci of political contestation." Without neglecting the importance of public institutions, late-twentieth-century identity politics also acted, though, on "the belief that identity itself—its elaboration, expression, or affirmation—is and should be a fundamental focus of political work." Political activists—even among African Americans and women, whose movements' roots rested firmly in an earlier century—now came to prioritize a language that emphasized "self-esteem," "self-fulfillment," and individual "authenticity." "Freedom," as one scholar explained, "lay in being able to decide for oneself what and who one was and what choices were appropriate or fulfilling." Echoing Chief Justice Earl Warren's 1954 opinion in *Brown v. Board of Education* that segregated schools created "a *feeling* of inferiority," these new identity politics underscored the feeling and deep experience of identities; the harm done by demeaning language, images, and politics; the necessity of cultivating positive identities; and the nurturing value of distinct identity-based communities and cultures.[9]

Thus, for late-twentieth-century Americans, identity carried two seemingly distinct meanings. One was private, interior, and uniquely idiosyncratic; the second was public, political, and communally shared. One seemed to express the modern turn toward interior subjectivity; the other carried forward traditional liberal debates about the multiple factions of a pluralist society. Late-twentieth-century identity politics marked the convergence of those two trends, wherein the pluralist politics of the public sphere focused extensively on personal identities and their inner meanings. The "identity politics" that buffeted the United States in the later twentieth century were simultaneously deeply private and fundamentally public.[10]

That convergence began well before the end of the twentieth century. Indeed, the transition from Eltinge to Hay—from the 1910s to the 1950s—suggests how these two trends in American life became intertwined: how, that is, the inner life became the subject of heated political action. Typically identity politics are viewed as a by-product of the student and civil rights movements of the 1960s and '70s. This book argues, however, that their roots lay much earlier, in the first half of the century. The emerging emphasis on internal "authentic" identity took on political significance in the years between Eltinge and Hay.[11]

As a window onto that transformation, this book focuses specifically on the politicization of homosexuality and the rise of gay politics. Gay politics, both because they were relatively new in 1950 and because they emphasize precisely the importance of emotions and inner desires, offer a powerful case study for thinking about the emergence of American identity politics. In the transition from Eltinge to Hay, homosexual desire and politics collided, and that collision demonstrated fundamental changes in American political life.

Those changes can be seen in two important differences in how Eltinge and Hay understood their lives. First, while both Eltinge and Hay had sexual affairs with men, Eltinge resisted any efforts to suggest that those affairs revealed some fundamental truth about who he was. By contrast, the handful of men that gathered with Harry Hay in 1950 for the initial homosexual rights meeting came to agree that their interpersonal sexual and emotional desires—their lusts and affections for other men—were central to, if not the centerpiece of, their personal identity. Calling themselves the Mattachine Society and labeling themselves individually as "homophiles," they embraced the project of crafting a collective perception of their lives in which their sexual desires—conceived as a "sexual identity"—formed the fundamental or essential core of who they were. While not the first Americans to think of themselves in those terms, they were the first to articulate that identity so self-consciously and to organize a community around it so successfully. Unlike Eltinge, who seemed to celebrate the very multiplicity of his identity, the Mattachine members understood their sexual activities to be directly connected to who they fundamentally were, as individuals and as a community.

Second, the Mattachine members agreed for a time that their singular identity had immediate political implications. It was the cause for their uniting in a community, and it provoked them into significant acts of political activism. The organization lasted well into the 1970s and inspired several other groups that formed a network of activist chapters which quickly spanned the country. Mattachine and its cohort of organizations eventually called themselves the "Homophile Movement." While Eltinge did not see himself as either a political player or a political subject, Mattachine members marked their sexual activity as both central to their personal identity and the basis for communal political action. Beyond simply discussing their sexual lives, the members devoted their efforts to meeting with police, psychologists, clergy, and occasional legislators in order to challenge medical, religious, and legal sanctions against homosexual activity. In California at the time, for example, arrests for acts of same-sex flirtation or sexual activity regularly landed men in prison for several months or years. These were conditions that Mattachine and the homophiles hoped to change.

For Harry Hay and the members of Mattachine, then, their sexual lives gave them both an identity and a political agenda. But if the Eltinges of the 1900s did not have or require such a notion of identity, where did one come from? And if Eltinge was so celebrated, why did Harry Hay feel so embattled? Why and how did a culture of celebratory titillation become a politics of conflict and demand? What ultimately produced homosexual identity politics? Those questions about changing notions of identity and communal politics lie at the heart of this book.

Asking such questions builds on the work and ideas of other scholars. American historians have illuminated increasingly well, for instance, the early-twentieth-century urban subcultures in which men frequently had sex with other men without perceiving themselves as possessing a homosexual or gay identity.[12] When distinctly homosexual identities eventually did emerge, some have argued, they did so principally as a result of wider economic changes. Like John D'Emilio, these scholars insisted that capitalism and the wage-labor system allowed individuals to separate from the family economy and construct lives around non-procreative sexual desires: they could, essentially, leave the family farm for the city and become homosexually active without suffering dire economic consequences. Capitalism, D'Emilio wrote, both "created a social context in which an autonomous personal life could develop" and "provided the conditions for a homosexual and lesbian identity to emerge."[13] What is more, others have claimed, American gay identity became distinctly political because as more and more homosexually active men and women moved to the city, they faced increasing police oppression; that oppression politicized them, both teaching them strategies of resistance and cultivating a sense of community.[14]

These are important arguments, and they provide a vital framework for this book. The tale here certainly begins with a homosexually active subculture not unlike what other scholars have found in New York or Portland, Oregon—a world devoid of gay identities, for which Eltinge was somewhat emblematic. And embedded here as well lies a narrative of oppression, loss, and collapse, for Eltinge's world was attacked and unmade in the years that this book covers. At the same time, however, the Mattachine Society was more than a reflexive response to growing police hostility. Harry Hay's identity politics represented a far-reaching effort of creation and construction that was generated by more than blackjacks and police boots. The drive toward identity politics lay deeper and wider in the culture than that. Its roots lay in a broad array of social arenas where fundamental questions about the self and politics were renegotiated in the middle decades of the twentieth century. Those negotiations were powerful enough that we carry their legacy well into the next century.

The broad cultural transformation that yielded gay identity politics involved many more people than Hay and Eltinge: they are simply the iconic figures—the bookends—who mark a start and finish for this project. But in between them, this book investigates Los Angeles, and particularly Edendale, to demonstrate the wide cultural change.[15] That broad transformation is clear in the two distinctive "nonsexual" communities that settled among the hills of Edendale in the period between Julian Eltinge and the beginnings of Mattachine. The first was an arts community. Even in the 1910s, Edendale housed some of the first film studios in Southern California. But beginning in the mid- to late 1920s, a large number of painters, writers, sculptors, and architects—and their clients and promoters—also began to settle in the hills of Edendale, even as the film companies departed. Among them were painters like Millard Sheets, who captured the look of the rapidly growing city; printmakers like Paul Landacre, who created a new vocabulary for wood-block printing to portray the geography of California; and supporters like Jake Zeitlin, whose bookstore became a gathering place for creative conversation and inspiration. The principal art schools of the city were located in a cluster just south of the neighborhood. Some graduates took studios—others made homes—in the foothills north of them. One of the schools, the Chouinard School, funneled students into the animation offices of the Disney Company, which remained in Edendale until the 1930s. The others formed a network of sketch clubs, galleries, and publishing teams.

The second community consisted of leftist progressives with Communists at its core. The fellow travelers far outnumbered the Party faithful, but in the 1930s and 1940s the Edendale hills became littered with union organizers, civic activists, and Party leaders. Among the most active were people like Miriam Brooks Sherman, a pianist, wife, and mother and one of the strongest leaders of the Los Angeles Communist Party, and Carey McWilliams, never a Party member but a progressive activist and intellectual who helped frame the fight on behalf of migrant farm workers and Mexican immigrants and went on to become editor of *The Nation*.

The period at the heart of this book, especially the Depression years, represented a vital phase for each of these groups. For Communists, the 1930s have been referred to as the "heyday" of American Communism, when communist ideals—if not Party membership—became more widely embraced by the American public. And yet, we know far too little about what it felt like to be a part of the Party, why people were drawn to it, and why they stayed. We are used to hearing about the dogma and strategies of

Communists, but we hear much less about their emotional and expressive lives. And even though self-expression or emotion might seem the bailiwick of artists, it was a vital component to the experience of political participation in the Communist Party.

For artists, these decades were filled with a significant struggle over the purpose of art, with some artists pushing for an art that spoke directly to the public and addressed larger social concerns, while other artists advocated an art that was deeply personal, idiosyncratic, and emotional and often quite abstracted from the realm of representation. While art histories analyze changing forms of expression and content, they generally tell us much less about the organizing efforts and community-building projects of artists. Nevertheless, those endeavors, which we might expect in a history of Communists, were vital to the lives of Edendale artists. Indeed, in the throes of their representational battles, artists built communities for themselves that increased their impact on the larger American community.

Finally, for homosexuals, these decades mark a transition between two fairly well documented eras: an early one when sexual activity between men was rarely read as indicative of a singular personal identity and was indulged in by a host of men who little contemplated the unity or disunity of their desires; and a later period when sexual activity did seem to demonstrate a particular identity and that identity had growing legal and political ramifications. The how and why of that transition, however, remains elusive for historians.

For each of these communities, these decades marked a vital shift, and the relative simultaneity of these shifts is more than a mere coincidence. These shifts were deeply connected. They were each a piece of a larger shift, a shift from one world to another, a shift from Eltinge's vaudeville success to Hay's political battleground. All three neighboring groups were working through related questions of self-understanding, articulation, and public presentation. All three communities strove to reformulate the relationship between the private self and the larger polity. The Mattachine members' story is part and parcel of the wider stories. Ultimately, their politicization of sexual identity was directly influenced by the debates about the abstract notions of "self" and "politics" carried on by their neighboring artists and leftists.

Curiously, Los Angeles is rarely mentioned as the launching pad for serious American political movements, let alone gay history. And yet, as urban scholar Moira Kenney wrote, "Los Angeles is the greatest hidden chapter in American gay and lesbian history." Well ahead of New York or San Francisco, it provided a starting point for the nation's political movement for homosexual rights—as well as the first gay scholarly group, lesbian publication, and gay religious organization. Los Angeles was a crucial cauldron, but not simply Los Angeles. The impulse to narrate the transition from Julian Eltinge to Harry Hay and Mattachine by way of artists and Communists rests on the fact that these groups not only lived in Los Angeles in general but also specifically shared Edendale: they all lived, quite literally, among the hills and valleys surrounding Eltinge and Hay. Edendale mattered because Edendale—as a place—was fairly unique compared to the rest of Los Angeles.[16]

Even though Edendale lay only a couple of miles from downtown, its physical make-up was quite distinct from the city's extensive flatlands. The neighborhood was overrun with hilly lots and streets that were precariously steep. When much of the area was developed, engineers had not devised sophisticated street grading techniques. Thus many steep roads simply ended in the long stairwells that provided the only access to the homes farther up the hill. Residents, in a sense, were locked in, and even after the streetcars began carving their way into the neighborhood, the area retained a sense of near-rural seclusion: it was that very isolation that had attracted most of the city's first film studios to settle there in the 1910s.[17]

Amid the land booms that repeatedly swept Southern California from the late 1880s to the 1920s, campaigns to attract residents to Edendale consistently spoke out against the perception that the area would be forever inaccessible. In 1887, for instance, developers Byram & Poindexter advertised their "Ivanhoe" project with boasts that the center of Ivanhoe was only four miles from the downtown courthouse and that the route could be traveled (for only five cents) by steam dummy railroad "OFTEN enough and FAST enough to accommodate business men." More than thirty years later, when nearby Silver Lake Terrace was completed, its promotional brochure still shouted from the cover that it was a mere "15 minutes from Broadway [in downtown Los Angeles]" and that a new thoroughfare, Silver Lake Boulevard, connected the neighborhood to the pulse of the city.[18] Nevertheless, Edendale long seemed somewhere else, not of the city.

Geographers have steadily argued that human experience is profoundly affected by its placement in particular spatial contexts, that "the social, the historical and the spatial" are all intertwined. Indeed, according to Edward

Soja, the places where people live and how they live in those places distinctly affect how they understand themselves and their world. Edendale certainly seems to have enacted that power. Because of its rural-like isolation, it became what Soja deemed a "thirdspace"—a space at the margins of society that can be adopted as a site for contesting power, a place where new identities, actions, and opportunities can be constructed.[19]

In other contexts, thirdspaces have often earned the label "bohemias." Typically, historians of bohemias have underscored their counterhegemonic qualities. Jerrold Seigel's seminal study of nineteenth- and early-twentieth-century bohemian Paris, for instance, deemed bohemia the "reverse image and underside" of the rising bourgeoisie. It was the place within the bourgeois social structure from which that new order could be critiqued. "Bohemia was not a realm outside bourgeois life," he explained, "but the expression of a conflict that arose at its very heart . . . it was the appropriation of marginal life-styles by young and not so young bourgeois, for the dramatization of ambivalence toward their own social identities and destinies." More recently, Ross Wetzsteon wrote of Greenwich Village that it "existed in an almost symbiotic relationship with the middle class," much like "an adolescent rebellion against the adults."[20] Edendale was Los Angeles' bohemia in the decades following the First World War—a site that, while within the city, was also a space of marginality and possibility, a space from which the city's social and political structure could be critiqued and challenged.

Historians of bohemias—and certainly of artistic movements—have not always given serious weight to the politics of their participants. Usually they are viewed through their creative impulses and judged for their resistance to larger societal mores. Yet linking the artists of Edendale with local activists offers the possibility of understanding how, within the distinctive confines of the neighborhood, one bohemian world was engaged in a broad counterhegemonic social and political movement. Sidney Tarrow, in his classic analysis of political movements, examined how movements "build organizations, elaborate ideologies, . . . socialize and mobilize constituencies, and . . . engage in self-development and the construction of collective identities." In many ways, Edendale, from the 1910s to the 1950s, was the site of such a movement wherein a new ideology of identity was constructed and elaborated around organized and mobilized constituencies. It took years before the constituency, in the form of Mattachine, formally entered the political arena, but the cultural construction of an ideology and identity that was this movement's foundation was already well under way.[21] Mattachine, as representative of a new kind of identity politics, was very much a product of that place.

This book, though, is not just about Edendale and its communities. Identities have rarely been the exclusive product of like-minded individuals. While each of the major identities in this project—artist, Communist, and homosexual—were negotiated in part by groups of individuals who engaged in similar activities and sought to adopt a shared self-definition based on those activities, identity construction was also the product of oppositional relationships between those individuals and the larger society or state. The philosopher Louis Althusser suggested that people received an identity definition as soon as society called out to them, "Hey, you there!" and the people turned to respond, accepting, in a sense, society's label.[22] Although Edendale operated as an engine of change, the ideas generated and sustained there sparked powerful reactions from the city at large. As Edendale locals imagined new notions of self-expression, politics, and community, Los Angeles officials responded with their own ideas about the political significance of identity. Those responses, often in the form of crackdowns, shaped the emergence of identity politics just as much as the progressives and bohemians of Edendale did. City and neighborhood carried on a dialogue, a call-and-response, about what identities meant, and this book echoes that exchange.

There are, of course, many ways to tell this tale, many ways to traverse that Edendale hillside from Eltinge to Hay. But because of that back-and-forth, this book casts both a wide and a narrow net, sometimes looking at the city as a whole, sometimes just Edendale. It begins with a prologue, a brief account capturing Julian Eltinge as a vaudeville star at the height of his success—just prior to his move to Los Angeles. The chapter presents the mystery and excitement of gender play as Eltinge performed it. It explores the audiences' interest in Eltinge and the messages about gender and identity that he seemed to be sending them.

The opening chapter presents Los Angeles in the 1910s, on the eve of Eltinge's arrival. The city is seen from the perspective of homosexual activity, not just its occurrence, but also the ways it was understood. When Eltinge arrived in Edendale in 1918, Los Angeles was similar to New York, and gender remained the dominant personal identity code for understanding sexual activity.[23] Indeed, as the first chapter reveals, even when Angeleno men were arrested for engaging in same-sex activity, their behavior was not perceived as indicating a fixed core identity. At least in terms of sexual activity, the city behaved like Eltinge: happily sexual, but untouched by and resistant to a conception of a sexual identity.

Eltinge settled in Edendale. It was, for a few years, the playground of the new film industry. But when the industry left, Edendale continued to sustain a creative life, though one populated by painters and sculptors and writers. These creative individuals eagerly plumbed the soul of identity. Indeed, the artists of Edendale during the 1920s and 1930s devoted themselves to the task of finding their inner emotional lives and portraying them through art. The second chapter documents how, during these decades, a cohort of artists and their supporters settled into Edendale's hills. They quite self-consciously constructed a community for themselves, establishing various clubs and organizations. Within those structures, they began to construct and debate a definition of artists as individuals who gave loud public expression to their inner emotional lives. Whereas Eltinge had reveled in gender as a play of costume and make-up—of surfaces—these artists set out to explore their psychic depths and attach public meaning to what they found.

The Depression wrought a powerful change to both these worlds as the shared public life of political action and significance began to impinge on creative and sexual activity. Among the artists of Edendale, the Depression and international politics forged a second debate about the need for artists to engage with the social and political situation that surrounded them. For some, the government, through the Public Works of Art Project and the Federal Art Project, intervened quite directly to sustain their careers. But many artists attempted both to articulate their inner lives and to engage in political action.

At the same time, the political touched on the world of lusts and affections. Homosexual activity increasingly came to be viewed as constituting an identity. That notion was both state imposed and individually and communally conceived. Thus, while same-sex behavior became more visible throughout the 1920s and into the 1930s, the city administration now intervened aggressively. Los Angeles police initiated a series of crackdowns on the gathering and performance sites of lesser Eltinges. Bars were closed; impersonators were arrested. The city began to identify gender play as a sign of sexual deviancy and a disturbed inner essence. Additionally, the government deemed sexual deviants as politically dangerous. The implications of the policing drive and its process of labeling became clear during a contemporaneous campaign to unseat the mayor. By the end of the 1930s, as the third chapter explains, Eltinge and his kind were seen as enemies of the state: they had a political identity, even if not one of their choosing.

During the years of these crackdowns, the artists of Edendale were joined in increasing numbers by Communist Party members and their progressive colleagues. The fourth chapter returns to Edendale and documents the network of organizations the Left established there. Much like the artists, Communists of the 1930s and '40s were forging a powerful relationship between their interior lives and political action. In part, they lived out their political identity in the most intimate corners of their lives. The Party functioned on a powerful emotional base of ardent connection among its members. That connection was enacted at one level in the housewarming parties, anniversary parties, even Halloween parties that were as much a staple of Party life as the planning meetings and demonstrations. At a more intimate level, love and passionate friendship were the glue of Party life well beyond principle. Marriages were made and unmade by the Party. One woman told me that if someone was married outside of the Party, either the spouse joined the Party or eventually the marriage collapsed.[24] The people you agreed with, and picketed with, and got arrested with—these were the people you loved and fell in love with. Much more than the artists, the Communists wedded their political identities and their personal lives.

Additionally, Party activists became intently focused on the political significance of racial identities and fought quite aggressively against racial discrimination. For instance, the defense of a group of young Mexican Americans convicted on a spurious murder charge—the notorious Sleepy Lagoon case—was organized by the Edendale left. The left leadership there also coordinated a successful recall of the area city councilman in 1946 for his support of Gerald L. K. Smith and the Ku Klux Klan. They argued vehemently for the political integrity of racial minorities.

Those arguments carried greater and greater significance in Los Angeles as violent conflicts over racial identities began to dominate the city's political landscape during and after the Second World War. While gay historians like Allan Bérubé and John D'Emilio have argued that the war spawned an explosion of gay urban communities because of the concentrations of homosexually active men and women it produced, in Los Angeles the most dramatic changes the war wrought were racial.[25] As the fifth chapter demonstrates, race relations were one of the central dilemmas that weighed on Los Angeles as war spread from Europe and Asia and finally engaged the United States. In fact, the specter that haunted Los Angeles throughout the war years and well into the Cold War was that international warfare abroad would come home to roost as race warfare in the city's streets. The fluctuating deportation, importation, and riots against Mexicans and Mexican Americans; the mass evacuation of local Japanese and Japanese Americans; and the anxious negotiations for African American housing following the war—all combined to place categories of racial identity and their concomitant danger at the forefront of Los Angeles political and social culture.

Out of those public battles emerged a conception of city politics as international politics in microcosm, with racial groups standing in for nations. Maintaining harmony in the City of Angels required recognizing racial minorities, albeit grudgingly, as political participants. If the United Nations would maintain peace among the world's nations, city politicians needed to accept minorities as equally independent political constituencies. Race relations were not simply a political problem. Racial identities became significant political identities.

Mattachine embraced the construction of these new political identities. As the final chapter argues, its members took equally seriously the implications of the artists, the crackdowns, and the Communists. The group's founders saw their inner lives as vital and as carrying a political valence. Reversing the Communists' equation, they lived their personal identities in the most public corners of their lives. They constructed a political identity and organization around them. The shape of those identities they borrowed from both their leftist neighbors and the city as a whole: they conceived of sexual political identity as comparable to racial identity. To be homosexually active in Los Angeles in the 1950s, they argued, was equivalent to belonging to a racial minority group. It conferred the same kind of identity, resulted in the same kind of oppression, and demanded the same kind of political action. The "homosexual" identity that they conceived was, at its core, a political identity.

The Mattachine founders' notion of "homosexual" or "gay" identity undergirds much of today's gay American community. Nevertheless, the founders' view was not easily accepted by the wider membership. Their notion of a "homosexual" was hardly seen as natural or predetermined. Instead, it was the focus of heated internal debates that both echoed many of the earlier debates in Edendale and foreshadowed many of the battles that continue to swirl around the politics of identity, most recently as "queer" activists have challenged the utility of notions of "gay" and "lesbian." Indeed, the birth of Mattachine represented the birth of a politics that can be defined specifically by such battles over who counts as a minority in

American life and what such a minority status ensures. Those battles certainly rage on.

That is the arc of this project. It follows, as closely as possible, the politicization of sexual identity, but does so within a larger framework of changing notions and practices of selfhood. Fundamentally, it argues for the complexity of that process, tracing both the intellectual developments and the application of those ideas in how people built individual lives and communities.

In each of the cases at hand, identity construction emerged from a complex interaction between individual volition, like-minded concurrence, and state imposition. The emergence of homosexual politics, and identity politics in general, was not merely the creative product of several homosexually active individuals. It was shaped as well by a neighborhood that, in a variety of ways, was reimagining the relationship between politics and emotions. Equally, Los Angeles itself, captivated by the ties between vice, race, and politics, participated in that transformation. Along the way, one cultural world was destroyed and another—a political one—was born.

In the heart of downtown Los Angeles, at the corner of Seventh and Broadway, as the city steadily grows, 1927. (Automobile Club of Southern California Archives.)

Prologue
A World Left Behind

THEY ARRIVED BY THE HUNDREDS and thousands, new migrants pouring into the city every day. In 1900 barely 100,000 people lived in Los Angeles, making it only the thirty-sixth largest city in the country. San Francisco, by contrast, had a population of nearly 345,000 and New York, 3.5 million. By 1910 Los Angeles had grown to 319,000; by 1920 it had nearly doubled to 577,000; and over the next ten years it more than doubled again, to 1.2 million residents. Invaded by newcomers, in only thirty years Los Angeles became the fifth largest city in the country. And unlike New York or San Francisco, which witnessed dramatic levels of foreign immigration, the majority of Angeleno arrivals were native-born Americans, lured out West by what they heard about the City of Angels. In fact, between 1920 and 1930, 1.5 million Americans, many of whom helped create the city's bohemia, moved to Southern California.[1] Why? What was so appealing?

For some it was the sun and the air and the health their doctors promised the new climate would bring. Southern California became a dominant health destination in the late nineteenth century, when doctors insisted that climate change was the answer to many respiratory ailments. But even as medical practice changed, migrants continued to seek out the rejuvenating sun and warmth of Los Angeles.[2]

Peggy Dennis, soon to be a leading figure in the region's Communist movement, came by train from New York City with her parents and sister.

Her parents worked in the sweatshops of the Lower East Side, but in 1912, when Dennis was barely three years old, her mother developed a virulent form of asthma that left her permanently incapacitated. Peggy herself had similar bronchial troubles, and so the doctor prescribed life out West.[3]

Miriam Brooks Sherman, who would follow Dennis in her activism, moved with her family from Albany, New York, in 1927, when she was twelve. Her parents, Russian-born immigrants, had been planning to move the family to the Soviet Union to join a laundry cooperative. At the last minute, though, the plan collapsed. Her father, Isidor Brooks, a dental supply salesman, had long suffered from hay fever, and so, with their trunks packed, the Brookses considered moving to Southern California. Her mother, Bessie, had a distant cousin in Los Angeles, and Isidor set off to investigate; eventually he settled with his wife and three daughters in the Boyle Heights neighborhood.[4]

Even Harry Hay's family came for health reasons, though not for the sunshine. When Hay was only four, his father lost his leg in a mining accident in Chile. He brought his wife and children to Southern California so that he could obtain proper medical treatment; eventually, he bought a house just south of Hollywood and some farmland to the east, and the family stayed.[5]

For others, Los Angeles was a retreat from hardship, especially for midwesterners, the farmers and ranchers, who were ready to give up rural life and were attracted by the lure of home ownership in an easier climate. They constituted the "folks," according to writer Louis Adamic, these "floods of Middle Westerners" that Hamlin Garland observed "filling the streets." As Carey McWilliams wrote in 1927, Los Angeles became "a sort of higher heaven of middle-west plutocracy."[6]

Yet for many more of these migrants, economic opportunity remained Los Angeles' principal draw. During the 1920s the city's trade and service sectors were booming. Los Angeles emerged as the major oil equipment and service center in the country, the number-two tire manufacturing center, and the locus of the western steel, furniture, and transportation industries. Those prospects were magnetic.[7]

Jake Zeitlin hitchhiked out from Fort Worth, Texas, in the spring of 1925, having no idea how central he and his bookstores would be in cultivating artistic community. He had sent his pregnant wife on ahead and had only a dime in his pocket. But he was twenty-two and believed he would succeed in Los Angeles. Paul Landacre, not yet a wood-block printer, was an advertising illustrator in San Diego; in 1923, though, at age thirty, he decided to broaden his horizons and moved to Los Angeles to attend art school.[8]

Serril Gerber was only sixteen and halfway through high school in Sioux Falls, South Dakota, when he, his brother, and two friends decided to head out to Los Angeles. He could not have imagined how leftist activities would transform his life, but it was 1929, and "we had no future in Sioux Falls," recalled Gerber. "We had to go somewhere to make our way in the world, so what would be more perfect than Los Angeles?" For a dollar a night, they lived out of a tent in the back of a motel, cooking on a Coleman stove and looking for work until Gerber got a job as a busboy. While this was hardly an auspicious beginning, Gerber later said, "when you're sixteen, wherever you went away from home would be magic, but L.A. was super magic. . . . It was paradise."[9]

For Gerber and others, part of that magic derived from the allure of the movie business. According to various histories of Hollywood, a nickelodeon was running in downtown Los Angeles by 1896 and a full-blown movie theater opened in 1902—events which made Los Angeles little different from other American cities. But in 1907, when a few employees of the Chicago-based Selig Company came to Los Angeles to escape the clutches of winter and finish shooting *The Count of Monte Cristo,* Los Angeles stepped forward as a possible home base for movie-making. The following year, William Selig sealed that fate when he brought his whole company out West and built the first "real" studio in the city. He set up shop in Edendale.[10]

Edendale at the start of the twentieth century was a dusty, lightly inhabited corner of the city. A horse-drawn coach plied up and down the slope of Echo Park Avenue. There was a horse ranch, a dairy, and herds of cattle grazing in the hills and in Echo Park itself, and residents kept horses, cows, and other farm animals on their property. In 1907 the city completed construction of a 770-million-gallon reservoir on the edge of the neighborhood and named it after a former city council president and water commissioner, Herman Silver. Silver Lake, not four miles from downtown, marked the border of the city, where it dropped off into the countryside. Indeed, the wealthy used the hills of Edendale as "a resort and weekend recreational area" where they "built shacks as overnight shelters for camping and horseback-riding parties."[11]

But Selig put Edendale on the map. He invested in his studio, building permanent sets, digging a large concrete swimming pool for water action scenes, and constructing a frosted-glass studio for shooting interiors. It was

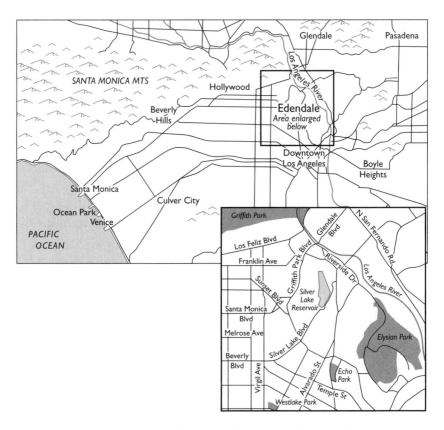

This map of 1930s Los Angeles places Edendale just northwest of downtown Los Angeles. The inset shows the heart of Edendale, lying between Temple Street to the south and Riverside Drive to the north, with Elysian Park marking the eastern border and Virgil Avenue the western border.

an ideal spot, readily accessible to the business and residential parts of the city, yet offering a small-town feeling. And it sat immediately adjacent to the open acreage of Griffith Park, the largest urban park in the country, and a perfect setting for countless outdoor dramas. By 1912, some seventy-three companies were at work making movies in the city as a whole, and the heart of the new industry lay in Edendale. For a time, Mack Sennett, Tom Mix, Essanay Films, Pathé, the New York Motion Picture Company, and Vitagraph were all making films in the area. In fact in a few years, Sennett took over Selig's Edendale studios and began filming comedies on the lot, most famously those featuring the Keystone Cops.[12] According to one

Selig Studios, the first "real" movie studio in Los Angeles, transformed dusty Edendale into the heart of the new film industry. (SECURITY PACIFIC COLLECTION/ Los Angeles Public Library.)

account, Edendale became "one of the most unique villages in America." A visitor suddenly arriving in the neighborhood "might well believe that he was visioning a jumbled dream of the Santa Fe or the Overland Trail, what with near-naked Indians, some dismounted, some still riding; dusty cavalrymen, covered wagons, leather-jacketed scouts, stage coaches, women in crinolines, and so on, all converging . . . at the end of a day's work."[13]

Many recollections of Edendale in the 1910s involved "goggle-eyed neighbors" pressing up to the gates of the studios or climbing nearby lamp and telephone poles to watch the filmmaking. "When big scenes were going on," wrote one contemporary, "the local public school was sometimes almost disrupted, particularly the afternoon sessions, when the kids would crowd the gates and the phone poles during the noon hour and ignore summons back to school." Some in the crowds hoped to be hired as extras; others tried to talk to the actors, many of whom lived nearby and walked home for lunch or grabbed a bite at the local drug store. And as the extras and bit players sat around munching their sandwiches, "the kiddies swarmed around them, getting a close-up of wild Indians, Chinamen, cowboys, soldiers, barroom gals and God knows what, in the crude makeup of the early movie period."[14]

As the studios became more settled, they began to expand their reach for talent and tried to lure vaudeville stage stars to lend their gifts to moving pictures. Among the hundreds who answered their call were Roscoe "Fatty" Arbuckle, Mabel Normand, Charlie Chaplin, Louise Brooks, and Rudolph Valentino. And, of course, in a development that even the *New York Times* paid close attention to, the movies lured Julian Eltinge as well.

Like so many others, Eltinge was a newcomer to Los Angeles. He was part of that cohort of Americans who sold or abandoned their possessions, said good-bye to friends and family, and set out for the West Coast. Like immigrants everywhere, they carried with them their values and ideals of what life should be, and they continued to pursue those values once they settled. But at the same time, their lives and ideals were dramatically altered by the world they encountered.

Despite the extraordinary nature of his career, Eltinge shared much with his fellow migrants. He came with a vision of the good life and what was essential about it. Indeed, he made his living by dramatizing the country's ideas of what was right and true about gender and gender roles. As a result, his career offers up a snapshot of how significant those notions were for Americans. And yet, while he rode those gender ideals to tremendous success well into the twentieth century, fundamentally they were vestiges of an older world—a world that is worth remembering because it began steadily fading away, even as he settled in Edendale.

JULIAN ELTINGE AND THE ART OF GENDER

"Julian Eltinge" sprang to life just before the turn of the century, in 1898 or 1899. Young William Dalton—himself born fifteen years earlier—appeared as a little girl in a local Boston revue and, quite by surprise, stole the show. It was an auspicious time for such a debut: vaudeville still ruled the boards and "female impersonators"—men who explicitly inverted the gender code by dressing as women and singing or acting in sketches and shows—were considered family entertainers. The white, Montana-born and Boston-bred Dalton assumed the name "Eltinge," and Eltinge quickly became the most renowned impersonator in the nation, if not the world.[15]

By 1904 the twenty-one-year-old was performing professionally on the stages of New York, and two years later, debuted in Los Angeles and London. Photographs of him as a woman appeared in newspapers and magazines across the country. He gained international acclaim in the musical comedies *The Crinoline Girl* and *The Fascinating Widow* (both written for him); was dubbed "the loveliest woman on stage"; gave a command performance at Windsor Castle for King Edward VII (for which he was gifted a white bulldog); and lent his name and financial backing to a very successful Broadway theater. Julian Eltinge was, quite simply, a star.

An early Eltinge stage performance was often a display of refinement. Singing famous songs of the time in falsetto while dressed in the latest and most opulent gowns, Eltinge did not mock an ideal of womanhood; instead, he tried to embody it. As Harry Hay later reported, based on his conversations as a young actor in Los Angeles in the 1920s and '30s, Eltinge did a "magnificent job of the impeccability, where he would actually use beautiful clothes . . . doing a perfectly beautiful woman. . . . [Y]ou simply couldn't tell he wasn't a woman." Indeed, Eltinge the stage performer was embraced for his rarefied skill, for the Houdini-like miracle of creating so appealing a female from a male. As one prop man famously insisted, "I'll never forget the first time I saw him. I couldn't believe it was a man. He was the most beautiful woman I ever saw on Keith's stage and that includes Lillian Russell and Ethel Barrymore and all the rest."[16]

Eltinge's artfulness placed him at the center of a much beloved entertainment milieu, one that thrived from the early 1880s to the late 1920s and viewed female impersonation as "wholesome amusement, particularly suitable for women and children." That art distinguished Eltinge from some of his contemporaries and from the post–World War II "drag queen," the bawdier portrayer of womanhood who mocked the ideal even as it was presented.[17] As an impersonator, Eltinge was no tawdry burlesque performer: he was demure, delicate, refined, and eminently successful. Part of the admiration of his performances came from how convincing they were and how seriously he took them—his carriage, his make-up, his fashion. Eltinge both displayed the highest standards of the gender code and showed that it could be taken apart—and to a good, fun effect.

Eltinge's performances, then, toyed with the gender-specific behaviors one might expect from someone of the male sex. If "gender" constituted all those gestures, styles, and attitudes that were assumed to emanate naturally from male and female bodies, Eltinge revealed that the markings of gender might not be so natural after all. By inverting the gender code—that is, by presenting himself as a man being a woman onstage—he suggested that femininity and masculinity were not the natural by-products of female and male bodies, but something else entirely.

The existence of an enormously successful female impersonator does not fit easily into our notions of what American society was like one hundred

Julian Eltinge appeared as both a woman (above) and a man (opposite) in his publicity stills. The image of him in a dress is from his hit vaudeville show *The Crinoline Girl* in 1912. (Billy Rose Theatre Collection, The New York Public Library for the Performing Arts, Astor, Lenox and Tilden Foundations.)

years ago. Eltinge's success alone begins to reveal how different the start of the twentieth century was from the middle of the century, or even our own time. Yet what was the spark that drew crowds to his shows and that film-makers wanted to capture?

Certainly, part of Eltinge's appeal came from the aura of romance that surrounded him. In his shows he regularly sang songs about flirtation and intimacy. In the song "If Only Some One Would Teach Me," Eltinge sang how he was ready to go swimming, if someone would teach him how: "I've donned my newest bathing suit / They tell me it is trim. / One fellow said it was a 'beaut,' / And looked, well, good, to him. / Another said, with a knowing wink: 'The fit is perfect, yet. / I somehow cannot help but think / 'Twould be more perfect wet."[18]

The media also consistently described the audiences' affection for El-tinge in terms of romance. There were regular tales in the press of men and women alike falling hard for the performer. A long-running joke described the drunk or spectacle-less men who waited backstage for Eltinge after see-ing his show, believing he was truly a woman. One extreme version ap-peared in *Vanity Fair* in 1912 when the editors ran a full-page photo of Eltinge and a poem entitled "A Tribute to Art." The speaker of the poem explained how, "O, Julia (n), Julia (n),"

> When thou wert on the stage just now,
>   A longing gripped my heart.
> I heard thy silvery voice ring out,
>   I never had a single doubt,
> But when 'tis over—only then
>   I realize you end in "n"!

But the men were hardly always dupes. A Cincinnati reporter wrote about a man waiting in line to buy a ticket to Eltinge's show who insisted, "I want to see him . . . because I think he's the swellest looking dame that ever wore down the boards, tripping the light fantastic."[19]

Similarly, women of all types were said to fall in love with Eltinge. In Buffalo, New York, for instance, one man allegedly asked the mayor to for-bid Eltinge's show, claiming that two wives had already left him to pursue Eltinge. Women were the staple of his audiences. As one commentator pointed out, "It is women who have made him. And it isn't the matinee girl alone who has been so helpful to his plump bank account. Married women and bachelor girls, and those who are brave enough to admit that they are spinsters, fall victim to the Eltinge stage ways."[20]

But Eltinge was not simply another stage star with whom audience members fell in love: he offered a quite specific performance. In an era in which gendered behavior was understood as the natural, inevitable expression of physical sex and in which adhering strictly to the code of gender roles remained powerfully important, Eltinge delighted audiences by offering the unbelievable possibility that womanhood, in specific, and gender roles in general were not truly fundamental or essential. He was successful because he mocked and inverted the very thing they held so dear. He did not mock womanliness per se; he mocked its naturalness, its essentialness, and the distance that allegedly lay between femininity and masculinity. Spectators reveled precisely in how he flaunted gender as a natural and fixed code of identity.[21]

Certainly the media around Eltinge remained endlessly fascinated with precisely how this man became a woman onstage. As one corset promoter wrote:

> Women are constantly inquiring of Julian Eltinge by what means a man so sturdy and robust as he, can so wonderfully impersonate a woman of singular grace and poise. It is, indeed, a veritable transformation, almost uncanny if it were not beautiful. At one moment we see before us a strong, broad-shouldered swaggering man, deep voiced, thoroughly masculine—such as one associates with the feminine ideal of the college athlete.
>
> Suddenly, as though by magical metamorphosis, in his place stands a sylph of modern society, a woman sumptuously and fittingly gowned and graceful in every move.

The *Chicago Tribune* in the fall of 1908 devoted a nine-image photo essay to Eltinge under the headline "How a Man Makes Himself a Beautiful Woman." The photographs documented the stages of the transformation, from Eltinge as a man to his putting on make-up, wig, outfit, and eyebrows, and finally being cinched into a dress by his valet.[22] That transition was captivating.

One Boston reporter wrote that "the transmogrification of the actor into character is deadly familiar to me, but nothing I have ever assisted at, as the French say, made me feel *de trop* like this." Indeed, he said, "The first glimpse of Eltinge was bewildering. He was seated before a huge mirror engaged in whitening his neck and shoulders and arms, and he was so plump and velvety and so—yes, I must say it—so curvilinear that I gasped."[23]

Some critics did make quite a show of their *"de trop"* disdain for Eltinge and other female impersonators. Regularly enough they framed their

BEFORE   HIS WAIST LINE AND   AFTER

The press and the public were captivated by the way Eltinge could change from a man into a woman so quickly and convincingly. This cartoon appeared on February 24, 1912, in the *Toledo Blade* and accompanied a rave review of *The Fascinating Widow*. The text alongside stated, "For the benefit of those who would like to get into the secret of hasty toilettes, Mr. Eltinge has made the accompanying sketches. The actor says it's all nonsense, this two and three hour thing which most women say is necessary to look right. If a mere man can look right in ten minutes—or a little more—why cannot woman accomplish the same feat?" (Billy Rose Theatre Collection, The New York Public Library for the Performing Arts, Astor, Lenox and Tilden Foundations.)

praise of him in the context of a general disgust for the "little brotherhood" of "average" female impersonators who filled them with a "horror akin to that which a fellow convict must feel for the gallows." A Pittsburgh critic insisted that "the sight of a female impersonator, who in private life called himself a man, would send me out into the world perfectly willing to murder my best friend if by that act I might assuage and calm some of the tumultuous disgust that surged madly through my bosom."[24] Clearly the dismantling of the gender system that Eltinge represented was terribly frightening to some.

Yet those critics' disdain was far from typical, and hundreds of thousands of audience members nationwide flocked to see Eltinge perform. As vaudeville historian Robert Toll pointed out, "In the first thirty years of the twentieth century . . . performers impersonating the opposite sex—men portraying women and women portraying men—numbered among the most popular and most highly paid stars in American vaudeville." And Eltinge was, without question, at the top of their ranks, both in terms of dollars and popularity.[25]

The particular excitement that Eltinge generated emerged in a 1912 article analyzing the Boston run of Eltinge's *Fascinating Widow*. The show lasted thirty-nine weeks there, grossing over one-half million dollars, and the unsigned article suggested that its success was tied to the widespread fantasy that Eltinge was living out. As the writer explained, "There have been men who wished they might be beautiful women in order to experience the joys of having a world of men at their feet, but it is safe to say that few of these have become fascinating widows." They had been held back by "too many difficulties," quite a number of which seemed to be "matters of mere obvious appearance and outward show." Nevertheless, the desire for escape that Eltinge expressed could easily be shared. The writer suggested that "a man who can pass for a woman has, of course, chances for entrancing adventure," although what those offstage adventures might be the author did not say. Yet the fact that becoming a woman might open up the world in a new way for a man was very much the alluring, confusing, and playful possibility that Eltinge's performances suggested.[26]

Eltinge's appeal was not that everyone could become an impersonator—far from it: his success could hardly be imitated. But he tickled audiences by making the impossible seem possible, by making gendered appearance and behavior seem merely artifice, divorced from physical sex.[27] For us in the twenty-first century, his performances highlight just how central—and perhaps even onerous—gender roles were one hundred years ago; and for those audiences, he raised the dizzying possibility of escape.

In *The Crinoline Girl*, as in many of his musical comedies, Eltinge portrayed a young man forced into a female masquerade. Before Eltinge underwent his transformation, his character and the character's sister discussed a thief who had used female impersonation to stage his crime. "No man could dress as a woman and not be detected," the sister asserted. "Why not?" Eltinge, as the brother, responded. "Any ordinary chap with a little skill in painting can make himself a good looking woman." "You're complimentary!" his sister snorted. "I mean it," he replied. "Nowadays, a woman is only ten per cent nature. The rest is art."[28] The plot, like Eltinge's career, unfolded from there. But it was on that premise—the art of gendered appearance—that Eltinge's stories and success were built.

Part of what is captivating about Eltinge is that in addition to being an internationally celebrated impersonator, he also cultivated sexual and affectionate intimacy with other men. Actor Hay recalled many male friends who had affairs with the star. Additionally, according to scholar Joan Vale, he lived for several years outside of San Diego with at least one long-term male companion.[29]

In the late nineteenth and early twentieth centuries, many psychologists and sexologists insisted that homosexually active men were, essentially, women trapped in male bodies. They were "inverts," they explained, and thus women in almost every way, from how they acted and moved to whom they desired: their bodies were the only unwomanly thing about them. By the latter half of the twentieth century, many academics and nonacademics alike had come to imagine that men who dressed and acted feminine were displaying this "inner woman" and must also possess inverted sexual desires. For them, female impersonation was the flip side of male homosexuality. And the increasing recognition of gay "drag queens" seemed only to strengthen the tie between gender inversion and homosexual identity in the public's imagination. As Esther Newton pointed out in her study of drag queens, "homosexuality is symbolized in American culture by transvestism."[30] In such a context, Eltinge the female impersonator seems to be merely another version of Eltinge the homosexual. Yet should Eltinge's gender play from the turn of the century be read as a sign of a homosexual identity?

Eltinge was certainly vociferous about his masculinity. One typical press notice from the 1910s boldly announced that "JULIAN ELTINGE ISN'T EFFEMINATE WHEN HE GETS HIS CORSETS OFF" and proceeded to describe both his "bubbling" manhood and his career as "a strong young athlete who covered right garden for the Harvard baseball team." For years he told stories of how he was forced into the role of impersonator, of how he performed only for money, and of how happy he would be when he could give up impersonating. He complained about the corsets, calling them "physical torture" and insisting that "the best part of my act is getting rid of them." He emphasized that "feminine impersonation is to him only a means to an end and that end is the accumulation of a competency and accumulating it quickly." And he consistently told reporters about his goals to appear as a man onstage—"in the toga virilis."[31]

At the same time, he generated bountiful publicity about his offstage manliness. He regularly circulated stories and photos of himself on his Long Island farm, sawing wood, feeding chickens, or playing with his bull-dogs in the lake. Out there, said one journalist, "he gets right down to things masculine and earthy." He staged encounters with famous boxers and also released an endless public relations litany about fishing expeditions and bare-knuckle brawls. One press notice, for instance, explained how "when off the stage he will get into a game of poker, can beat Bob Hilliard playing pinochle, can row in a varsity eight, or can eat chop suey with the sticks and talk nonsense with the ladies. Julian is certainly all right."[32]

Other contemporary female impersonators, like Bert Savoy and The Great Richards, made far less show of their masculinity. Richards, for instance, told *Variety* in 1911, "You don't hear of me giving up dresses. I know how to wear them and am going to stick." Likewise, the much more comic Savoy was "notoriously effeminate both in private and public." Eltinge, by contrast, was notoriously aggressive about his masculinity. As one male fan told a reporter, "A lotta guys think he's in the sis class. Jes' let 'em say that in front of him. I seen him fight once in Pittsburgh and I'm for him, right from the ace to the king." Stories circulated so frequently about him defending his good name with his fists that a 1925 Buster Keaton film even included a joke about his pugnaciousness.[33]

Most historians have interpreted Eltinge's masculine strutting as a cover for a clear homosexual identity. The success of gay liberation politics and its ideology of essential "gay identities" hidden in "closets" may make it difficult *not* to see Eltinge as a man both aware of and hiding his sexual identity. Early in the twentieth century, however, gender play was not popularly understood as the surface marker of some perverted inner sexual identity. An effeminate man may have been a member of "the sis class," but he was not understood as "a homosexual": the latter category barely existed in popular consciousness. Sexual activity alone was not understood as constituting an identity. Similarly, defending one's masculinity did not necessarily indicate anxiety over perceptions about sexual identity. In the Teddy Roosevelt era, anxiety about masculinity was widespread and little focused on homosexuality.[34]

The Fascinating Widow, Eltinge's successful show that toured the nation for some three years between 1910 and 1913, provides a window into these distinctions.[35] Eltinge played Hal Blake, a college man in love with Margaret Leffingwell who punches his rival for her affections, Oswald Wentworth. Facing possible prison time for the blow, Blake disguises himself as Mrs. Monte, the eponymous widow, to elude the law, and also then proceeds to foil Wentworth's efforts at wooing. He so delights Wentworth along the way that at show's end, Blake in bridal gown prepares to wed Wentworth himself. Then, at the last moment, he changes into groom attire and marries Leffingwell.

Setting aside Eltinge's impersonation, the rivalry between Blake and Wentworth framed a debate about heterosexual masculinity. Wentworth, who wears glasses, was identified by at least one critic as "the college student cissy." Eltinge as Blake, by contrast, was described as a "handsome, athletic, manly fellow." While the "cissy" was fooled by Eltinge's impersonation, he was not deemed a "cissy" (or sissy) for his sexual object choice. After all, he was hardly unique in being smitten by the feminine-attired Eltinge. Rather, it was Wentworth's gender style—his bookish weakness—that marked him as a sissy.

The same rivalry appeared in a 1925 Eltinge film, *"Madame, Behave!"* There the sissy rival, who had been handpicked by a guardian to wed Eltinge's character's sweetheart, was deemed a "cake eater"; not only was he tall, wispy, and monocled, but he also exuded aristocratic wealth and heritage. He was after the same woman as Eltinge's character, so his effeminacy was a statement about his weakened masculinity, not his sexual desires, and it was expressed through the class-conscious framework that dominated Progressive Era understandings of manliness. If Eltinge punched anyone who called him a sissy, he was fighting off similar charges of gender effeminacy, not an identity as a homosexual. In fact, as one historian pointed out, while some close friends and certain associates knew about Eltinge's homosexual affairs, many theatrical workers and members of the press did not think of Eltinge in such terms.[36]

What complicates the picture, however, is that some homosexually active men in turn-of-the-century New York City did begin to use gender inversion as a code to express their sexual desires. As George Chauncey has demonstrated, most men who participated in the homosexual subculture there possessed little sense of sexual identity. By and large, to the degree that they upheld gender norms and acted as the "inserter" in sexual interactions, they perceived themselves as normal masculine men; their gender identity seemed to be their full identity. A fraction of these men, however, began to use various versions of female gender impersonation to convey homosexual desires. Calling themselves "fairies" and adopting tactics ranging from dandy-like fashion to wearing make-up and even women's clothing, these men tried to mark their display of feminine gender as connected to their sexual desires for other men. For these men, Chauncey argued, effeminacy became "a deliberate cultural strategy . . . a way to declare a gay identity publicly." In doing so, they echoed the opinion of many late-nineteenth-century scholars that homosexual desires were "symptoms" of a larger "inverted" personality in which a homosexually active man was fundamentally a woman in all but body. The fairies' style, in a sense, argued that an effeminate male *did* have inverted sexual desires. And in a way, fairies were the first Americans to clearly express some identity tied to fixed sexual desires. Even so, what was fundamental for the fairy was that despite his male body he was female in *all* his behaviors and desires: he had a fully inverted gender identity, not just an exclusively sexual identity.[37]

That Eltinge was both homosexually active and a female impersonator does not make him a "fairy," though. Indeed, if we accept Eltinge's own declarations—and why shouldn't we?—he saw his maleness as the essential truth about him much more than either his stage shows or his sexual activities. Certainly his masculine behavior was the key to his stage success. By being believably masculine offstage, he both affirmed the notion that a male body produced masculinity and made his appearance as a woman onstage that much more miraculous and exceptional. Female impersonators like Richards and Savoy who were equally feminine offstage achieved none of Eltinge's fame. In fighting for his masculine identity, Eltinge was fighting to retain the greatest drama for his performance.[38]

Indeed, the one tale of Eltinge apparently interacting with "cissies" or "fairies" marked him as a man of a very different order. It appeared in a 1913 column by Amy Leslie, who was unabashed in her disdain for typical female impersonators, "the usual creeping male defective who warbles soprano and decks himself in the frocks and frills of womankind." Leslie distinguished Eltinge quite clearly from the "male orchids," however, explaining that he shared her contempt for them and was "brawling and stampeding and roaring out his fury half the time because these creatures who always flock together are 'crazy about him.'" Eltinge, she insisted, "would just as soon see a detached freight train plunging at him as one of these pariahs with the wrist watch coming at him with a puny grin." Once a New York stagehand brought "two nattily dressed youths with hand painted joy on their faces to the barred door of the tawny Eltinge. Julian stepped out, caught sight of their fanciful ensemble, and let a roar out of him that shook the scenery. His pretty wig was off, his black jet sleeves rolled up to fight and he looked like a stricken bull in the arena. The prim gentles fled. One of them yelled: 'Somebody throw her a fish; she's a sea lion!' "[39] Here was Eltinge ready as ever to defend his manly identity against any aspersions, even by mere association. He refused to be seen as a "cissy," certainly not by obvious ones.

How much, though, was Eltinge's roar about masculinity, and how much about sexuality? Was his, and Leslie's, disdain caused by the men being "cissies" or actual "fairies"? The answer is decidedly ambiguous. For even while fairies may have understood their gender play as an indicator of sexual desire, that connection between gender inversion and sexual practice was not widely shared by the general public.[40]

The only thing that is clear is that in his roaring, Eltinge was plainly resisting being grouped with the "prim gentles." His performances on stage and screen mocked such "gentle" men no matter what kind of sexual desires they had. If he mocked the sissies for being unmasculine, he equally roared at these "gentles" for being so feminine. Masculinity and femininity were his concerns, not sexuality. And while the "prim gentles" may have seen in Eltinge just another "fairy," it is likely that few others, Eltinge included, would have seen their common sexual practices as unifying them into a shared category. Eltinge's resistance, ultimately, speaks not to fears of relinquishing the closet; it speaks to his unwillingness to relinquish his offstage masculine gender identification. He refused to allow gender play or even inversion to be read as a mark of something else—a hidden sexual inversion or even sexual identity. Gender identity was the essential thing.

Eltinge was a larger-than-life figure. His gender role-playing, on- and offstage, was not exactly typical of early-twentieth-century Americans. Rather, his performances exaggerated and made explicit the centrality of gender as a code of identity and the deep tie between sexed bodies and gendered behavior. Eltinge's vaudeville career reveals the attention—even celebration—accorded to the gender code early in the twentieth century, much more than to a code of sexual identity. Eltinge's shows did not suggest that "beneath" gender lay a more "fundamental" identity based around sexual desire. In Eltinge's era, sexual identity did not exist as a widely accepted notion. And except perhaps for some "fairies" and their peers, the inversion of gender—Eltinge's female impersonations—did not connote a comparable inversion in sexual object choice.

Ultimately, of course, Eltinge's roaring at the "prim gentles" could hardly stop the cultural transition that was to come, one that first paired gender inversion with inverted desires and then affirmed desire alone as the narrow basis of identities. But for the moment—this moment of Eltinge's heyday—sexuality had yet to be conceived as a system of identity. As such, his performances delighted America and much of the world, and so, of course, the movies came calling.

For a time, Eltinge resisted. In 1913 Eltinge told a Cincinnati paper, "I feel that I owe something to that public which has recognized me as a legitimate star, and inasmuch as I expect to continue appearing before the same public for many years to come, it would hardly be fair to permit even moving picture likenesses of myself to be exhibited in the moving picture houses." But his resolve weakened. Between stage shows in the spring of 1915, Eltinge ventured briefly out to California. While there, according to a succinct *New York Times* headline, he experienced a change of heart: "Eltinge an Actors' Colony Founder."[41]

Eltinge, like so many other Americans, decided to make the great move West, and he chose to settle in the hilly center of the movie industry, Edendale. Many of the movie studios were already based there, shooting Westerns among the undeveloped hillsides, recruiting extras from the local residents, and sending madcap police officers racing along the neighborhood's streets. In those earliest years of Hollywood, Eltinge developed friendships with the likes of Mary Pickford, the DeMilles, and later, Charlie Chaplin. He signed a contract to begin making films and set his sights on becoming a movie star. By 1917 he was acting in three movies, being cooed over by the Hollywood media, and constructing a mansion in the hills of Edendale. For the moment, he quite successfully carved a place for himself in a world that was in flux.[42]

The view looking west from Eltinge's dining room terrace, as it appeared in *The Architectural Record,* February 1921.

ONE

"A Most Lascivious Picture of Impatient Desire"

AS ELTINGE SETTLED INTO EDENDALE and the new phase of his career in the 1910s, he quickly found himself at the center of a flurry of activity. Movie-making was a busy business. By a conservative estimate, the film companies in and around Los Angeles were already spending more than 30 million dollars a year. At least twenty thousand Angelenos were permanent employees of the industry. Part of the excitement in the film world focused on just the sort of entertainment that was Eltinge's specialty: playing with and challenging gender roles. In fact, in 1917 the popular fan magazine *Motion Picture* ran an article entitled "He, She, or It" that described how more actors were wearing dresses and actresses sporting pants for the movies. "In these days of suffragets and long-haired poets, bifurcated skirts and lisping laddies, it's hard to know who's who and what's what. It's getting to be quite the rage—this exchange of identities."[1]

Thrown into the center of all that action, Eltinge nonetheless attracted more than his fair share of attention. Louella Parsons devoted a column to "the deft impersonator of feminine charm," and *Photoplay* magazine published its account of "the studio sensation." In fact, *Photoplay* gleefully reported in 1918 how Eltinge

> has a habit of forgetting he is a lady going to and from his dressing room and the stage. . . . So when a handsomely gowned young woman crossed

the stage with her beautiful evening gown hiked up so as not to interfere with her knees, traffic stopped; one property boy dropped a perfectly good vase so he could signal with both hands to his mates; a carpenter paused to look, but not in hammering, so took a smashed thumb to the doctor; three juveniles nearly swallowed their cigarettes; and "gossips' row" gave three cheers, because there was somebody new on the lot to talk about. Everyone ran toward the Eltinge set as if it was on fire.[2]

Indeed, Eltinge's fire burned brightly, and the interest did not stop when he left the studio at day's end. For months, the press also followed the construction of his Edendale manor, the Villa Capistrano. By the time the villa was completed in 1918, Edendale no longer dominated the film industry the way it had five years earlier. More studios were setting up in Hollywood, Burbank, and Culver City.[3] Nevertheless, Edendale remained a geographic hub of the industry: the new Hollywood locations were only one or two miles west of the neighborhood, and Universal's Burbank lot sat just to the north on the other side of the Edendale hills. At the same time, the neighborhood retained its sense of both rural isolation and, especially with Eltinge's arrival, glamour.

As soon as Villa Capistrano was completed, various papers and magazines sent reporters and photographers to take a look. Sitting high on its Edendale ridge with a panoramic view across Silver Lake, the villa was spectacular, and no doubt some of the interest genuinely related to the house itself. At the same time, the movie industry had already begun to transform the nature of celebrity, using publicists to market the true and invented tales of actors' personal lives, and the interest in the villa—and through it, in Eltinge—had a particular focus: his "true" gendered identity.[4]

Among the first to arrive was *Photoplay* magazine. *Photoplay* largely restricted itself to publishing photographs of the house—though they did deem the villa "the most beautiful and unique ever built for a motion picture star." But its sequence of four photos, beginning with an external view of the house from across the lake and ending with a shot of Eltinge in his bedroom, pensively standing by the window in a silk robe, suggested a narrative of increasing intimacy. Indeed, much more than the theater columnists who reveled in Eltinge's backstage transformations, the movie journalists seemed keen on getting to the heart of who Eltinge truly was in private. While one writer said that the steepness of the drive to the house gave the impression of "mounting to some medieval baron's home or to some impregnable fortress that had been so placed for defensive purposes," the journalists all seemed eager to penetrate those defenses.[5]

Predictably, their questions focused on masculinity, and they interpreted the house as an expression of Eltinge's maleness. *Photoplay,* for instance, introduced the four intimate photos with the line "It's too beautiful for a bachelor—it's a shame." Louella Parsons agreed, adding, "It looks suspicious, and it would not surprise his host of friends if one day a beautiful lady would sit at the head of that table." Elmer Grey of *Architectural Record* insisted that the house was "so distinctly a man's house," and he noted the multiple stairways in the house: "Some women might not like them—but this is not a woman's house!"[6]

The journalists' declarations about Eltinge and the house's gender echoed his own insistent claims about his offstage masculinity, but they also reflected a growing cultural demand for the hidden truths of human nature. The editors of *Photoplay* underscored that demand in the editorial that framed that month's issue. The essay, entitled "The Melting Pot," argued that a new age of clear and essential identities lay ahead. After passing through the crucible fires of World War I, the editors insisted, "prejudices are sweeping out like ash on the furnace winds." Humanity was becoming unified and soon there "will be a shaking of the conventional codes to their foundations." National and ethnic identities, for instance, were going to be cast aside, and human identity itself, pure and unadulterated, was going to bubble to the surface. "Five years ago, people were pretty generally accepted for what they *seemed* to be. For the rest of our lives, people are going to be accepted for what they *are*."[7] Appearances be damned, the editors seemed to be insisting; costume and make-up did not show who people were. Their new goal of authentic identity—or what might be called *essence*—was something more fixed, perhaps hidden, but soon enough within their grasp.

Reportage on Eltinge, the gender-playing centerpiece of the issue, expressed this quest for identity. Perhaps by including him in an issue about accepting people for who they *"are,"* the editors were indicating a continuing tolerance for his gender play. But the tide was shifting. The tone of all the journalists conveyed a demand for essence, for true identity, not for a playful performance that seemed to mock identity codes. And a steadily pressing set of questions focused on the relationship between sexual desire and identity, particularly gender identity. Was gendered behavior actually an expression of sexual desires? That is, did men who dressed like women in fact desire other men? Were such desires consistent and never changing? And if so, did their desires constitute the more profound truth—the essential truth—about them, and not the surface play of clothing and cosmetics?

Such questions began to circulate more widely in Eltinge's Los Angeles, yet in the 1910s, '20s, and early '30s, the city lacked a single answer, a single governing paradigm for explaining sexual desire and sexual behavior. Instead, multiple paradigms prevailed. Some held that the objects of men's sexual desires could and did change over a man's lifetime—perhaps even over the course of an afternoon. Others held that sexual behavior was an expression of gender identity and was fairly static. Some began to believe that sexual desire marked a fundamental truth about people; others scoffed at such a notion. Fundamentally, in Eltinge's new hometown, widely different notions competed to explain the relationship between desire, gender, and identity. At the same time, the city's homosexual activity became steadily more visible.

"96" CLUBS IN THE CITY OF ANGELS

In November of 1914, in a series of arrests across the Los Angeles area—both within the city proper and in Long Beach, the independent port city to the south—police jailed between fifty and one hundred men on charges of sexual misconduct. Long Beach, one of the few streetcar suburbs of Los Angeles that had resisted being incorporated into the city, prided itself on its midwestern values and small-town atmosphere. But apparently it was not immune to sexual impropriety.[8] Specifically, the arrested men had been caught engaging in or attempting homosexual oral sex. The state's criminal code did not criminalize any oral sex at the time—though that soon changed—and felony sodomy laws were understood as referring only to anal penetration. Sodomy punishments could be very steep: men in the 1910s and '20s were sent to prison for sentences ranging from five to fifteen years—though the law allowed for a life sentence—for sodomy convictions.[9] The men arrested in Los Angeles and Long Beach, however, were charged with the much more nebulous misdemeanor of "social vagrancy" and either fined between one hundred and five hundred dollars or sentenced to the county jail for six-month sentences. Despite the much less grievous punishment, the misdemeanor charges still provoked the suicide of two of the arrested men, the suicide attempt of a third, a lengthy court battle between the publishers of the *Los Angeles Times* and the *Tri-*

bune, and an investigation by the *Sacramento Bee,* the state capital's major newspaper.[10]

The cases may well have avoided this heightened level of public attention—even considering the suicide of well-regarded Long Beach banker John Lamb—if one man, a florist named Herbert Lowe, had not decided to resist the charges.[11] As misdemeanor arrests, they were unlikely to warrant much press attention, and most of the men simply pled guilty and paid their fines. Lowe's defiance, however, attracted coverage. His story piqued the curiosity of the *Los Angeles Times* along with *Bee* editor C. K. McClatchy. McClatchy sent undercover reporter Eugene Fisher to find out what the local press was not reporting, and Fisher left behind an intriguing file of handwritten notes and article drafts first reported on by historian Sharon Ullman.

Fisher's notes, the arrests, and the court case offer a captivating window into the possibilities of homosexual interactions in the 1910s. Taken as a whole, the sources suggest clearly that a network of homosexual activity spanned the Los Angeles area in the 1910s. At the same time, the sources raise provocative questions—much as they did at the time—about how codified that network was, who participated in it, and how those participants should be understood.

In his own investigation, reporter Fisher stumbled upon a remarkably chatty fellow named L. L. Rollins, a Los Angeles resident who was among the arrested men. Rollins lived just west of downtown and just south of Edendale in a Bunker Hill apartment building. Rollins apparently hoped to be the principal informant for what he assumed would be a massive police crackdown, and so spoke fairly freely with Fisher. Between Rollins's revelations and various police officers' confirmations, Fisher felt confident in writing back to his editor "that 'degeneracy' is organized in Los Angeles, that there are in actual existence today in the 'City of the Angels,' clubs known as '96' clubs existing solely for the practice of degrading forms of sexualism, and that these social vagrants, calling themselves the 'society of queers' flaunt their vice to heaven in this and other civilized communities." All this, Fisher wrote, "is now positively known to the officers of Los Angeles and Long Beach."[12]

Most of the men who were arrested were detained by the police in the Long Beach Bathhouse. Nevertheless, Rollins described for Fisher more elaborate and exclusive assignation spots around Los Angeles. Two private clubs, he said, were within two blocks of City Hall and hosted evening events. (Apparently, he and a friend had forced their way into one such

This photograph, circa 1915, discovered in *Sacramento Bee* editor C. K. McClatchy's file about the Long Beach and Los Angeles arrests, bore the label "L.A. fairy." (Sacramento Archives and Museum Collection Center.)

club on Main Street, after proving to the others that they were "queer.") Rollins also described a Venice Beach party, hosted by two cohabitating multimillionaires, where thirty prominent young male guests were each given a kimono, a pair of high-heeled shoes, and a wig upon arrival and shown to a room to change. "These two multi-millionaires, and their friends," Fisher later wrote, "cared absolutely nothing for women, but resorted to all sorts of unnatural practices with men, especially young men and with them the 'twentieth century way'"—allegedly their term for oral sex—"was preferred."[13]

Similarly, Rollins detailed a party at a wealthy Los Angeles man's apartment. Fourteen young guests were invited, Fisher recounted, "with the promise that they would have the opportunity of meeting some of the prominent 'queers' of the 'Angel City' and the further attraction that some 'chickens,' as the new recruits in the vice are called, would be available." The city's finest attended: politicians, businessmen, and churchmen. There was food and chatter, and in lieu of place cards, each place setting had "a candy representation of a man's private which was sucked and enjoyed by each guest to the evident amusement of all." One or two young men entertained the others with music and singing, while costumed in women's clothing. No sexual activity occurred at this party until after most of the guests had left. Then Rollins played ragtime music on the piano while the host had his way with one of the young men. Beyond the fairly public site of a bathhouse, there lurked the much more private and restricted world of such parties and clubs.[14]

Rollins estimated the number of "queers" in Los Angeles to be five thousand. Fisher's police informants inclined more toward two thousand, but he himself thought the larger figure more likely. Rollins claimed to know at least two hundred personally. In a city of some four hundred thousand, five thousand was a significant portion of the population. There was a world, it seemed, of social-sexual activity that involved one in forty Angeleno men—or perhaps one on every street car.[15]

How should we understand such a world? On the one hand, Rollins's descriptions and Fisher's calculations suggest a network of sexual and social activity that seems familiar—that is, it seems as though it could have been lifted from twenty-first-century gay American culture. Did these social encounters constitute so coherent a community and subculture? Was it really "a world"? On the other hand, how did the participants in these events understand themselves—and in turn, how were they understood by others? Did they share a distinct identity based on desire?

Sharon Ullman explored the implications of Fisher's report for her 1998 volume *Sex Seen*. She argued that Fisher's investigative efforts revealed "a large community of self-identified homosexuals," or what she elsewhere deemed "a robust, complex homosexual community that saw itself as quintessentially modern and progressive and had its own culture and institutions." Such a claim is buoyed by the testimony of a police officer at the principal Long Beach trial who alleged that Herbert Lowe had made confessions similar to Rollins's. Like Rollins, the officer said, Lowe had also described exclusive clubs where men met and insisted that

> the Ninety-six Club was the best; that it was composed of the "queer" people, that they got together every week. I asked why they called it the Ninety-six Club, and he said something about turning the letters around, before and behind. He said that the members sometimes spent hundreds of dollars on silk gowns, hosiery, etc., in which they dressed at sessions of the club. He said that at these "drags" the "queer" people have a good time, but no one could get in without being introduced by a member in good standing.

If true, the officer's description adds to the sense of an exclusive network of parties and special events that those in the know—and with the cash—could join.[16]

Yet claiming the existence of a "large community" based simply on Fisher and the officer's secondhand testimony may be too broad a stretch. Fisher certainly tended toward the melodramatic, writing at one point that homosexual activity constituted a "damning mind-dwarfing, soul-blasting blight." At the same time, the clubs and parties of city luminaries that Rollins and the officer described are hard to corroborate from court records. (Fisher thought the well-off bought their way out of the police records.) Instead, court trials from the 1910s and 1920s focused mostly on isolated pairs of men found in public spaces, such as streets, parks, and bathrooms, and occasionally a hotel room.[17] Such sexual activities were hardly at the center of a rich social life, let alone a community—a cohort of people who recognize themselves in one another and strive toward a variety of shared goals. Rather, they revealed a network or circuit of sexual meeting spots. That network expanded and diversified in the years between the First and Second World Wars.

LIFE ON "THE RUN"

Across the 1920s, '30s, and '40s, men regularly met one another for sex in the very public locales of bathhouses, shops, streetcars, and parks. The experiences of a man like Don Greenfield are representative. Greenfield was born in late 1909 in San Francisco, but settled with his parents in Los Angeles in the 1920s. By 1930 he was working in a print shop and had his own place in Bunker Hill, by then a neighborhood full of Victorian homes that had been largely converted into boardinghouses. While living there, Greenfield began to discover that men were interested in him sexually. "I was never the aggressor, but people would come up and suggest," he recalled years later. As a volunteer usher at the Philharmonic Auditorium, he was picked up by the head usher. While trying on shoes at Bullock's downtown department store, the salesman began caressing his leg. Standing on the streetcar, men would rub up against him. The city was rife with opportunities for knowing eye contact, gropes, and even full sexual interactions. Asked if he dressed in a certain way to signal interest—something that had been suggested by other historians—Greenfield said no. Jokingly he insisted that the men hit on him "because I was so good looking," but then suggested that "there was something about me that said there was a possibility there." Other men met sexual partners in classrooms, movie theaters, and restaurants. Assignations and flirtations could and did occur anywhere.[18]

Increasingly, a steady portion of homosexual assignations occurred at a network of very particular known public meeting spots that developed around Los Angeles. By the late 1930s, Pershing Square, Main Street, Hill Street, the park at the public library, the bathroom in the subway building, the bus depot—all were stopping points on a downtown circuit of male same-sex activity that some referred to as "The Run." In addition to these very public places, the circuit of the Run also came to include the slightly more private spaces of a few bars and bathhouses.[19] What historian John Howard wrote about Mississippi also applies to Los Angeles in these years. The Run was not an "enclave—in which gay men regularly interacted with other self-identified gay men, mostly patronized gay establishments, and frequently participated in gay community rituals." Rather, it was part of a network or circuit—a "broader expanse of terrain" in which men "with stealth and cunning moved in, across and out of these spaces." Despite the absence of a clear community, however, from the 1920s through the 1940s, these pockets of homosexual activity and socializing became entrenched in Los Angeles life.[20]

A fair portion of encounters along the Run occurred outdoors, along specific streets and in certain parks. As one man recalled, you had to have money to hang out in bars: those were for the "affluent" who could spend a quarter or fifty cents on a dime's worth of beer. The parks, however, were open for all. Pershing Square, the busiest site on the Run, occupied a square block in the heart of downtown and was flanked by some of the finest hotels, stores, and theaters in the city. Officially known as Central

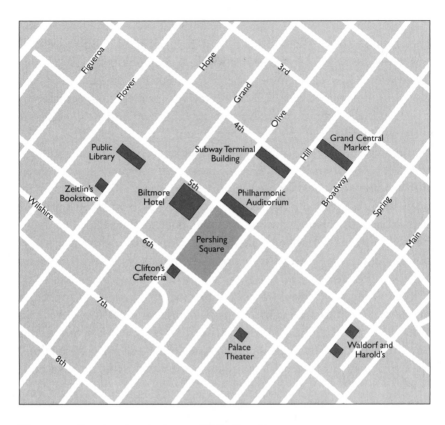

Downtown Los Angeles, the heart of "The Run."

Park until 1918, the square was given a formal design early in the century, with a central fountain and symmetrical paths. Landscaped with lush vegetation, the park became a daytime site of free-speech activity with a bevy of soapbox orators drawing crowds throughout the day; in the evenings, at least since the 1910s, the square also became a magnet for male homosexual contacts. Harry Hay moved with his family to Los Angeles when he was four, in 1916. As an avid student at Los Angeles High School in the 1920s, he heard rumors about the drunks and perverts in Pershing Square; he confirmed those rumors before the decade ended, meeting his first long-term lover in the square's underground bathroom.[21]

Pershing Square attracted a wide variety of men for a multitude of tastes. Fred Frisbie, an engineer who moved to Los Angeles in the late 1920s, observed that since the square "was convenient to downtown and it was comparatively safe," it attracted men from the city's financial district: "there

Pershing Square in the late 1930s, dense with men sitting, talking, debating politics, and cruising. (SECURITY PACIFIC COLLECTION/Los Angeles Public Library.)

were elegant people, there were professional people who were very discreet and just stood around, but made contact." By contrast, a social-work student from the University of Southern California who studied the square's habitués in the late 1930s decided that most of the interactions there involved prostitution between young men and older "deviates" who lived nearby. He thought that the prostitutes were clearly identifiable: "They were slender, smooth skinned, pink cheeked young men whose actions were effeminate. They wore men's clothing which was neatly pressed and tailored, bright ties and flowers pinned to the shirt or coat on the left lapel." Many other accounts of Pershing Square featured a still wider swath of cruising men—including rougher men and marines looking for action. Even the soapbox orators joined in at times: Jim Kepner remembered a "lanky old atheist who slashed believers with stinging scorn," but when he had finished his harangue, invited Kepner out for donuts and then up to his room in neighboring Bunker Hill. The park thus displayed the variety of participants in life on the Run—even the multiple sexual subcultures that overlapped and interacted there.[22]

Park cruising spread well beyond Pershing Square. The park surrounding the public library (two blocks to the west) and Westlake and Lafayette parks (nearly two miles further west, near the city's best art schools) were all well known and well trafficked. And Echo Park, along the southern end of Edendale, also saw significant homosexual activity. Screenwriter and later Mattachine activist Dale Jennings recalled Echo Park as "quite active" and "rather exciting," with most of the encounters taking place at night.[23]

Beyond these outdoor adventures, men also began to find each other in particular bathhouses, restaurants, and bars as a network of indoor homosocial and homosexual venues expanded across the city. Bars, in particular, appeared in downtown Los Angeles, along Sunset Boulevard near Hollywood, and out west along the Santa Monica beach.

These venues were often far less elegant than the kimono parties that Rollins described. Photographer Edward Weston stumbled onto one such place early in the spring of 1923. Weston became famous later in his life for his sensual photographs of the southwestern landscape and nude women and for his participation in the arts community of Carmel, California. In 1923, however, he made his living as a portrait photographer and worked out of his studio over the hills north of Edendale in a neighborhood called Tropico. One spring night, Weston ventured into a Greek coffee shop on Los Angeles Street in the city's downtown. He and a friend had been led there by Weston's assistant, Margarethe Mather. She had heard that it was a place where sailors gathered, that a murder had been committed there, and that fights were a nightly occurrence. As Weston later wrote in his daybook, "though not favored with a murder or fight had a sufficiently exciting night—yes a fascinating night."[24]

Four or five waitresses were working in the diner that night and, aside from Mather, there were no other women present. An African American man played the saxophone, while another strummed the banjo. Otherwise, a mix of white sailors filled the room, Weston observed, with

here and there a collarless nondescript—but mostly those not in uniform were that type of effeminate male who seek the husky sailor to complement their lacking vigour—One such fastidiously-dressed—unmistakable person—presented to us a most lascivious picture of impatient desire—his foot twitched continually—his whole body quivered—his lips fairly drooled—until finally with several others of his kind—a bunch of sailors were "dated up" and off they went in a limousine—Sailors danced together with biting of ears and open caresses—some sprawled over their tables down and out—every one had a bottle on the hi—while an officer of the law amiably overlooked his opportunity to enforce the 18th amendment.

One sailor stumbled over to their table, sputtering out his life story. He invited them to feel his muscles, while he whined about the "gold digger" with whom he had quarreled. Weston was captivated. Though he felt that he and his friends stood out, "I should like to go again," he wrote, "under different circumstances."[25]

Like Weston's diner, few of the Run's indoor venues were set aside exclusively for homosexual interactions. Much more consistently, men interested in homosexual affairs were mixed together with other men, often in predominately male settings. According to the social-work student, some men, for instance, pursued sexual encounters in the cheap movie theaters along Main Street, where men outnumbered women by ten to one. Sexual encounters also occurred in the homosocial setting of bathhouses. Urban bathhouses emerged around the turn of the twentieth century, providing swimming and bathing facilities for city-dwellers who lacked indoor plumbing. In addition, entrepreneurs established Turkish or Russian bathhouses that offered some middle-class comforts. Thus the clientele at a bathhouse could be the urban poor and working classes, most of whom were not there for a sexual encounter. But men interested in sex also succeeded in making several middle-class bathhouses sites of regular rendezvous.[26]

During the 1920s and '30s, the management of at least one downtown bathhouse allegedly "pretended not to know what was going on" and so, reported bathhouse aficionado Harry Otis, "the action was wild." Famously, the Palace Baths operated for several decades with communal steam rooms and private changing rooms. Otis insisted,

The Palace Baths in Los Angeles should be named the Palacio de Bellas Artes for the reason that many of the men who perform there are really artists in satisfying themselves as well as others. Some with hidden talents develop them by the trial and error system, whereas others keep alive and improve the technique they developed thru years of experience. To men of the reserved type the Palace is a second home where they can let down their hair, if they have any, and do what they wish without fear.

On some nights, according to Otis, the Palace was rented out for private parties. In later decades, its reputation was far less glamorous. Asked if the

Palace was fancy, even in the 1930s or '40s, Don Greenfield replied, "No, anything but." But it was busy, in his memory, with men looking for sex with other men.[27]

The Bimini Baths, just west of downtown, also saw a fair share of homosexual activity, though in a much less strictly homosocial setting. The Bimini attracted diverse crowds to its large swimming pools—separate ones for men and women. Harry Hay, who went to the baths as a child and youth in the late 1910s and early 1920s, said he was "molested several times by men" there who swam or dived beside him and initiated underwater oral sex. R. B. Harrison was arrested at the Bimini Baths in 1910, spied by a part-time guard while having sex with a thirteen-year-old in a changing room. At the preliminary hearing, the weekend guard, Wilbur Searles, reported, "In my previous work at Bimini I had discovered immoral conditions there on several occasions." In fact, he was so familiar with that kind of activity at the bathhouse that when he saw Harrison enter a changing room with the teenager, "I immediately thought there will be something wrong there." Searles therefore positioned himself to be able to see into Harrison's dressing room.[28]

By the 1940s the Crystal Baths near the pier in Santa Monica were also well known for sheltering homosexual activity. Jim Kepner, a Texas native, moved to Los Angeles in 1943. An avid science fiction buff and a jack-of-all-trades, Kepner eventually began the first ever American gay history archive. Before that, however, he eagerly explored Los Angeles' various homosexual offerings and remembered that in the 1940s the front desk clerk at the Crystal Baths sent clients to different floors depending on whether or not he thought they were interested in sexual encounters. The rooftop also allowed nude sunbathing, which often became a prelude to sex. "In spite of 'No Loitering' signs," Kepner recalled, "many customers spent hours in the dank, dark halls, lockers, showers, and changing room." By the 1940s, he said, there were three or four active bathhouses down by the beach, and a long stretch of beach had come to have a reputation, at least among certain men, as "Bitches Beach," "Queer Alley," or "Queens Beach."[29]

Like the bathhouses, in the 1920s, '30s, and '40s, the city's speakeasies and bars similarly contained a clientele with mixed sexual desires. According to Fred Frisbie, for instance, during Prohibition some Los Angeles speakeasies had extremely diverse crowds "because it was a liquor-oriented type of thing. But there was a camaraderie that embraced everyone. Even the screaming faggots were welcomed by the most untoward people you could imagine. There would be gangsters and mobsters and women hanging by their claws. . . . But they embraced the queens, and they would say, 'Well now sweetie pie, how's it today?'" In Frisbie's recollection, some speakeasies allowed homosexual flirtations and feminine-acting men. The customers "considered themselves passengers on the same train. They had their own little quirks. Everybody was united by breaking the Volstead Act," the federal law that enforced Prohibition.[30]

By the mid-1930s, a handful of well-trafficked bars became fixtures along the downtown Run and in Hollywood. The downtown circuit centered on Main Street, which was then the Bowery of Los Angeles, featuring cheap hotels and restaurants; pawnbrokers; dime and nickel movie theaters showing "pictures" that, according to *Reader's Digest,* "will certainly never reach *your* neighborhood theater"; burlesque houses; and cheap brothels. The street thronged with men—unemployed day laborers, men looking for sex, men out drinking or searching for cheap entertainment—men whom the USC social-work student confidently labeled "deviate personalities." Along Main and Hill streets, homosexually active men found one another in bars like Maxwell's, Harold's, the Crown Jewel, and the Waldorf. In Frisbie's recollection, these bars flourished because owners paid off the police to ignore them. They were mostly dives, he said, "in the sense that everything was sort of unfinished. It was rough and ready, so to speak. 'You want a drink, here's a drink.' No elegance. Excepting for that there would be entertainment." Someone might sit and play an organ or piano and offer some music.[31]

In many of these bars, the patronage changed over the course of the day. The Crown Jewel, for instance, was remembered as having a non-homosexual crowd in the mornings and at lunchtime; after lunch, homosexual socializing began. During happy hour, a non-homosexual clientele returned, only to be replaced by more homosexual interactions later in the evening. According to Frisbie, "We used to have a little joke about that. 'Are you going to the night shift?' 'What's that?' 'Oh you know, the Crown.'"[32]

Although this handful of places began to cater more and more to homosexually active men, they did not feel like especially safe havens. Vice officers patrolled them regularly, watching for inappropriate physical activity. At places like Maxwell's or Harold's, a man could get arrested if he put his arm up on the booth behind another man. According to several men, the owner of the Crown Jewel regularly pointed out customers to the police—and then offered his services to them as an attorney.[33]

Additionally, even though sexual prospects were pursued at a place like Maxwell's, and even though the bar was listed in a 1949 underground "primer for novices" called "The Gay Girl's Guide," neither the bar nor its clientele would have embraced an obviously homosexual identity. Harry Hay, looking back from the 1970s, explained that a typical Maxwell's customer behaved as "a straight who doesn't mind standing still for a minute for what you might have in mind." That is, while he may have willingly participated in homosexual activity, he did not self-consciously identify with that activity. As such, Maxwell's did not necessarily feel like a setting in which a shared identity was explored and articulated. In the vocabulary of the day, Hay said that at Maxwell's "you didn't let your hair down till the lights went dim, and even then not very far down." Indeed, he insisted decades later, "no one was ever forthrightly gay anyplace, anywhere, except maybe in the bathtub by yourself, or on those rare occasions when you could be totally alone for a long period with a lover; and such occasions were few and far between."[34]

During the 1930s, however, men did let their hair down rather more at a place like the 808 Night Club. Estelle Milmar began working at the 808 in the early 1930s. Milmar was born in 1905 into a circus and vaudeville family. After twenty years of performing, she married and, in 1930, moved with her husband to California and eventually settled in Los Angeles. Milmar worked around the city and then, in the early 1930s, got a job at the 808. Initially located at 808 Figueroa Street, the club boasted eight or ten tables, pinball, and a stage where female impersonators regularly performed. Nine out of ten of the performers, said Milmar, were homosexually active. By 1934 the club, which developed an international reputation, moved five blocks north into a building that was a full-fledged theater and could hold a larger crowd. The new building had a long bar with some thirty stools, a terrace, an orchestra pit in front of the stage, and an ice cream shop and restaurant that were open in the daytime. According to Milmar, the 808 was a bustling and exciting place.[35]

Other, more staid settings offered a similar opportunity to let one's hair down, if only slightly. Hay, for instance, recalled going to a former speakeasy turned bar in 1937 that had a grand piano. Situated on the border between Hollywood and Edendale, the bar encouraged old-time vaudeville folks to drop in to play and sing. Taking material that was available, "either songs that were not specific as to sex or gender, or the songs where you could change the name, or it would be a song to a man so that the singer didn't have to change the thing in any regard," the performers would sing songs that could be heard as expressing homosexual desires. In that way, said Hay, "they would be songs for us, songs that everybody knew." From that era, he remembered hearing songs like "(Along Came) Bill" from *Showboat* and "My Man," a torch song that Fanny Brice and Billie Holiday sang. Both songs detail a love of imperfection. The narrator of "Bill," for instance, sings, "And I can't explain— / It's surely not his brain / That makes me thrill. / I love him because, he's—I don't know— / Because he's just my Bill." Its lyrics tell of a plain and simple love, hardly outrageous or even unusual. And while clearly written to be sung by the lover, the lyrics could also be sung by a man, singing humbly about himself. It was perhaps this gap that made the song acceptable as discreet piano-bar fodder.[36]

Men let their hair down the most, however, at exclusive clubs and near-private social events. Harold Burton remembered small speakeasies in the late 1920s where a tiny clique of tightly connected patrons gathered to "camp" and drink, but he said that such speakeasies were extremely self-protective and it was quite difficult to gain access to them. Equally exclusive were the "te-dansant" parties, where, behind closed doors, men danced with other men. "They would go out on the Sunset Strip and be admitted, and people would sit down and have tea and dance." According to Fred Frisbie, "No one was admitted who didn't have a membership card" or was not known by the host or friends of the host.[37]

Such parties sounded like the exclusive affairs that Rollins described in 1914, and indeed could be very elegant. Harry Hay spent a memorable evening in 1930 at a speakeasy known as Jimmie's Back Yard that hosted its own version of a te-dansant. Hay was home from college for winter break in 1930. He ran into the brother of a friend and felt a mutual attraction. The brother invited Hay to attend a New Year's Eve party at Jimmie's in Hollywood. Having given the correct name at the door, Hay was allowed to enter. What he found—some two hundred formally attired same-sex couples of both sexes dancing to an orchestra—glowed still in his recollection seventy years later. He danced all night, he said, with a "beautiful, charming young black boy, probably not more than seventeen."[38]

This circuit of Los Angeles bars, parks, and bathhouses echoes what various historians have documented in other cities. Many of these historians have argued that these places cultivated fledgling gay communities. Seattle historian Gary Atkins described the bars of that city as "refuges" in which, during the 1930s and '40s, "the first traces of a public community of gay men and women . . . started to emerge." Elizabeth Kennedy and Madeline Davis wrote about lesbian bars in 1930s Buffalo as places "where patrons felt relatively safe" and could find a social group and even learn subcultural styles of dress and behavior. By the 1940s, bars there fostered "a common culture, community, and consciousness." Similarly the world of working-class bars in 1930s Chicago "led to a transformation of [the patrons'] self-identities" that was more significant, according to David Johnson, "than their sexual behavior."[39]

For some men along the Los Angeles Run, their encounters led to something larger that might merit a similar attribution of "community." For Jack Gard and Don Greenfield, sexual encounters spawned friendships and, from them, party invitations. Greenfield, for instance, met a fellow in the restroom of the Subway Terminal Building in the 1930s who began regularly inviting him to cocktail parties in the home that he shared with an older woman. Maybe six or eight guests, all men, attended those evenings (some of whom occasionally slipped off to the woman's closet and returned in drag), and they became for Greenfield a circle of friends. Gard, who was a student at UCLA in the late 1930s, attended similar parties, although such a friendship circle remained elusive for him and he went to the parties with trepidation. The parties "were clandestine, rather than out and out, because there was always danger involved . . . that maybe this could be raided, because things were raided. Suddenly the police would come in, 'All right you guys.' And of course the danger could be that somebody would be, perhaps, in a bedroom, and they could be caught having flagrant sex. Of course, that was not the thing to do—you'd never want that—but it sure did happen."[40]

But finding a social network and attending parties were not the same thing, as Montreal historian Ross Higgins pointed out, as belonging "to a large social group which shared common language, symbolic systems, interests and values distinct from those of the surrounding society"—that is, belonging to a clear community. Indeed, for the majority of the men of the Run, their experience likely paralleled that in San Francisco, where, in the 1930s, '40s, and '50s, an equally vibrant network of bars and clubs blossomed. Yet the participants in that bar scene, historian Nan Boyd wrote, "did not form a cohesive whole. They did not recognize each other, in the words of Benedict Anderson, as part of a 'deep horizontal comradeship.' " Instead, multiple constituencies met up, intermingled, and even had sex, without seeing themselves reflected in one another, without fully *identifying* with one another.[41]

For many men—perhaps most—a homosexual encounter constituted an end in and of itself that lead to nothing larger. According to Laud Humphreys's classic study of men having sex in public bathrooms, even in the 1960s, only a minority of the men were active in the "homosexual subculture": the majority were married and living with their wives. And certainly in the 1920s and '30s, if a sexual encounter spawned an individual relationship, it did not necessarily provide an entrée into some broader circle. Harold Burton, for instance, moved to Los Angeles from New York in the mid-1920s and soon began attending night school. He was just twenty-one or twenty-two and encountered a young man in his classes to whom he was attracted. The attraction was mutual, and the two men began having sex— often just at the school or behind the bushes of a neighboring home. They eventually developed a serious relationship that lasted for three years. But the two of them constituted their entire circle. "We were isolated," Burton later said. "We were not among the gay people. There was no such thing as a gay crowd. We only knew that we loved each other."[42]

Love, sex, and social activity were all available to homosexually interested men. From parks and bathhouses to bars and more welcoming clubs, a widely varied network of homosexual liaisons and meeting sites spread across the city. But a deep sense of community—which would rest on a fundamental notion of shared identity—was not yet among the offerings along the Run.

UNDERSTANDING HOMOSEXUALITY: ABERRATION OR ESSENCE?

As this network of sexual activity expanded between the wars, it came increasingly into public view. Briefly in the early 1930s that shift into the public eye was greeted with curiosity and even enthusiasm, as nightclub habitués became fascinated by homosexuality and "fairies" in particular. At the same time, the perception of the men within this milieu and their activities changed. If, at the turn of the century, there was little conception of homosexual desires constituting a fixed and constant identity, the idea of an identifying sexual essence began to be explored. In part, the fairies' paradigm— in which their feminine mannerisms were understood as signifiers of their desire for sex with men—began to gain wider cultural ground. But a second idea, that inverted sexual desires could exist separate from inverted gender behavior, also began to take root on the cultural horizon.

Importantly, these shifts did not happen all at once or even in a particularly coherent fashion. Different ideas circulated about how gender, sexuality, and identity were related. Rather than a single identity paradigm operating uniformly and ubiquitously in the culture, various notions competed for cultural dominance across the decades.

Two legal cases from the 1910s and '20s illuminate the nature of that competition. The first case—the arrests of L. L. Rollins and the Long Beach men—featured ongoing discussions about the constancy of sexual desires. Fundamentally, these were questions about whether homosexual behavior indicated a lapse into vice—a simple, one-time sin—or whether it revealed a fundamental and unchanging fact of character—a feature of a person's essence. The second case, a 1923 extortion trial, elaborated these questions further. At the same time, the extortion case also dwelt on the relationship between sexual desires and gendered behavior. Both cases point to the wide variety of ways that homosexual behavior was being interpreted in early-twentieth-century Los Angeles.

Discussions surrounding the 1914 Long Beach arrests repeatedly addressed the central question of sexual identity. One basic premise of any identity is its essential constancy: possessing an identity means that we are identical with ourselves over time. The arrested men, their neighbors, and the press all weighed in as to whether the men's homosexual behavior was an indicator of some unchanging personal quality. Most often, the majority opinion was a negative one, but within different contexts, the question itself was open for discussion.

First, to the degree that we possess the arrested men's voices, they inclined toward the argument that their behavior was a temporary aberration. Importantly, their voices remain only in Eugene Fisher's notes and the press accounts of their arrests and trials; they were thus recorded only in a period of extraordinary anxiety and were also filtered by police officers and judges seeking convictions, as well as by newsmen crafting colorful narratives. Despite these limitations, the men's insistence on their temporary failings can still be distinctly heard.[43] Only L. L. Rollins, the loquacious young man who proved such a rich source for reporter Fisher, described himself as having a constant, unchanging identity. At least in Fisher's reports, Rollins labeled himself distinctly as "queer." According to historian George Chauncey, in turn-of-the-century New York, homosexually active men would have used the term "queer" to describe men who were interested in sex with other men but who maintained a decidedly masculine gender; that is, "queers" were quite different from the feminine-acting "fairies." Despite his use of "queer," however, Rollins seems to have portrayed himself much more like a New York–style fairy. He presented himself as possessing a female gender and, because of that, female sexual desires. He implied that a code of gender identity was in use for some men in understanding their sexual desires.

The other arrested men whom Fisher described, though, discussed their homosexual activities much more as a kind of temporary vice, a sinful aberration. Men fell into these vice actions or lifted themselves from them without altering who they fundamentally *were*. "Degeneration" and "degeneracy" were viewed as processes that could be reversed or conditions that could improve. Herbert Lowe, the florist who refused to plead guilty, allegedly told the police about becoming "a degenerate from the time some person 'went down' on him in Los Angeles." He attended some of the clubs Rollins described, but he also explained that he married a beautiful woman "in an effort to reform" or, in a sense, "regenerate." Although repeated thirdhand, Lowe's sexual confession hardly seemed to have the tone of pride that Rollins's did, let alone the sense of identity. Rather, degeneracy appeared as a condition he had fallen into—like gluttony—but was hoping to escape.[44]

Similarly, Dr. Franklin Baker, a former Unitarian minister from Sacramento, was arrested for trying to "feel out" an officer and denied the accusations. Later, though, he allegedly confessed to the chief of Long Beach police that he was a "flutter," a term Fisher said was in vogue for fans of homosexual oral sex. Baker was married, however, and his wife remained with him during the accusations and the subsequent moves and career changes they provoked. Neither Baker nor his wife seemed to perceive him as possessing some kind of exclusive or central sexual identity. If he had degenerated into vice, he too could reform.[45]

Even Fisher suggested that the men's homosexual activities had been temporarily caused by external circumstances, not by their innermost nature. He explained, "It is the honest belief of those who have made a thoughtful and careful study of the situation, that the banishment of the segregated [red light] district in Los Angeles and the strict attitude of that and the surrounding cities of Southern California toward the 'social evil' [of prostitution] has tended to aggravate 'social degeneracy' and has brought to the surface this more degrading vice in a manner that probably would not have come out otherwise."[46] The absence of prostitutes drove these men to seek sex from other men. Much less than an explanation of fixed identity, Fisher and his contemporaries attached a situational explanation. Rather than simply *being* "queer," as Rollins suggested, these men had unmet sexual desires. By force of circumstance, they had degenerated to find a way to fulfill those desires. Thus they spoke of "degeneration" not the way historian Peter Boag did in describing similar events in 1910s Port-

Long Beach Bathhouse, 1915, where undercover police arrested dozens of men found in compromising sexual situations. (University of Southern California on behalf of the USC Specialized Libraries and Archival Collections.)

land, Oregon—as part of a larger conversation about social Darwinism and dramatic racial decline. For them, it contained the possibility of change and redirection. Akin to contemporary Progressive activists, they believed in the possibility of rescue and reform.[47]

The divergence between Rollins's identity language and Lowe or Fisher's situational vocabulary underscores that for the men who participated in it, the network of same-sex sexual activity and socializing in Los Angeles in 1914 was not held together by uniform notions of identity. As such, it is unlikely that Lowe would have placed himself in a "community" with Rollins. Issues of gender identity—let alone class—would likely have overruled any alliances based on sexual activity. That is not to say that, had Lowe and Rollins encountered each other in a park bathroom, they would not have indulged in the "twentieth-century way" together. Much more it is to say that they would have done little else together, let alone recognize each other as sharing a consistent identity.

The question of essence was also discussed by the men's neighbors and peers. To be certain, some Long Beach citizens were captivated by the

Lowe trial. The *Los Angeles Times,* which paid assiduous attention to the indictments and subsequent trials, noted that the courtroom was packed with spectators, who initially paid up to a dollar for a seat. The judge assigned a special police squad to stand guard at the door, as hundreds more "surged into and around the City Hall today to get seats in Police Judge Hart's court." Like the *Times* correspondent, the spectators likely expected the case "to be the most sensational trial ever held in this city."[48]

No doubt the trial was quite shocking. Spectators would have heard of the techniques used by Special Officers B. C. Brown and W. H. Warren during their month-long sting at the bathhouse. Officer Brown described to the packed courtroom how he allowed himself to be fondled by Lowe in his beach cottage while other officers watched through a peephole; the witnessing officers confirmed what happened. The public also would have heard about the "drags" at the 606 Club and the 96 Club and about Lowe's alleged claim that "the Ninety-six Club was the best."[49]

For C. K. McClatchy, the editor of the *Sacramento Bee,* the tidbits he heard about the arrests were an outrage. Even from his post in the state's capital, some three hundred miles away, he insisted that Fisher uncover the truth about these men and their clubs. And he called for a very public denouncement of the men, insisting that "the cause of common decency demands that these vile wretches be pilloried in the sunlight, so that they may be abhorred by all humankind." McClatchy did not see in Lowe's or Dr. Baker's actions the mere folly of an afternoon, or a slipping into vice. He saw something more fundamental and argued that "the good men and the good women of Los Angeles County—of every other section, in fact, should frown down every effort to soften by silence and suppression of news the punishment of these devils. To the contrary, they should encourage all publicity that does not clash with common decency, and should demand prominent publication of the name of every wretch convicted of a horrible enormity beside which ordinary prostitution is chastity itself."[50] For him, these men were hardly simple sinners: they were "devils" and "wretches," and their actions constituted an "enormity" that was profoundly awful. McClatchy saw the men's behavior as the outward sign of a reprehensible and unchanging essence.

The *Los Angeles Times* editors seemed to share McClatchy's view. The paper wrote avidly about the arrests and cases. Its publication of the men's names was thought to be the prime cause of banker John Lamb's suicide. The *Times* editors, however, defended their actions aggressively. "When upon good evidence an arrest is made," they wrote, "it is the duty of a newspaper to print the fact of the arrest and the evidence which warranted it." The *Times* insisted that its reporters were exposing "the human charnel houses that are fair on the outside walls, but within are the abode of lust-carnality, lechery and animal appetite for a devotee of pleasure." These men's actions revealed their true essence, and it was their job as journalists to expose that hidden inner truth.[51]

But to the Long Beach citizenry, these men hardly appeared devil-like. Despite the titillating testimony at Lowe's trial, after a first jury was dismissed, the second jury acquitted the florist. Historian Ullman read the acquittal as an expression of fear. The Long Beach jurors, she argued, did not convict Lowe because he appeared so normal, so un-fairy-like: it was too frightening for them to imagine that his degeneracy was not clearly marked with recognizably outrageous styles of dress or public behavior. Ullman's interpretation, though, presupposes that the jurors imagined degeneracy as a fixed inner essence; yet that very question was up for debate.[52]

Possibly the jury acquitted Lowe because they simply did not believe the astonishing revelations; Lowe, for one, did not repeat his alleged jailhouse confession in the courtroom, which may have made the case seem weaker. Or the jury might not have agreed that Lowe's vice was significant enough to warrant criminal action. Even if they thought he was guilty, they may well have interpreted his actions as the minor transgressions of an otherwise good man, not as indicative of a fundamental criminal nature.

Certainly the Long Beach citizens did not scorn Lowe. During the week between his two trials, Lowe's flower shop was mobbed. According to the *Times,* the crowds meant that he was often "unable to take care of the business which those who do not believe him guilty bring to him. . . . A large number of customers are women." Far from disdaining Lowe as an identifiable pariah, Long Beach seemed fascinated by, and perhaps even supportive of, its now infamous citizen. He was hardly a criminal they loathed. Thus while McClatchy looked at Lowe and saw a devil, his neighbors saw either a man who was not guilty or one whose sins hardly counted as a profound transgression. The dominant belief seemed to be that his behavior constituted an aberration.[53]

Ultimately, the Long Beach cases ended up before the California Supreme Court, but not because Lowe's acquittal was appealed. Instead, the *Times* and another paper devolved into a heated battle over whether it was appropriate for the *Times* to have covered the cases so closely. The editors of the *Los Angeles Tribune* argued that the *Times* staff practiced "brutal journalism" and had an attitude of "This story will wreck a dozen innocent lives but—I should worry!" The *Times* in turn mocked the *Tribune*'s viewpoint and instead taunted the paper's publisher, Edwin T. Earl, calling him the publisher of "The Morning Sodomite and Evening Degenerate." With that editorial in hand, Earl sued for libel and won $30,000 on the grounds that those terms damaged him personally and professionally; the *Times* appealed.[54]

The Supreme Court affirmed the lower court's decision, agreeing that the *Times* had libeled Earl with the terms "sodomite" and "degenerate." At the same time, the justices did not comment on whether or not the *Times* appropriately exposed "human charnel houses" in writing about the arrested men. "Whether or not such publications should be made is one of the difficult problems of all newspapers which claim to publish all matters of current interest," they stated. But they refused to resolve the dilemma, leaving unanswered the question of whether people's sexual lives were really significant enough to be newsworthy.[55]

Curiously, then, as the Long Beach cases lingered, the initial social disapproval attached to the "social vagrancy" charges dropped away. The focus shifted away from the original actors and onto those who identified them, giving them names and labels. The concern ceased to be the moral probity of the Long Beach citizenry or even that of Lowe and his fellow arrestees; Lowe, quite likely, continued to run his busy flower shop. Instead, the issue turned into worry about name-calling and the far too loose application of terms like "sodomite" and even "degenerate"—terms that seemed risky and perhaps freighted with too much meaning.

The spectators who crowded in and around the courtroom may have wished to see exactly what a sodomite was. Both Eugene Fisher and the *Times* reporter compared the case to that of Oscar Wilde, and the residents may well have wanted to see what a home-grown Wilde looked like. At the same time, they likely agreed with the jury that Lowe was not one. Rather than regard that determination as an expression of fear or ignorance, perhaps we do better to consider that the jurors were right. Even if we believe all the accusations lobbed at Lowe—from the fondling to the club parties—might we not also believe the alleged protestations of his own struggle? He did not see or conceive of himself as something so permanent as a "sodomite" or a "degenerate." He understood himself to be a married man who struggled to resist degeneracy or degeneration: these were events or situations—vices, not identities. He may have participated in degenerate acts, but they did not define him. As Ullman pointed out, Lowe's defense attorney convinced the jury that while they did not know the special officers hired to pursue this investigation, "you do know Lowe." That knowledge of who he was fundamentally—which he likely agreed with—did not include his sexual practices.[56]

The Lowe case underscores two clear features of the 1910s. First, it indicates how much the question of the meaning of homosexual behavior was beginning to be discussed, with particular emphasis on whether or not homosexual actions were indications of a fundamental essence. At the same time, it suggests that the dominant opinion was that homosexual behavior was not the mark of a "devil." Clearly, Lowe's arrest represented a state-run legal system that criminalized sexual activity between men—a position that both the *Times* editors and McClatchy evidently supported. Yet at the same time, the trial revealed not only great public fascination with Lowe but also a surge of support for him as a person, regardless of the charges. And the Supreme Court opinion implies that the tension between these two public stances was, for the time being, unresolved. The court made little effort to condemn Lowe, and left open the question of whether he should even be so profoundly condemned in the public eye.

HE SAID–HE SAID AND THE 1920S PARADIGMS OF SEXUALITY

During the 1920s, these discussions about the meaning of homosexual behavior continued and sharpened. To a limited degree the notion of a fundamental sexual essence or identity gained ground. But it did so, in large part, because the fairy paradigm—the linkage of behavior that inverted the gender code to inverted sexual desires—also gained more cultural credibility. Nevertheless, none of these understandings held cultural dominance. Male effeminacy and homosexual desires were certainly not perceived as absolute correlates. Instead, distinctly different conceptual paradigms continued to compete for dominance in the wider culture.

That ongoing battle can be seen in a revealing "he said–he said" court case that emerged out of a late-night encounter along the Run between Don Solovich and Macon Irby. The judges, lawyers, and jury battled over two interlocking questions. First, did inverted gendered behavior reveal homosexual desires, as the fairy paradigm seemed to suggest? And second, did past same-sex activity indicate a deep identity, as the mid-twentieth-century homosexual or gay paradigm would suggest, and thus predict future same-sex activity? The case reveals that by the mid-1920s three cultural paradigms offered quite different answers to these questions.

Don Solovich and Macon Irby met each other while peering into a department store window in the heart of downtown along the Run. It was around midnight on an August night in 1923. Irby painted signs for a living, and Solovich was working as a secretary for Julian Eltinge's friend Charlie Chaplin. The men struck up a conversation that carried them along the streets for a few hours and eventually to the Hotel Apex. There, using a false name that Irby supplied, they checked into a room for the night, where, each man later alleged, the *other* man initiated some kind of sexual activity.[57] That activity landed the two men in court.

Once before a judge and jury, Solovich and Irby offered very different accounts of what happened in the hotel room—most likely because even attempted homosexual activity (let alone if the two men actually had sex) constituted a crime. According to Solovich, the secretary, the case was one of brutal extortion. He claimed that Irby tried to have sex with him and then became violent, punching him in the mouth, breaking two of his teeth, and pulling out a gun to demand money. Not satisfied with the thirty-odd dollars that Solovich had, Irby insisted that they go to Solovich's own room at the Majestic Hotel to get another 150 dollars. At the Majestic, the men woke Solovich's long-term roommate, Lawrence Harrigan, who was able to provide only fifty dollars more, and while Irby took the money, he threatened that he would return the next day for another hundred. When he did return, Solovich went to the police to report the extortion, and the police arrested Irby when he came back yet again seeking more money. According to the secretary, Irby was an extortionist—a blackmailer—who not only initiated some kind of sexual activity but also brutalized him as a result. In Solovich's framework, the case involved a simple scenario of blackmail and robbery.[58]

Irby and the district attorney, however, both framed the case in terms of sexual desire and identity. Irby claimed, in his own defense, that Solovich was a fairy and that he had initiated sexual activity: his sexual desires were evident from his effeminate behavior, and those desires provoked Irby's violence. In a sense, Irby relied on a version of what has been labeled a "homosexual panic defense," though perhaps calling it a "fairy panic defense" would be more apt.[59] By contrast, the prosecutor claimed that Irby was himself fundamentally homosexual and that he was only too happy to meet Solovich's desire. Despite his masculine appearance and violent behavior, the prosecutor argued, Irby craved a sexual encounter with Solovich. Fundamentally, the defendant and prosecutor outlined two competing notions of 1920s sexual identity.

Testifying in his own defense, Irby did not deny his violence. Rather, he claimed that Solovich provoked it with his criminal degeneracy. Irby told the jurors that he let Solovich share his room because the secretary had said he was sick and low on cash. Within thirty minutes, they were undressed and in bed and then, just as he was falling asleep, "I felt something reach over and touch me. . . . Mr. Solovich had his hands on my sexual organs"— and thus initiated a crime. Irby jumped out of bed and grabbed Solovich by the hand and "asked him what was the matter with him—what made him do that. And he didn't answer right away. So I took him out of bed and I hit him in the mouth, and he threw up his hands . . . and says, 'Don't strike me; I have woman's blood in me.' " Irby hit Solovich again, then told him to sit down and gave him a handkerchief for his bleeding mouth. Again Irby asked "why he did this, what he did it for, and he told me he wasn't born as other men were, and that he couldn't help what he did, and after that I couldn't hit the man any more—I didn't want to beat him up, that that was his nature to do things like that—I didn't want to harm him any more." Irby said that he wanted to leave and that he wanted Solovich to pay for the hotel room. According to Irby, there was no extortion, and when Solovich said that he had no money, the two men agreed cordially to wait until it was late enough to ask Solovich's roommate for the necessary funds. Ultimately, Irby argued both that it was in Solovich's "nature" to pursue sexual activity with men and that, fundamentally, his nature was that of a woman. Irby presented Solovich as being feminine on the inside. His own violence was merely a natural repulsion toward the secretary's criminal behavior.[60]

Who can say with certainty what transpired between the two men, alone in the Apex? There is an undeniable sadness that the two men appear in the public record at all. That betrayal and alleged extortion brought them there underscores the sorrowful consequences of a legal system willing to fine and imprison men who engaged in homosexual activity. At the same time, the courtroom context meant that their comments may well have been intended to achieve conviction or acquittal. Irby certainly thought that he had a good defense by claiming that Solovich had made sexual advances.[61]

Once on the stand, to prove that Solovich was the provocateur, Irby alleged that Solovich was a fairy. In fact, he portrayed Solovich as a kind of Julian Eltinge, except he argued that Solovich's feminine mannerisms revealed a true womanly essence and concomitant desire to have sex with men. Irby claimed that while the two were walking, "I noticed that Mr. Solovich was displaying some feminine gestures; that is, he didn't act exactly like a man; and I asked him in front of the Marsh-Strong Building entrance why he acted that way, and he said he had acquired it by being a feminine impersonator." Allegedly, Solovich then launched into a description of his stage and screen career and talked at length. "I tried several times to butt in and stop him," Irby said, "but apparently he thought more about his career than he did about getting a room."[62]

During cross-examination, the district attorney asked Irby to specify how Solovich was acting. Irby said he could demonstrate it. His own defense attorney objected, but the judge overruled. The court reporter transcribed Irby's comment as "When he was walking down 9th Street towards Main, he had one hand on his hip that way (indicating) and he was walking along something like this (indicating)." Whatever those movements and gestures were, they were the pieces of the gender code of behavior that were to be understood as some version of "femininity." According to Irby, those external feminine gestures revealed Solovich's internal sexual desires, and he used them to try to establish Solovich as a true homosexually active fairy.

The district attorney never challenged Irby's assessment of Solovich's feminine nature. Indeed, when Irby demonstrated how Solovich walked, the DA insisted, "You felt then you were right in clover, didn't you?"[63] Part of what the DA was suggesting by such a comment is clear: he too read trans-gendered behavior as a sign that Solovich had sexual desires for men and therefore would be a good target for Irby. What is a little less clear is what the DA believed Irby would get out of the transaction. He might have been suggesting that Irby could have thought he was in clover having found an easy target for extortion or blackmail. But in addition, he seems to have been suggesting that Irby shared Solovich's interest in sexual activity with men. Although he never argued that Irby also had "woman's blood" in him, the DA flatly implied that Irby invited Solovich back to the hotel because Irby was a degenerate as well. In fact, the DA made reference to—and fought hard to include in the trial as evidence—the fact that Irby had been arrested on a separate sodomy charge six weeks earlier. He seemed to be arguing that Irby, without being a fairy or behaving in feminine ways, had his own consistent sexual desire for men.

In pushing that argument, the DA got Irby to spell out a definition of a degenerate that fit this broader conception. During cross-examination, Irby claimed that in addition to trying to get money from Solovich, he "wanted him to get out of Los Angeles . . . because he is a degenerate." The DA quickly asked for his "understanding of a degenerate," and Irby replied, "My opinion of a degenerate is a man that will want another man to go directly against the laws of nature, and have sexual intercourse with another man, instead of a person of the opposite sex." Pressed to state if Solovich had tried that with him, Irby replied, "Well, I couldn't say that he came right out and says, 'Irby, will you do this?' but from his every action caused me to come to that conclusion." To which the DA asked, "Did you try to do it to him?" Objections kept Irby from responding yet again.[64]

Irby and the DA relied on two different ideas about homosexuality. Both men read Solovich's alleged feminine gender behavior as indicative of homosexual desire: they saw him as a fairy. By claiming that Solovich's "woman's blood" explained his actions, Irby essentially embraced the "invert" concept that some psychologists and sexologists used to argue that homosexually active men were fundamentally women "on the inside." Solovich's feminine behavior confirmed that he would have made the sexual advance, and implicitly, Irby's masculinity proved that he would have resisted it. In his schema, only a fairy would have had homosexual desires. The DA, however, not only seemed to accept that Solovich was a fairy but also suggested continually that Irby was equally interested and likely tried to have sex with Solovich; for the DA, who separated homosexuality and gendered behavior, both men were equivalent "degenerates."[65] Although Irby may have been more masculine—and more violent—the DA wanted the court to see that he was just as interested in homosexual sex as Solovich might have been. Thus while the DA did not challenge the gender focus of the fairy paradigm, he also suggested an alternative paradigm in which there need not be a correlation between gender-specific behavior and sexual desire. Degenerates might well be gender neutral.

The jury convicted Irby on two counts of robbery without commenting on his or Solovich's sexual desires.[66] Clearly, though, they were not won over by Irby's notion that Solovich's femininity was likely evidence of an initial crime—an initial sexual advance—that Irby only attempted to ward off. Had they been, it is unlikely they would have found him guilty. Why did they convict him? The jurors may well have accepted Julian Eltinge's insistence that gendered behavior did not indicate anything about sexual desire: a feminine-acting man, they might have assumed, was not necessarily a degenerate, even if, like Solovich, he had been roommates with another man for several years. Or, they might have been convinced by the DA that Irby, despite his masculinity, was just as degenerate as Solovich. Or perhaps, without trying to decide what had or had not happened in the hotel room, they simply agreed that Irby had robbed Solovich and his roommate of eighty-odd dollars.

Interestingly, Irby appealed the decision and was quickly granted a new trial by the appellate court. His success at the higher judicial level is intriguing because the appeals court concurred that the DA had unfairly prejudiced the jury by making reference to Irby's history of sodomy charges. That allegation, the court insisted, bore no relevance to the case. That history did not indicate, as would have been readily accepted later in the century, that Irby possessed a fairly consistent set of sexual desires focused always on men as sexual objects. Such an idea of consistent sexual desires, let alone a sexual identity, had no traction for them. If anything, the justices insisted that Irby's arrest was merely evidence for a charge from a prior crime and shed no significant light on whether or not he would have been disposed to commit the current crime.[67] This represented yet another notion of sexual identity.

In the final tally, then, three plausible paradigms of sexual identity surfaced in the case. One, inherent in the appeals court's decision, saw little continuity between past sexual acts and desires and future ones. In this framework, none of the previous sexual escapades of Irby foretold his future desires. Even if a man, like the Long Beach florist Herbert Lowe, had degenerated today, tomorrow was a new day. He could re-generate, as it were. Within this paradigm, as well, if past sexual acts were not indicators, neither was gender-specific behavior. Solovich's "feminine" walk and posture revealed nothing about how he might have behaved at the Apex. In this "re-generate paradigm," gender was independent of sexual desires and those desires could be variable.

In the second paradigm, the fairy or "gender paradigm" that Irby used, sexual desires did appear fixed over time: fairies always desired men. But to some degree, those desires were a feature of a larger gender identity that was expressed by gendered behavior. The truth of the fairy, as Irby articulated it, was that he had "woman's blood" in him: this was his inner truth. And with that womanly essence came certain mannerisms, certain styles, and the subsidiary desire to have sex with men. In this paradigm, gender deviance was the overarching category that explained sexual degeneracy.

The DA clearly accepted this paradigm, yet he offered a third paradigm that subsumed it: the degenerate or "desire paradigm." While the justices of the Supreme Court had resisted the use of the term "degenerate" just a few years earlier, the DA embraced it. As with fairies, this paradigm contended that sexual desires were consistent over time. However, in this framework those desires were independent of and more significant than gender: Irby could be a degenerate even without displaying feminine gestures. Degeneracy, rooted in consistent desire, was viewed as a broader category than mere gender; it formed an identity unto itself.

Significantly, the fairy/gender and degenerate/desire paradigms shared the notion of consistent desire. This meant that as sexual desire became underscored as the question of greatest importance, the fairy paradigm could be subsumed into the degenerate paradigm: fairies would become simply another version of degenerates, sharing the more important common feature of homosexual desires. Yet that very notion of consistent desire was not convincing to the appellate court. For the time being in the mid-1920s, the notion of essential and consistent sexual desires was not a culturally dominant perspective. Instead, the re-generate paradigm, which maintained a separation between past desirous acts and future ones, and between desire and gender-specific behavior, persisted in its prevalence.

Importantly, these three paradigms and the questions they framed operated as more than courtroom strategies. To a degree, they echoed the divide among medical professionals: some included sexual desire as part of gender identity and argued that men who desired other men were fundamentally women on the inside, while others, influenced by Havelock Ellis and Sigmund Freud, began to conceive of sexual desire as separate from gender identity.[68] More significant, though, these paradigms represented what was imaginable in 1920s Los Angeles, and versions of them circulated broadly in the culture. At one extreme, for instance, echoes of the re-generate paradigm—in which there was little continuity between past sexual acts and desires and future ones—appeared in the pornography of the era. The still and moving pictures—largely intended for male audiences—were certainly rife with images of male eroticism and homosexual activity. Yet from several pornographic films that have been preserved, it seems clear that, at least as fantasy, one dominant idea held that any man might happily engage in a mixture of homosexual and heterosexual activities without possessing some fixed sexual identity.

The Exclusive Sailor, for example, a silent film from the mid-1920s, follows Adam, a sailor, while at sea. Eve, the captain's secretary, invites Adam into her cabin, where she proceeds to seduce him. The captain discovers the two having sex, however, and is outraged. He forces Adam to perform oral sex on him, though Eve also helps out. Soon thereafter, the captain takes turns penetrating first Eve and then Adam. While the title cards indicate that this is "sweet revenge" for the captain, no one seems unhappy or disgusted by the turn of events. There is no portrayal of awkwardness or discomfort as the captain moves from intercourse with Eve to intercourse with Adam. Indeed, both the captain and Adam—both of whom have homosexual and heterosexual experiences on camera—seem quite pleased with the arrangement; homosexual activity, in and of itself, does not constitute a punishment. As Thomas Waugh pointed out, while there is an implicit hierarchy of sexual activities in the film, the characters "partake of a generalized erotics" that he deemed "pansexual." A similar trading of sexual interactions occurs between a monk, a nun, and a male farmer in a 1935 film called *Monkey Business,* in which the monk and the farmer trade oral and anal sex with each other as well as with the nun. While these films certainly shared the stag film practice of confronting taboos, both conveyed the popularity that the appeals court paradigm held. In that conception, none of the previous sexual escapades of Irby, the sailor Adam, or his captain foretold their future desires. If they possessed a sexual identity, it was merely that they were pansexual—not that they had an unwavering desire for a particular sexual partner.[69]

Elsewhere in the culture, the debate about the relationship between gender identity and sexual identity continued as starkly as it had between Irby and the DA. To some degree, this debate was a version of the battle Eltinge waged against the "prim gentles," not wanting to be grouped with feminine-acting men. More surprising, the chasm between the different paradigms also came up in Harold Burton's relationship with his boyfriend Jerome, whom he had met in night school late in the 1920s. Jerome was Burton's second or third serious boyfriend, and he described him as "a regular-acting young man," adding that "there was nothing sissy about him." Yet as their relationship proceeded, "it was dawning on us that there were sissies around"—meaning fairies who, because of their inversion of the gender code, the young couple perceived as very different. "We could see the feminine gestures and the feminine behavior." One time, Jerome pointed to a group of young men, cursing them as "faggots" and "fairies." Those "faggots," Burton recalled him saying, "they use paint and powder, they use lipstick, and they act like sissies." For Burton and Jerome, the femininity of the "faggots" marked them as a completely different species from the two young students.

Asked if he had a sense that he and Jerome were "faggots" as well, he explained, "It never occurred to us. . . . *They* acted sissyish. *We* were butch boys. I put it together this way in my own mind: So these are faggots. Why are they faggots? Because they act like faggots. And how do faggots act? They act like sissy girls. They go tripping down the street, and they have little gestures, they can't catch balls, and they can't do that. They're just not boys."

Asked if the "faggots" also wanted to have sex with men, Burton replied, "That came as one of their primary functions. That's why they were faggots, because they wanted sex with men. . . . And we, men, we men who did not want to be sissies, disdained them. We would have nothing to do with them. We would never want to have sex with them, never. We wanted to have sex with each other, because we were men."

To a contemporary ear, Burton's distinction between men desiring men and fairies desiring men seems tenuous. Looking back across several decades, Burton described his thinking as "ridiculous," suggesting that he eventually came to see himself and the faggots as fundamentally the same. But in the 1920s, he felt an enormous distinction between himself and Jerome as "butch boys" or "men" and the "sissified" "faggots" and "fairies." While they may have shared certain sexual desires, the gender differences between them remained paramount. Gender identity overrode any notion of a common sexual essence. Like Irby, Burton and Jerome would have resisted the DA's suggestion that they and the fairies were fundamentally the same: that paradigm did not hold cultural weight for them.[70]

A WORLD IN FLUX

Thus, as Eltinge arrived in Los Angeles and settled into Edendale, launching his film career in the late 1910s and early 1920s, he arrived in a world in flux. On the one hand, a network of locations where men met other men—certain streets, certain parks, certain speakeasies—was expanding around him. Public opportunities for finding other men interested in homosexual encounters were growing. On the other hand, while there was an emergent interest in understanding fundamental selves—in what *Photoplay* magazine said was the effort to reveal people for "what they *are*"—no definitive answers emerged for how to explain who people fundamentally were in terms of sex. Multiple paradigms circulated in the culture to explain the importance of sexual activity, the consistency (or inconsistency) of sexual desires, and the relationship of sexual behavior to gendered behavior.

Yet the demand for inner essence, for true identity, continued unabated. In thirty years, Harry Hay and Mattachine would argue that sexual desire did constitute an answer to the question of essential identity. Much more than Rollins's fellow arrestees, the Mattachine members would demonstrate that a rich identity and even political organization could be built around sexual desires. Additionally, while "fairies" implied that there was a correlation between inverted gender roles and sexual desire, Mattachine would insist that sexual identity had no gender coding: it was a full identity unto itself.

In order for that to occur, however, the arena of lusts and emotions—the inner life—itself had to become conceptualized as a foundation of selfhood. In Edendale, Eltinge's new home terrain, the examined articulation of the inner life was most eagerly embraced by a community of artists who settled among the hills. Unlike Eltinge, they were not performers; they were painters and sculptors. Yet they took up the questions that he and *Photoplay* had raised. If 90 percent of womanhood was merely "art," as his character in *The Crinoline Girl* declared, what lay beneath the surface? If, as *Photoplay* implied, people were no longer to be "accepted for what they *seemed* to be," what in fact were they at their true cores?

Eltinge's performances offered no answers to such questions, and he seemed to scorn such a request for an essential self. For a time, that did not matter. Hollywood was still happy to put Eltinge on screen as a female impersonator: he appeared in at least eight movies, and numerous other silent films included clearly feminine-acting men. In the 1926 film *Irene,* for instance, actor George Arthur played the owner of a dressmaking shop. At one point, he snidely tells the new model Irene, "You walk almost like a man!" to which she replies, "So do you!" *Variety* enjoyed the laugh, saying, "Nothing fresh, vulgar or objectionable about the way Arthur plays it, just 'sissified' and funny."[71]

But the joke began to weaken. The demand for authenticity and the interest in desire became too great. In part, the fairy paradigm gained wider popularity. While audiences laughed at male effeminacy in the 1900s and 1910s, increasingly they began to believe that the hidden truth of male effeminacy was homosexuality; sexual desires constituted something fundamental. As a result, as film scholar Anthony Slide pointed out, "the effeminate male character dropped from the screen." And Eltinge's success in the 1900s and 1910s was never matched in the 1920s, and his public stature declined dramatically in the 1930s.[72]

Yet searching for the essential authentic self was a much broader project. It involved more than an effort to distill human sexuality, let alone the relationship between sexual desires and gender expression. The other Edendale artists, the nonactors, structured their lives around that ambitious undertaking.

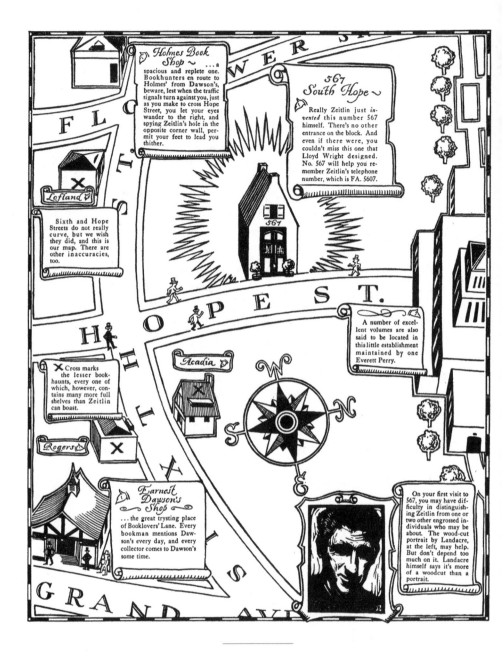

Jake Zeitlin published this "Unofficial Map of Booklovers' Lane & Environs" in order to promote his business on Hope Street. Paul Landacre drew the map and, in the bottom corner, a portrait of Zeitlin himself. (Estate of Paul Landacre/William Andrews Clark Memorial Library.)

TWO

Together against the World

Self, Community, and Expression among the Artists of Edendale

IN 1927, IN THE FEW MOMENTS it took Margaret Landacre to wander into Jake Zeitlin's rare-book store and ask a question, she dramatically altered her and her husband's lives. In part, she simply discovered the Zeitlin scene, one of the central flash-points of Los Angeles cultural and intellectual life. Even more, she discovered Edendale and its community, which placed both her and her husband, Paul, in an entirely new world, socially, geographically, economically, and aesthetically. Within that world the Landacres encountered both an organized communal life that sustained artistic effort and a new aesthetic sensibility that privileged art which plumbed and revealed the emotional life. That expressive community created the first template that Mattachine used in organizing around sexual identity. While the Landacres' experiences were unique, they were also indicative of the possibilities within the Edendale arts world and of why the neighborhood became such a magnet to many Angeleno artists.

Margaret was on lunch break from her job at the Barker Brothers furniture company, where she worked as a copywriter in the publicity department. She and Paul, a struggling artist, were in their early thirties. They had met while working at a San Diego advertising agency and had been married for nearly two years, but were living in cramped rooms not far from her downtown Los Angeles office. What little money they had came largely from her salary; Paul, who had serious physical handicaps, had turned his focus exclusively to fine, not commercial, art. Despite their small income, they were in search of more comfortable and more accommodating quarters.[1]

They had already spent many Sundays that year searching for a new home. As Margaret later remembered, "In those first days we would take a street car or bus on Sundays and ride to the end of the line, hoping to find a quiet, open space somewhere, but the ride would end in a dull, newly settled 'tract.' " A new suburb was not what the Landacres were looking for: they wanted a retreat. As Margaret wrote, "When Paul and I first met, both of us had been badly hurt in different ways and we felt quite sorry for ourselves." Both had found adulthood to be extremely isolating, and Paul especially, robbed of his youthful dreams by a disease in college, was fighting to find any value, let alone achievement, in his work. "When we were married," she felt, "the adjustments to life in this huge, clamorous city added to our attitude of 'we two against the world.' " They wanted a home which echoed that very sense that together they stood alone against the world.[2]

So Margaret wandered into Zeitlin's downtown shop. Sixth Street near Grand and Hope streets was a mecca for participants in the city's cultural and intellectual life. Just one block west of Pershing Square at the heart of the Run, and half a dozen blocks from the store windows where Macon Irby and Don Solovich met, Sixth and Grand contained a warren of secondhand bookshops and a steady flow of browsers moving from store to store. As one writer recalled, "This small realm of booksellers that was concentrated on Sixth Street, with fingers into the surrounding blocks, was the cultural center of Los Angeles in the twenties and thirties. . . . After lunch those days, doctors, lawyers and business men who ate at the California and University Clubs would wend their way back to work by way of Sixth Street, loitering and reconnoitering to see if they could find something of interest for their library or reading pleasure."[3] Zeitlin's shop, while one of the newest, was destined to become one of the best regarded in the city and country. On a whim, Margaret asked one of the clerks, Fay Fuqua, if she knew of any places available for rent. Indeed, Fuqua said, she did; the house across from her on Walcott Way was for rent. The house, a small bungalow, lay nestled in the hills of Edendale.

As the Landacres moved onto "The Hill," as the locals called their immediate street, and as they settled more and more into Zeitlin's circle, the Landacres found more than a retreat: they found a fairly well organized community, albeit a contradictory one. It was decidedly artistic, although not made up exclusively of artists. It was hidden, yet vibrant. It brought them isolation, yet it tied them to the extensive cultural and economic networks of Los Angeles. It brought them the freedom to revel in a solipsistic search for the self, and it brought them into a circle of similarly inward-turning individuals who became their friends: Jake Zeitlin, Fay Fuqua, Ward Ritchie, Grant Dahlstrom, Delmer Daves, Kay Francis, Merle Armitage, Fillmore Phipps, and Sueo and Mary Serisawa, among many. Emotional, economic, and creative—such were the roles that that community played in the Landacres' lives.[4]

In the 1920s and '30s, as the film industry left for other neighborhoods, a host of writers, painters, sculptors, and printers—and their supporters—settled in their wake among the hills of Edendale. Contrary to the myths which insist that Los Angeles was devoid of any arts communities before the 1950s, Edendale artists quite explicitly constructed a community for themselves around the passion of artistic expression. That passion was the self-conscious focus of their organizing efforts. Their community nourished them emotionally, sustained them economically, and provided a locus for their aesthetic debates. Consisting of sketch clubs, discussion groups, and various social events, the community organizations created a vibrant local structure within which the significance of being an artist in 1920s and '30s Los Angeles could be explored. In fact, when the Public Works of Art Project and Federal Art Project arrived in Los Angeles, they were established on the organizational foundation of the Edendale artists.

Within their community structures, the artists of Edendale grappled with a host of questions about how much and in what way the artist could strip life down to its fundamentals and convey those through art. In doing so, the artists framed a discussion parallel to the courtroom arguments about the continuity of sexual desires and the relationship between those inner desires and external behavior. While they did not focus exclusively on desire, they wrestled with the related task of expressing the artist's "essence"—an "inner self" they saw as constituted by feelings and psychological constructs. Such a formulation of essence contained more than sexual and gendered behavior, but it shared the notion that an interior truth about people spoke the most about who they were. They investigated expressionist techniques for conveying the inner life. Rather than resist the *Photoplay* quest to get past appearances, Edendale artists worked hard to join the effort.[5]

At the same time, under the shadow of the Depression and international conflict, the artists added a second set of questions. Even as their debates about self-expression remained unresolved, Edendale artists began debating the relationship of artists to the surrounding social and political context. Partially in reaction to the inward focus that an expressionist aesthetic encouraged, many called for artists to turn their gaze outward and interact more with the world around them than with one in their heads or hearts. Formulating what might be deemed an aesthetic of politics, they called on artists to become activists. These two aesthetic projects—expressionist and political—framed the debates about the artistic self within the Edendale artistic community.[6]

Questions of expression and politicization were not simply the private ruminations of individual artists, explored in diaries and art, but the stuff of their shared discussions. Much more than the men who found one another on the Run of the 1910s and '20s, the Edendale artists quite self-consciously constructed a vibrant, nurturing community. Thus, while the courtroom battle of Don Solovich and Macon Irby suggested that multiple ideas were circulating to explain the significance of emotions and desires, the artists of Edendale explicitly fashioned a community and a set of organizations to sustain them in the project of being artists and in their efforts to pin down precisely the importance of the inner self. In doing so, they forged a template for building a community around a shared passion and shared identity.

Two overlapping Edendale networks demonstrated how self-consciously the artists of Edendale set out to organize their lives around their creative passions. The first was a network of artists and intellectuals that centered on three men: Jake Zeitlin, the bookstore owner; Ward Ritchie, a printer craftsman; and Paul Landacre, a wood-block and lithograph artist. All three men lived in the hills of Edendale, and between their homes, studios, clubhouses, and Zeitlin's downtown bookshop, they unfurled a rich variety of informal but powerful community-building activities. The second network lay at the heart of the Los Angeles Public Works of Art Project and Federal Art Project. Edendale offices not only served as headquarters for much of the PWAP and FAP organization, but, not surprisingly, several Edendale artists were hired to fill the organizational ranks, from assistant mural painters all the way up to project directors. Many were hired straight out of the studios and clubs that figured prominently in the first network of relationships.

Through their art and within these networks, these artists and intellectuals grappled with a set of questions parallel to the Solovich-Irby debates. They examined what it meant to be artists, asking questions about art, representation, meaning, and social responsibility. What was an artist's job: to imitate the world he or she saw or to interpret it in her or his own fashion? Re-creation or self-expression? And what kind of relationship was an artist supposed to have with the surrounding society—observer, participant, instigator, leader? In asking such questions, they were exploring the importance of the inner life, its validity and significance in a broader political and social context. As the 1920s and 1930s unfolded, the answers to their questions shifted increasingly toward an inner self more publicly revealed and a society more directly engaged. That is, they began to argue that the life of emotion and desire did matter, was worth expressing, and had relevance for the larger world.

DISCOVERING EDENDALE'S BOHEMIA

To visit Jake Zeitlin's bookshop in the 1920s or 1930s, as Margaret Landacre did that afternoon in 1927, was certainly to step into one of the pulsing points of Los Angeles cultural life. Zeitlin, a Jewish, Texas-born poet, had hitchhiked his way to Los Angeles in the spring of 1925 and had settled with his wife and child in a shack on a dirt road in Edendale. He began selling books for local department stores, but soon ventured out on his own, first selling directly to customers he had met through the stores and then opening his own store in 1927. His shop offered an enticing selection of used and rare books, and he moved it repeatedly around Sixth Street before settling for a time near Westlake Park and then farther west. Committed to the visual arts as well, Zeitlin always reserved one wall in his shops as gallery space and often gave the first West Coast showing to international artists, like Käthe Kollwitz, as well as the photographs of the then little-known Edward Weston, and the more locally recognized paintings of Millard Sheets, Tom Craig, Phil Paradise, and Milfred Zornes. Zeitlin also believed in the power of the well-chosen word, and so each of his shops became a mecca for a generation of unproven young artists, writers, and bibliophiles who found inspiration in Zeitlin's enthusiasm, as he encouraged them to write this, print that, publish something.

The young bibliophiles Lawrence Clark Powell and Ward Ritchie were seduced by Zeitlin's world. As Powell recalled, they "loved Jake's shop, stocked with books on literature and the arts. It smelled good, too, from the Turkish cigarettes he smoked, blended with paper, ink and leather, a perfume more exciting than 'My Sin.' " And Ritchie and Powell were far from alone: professors and architects, editors and photographers, radical thinkers like Louis Adamic and Carey McWilliams, opera singers, impresarios, and wealthy collectors—all hovered around Zeitlin like bees before their hive. Zeitlin hosted weekly evening gatherings, with talks by local writers and artists, poetry readings, and Shakespearean performances. "Those were memorable soirees," Powell wrote years later, "when it was 'very heaven to be young,' the shop packed to suffocation, the sidewalk crowded with people trying to get in. Jake was then short and slim with thick curly black hair and the face of a young satyr. He was agile, too, given to graceful calisthenics, space permitting. Sometimes he took down his guitar and sang 'The Yellow Rose of Texas,' then with a final yippee he would clear the shop, lock the door, and add up the day's sales."[7]

Within a year of Margaret's encounter with Zeitlin's shop, the Landacres were decidedly part of the buzzing there. Margaret had joined Fuqua as a clerk for Zeitlin, placing them well within the Zeitlin radius. That summer, Margaret wrote a profile of Zeitlin for *West Coaster* magazine, and Paul supplied the illustrations. Zeitlin was taken enough with Paul's work as a wood-block printer that at the start of 1930, Zeitlin put up the first Paul Landacre one-man show on his gallery wall in the shop. It was the start of a prestigious career that, by the Second World War, found Landacre heralded by critics and artists alike as the finest block engraver in the country, with his work sought by galleries, print clubs, private collectors, and museums from Texas to New York and back to California.

To know Zeitlin was to have an invitation to find a little room among the city's intellectual and creative enthusiasts. And while there was transience in the bookstore crowd, many of the store's denizens fashioned a more fixed and ultimately more significant communal life in Edendale. When Margaret went to work for Zeitlin, she became the third Edendale clerk in his employ; Zeitlin lived there as well. During the early 1930s, the boyhood friends Ritchie and Powell, who both worked for Zeitlin, also took a stab at life in the hills, as did attorney-writer McWilliams. Hundreds of little-known artists filled the hills, and there was a world of book enthusiasts up there as well, many of them steady Zeitlin clients. The writers Sarah Bixby Smith and Paul Jordan Smith, himself a former professor, moved to the edge of Edendale. Architects Rudolf Schindler and Richard Neutra dotted the hills with visionary designs that became icons of California modernism, including Neutra's own home. In 1939 Peter Yates and his wife, Frances Mullen, began an "Evenings on the Roof" chamber music series in their own Schindler-amended home; the series provided a venue for unheard music—like that by Los Angeles immigrants Arnold Schoenberg and Igor Stravinsky—and after many years was relocated to the County Museum of Art. The Edendale hills were truly dense with cultural activity, both creation and appreciation.[8]

Historian Kevin Starr once deemed Edendale Los Angeles' "bohemian quarter of the 1920's and 1930's" and described it as "the closest thing Los Angeles had at the time to an artists' quarter." Certainly that was book dealer Zeitlin's sense as he settled into the hills in 1926 and stayed on for a dozen years. The neighborhood attractions, he said, were not unlike those that had drawn the early filmmakers: cheap rents, privacy among the trees and hills, and peaceful independence. In an interview in the early 1980s, Zeitlin explained:

> Bohemianism thrives on adversity. It's not a movement, but a consequence of certain conditions. You have to have a concentration of people practicing their arts, people with superior endowments who don't necessarily fit into society, and who are, in fact, often engaged in rebellions against convention, creating a symbiotic society where not only can they go and eat at each other's houses when they're hungry, but where they can also spark each other and be each other's critical audiences. To such people, money is not the main motivation; they may like spaghetti and wine and women and conversation and not getting up in the morning to go to a job; but all believe in practicing something that is their justification for being, whether it be dancing, writing, sculpting, or music.[9]

Edendale had just such sparkling creators and audiences. Carl Sandburg visited Zeitlin there. Abstractionist Ben Berlin and filmmaker John Huston hung out there, often in the home of Miriam Lerner. She herself was the secretary to oil mogul E. L. Doheny, an activist in the Young People's Socialist League, and a favorite model of Edward Weston. In addition to the artists, part of the bohemian flavor of Edendale came from the higher percentage of foreign immigrants who settled there than elsewhere in the city. Much like Greenwich Village early in the century, the artists and immigrants stimulated each other, creating, in one scholar's account, "a place that reverberated with Bohemia."[10]

Edendale was, not surprisingly, one of many artistic centers in the region.[11] Pasadena, just north of Los Angeles, hosted an arts colony dating back to the 1890s, and Laguna Beach, south of Long Beach, had been a painters' mecca since the turn of the century; even in the mid-1930s, *Los Angeles Times* art critic Arthur Millier described Laguna as a "seething art colony" where the "entire population . . . paints pictures when not selling building lots or writing poems."[12] Within Los Angeles proper, there were also several loci of art activity. One group centered on painter Stanton Macdonald-Wright and the Los Angeles Art Students League, which he directed. There were "smatterings" of artists in Hollywood, according to painter and art educator Millard Sheets, but a steadier stream of artistic activity emanated from Westlake Park. Not only was the park the scene of much male sexual cruising in those years, but the area also served as home to Los Angeles' three major art schools—the Chouinard School, the Otis Art Institute, and the Los Angeles Art Institute—as well as the supply shops they supported and one of the city's major art galleries, the Dalzell Hatfield Gallery. And up in Edendale, recalled Sheets, "there were quite a lot of artists that lived right around in there."[13]

Westlake Park sat just beyond the southern edge of Edendale, and there was no clear line of distinction between the areas. As a result, there was a kind of push and pull between the educational resources of the Westlake area and the greater independence and freedom of Edendale. In the fall of 1925, fresh out of high school, Sheets started taking art classes at the Chouinard School, just off Westlake Park. At the end of the second year, he and Phil Dike, destined to be another impressive local painter, decided, "We should not just take every class every day; we should start to become painters." They decided to set up a studio and rented a "funny stable" up on North Alvarado—away from the park area and up into Edendale. They fixed it up, stretched a stack of canvasses, and determined to begin painting.

> We each started painting, but couldn't see each other on the opposite sides of this little partition. I think it was about ten o'clock, and I don't know whether he came over to my side or I went over to his side, but we thought it would be so much fun to go down to the coffee break at the school. The idea of being absolutely alone in a studio after being around all these people was so difficult. I can't even begin to tell you what a blow it was really to be confined there just with yourself to fight these things out. We managed to go down there about once or twice a week for maybe a month or two before we housebroke ourselves, and then we really had a ball working.[14]

In Sheets and Dike's experience, there was something necessary and obtainable in the camaraderie of school and classmates, something specific there in the neighborhood of Westlake Park. At the same time, there was something attractive at the north end of Alvarado, something that drew them up toward the city's hills, away from the center. For many artists in

Los Angeles, Edendale won that competition. The lure of shared isolation was too great to resist.

Edendale's very geography created that sense of remoteness that Sheets and Dike cherished. It was a spot of seclusion in the midst of a busy city, remaining for many decades a rural outpost with a panoramic view of downtown Los Angeles. Walcott Way, the street where Paul and Margaret Landacre first settled before moving further into the hills, was unpaved, becoming a wading pool of mud in the winter, a ribbon of dust in the summer. The area possessed an un-urban setting, with simple homes surrounded by trees, bushes, wildflowers, raccoons, possums, and birds.[15]

Being removed from the bustle of the denser city flats was somehow essential for Paul Landacre's pursuit of art. It took several years for Landacre to immerse himself happily into art. Born in Ohio in 1893 and both highly athletic and interested in horticulture, the young man's plans were crushed when a series of infections left him drastically handicapped at the age of twenty-two. Following his father out to San Diego, Landacre began sketching the countryside as part of his recuperation; much to his surprise, a local advertising agency soon hired him as an illustrator. Landacre tired of the work, though, feeling that "there wasn't any art in commercial art; at least, there was no satisfaction in it." He decided to move up to Los Angeles in 1923 and to focus more seriously on his artwork. He enrolled at the Otis Art Institute, off Westlake Park, and settled on wood-block engraving as his medium. Yet during those "first few years of trying to become an artist," Margaret later wrote, "he felt himself somehow an exile in a teeming restless city. Fortunately, just when his ideas of technique began to shape themselves he managed to find a place where he felt he belonged, an environment of simplicity, seclusion and natural beauty."[16] That place was the Hill, where he and Margaret settled. Yet even in their seclusion there, the Landacres were hardly alone.

According to urban sociologist Suzanne Keller, personal connections are a key factor in distinguishing a simple geographic area from a "neighborhood." Such connections were certainly vital for Greenwich Village bohemians of the 1910s. Studying the likes of John Reed, Louise Bryant, Emma Goldman, and Randolph Bourne, Christine Stansell argued that the relationships the artists and intellectuals formed with one another—and how they defined those relationships—were vital to their bohemian revolt.

Their personal relationships provided the crucial testing ground for their ideas on modernism and democratic living. Their "free love" affairs expressed their commitment to equality between the sexes; they continually talked and wrote about sexual activity as part of their efforts to focus on individual expression and heightened subjectivity; and their cultivation of the arts of friendship—particularly the endless open empathic dialogue— made them sympathetic as journalists to the struggles of Mexican revolutionaries and striking miners. The human relationships at the center of their community provided a foundation for their cultural revolution.[17]

In Edendale, as well, emotional ties provided vital sustenance for the work of art-making. The first night after moving to Edendale in 1927, Margaret was filled with regret. She and Paul no longer lived an easy walk from her office at Barker Brothers: now their home lay a streetcar ride away. That night on the streetcar—and on the quarter-mile hike up the hill from the train stop—she began to reconsider. No doubt, Paul sat at the forefront of her considerations: her husband not only could not drive but could barely raise one of his arms and could walk only with a cane. Certainly the Hill was only going to make life harder for him. Of all things, as she finished her climb, she dreaded the thought of unpacking enough boxes to make a suitable dinner there in their hideaway.[18]

Moments after she arrived full of her doubts, though, a new neighbor from down the road appeared with a hot casserole and fresh biscuits. And so began the Landacres' romance with what Margaret would call "The Clan," the participants in their communal isolation who sustained them emotionally. Over the years, those same neighbors took them driving (before they owned a car) and on road trips; they came to their parties; they helped fix their roof when it was giving out; and eventually they were family enough that one couple left their daughter to live with the Landacres so she could finish school in the same district. There developed what Paul's biographer deemed a "remarkable camaraderie" among the Hill people.[19]

Music and song were an important part of that camaraderie. The Landacres were great fans of the fairly new Los Angeles Philharmonic, attending concerts when they could afford to or were given tickets. Often, though, they were guests of Margaret's coworker at Zeitlin's shop, Fay Fuqua, and Ethel Ingalls, her housemate and a teacher at Garfield High School. The women had a record player and a large classical music collection that easily provided an evening's entertainment. Just as frequently, Fuqua and Ingalls hosted songfests where the Clan gathered round the piano and belted out tunes, their voices well lubricated by Fuqua's ever reliable bootlegger.[20]

Margaret wrote earnestly about the importance of the Clan. Significantly, Clan members invited the Landacres into deeper explorations of their emotional and psychological lives. Despite the Depression's often "really grim times," Margaret noted, the Landacres were not only surviving but enjoying themselves and "getting ourselves 'sorted' emotionally." While the couple was reticent about their own inner lives, their "new friends" were "a group of young people with so much warmth and 'bubble and squeak,' they broke down our barriers and swept us into their circle." Margaret stressed that these young people "had problems, too, and they could talk about them as we could not." At the same time, their emotional lives seemed less overbearing. "Some of them had known bitter disillusionments," she wrote, "but how they could forget them as we got together after a concert or around our bonfire! We talked and laughed and sang—one foggy night we even heard a round of applause from somewhere across the canyon. From these friends we began to learn how to enjoy *now* without being afraid."[21] They were a community exploring the inner life and sharing it over the fire.

But as would prove true of most of the Landacres' social networks, the Clan provided professional connections in addition to emotional support. Paul's first major publication, his 1931 book *California Hills and Other Wood-Engravings,* was in a large sense an outgrowth of the interweaving of the Clan and the Zeitlin world. The book began in 1930 when Fuqua and Ingalls invited Paul and Margaret on a road trip to Carmel and Big Sur. The Landacres owned no car, so this was a boon for them. At the northern end, they stayed in the rental house of Edward Weston, who was also friends with Fuqua. Along the way, they stopped so that Paul could sketch and absorb the California coast. Soon after, Fuqua took the couple to Indio in the Coachella Valley; again Paul sketched. These sketches together formed the basis for the wood-block prints that made up that first volume. The book was ultimately published by local printer Bruce McCallister, a working colleague of Zeitlin's, who two years later advanced the Landacres the down payment on their own Hill home.[22]

PROFESSIONAL AND ECONOMIC SUPPORT

Part of the mythologized lure of artistic isolation suggests that it provides an escape from a money-obsessed world. Historian Richard Cándida Smith pointed out that many California artists of the 1930s, seeing themselves as a new avant-garde, deemed it necessary to be in some kind of isolation, at least from the brutal world of financial gain. In fact, Smith suggested that any artist who sought out fame or fortune was generally viewed as suspect by other artists. The Landacres expressed that belief. Writing about the coterie of artists Paul had encountered in the 1920s, Margaret said he sensed himself to be "something of an irritation" for a group in which "it was difficult to tell just where loyalty to the muse left off and a frank adoration of the golden calf began." Escaping that milieu had been crucial for his art to blossom.[23]

Nevertheless, the social and emotional ties of the Landacres' arts community had significant professional value. As they settled into their lives there, the couple took on additional memberships in a series of organizations that created a structured community devoted to artistry. Although seemingly only creative in intent, three of the more formal memberships demonstrate how purposefully the Edendale artists organized their camaraderie and built lives around their artistic passions. These artists self-consciously created organizations that facilitated their investigations into the self and expression, provided economic sustenance, and allowed them to develop quite explicitly "as artists."

The most purely artistic of the three memberships was the Rounce & Coffin Club. A rounce and a coffin are each part of a printing press, and the Rounce & Coffin was devoted to fine printing. It was not the first such club in the city: that honor fell to the Zamorano Club. The Zamorano was slow to welcome new young members like Ward Ritchie or Jews like Zeitlin, however, so they formed their own club. Although there is some dispute about exactly when the club started and who were the original members, its membership centered around Zeitlin, Ritchie, Landacre, print designer Saul Marks (who had his shop in Edendale), and printers Grant Dahlstrom and Gregg Anderson. A love of printmaking was central to their friendships already, and they started meeting as a group simply to study the woodcuts and engravings of Dürer and discuss the art of printing. When they formalized their association, they began meeting in rotation at each other's homes. They would eat and then, Zeitlin recalled, "we would show each other what we had found in the way of interesting specimens of printing and talk about them." Additionally, the members of the Rounce & Coffin were regularly expected to print something for the other members. The original members were soon joined by librarians from the local and prestigious Clark and Huntington libraries and later by Lawrence Powell, Ritchie's childhood friend and Zeitlin's former employee, then well on his way to becoming UCLA's most esteemed librarian.[24]

Unlike the Zamorano Club, the Rounce & Coffin was informal, its meetings tended toward the disorderly, and it was far from exclusive in its membership. The draft bylaws stated that the club had "no definite purpose other than to provide a reason for the meeting of its members, and for the exchange of ideas between the members. These members shall be men interested in various aspects of books and printing." In Zeitlin's recollection, that intellectual exchange "sparked us all, and the Rounce & Coffin Club remained a sort of medium through which we all communicated. We stimulated each other, we brought ideas to each other, and I think every one of us benefited greatly, even the ones that weren't printers."[25] It was, in a way, an ideal-type of what we imagine the camaraderie of artists to accomplish.

The club's disorderliness belied its actual impact: cultivating friendships but creating work as well. Powell wrote laughingly much later that "only one fact" was "irrefutable" about the club's origins: "it was founded by an itinerant book-peddler and a band of starveling printers. . . . Thus it would seem to have been the product of social unrest and unemployment. Or, in other words, the materialized figment of a group of disordered young brains, all of them hungry for business." And indeed, the ties formed through the Rounce & Coffin did turn quickly into economic ones. Ritchie and Anderson soon enough went into business together as printers, a venture altered by the war and Anderson's subsequent death at Normandy; Anderson's widow, however, joined the firm, which became one of the best fine-printing companies in the city. Similarly, Zeitlin linked forces with Ritchie, Powell, Phil Hanna (editor of the Automobile Club's *Westways* magazine), and Carey McWilliams to start up their own press label, the Primavera Press. Not surprisingly, one of their first books was illustrated by Landacre. The club generated business for the men.[26]

This combination of artistic, social, and professional goals is perhaps clearer in the second important group Landacre joined in the 1930s: The Club. The Club was started by printer Ward Ritchie, who had the energy of several men. Born in 1905, Ritchie, like Lawrence Powell, grew up in Pasadena. The two became friends in elementary school, when they biked to the library together, and by senior year of high school, they were co-editors of the school paper and yearbook.[27] Powell and Ritchie both decided to go to Occidental College in nearby Eagle Rock, and although Ritchie entered law school afterward, he dropped out and, with encouragement from Zeitlin and the printer Bruce McCallister, began studying fine printing—which in turn became his life's passion and his profession.

Ward Ritchie (right) in the print shop of Ritchie's Roadhouse, where members of the Club gathered for their meetings. It was here that the noise of the press inspired composer John Cage. (Ward Ritchie Collection/William Andrews Clark Memorial Library.)

In the early years of the Depression, Ritchie's parents died, and he and his brothers bought an old ranch house nestled among the Edendale hills. While Landacre lived in the hills just north of Eltinge, Ritchie's place was on the opposite side of the Silver Lake reservoir. In one of many memoirs, he described his home as "a semi-historic building, once the foreman's house on the extensive cattle ranch that covered the hills of east Hollywood. It was perched on a hillside looking down onto a stream and a small mill." The ranch had belonged to Charles Canfield, a partner with oil magnate Doheny, and had also figured in Edendale's movie past. When Jesse Lasky was still filming Westerns at the southern end of the lake and was typically in need of a cowboy, he allegedly hired the ranch's foreman, William S. Hart, who soon became a major star.[28]

For many years Ritchie lived and worked in the ranch house. Set up with large windows peering down into the valley, two printing presses, and a grand piano, the house became a gathering point for what Ritchie deemed "a varied group of salesmen, artists, and loafers." His friend Powell dubbed it "Ritchie's Roadhouse," suggesting its allure as a place far from civilization where just about anything could happen.

Like the view from Zeitlin's hive or the Landacre's hill, the view from the Roadhouse was of a creative world. Ritchie printed all the early Primavera books there; in fact, Powell and his wife, who took on the shipping duties for Primavera, regularly joined him there to wrap and ship their products. According to Ritchie, avant-garde composer John Cage also came frequently to the Roadhouse. Cage, whose percussive compositions were just beginning to find an audience, had recently married and settled down the street and "would appear almost daily to create and practice amidst all of our noise and bustle. With the presses clanging, the compositors pounding forms, the clock ticking, and the fire crackling, he would be creating a melody." Ritchie added, jokingly, "Some of this experience may have influenced his later compositions."[29]

The actress Gloria Stuart (much later to be Ritchie's girlfriend) bought a house across the way for her then husband, sculptor Gordon Newell, to use as a studio. Newell had attended Occidental with Ritchie and Powell and remained good friends with them. The Walt Disney Company was still located only a few blocks away, so Disney artists also began to stop in, "gathering there after work for a beer and conversation." Soon enough a group of Disney employees set out to publish a magazine spoofing the company, called *The Mousetrap.* They included articles from a handful of writers, caricatures, even erotic nude drawings, all run on the Roadhouse press and hand-colored by a half-dozen artists. In fact, according to Ritchie's recollection, there were at least a dozen working artists living truly close by, and the Landacres, Zeitlin, and Paul and Sarah Smith lived not far away. (Ritchie soon married the Smiths' daughter, Janet.) The Roadhouse plainly offered the interactive bustle of artistic community.[30]

The critical organized gathering that the Roadhouse inspired, however, was the Club. Formed in the summer of 1937, the Club lasted some four years until the Second World War pulled it apart. The idea, apparently not Ritchie's, was to formalize the social and artistic camaraderie that was orbiting around the Roadhouse and form a club not unlike one of the prestigious downtown clubs. The men briefly hired a cook to serve lunch every day, but the elaborateness of that effort doomed it. Instead the organizers settled for a weekly Thursday-night gathering of the twenty-five members—all men, the bulk of them Edendale residents. They would bring with them a case of beer and a model, presumably a woman, to pose. For a solid hour, everyone would try to sketch the model, and then, artistic chores completed, she would be sent home and the Club would devolve into steady drinking and conversation.[31]

Ritchie—who remembered that the first time he walked into Zeitlin's shop, Paul Landacre's prints were on display—became friends with Paul in 1933, right at the time of Ritchie's own move to Edendale. Paul was a charter member of the Club and was faithful in his attendance. He was also a bit of a prankster. One favorite story from club lore detailed the time Ritchie hauled an old carved chest up to the Roadhouse for the model to sit on. Paul, arriving early, climbed inside, insisting no one be told. Once the rest of the Club had arrived and the model taken her perch, he began slowly and then more loudly to scratch and moan, until the model went running off into the night and he emerged beaming and triumphant.[32]

Evaluating the importance of the Club for Landacre and the others points to a series of questions about what constitutes community and what value is gained from it. Landacre was never considered a good sketcher, and one of the club rules was that no one could ask for criticism of his drawings; it seems unlikely, therefore, that the appeal of the Club was purely aesthetic. At the same time, its allure must have been significant enough to counterbalance Landacre's confirmed preference for solitude and the physical challenge for him of getting around; both of those factors could easily have kept Landacre at home. The cover illustration that he made for a printing of the Club's roster included a beer bottle, a few loose sheets of paper, a pencil, and a nude woman, and perhaps that combination was enticement enough.[33]

Certainly the Club, like the Clan and Rounce & Coffin, fostered powerful emotional and playful bonds among its male members. Their self-mocking yet earnest tone was apparent in a party invitation that Delmer Daves and his pregnant wife sent out in the summer of 1939: "A Time Capsule of rare and well-matured sewer pipe, now deemed capable of resisting any and all ravages which time may introduce for the next five thousand years and thus well able to preserve an account of the Club's universal achievements, will be embedded in a building being especially constructed for the purpose on the grounds of Mr., Mrs., and Miss/Master Delmer Daves. The ceremony will take place, with a flourish of cocktail glasses and the swish of mortar. . . ." Wives, read the card, were "encouraged to come, and if you are a gentleman you might inform either Mr. Daves or Mr. Ritchie of your intentions."[34]

Beyond the playfulness, however, the Club also indicated how broadly Edendale artists defined their notion of a shared artistic project and community. While esteemed local painters belonged to the group—like Barse Miller, Fletcher Martin, and Tom Craig—various club rosters also included sculptors like George Stanley and Gloria Stuart's husband, Gordon Newell, architect Theodore Criley, printer Dahlstrom, screenwriter Delmer Daves, and composer Leigh Harline (writer of Disney's *Pinocchio* music, including "When You Wish upon a Star"). For some of these men, sketching was ancillary to their primary creative projects. But beyond even the range of artists, Club members also included men who made their living promoting and selling art—like Zeitlin, one of his Edendale-resident assistants, Karl Zamboni, art dealer (and former Zeitlin employee) Fillmore Phipps, and impresario-writer-editor Merle Armitage. Additionally several of the men, including Ritchie's brothers-in-law, were much more art aficionados than artists in their own right. For many of these men, then, the sketching at their sketch club could hardly have been the only point. Rather, like the nexus of Zeitlin's shop, the Club also brought together purchasers with purveyors, dealers as well as clients.[35]

Fundamentally, the networking at the Club revealed the practical value that the Edendale artists gained by constructing an organized community. In part, as Ritchie pointed out, "the club was more than fun and entertainment. Most of us were getting help working on various of the WPA projects of murals, sculptures, and designs for schools and post offices." Merle Armitage was initially the key local coordinator for the Public Works of Art Project and remained active as well within the Federal Art Project of the Works Progress Administration. Time spent with Armitage at the Club was thus potentially time spent getting a job. In addition, though, "we also promoted the sale of one another's work." The art dealer Fillmore Phipps and Landacre, for instance, became lifelong friends. Armitage donated Landacre prints to the Museum of Modern Art in New York. Daves and Ritchie arranged for some Landacre commissions, as did Zeitlin, who also displayed Club artists on his walls. Landacre's account books show several purchases made by a doctor who joined the group. In fact, the Club as a whole commissioned Landacre to do an engraving just for its members; those who could afford to do so paid him twenty-five dollars a copy, a handsome price for a Landacre print in those days. Membership in the

Club, then, was distinctly membership in one of Edendale's most vibrant arts communities, but such a membership provided some necessary economic support to facilitate aesthetic exploration.[36]

The supportive power of the Edendale arts community was perhaps clearest in the formation and success of the Paul Landacre Association, the third of his memberships.[37] Landacre, despite his achievements, was never rich. He was loved and admired, though, and in this way he was connected. The Landacre Association started in 1936 and folded in 1939 and was largely the brainchild of Zeitlin and Delmer Daves. Daves, more then anyone else, was the Landacres' benefactor. A talented and productive Los Angeles youth, Daves attended Stanford before launching a terrifically successful career, writing and directing for Hollywood. He also maintained interests in other arts, and when he met Landacre at Zeitlin's shop in the early 1930s, he asked to be taught wood-block engraving. Not only did a friendship ensue, but Daves also consistently paid for the Landacre kitchen or bathroom to be remodeled, their insurance premium met, or their roof fixed. Asked by the *Los Angeles Times* why he contributed so steadily to the Landacres' welfare, he replied, "I bought stocks and where are they? I put money in the bank and who knows what will happen to it? But I can look at this roof ten years from now and see what my money did."[38]

The Landacre Association was artistic only in the form of appreciation; fundamentally it was a financial association. In 1936 Zeitlin and Daves wanted to find a way to provide Landacre with greater financial security while still leaving him his artistic and emotional freedom: the solution, in those Depression years, was to create a group or corporate patron. In a later statement, the founders wrote, "Realizing that none of us could individually afford to emulate the patrons of the Renaissance, and yet desiring to help an important artist to live by his work and leave him free to develop his art to a greater expression, twelve of us joined to do as a group what we could not do separately." Each paid one hundred dollars for which they were guaranteed twelve prints a year. In return, Landacre received a guaranteed income of $1,200, which in the third year, when the membership expanded to twenty, grew to $2,000.[39]

The list of sponsors is intriguing and suggests both the clear influence of Zeitlin and Daves and the wide community of economic support extending out from Edendale. On the Zeitlin side, sponsors included Elmer Belt, a doctor and book collector and one of Zeitlin's consistent customers, and Richfield Oil executive Homer Crotty, who was also one of the investors in Zeitlin's 1936 shop and a lawyer affiliated with the Huntington Library.

Paul Landacre studies the block he has used to make a print of his home. (Estate of Paul Landacre/William Andrews Clark Memorial Library.)

They were joined by Carrie Estelle Doheny, wife of E. L. Doheny and a client of many of the rare-book dealers in town, and Ruth Maitland, a major supporter of local artists. Daves's Hollywood was represented by Frances Howard (Samuel Goldwyn's wife), Daves's former girlfriend the actress Kay Francis, movie producer-director Frank Borzage, and cinematographer Karl Struss and his wife.[40]

By and large the Association's members were Los Angeles–area residents, and Landacre was good friends with a handful, like Daves, Francis, and Zeitlin. Yet members like Maitland, who operated out of the Beverly Hills Hotel, or Richard Millar, an aircraft executive who belonged to the exclusive California Club, moved in economic circles well beyond Landacre's realm. And some of the members who were based in New York and Boston seemed completely unknown to him.[41]

In essence, the Landacre Association represented an expansion of Edendale. It expressed a stretching of the close ties of Zeitlin and Daves to the less personal, more economic connections to Belt, Doheny, and Borzage. From the loving heart of Edendale, they flung a net of expanded economic relationships that stretched the Edendale arts community widely across the landscape of the city. Much more than either the Rounce & Coffin or the

Club, the Association was expressly economic in its goals. But like the Club, it contained a similar balance of economy, artistic enthusiasm, and emotion. After all, what could have been a more loving gesture than that of the men who conspired and marketed the idea of a Landacre subscription simply so that their friend might live more easily and more creatively? And what more pragmatic an action?

The importance of these small organizations is hard to overstate. Clearly, these groups, intimately imagined, constructed, and sustained, were powerful in shaping the emotional and financial condition of their members. They reveal the significant organizational structure Edendale's artists built for themselves and the seriousness they attached to their investigations of expression, emotion, and relevance. These were not simply occasional parties or random get-togethers. The artists were not just discovering each other at the local bathhouse or park; their gatherings were more consistent than that. These events were more ordered, more regular. The artists and their supporters quite self-consciously constructed a social world for themselves around their artistic identity. In this way, they transformed individual self-consciousness into a larger social phenomenon: a community.

IN SEARCH OF A NEW AESTHETIC

At the heart of this community lay profound aesthetic debates about the purpose of art and artistry. As years later Mattachine would debate the significance of homosexual activity, Edendale artists wrestled with fundamental questions about the goals and meaning of making art. Like Mattachine, they tackled two basic sets of questions. The first set extended the *Photoplay* demand for authenticity and pushed some artists to explore their inner psychological life in their artwork, much as the Clan had around the campfire. The second asked about the relationship of the artist to society, with many calling increasingly for art and an arts community that was socially and politically engaged. These questions were not unrelated, turning on fundamental concerns about art as communication. Yet the quest for essence and the drive toward political engagement could and did push artists in quite different directions. At the same time, these dual projects framed a larger shared endeavor of being artists and wrestling with the significance and meaning of that identity.

The efforts of Edendale artists fit into the large international project of modernism. Broadly speaking, modernism among visual artists encompassed a variety of changing emphases in the nineteenth and twentieth centuries as photography and other technologies seemingly liberated art from the task of merely imitating reality. Freed from that burden, artists began to examine new and even contradictory possibilities in the creation of art. Artists from Impressionists to Cubists and Synchronists like Macdonald-Wright examined the very tools of painting—light and color and perspective. They saw their art, as Richard Cándida Smith explained, as "basic research into the components of aesthetic expression and reception." Others such as Symbolists and Surrealists focused on meaning, fantasy, and the unconscious. For these artists, as scholar Victoria Dailey wrote, art "became an arena in which individuals expressed their private visions."[42]

Eltinge, of course, was himself an artist and performer. While his emphasis was on the art of gender play, Eltinge can be read as representing a particular late-nineteenth- and early-twentieth-century aesthetic that some might interpret as modernist in its impulses. In part, it was an aesthetic tradition tied to nineteenth-century dandies, like Beau Brummel and Oscar Wilde. As scholars like Richard Pine have explored, the dandies' aesthetic treated the public self as fundamentally a work of art. Like Eltinge, the dandies played quite consciously with their superficial presentation, fashioning their appearances as much as their words. The dandy, Pine explained, was "concerned with *style*," and his aesthetic was characterized by pose, display, and insincerity.[43]

Eltinge rode that aesthetic to unprecedented vaudeville success, to international fame, and, ultimately, to Edendale. But much as the movie magazines came in search of Eltinge's true self, the broad aesthetic of surfaces also came under attack. Many artists began to dig for deeper meanings and more fundamental forms. One version of the new aesthetic, which Pine deemed that of the "herald," sought to get beneath surfaces: "For the herald the principal concern, beyond style, is with *identity*, with an accomplishment of mind and morals, with renewal of self-knowledge rather than the mere proclamation of an ego."[44]

Pine's ideal-types are useful in analyzing the aesthetics of Edendale. While Eltinge was no Wilde, he did live in the realm of styles, manners, and taste. His roaring at the "prim gentles" expressed his refusal to have the surface be made symbolic of some deeper identity. In a sense, Eltinge operated in the realm of "form" as opposed to "content." By contrast, many of the Edendale artists—from their bonfires to their studios—took up the very different project of heraldic self-knowledge. They determined to examine the content of their "personal landscapes" and share what they found. And, at the same time, they worked to understand how much the artist's individuality determined his or her form of expression. These were some of the fundamental questions occupying artists the world over, and much of the modernist impulse in the visual and written arts of the century was motivated by questions about the artist's unique vision.[45]

Painter Lorser Feitelson, looking back in a 1950 letter to *Los Angeles Times* art critic Arthur Millier, commented on this fundamental shift in art in the modern age. Traditionally, he said, the artist had been an iconographer, drawing on the canonical symbols of his state or church and "giving form to the ideology and culture of his community." Because of this "adherence to the group-ideology, the artist's work was assured of communicability, approval, and, therefore, patronage." However, according to Feitelson, as the nineteenth century unfolded toward the twentieth, the wider cultural emphasis on individualism hit the arts, and traditionalism collapsed: "originality and integrity of the creative *personality* were stressed. . . . Unlike the almost anonymous artists of the past, who gave form to the thought-world of the group, the contemporary creative artist is often concerned uncompromisingly with externalizing a completely personal world, which he expects the group to make the effort to enter. Since his work is untraditional in its methods and imagery, his comprehending audience is often limited to a few friends and 'initiates.' "[46] The Edendale artists of the 1920s, '30s, and '40s navigated precisely this shift into the individualism of internal expression. They did not always agree in their approaches, but then they rarely developed philosophies, as Sheets put it, or formed explicit social alliances around those negotiations. Instead they simply shared the joint undertaking of investigating the transition into the internal individual.

One of the clearest voices in the midst of these developments was that of Grace Clements. Clements, who moved to Los Angeles in 1931 and to Edendale shortly thereafter, was born in Oakland in 1905 and studied painting there and in New York. She had a one-woman show at the Los Angeles County Museum the year she arrived, and rose to national prominence a few years later when she joined Feitelson, Helen Lundeberg, and Knud Merrild as a member of the Post-Surrealist group. By the 1940s, she was writing regular articles and reviews for *Arts and Architecture* magazine and delivering radio commentaries as well.[47]

In the late 1960s, Clements gathered materials from her personal journals and columns and wrote a memoir, —*but is it ART?*, that she never published. In it she traced the vicissitudes of the negotiations of aesthetics and meaning. She recalled her questions as a twenty-something art student, pondering the purpose of art. Sensing the gulf between artists and "the layman," she wondered where artists should invest their energies, whether in the traditional communal codes of communication or the individualist one she alone could develop. She framed her question as "Was art a matter of *feeling*—of what the artist could 'say' about his response to things outside himself? Was art *interpretation* rather than *imitation?* The affirmative to these questions provided my first conviction that I had the answer to the puzzle. I defended the distortions that began to appear in my work on the ground that this was the way I *felt* about it." In her studies, she understood the distinction between interpretation and imitation as paralleling the difference between Gothic and Renaissance art styles. While Renaissance artists had focused on imitating the external world of physicality and dimension, their Gothic era predecessors, she decided, emphasized the personal and "internal motion" in their work. Clements steadily pushed for an art that returned to its Gothic origins and once again examined and articulated the individual inner world.[48]

These were subjects of great debate among artists, these negotiations between "imitation" and "internal motion." As Los Angeles painter and instructor Stanton Macdonald-Wright wrote in the mid-1920s, "The serious painter must realize that his subject is merely an inspiration to the end of making a work of art . . . an ordered and harmonious canvas. To copy nature . . . implies many kinds of ignorance." Even in 1917, painter Mabel Alvarez's notes from a lecture at the Los Angeles Academy of Modern Art contained several aphorisms on expressing the "inner life": "Create everything from the inside out"; "Listen to the *inner* self all the time"; and "Listen to the Master within." In the 1960s, Lorser Feitelson was asked if he remembered being challenged on issues of expression by a young Jackson Pollock at Los Angeles' Stendahl Galleries in the late 1920s. Feitelson was unable to recall the specific incident, he said, "but it is possible since hot polemics with the youngsters about traditionalism, individualism, etc., was an everyday occurrence."[49]

By 1934 Clements had joined Feitelson and his former student turned wife, Helen Lundeberg, in their new movement of New Classicism, later dubbed Post-Surrealism. Feitelson, who had been educated in New York, arrived in Los Angeles in 1927 after already having had a one-man show in New York and being featured in a major exhibit in Paris. He became a leading figure in the local art scene and soon began teaching at the Chouinard School in the Westlake Park area, as well as out in Pasadena. Lundeberg, who grew up in Pasadena, started taking drawing classes with Feitelson in 1930 after obtaining a bachelor's degree in English from the local college.

Quickly they began inspiring each other and soon launched their Post-Surrealist movement.[50]

As Post-Surrealists, Clements, Feitelson, and Lundeberg set out to convey the emotional experience of confronting life's great dilemmas and questions. Rather than exploring the chaotic world of dreams and the unconscious, as the Surrealists had, they wanted to show how the conscious mind functioned, creating order and analogies. What is more, they wanted that experience to be communicable and understood. Their tactic, in part, was to paint sets of representational images whose size and sequence would lead viewers on an emotional journey. As Lundeberg wrote in a catalog essay, "The pictorial elements are deliberately arranged to stimulate, in the mind of the spectator, an ordered, pleasurable, introspective activity." One typical painting from their cohort, for instance, showed large hands interlocked, a smaller couple, a man adrift, and an iceberg; by perusing these recognizable images, the viewer was invited into an emotional experience. As Feitelson explained, "The Postsurrealist endeavors to direct an ordered movement of flow of the observer's attention through a planned series of objects, or configurations of objects, which unfold and develop a universal idea in a manner analogous to the development of a poem or symphony." By offering up a new set of symbols, the Post-Surrealists attempted to share their own emotional experiences with the viewer. According to at least one local critic, they succeeded. "Post-surrealistic beauty," Harry Kurtzworth wrote, "deals with the splendors of the inner world of thought and feeling . . . explaining the classics, those vast queries, hopes and fears which constitute life." Indeed, the Post-Surrealists were granted major shows at the San Francisco Museum of Art in December 1935 and the Brooklyn Museum in New York in 1936, and that same year Lundeberg and Feitelson were invited to participate in the Museum of Modern Art's exhibit "Fantastic Art, Dada, and Surrealism."[51]

Post-Surrealism—like Surrealism itself—was but one of the many stops that Los Angeles visual artists took in this investigation of individual expression. While some local artists ventured into much more abstract territory than the Post-Surrealists did, many remained committed to representational art that they also deemed deeply expressive. As art historian Bram Dijkstra explained, "influenced by the principles of abstraction, but rarely focusing on abstraction for its own sake, these painters continued to emphasize the expressive potentialities of content."[52]

For many of the artists around Paul Landacre and Ward Ritchie, the quest to express individual feelings often pulled them into representational

Lorser Feitelson, *Genesis #2*, 1934. Feitelson's painting shows the kind of legible imagery that Post-Surrealists used to lead viewers on an emotional journey. (Smithsonian American Art Museum, Museum purchase.)

studies of the natural landscape. These men were particularly inspired by the poetry of Robinson Jeffers, who epitomized for them the possibility of nature-based art conveying the individual encounter with the cosmos. Jeffers, born in the late 1880s around the same time as both Zeitlin and Eltinge, was considered one of the great poets of modern America and certainly of California. He wrote dark, moralistic, and didactic poems that drew on the California coastline—especially around Big Sur and Carmel, where he lived—for metaphor and inspiration. He offered epics of human failing, cruel nature, and destructive sexuality. As one critic wrote, Jeffers's "intent was to instill in his verse the cyclic rhythms that make the world divinely but terribly beautiful . . . a universe in which cycle ruled everything, and violence and pain were the inevitable price of continuance." One contemporary saw truth in Jeffers's harsh vision and deemed him a "veri-poet," praising the fact that, "with the courage that it takes to be a veri-poet [Jeffers] dares to gaze at the sun with naked eyes and not through the dark glasses of life-escape."[53]

In 1928, when Ward Ritchie, Lawrence Powell, and their sculptor friend Gordon Newell were all finishing school at Occidental College, Newell purchased a Jeffers volume by accident and passed it along to Ritchie. Ritchie, "in the thrill of discovery," shared the book with Powell, and Jeffers quite quickly became the mythic figure who hovered over their own endeavors, inspiring them. Powell determined to write his doctoral thesis on Jeffers, and Ritchie, having discovered the pleasures of fine printing, began printing up versions of his favorite poets, starting with Jeffers. By 1932 Ritchie printed a Jeffers autobiographical essay for *Colophon,* a New York–based journal of fine printing, and invited Landacre to illustrate it. In 1934 Zeitlin determined that Powell's dissertation should also be a book and arranged for the Primavera Press (his partnership with Ritchie, McWilliams, and Hanna) to publish it.[54]

Jeffers spoke deeply to these men. He demonstrated how the natural environment could offer an artistic vehicle for emotional expression. Asked years later why Jeffers was so important for them, Powell explained, "It was both the form and the content and the relationship to a landscape—I think, and maybe that latter most of all—the sense of place that you always feel when you go to Big Sur, even today, that, my God, here's the inevitable spokesman for this coast—the granite, the hills, everything about it—here is the inevitable expression of it."[55]

Jeffers represented an artistic investment in California's natural texture and beauty that was also an investment in passion and expression. These men—Landacre, Powell, Ritchie, and Zeitlin—all shared his faith in the expressiveness of the environment, as did many of their contemporaries from Edward Weston to Millard Sheets. Indeed, many histories of California art point to the centrality of the local landscape, even among modernists. As Victoria Dailey underscored, the embrace of the natural distinguished California modernists from others around the country: "While some of the modernists in New York and the East Coast had become enamored of the machine and its manifestations—bridges, skyscrapers, factories—the California modernists, living in a place where nature was still so apparent, continued to explore the natural world with a new vision. . . . Modernism in Los Angeles celebrated nature, not machine, and thus took a significant turn from American modernism in general."[56]

The major local landscape painters among California artists were people like Sheets, Dike, Milford Zornes, Emil Kosa, and Tom Craig: men who

Paul Landacre, *Indio Hills,* 1933. Landacre drew the preliminary sketches for this print, along with the other modernist landscapes in *California Hills,* while on a road trip with Margaret, Fay Fuqua, and Ethel Ingalls. (Estate of Paul Landacre/ William Andrews Clark Memorial Library.)

had studied together at the Chouinard School and whose work Zeitlin exhibited on his walls. They went into the hills or the desert or even the side streets of downtown, camped out for days, and just painted. "Our work had a whole new kind of punch," Sheets recalled. In part the newness emerged "because we were just so damn interested in the places we loved." But beyond that enthusiasm, these young painters were investigating the landscape with new questions about "the fundamental problems of aesthetics and meaning of painting."[57]

While Sheets and the others were nationally recognized as the key figures of a "California School"—regionalists in the era of American Scene painting—their work still looked fairly representational. Indeed, Sheets's version of modernism shared much with Edward Hopper and George Bellows—a kind of Angeleno Ashcan aesthetic. The power of a modernist approach to landscapes, however, shone through the prints of Paul Landacre. If part of the modernist effort entailed stripping back both the natural world and art to their bare essentials, the power of that minimalism leapt from the images of Landacre's wood-block prints. Victoria Dailey recently deemed his prints among the most "evocative" of "all the artistic views of California. His simple, sinuous lines, his ability to render sunlight and shadow and the palpable weight of his images are unrivaled by any of his contemporaries." "No one else," she pointed out, "had conceived of sunny California in such black and white terms."[58]

For Landacre, these prints were not intended as merely an imitation of nature. Even as he set out to capture something true about the California landscape, he also told a journalist in 1936 that individual expression remained for him the ultimate goal of art. The thing he strove to express was the very same thing he and Margaret were discovering at boisterous songfests with the Clan: the emotional self. Art, he explained,

> finds its real value in self-expression for the person doing it, and for the person re-experiencing it. . . . We can examine it closely, line by line, concept by concept; but the real essence eludes our critical faculties. It escapes analysis because it has an emotional basis. Real art is the simple expression of the self, and the self is expressed by feeling. Hence the individual experiences the reality of art only through feeling. He can't re-interpret in terms of concrete analysis, therefore, but only by a re-expression of feeling.[59]

The drive toward self-expression, especially abstraction, generated heated resistance from organizations like the anti-abstraction Sanity in Art group. At the opening of her 1931 show at the county museum, Clements had to plead with her audience to "discard all the blind prejudices you have dragged along from the generations that precede you. . . . If you are one of those people who say 'I don't know anything about art but I know what I like,' be ashamed to boast of your ignorance." Even Stanton Macdonald-Wright, who had been crucial in leading Los Angeles artists to explore pure color in his Synchronist movement, much later bemoaned the "wave of 'expressionists' who are expressing nothing but the frayed tassels of near-neurosis."[60] Yet these artists continued to push for new ways of seeing and new forms of expressing the inner self.

ART AND SOCIETY

Part of the resistance to near-neurotic self-expression emerged from artists themselves who were exploring questions about the relationship of the artist to society. If, as Clements believed in the late 1920s, the role of the artist was to express his or her inner feeling, then what should the relationship be between artist and audience, or artists and the larger world? Was it, as Feitelson suggested, that the artist would simply await his or her audience, and even then not be understood? According to art historian Annette Cox, while European artists in the mid-1800s embraced an ideal of social importance, by the end of the century the notion of the avant-garde "tended to be more closely associated with an aesthetic radicalism with little concern for the external world." Thus to raise questions about the artist's role was to revive old issues that had lost their importance on the world stage. At the same time, for American artists such questions became compelling early in the twentieth century and certainly during the 1930s. In fact, despite his comments on the isolation of the artist, Feitelson set out on a lifelong campaign to create a mass audience for modern art, most significantly hosting his own television show about art on Los Angeles' KNBC from 1956 to 1963. But before that, as the Depression hit Southern California ever harder, questions of communication and engagement weighed more and more on the consciences of Edendale artists.[61]

In Clements's experience, the economic depression pulled the security rug out from under artists and intellectuals just as much as from under industrial workers. She perceived, therefore, that "the artist's lot was inevitably bound up with the lot of his fellow man; that all together they were affected by the health or disease of the social structure of which they were a part." Thus, as the 1930s unfolded, Clements's sense of purpose shifted. She increasingly believed that the task of the artist was "to find his place in the present social upheaval and to become the revolutionary instrument to carry on the tradition of great creative art." That belief drove Clements out of what she called art's "Ivory Tower" and into the "Class Struggle," or into the social and political arena. "To the artist who still insists that he is only interested in art and does not want to be annoyed by other matters," she said in a 1936 speech, "it is necessary to point out that we too are interested primarily in art, but we realize that the creation of important art is a social phenomenon and does not begin and end in the studio." She raised her voice, entered the ranks of the Los Angeles branch of the left-leaning John Reed Clubs—organizations devoted to uncovering the political power of art—and led the drive to form a Los Angeles chapter of the American Artists' Congress. She pushed for an art that was socially engaged and ultimately political.[62]

Many Los Angeles artists shared her view. One figure who put political and social criticism at the center of his work was dancer and choreographer

Lester Horton. Horton, who founded his own dance company in 1935, led the modern dance movement on the West Coast. Born in Indianapolis and trained in art and theater, Horton began performing and teaching dance in the Los Angeles area in the early 1930s. While he did not live in Edendale, several of his company members did, and his influence on them was profound. Universally, Horton is remembered as demanding that dance speak to the social situation that surrounded it. According to his great protégée, Bella Lewitzky, "Lester made dances about the things we were very concerned with, that dealt with our lives." In the midst of the Depression, for instance, when the city and state were being inundated by Dust Bowl families, Horton choreographed *Exodus from the Land,* which spoke to their plight. A later piece dealt with the Warsaw ghetto, and a longer work, *Chronicle,* had a section on the Ku Klux Klan.[63]

According to Lewitzky, Horton trained his dancers to dance in as expressive and direct a manner as possible, severely and without decoration. "To be decorative was to be corrupt. It was the ultimate compromise. . . . Glamour does not exist. Truth, with a capital 'T,' is here." Hands, she recalled, were fisted or absolutely flat. "We were talking about serious things: you didn't get pretty."[64]

Other artists were more ambivalent than Horton, though, and they wrestled with the twin demands of emotion and social relevance. Clements grappled with how to make her drive toward abstraction and emotionalism also a socially oriented one. Conversely, her good friend sculptor and painter Peter Krasnow saw the connection as implicit. Though his work was not representational—"I have no desire to compete with the illustrator or historian," he once wrote—he felt that the world explicitly shaped his individual expression. He wrote in 1937 that while his sculptures were hardly representational and certainly not "a specific delineation of subject, or a documented interpretation of episodes," still "the combination of forms" present in them was largely the result of "the impact received from these tumultuous days of advance and retrogression of the human scene."[65]

Nobody inspired Los Angeles artists to consider the political potential of their art more than "Los Tres Grandes," the three famous Mexican muralists Diego Rivera, José Orozco, and David Siqueiros, all of whom were intent on linking their artwork with larger revolution. While several Mexican artists lived, worked, and taught in Los Angeles in the 1920s and '30s, Siqueiros loomed largest and was briefly an important presence in the city. Siqueiros, a member of the Mexican Communist Party, was repeatedly jailed and deported from his country. He came to Los Angeles during one expulsion in May 1932 and quickly tapped into the city's art networks. At Siqueiros's request, *Times* critic Millier arranged for him to paint a commissioned portrait of film director Josef von Sternberg, and both Zeitlin and gallery owner Earl Stendahl organized exhibitions of his work. Millard Sheets, then a teacher at the Chouinard School, arranged for Siqueiros to teach a class there in fresco techniques. The class culminated in the creation of a mural on one of the Chouinard School walls. In August, Siqueiros was also commissioned to paint a mural at Olivera Street, in the downtown district close to City Hall known then as "Sonora Town" for its large Mexican population. Soon after, he painted a third mural in the garden of film director Dudley Murphy, assisted by Fletcher Martin and Philip Guston.[66]

In each case, painting the murals followed a similar formula. Siqueiros worked with a group of Los Angeles artists to design and paint the framework. Then, one night near the end of the job, Siqueiros stayed on alone and, in a surprise move, painted a final central figure that gave meaning to the whole mural. In *Workers' Meeting* or *Street Meeting*, the Chouinard mural, Siqueiros worked with Sheets, Dike, Phil Paradise, Paul Sample, and Lee Blair. Siqueiros wanted it to be a "collective mural," and they all determined to paint construction workers who were building a wall while peering intently down at an undetermined street scene. Among the onlookers were a white parent and child and a black parent and child, although the muralists did not agree about what was attracting their attention. On the final night, Siqueiros stayed late and, without consulting the others, painted a red-shirted soapbox orator as the central focus. The speaker was declaiming and pounding his fist, and in a lecture delivered shortly after completion, Siqueiros elaborated on the figure's political significance in terms of Stalinists and Trotskyites. *Street Meeting* was a mural about political activism and generating change.

In *Tropical America,* the mural at Olivera Street, the scene was Mexico and the surprise final figure was a peasant bound to a double cross over which an American eagle stands. Here art was speaking about international politics through a fairly transparent metaphor. Siqueiros was denouncing American imperialism and its overbearing influence in Latin American politics.

The implications of Siqueiros's work reverberated quickly around the city. Within a year, *Street Meeting* had been painted over. Some said it was done at the instigation of the police, others because the paint ran in the rain. Nevertheless, a similar fate quickly befell portions of *Tropical America* as well.[67]

Each mural and its subsequent demise fostered heated interest and controversy, as did Siqueiros himself. A lecture he gave at the John Reed Club incited vigorous debate about art and politics. Provoked by Siqueiros, artists divided over the question of how to respond to the fascist threat that was growing in Europe. The Post-Surrealists themselves split as Clements took a more political stand than Feitelson and Lundeberg. Herman Cherry, who moved to Edendale and became good friends with the Landacres, remembered that he and his friends, who had been very interested in the Siqueiros murals, argued constantly about politics. Cherry felt that art should remain clear of politics; his friends, on the other hand, were more aligned with the Mexican muralists. As a result, their debates were ongoing. "Politics was everywhere—anywhere you moved there was politics," Cherry remembered. And the consequences were significant: in 1932, when a group of Siqueiros-inspired artists displayed their own portable political murals, Los Angeles' anti-leftist police division (known as the Red Squad) raided the exhibition, shooting at and bashing in some of the paintings.[68]

Principally, Siqueiros inspired the Angelenos, foregrounding the political potential of art. Fletcher Martin remembered the two months he spent working with him on the residential mural as powerful. "It was a fabulous experience for me because he was a brilliant, eccentric, eloquent man, the most vivid personality I've ever met in my life. While not too much of the talk was about art, his talk inspired me in terms of art and it was tremendous." Indeed Siqueiros's impact in the city was on making artists think about how art related to the rest of life, and that impact rippled widely out beyond the muralist.[69] While there was no definitive answer to how art should be political, its political potential remained a focus of attention.

FEDERAL ART

During the 1930s, the communal organizing of Edendale artists became steadily more defined and more institutionalized. Particularly as the federal government made art production one of its New Deal priorities, the structures of Edendale artistic life became central elements within the expanding federal bureaucracy that supported artists. First through the Public Works of Art Project (PWAP) and then the Works Progress Administration's Federal Art Project (FAP), Edendale and Angeleno artists were drawn into a powerful new economic and social community. Not surprisingly, the main FAP and PWAP offices were mostly at the southern end of the neighborhood, right in the vicinity of the Westlake Park cluster of art schools. More significantly, though, the public projects were built, to a large degree, from the Edendale networks. The federal organizations not only provided Edendale artists with extensive support but also drew from them and their social networks to coordinate the projects. In a way well established by Paul Landacre's smaller communities, this broader effort knit area artists more closely together.

The national Public Works of Art Project was organized by a Southern Californian, attorney turned painter Edward Bruce, who was friends with many of the local cultural leaders. Started late in 1933, the PWAP focused on generating the best art for public consumption. It hired easel painters to create paintings that might hang on government walls or be sent around the country in traveling exhibitions, and it commissioned large murals to decorate public buildings. Officially, PWAP assignments were based on anonymous competitions, not need. By contrast, the Federal Art Project, which began two years later, devoted its energies to hiring needy artists.[70]

The PWAP staff and supporters were drawn from many of the same sources as Landacre's networks. Merle Armitage, the impresario, served as the regional director, chosen in large part because of the networks to which he already belonged. His executive committee included gallery owner Dalzell Hatfield, art critics Arthur Millier and Louis Danz, sculptor Merrell Gage, and former studio mates Millard Sheets and Phil Dike, all of whom also knew Edward Bruce independently to some degree. The general committee was chaired by Ruth Maitland (member of the Paul Landacre Association), as well as Occidental College president Remsen Bird and movie director Cecil B. DeMille. The PWAP maintained an office on Sixth Street, in an empty storefront near the Hatfield Gallery and the Chouinard School, and employed some 125 artists from all over the city.[71]

Two years later the FAP set up its offices nearby, on Seventh Street, a few blocks west of Westlake Park. The Federal Art Project supervision looked very similar, with Synchronist Stanton Macdonald-Wright in charge and an advisory committee that included Armitage, Nelbert Chouinard (director of the Chouinard School), Danz, Edendale-based architect Richard Neutra, Maitland, and photographer Edward Weston. The FAP, however, was a much larger operation. For several years, Lorser Feitelson worked as Macdonald-Wright's right-hand man and ran the painting program. Within a few years, Edendale residents Albert King and Jason Herron began running the ceramics and mosaics part of the city FAP. King soon became area supervisor for the whole project, and Gordon Newell—Ward Ritchie and Lawrence Powell's sculptor friend from Occidental College days—joined to supervise the sculptors.[72]

Predictably, the economics of the projects, sustained by the federal dollar, operated differently from those of the Landacre Association or the Club. Artists suddenly discovered themselves earning up to thirty-eight dollars a week, which constituted a powerful change in their economic condition. At the same time, they found themselves under a scrutiny that the smaller organizations did not involve. Dorr Bothwell, for instance, described having a WPA official stop by "to find out if you really were in need of being on the WPA and also if you, really, you know, were living in the style they felt you should." Bothwell remembered one WPA inspector hunting around her home, opening her drawers and refrigerator, and objecting to her slick art magazines.[73]

Nevertheless, a good portion of the FAP budget was spent very locally. For instance, King and Herron supervised the construction of an enormous mosaic at the Long Beach Municipal Auditorium. Designed in part by Grace Clements, it was the largest cut-tile mosaic picture in the country, if not the world, and when it was dedicated in January 1938, it was the single largest physical and manpower achievement of the FAP nationwide. For this record-setting project, over 90 percent of the tile came from Gladding, McBean, a ceramics company just beyond Edendale on the edge of the Los Angeles River. Some of the unglazed border tiles were decorated across the river by La Mirada Potteries. Coordinated by King and Herron from Edendale, constructed from Edendale goods, and designed by Edendale locals like Grace Clements, the mural was essentially an Edendale export. That was what the financial power of the projects allowed.[74]

To the degree that the PWAP and FAP could outshine the smaller artistic networks financially, they also could generate a much wider community. Both projects, largely because of the supervision they required, drew artists from around the city into a centralizing community structure. On regular Saturdays, the executive committee of the PWAP met with all the artists in the program at their Sixth Street office. The artists either brought in their work or reported on their accomplishments from the week in order to receive their pay. At the very least, that meant some one hundred artists were confronting and engaging with one another and their work.[75]

The FAP, because of its still larger scale, had much more extensive supervision and generated much wider communal ties. The project used several floors in its building by Westlake Park, and some of the art production, such as the lithography and printmaking, was done there in the building. Dorothy Jeakins worked in the lithography division and was in the building every day. Looking back, she remembered a great deal of laughing; "we'd draw each other at times and there was a certain camaraderie." Anton Blazek also worked at the lithography center and remembered, "Everyone had such a nice feeling, in all it was like a large family." In addition, the FAP organized educational exhibitions in its building on topics like gothic or baroque styles, intended for the artists as well as the general public. That kind of education also occurred in group sessions organized by Macdonald-Wright or Feitelson to discuss various features of design and art history.[76]

Being a painter on the project was especially engaging because the painters gathered regularly for critiques and discussions about art with Feitelson. Feitelson set out self-consciously to create the structures of an arts community. Every week, he gathered groups of easel painters with similar styles, ranging from the most progressive artists to the most conservative. That way, he said, "they felt that they had a little world of their own." Then every six weeks, he would call a meeting of all the easel painters. They would show their various paintings, and each painter was invited, "without trying to be eloquent or ostentatious," to "tell what he had been doing, so all the others could understand." The painters listened, and as a result, Feitelson said, he saw them admiring each other's work, sometimes defending it, even experimenting with each other's style. They built, he felt, a sense of shared purpose.[77]

Not all painters joined the Feitelson discussions or made community with the other painters they met there, but many did. The painter Herman Cherry said that through the FAP he met most of the artists living in the Los Angeles vicinity; at least 50 percent, he said, were unknown to him initially. "And so we began to see each other at least once a week, and so on, and of course became acquainted and made new friends and it started the ball rolling."[78]

Beyond forging community among artists, the projects also built a sense of connection between artists and the larger society, in a sense drawing them out of Clements's "Ivory Tower" and into the world. From Millard Sheets's point of view, the significance of the projects "wasn't just the fact that the artists were given money to live on—which sure as hell was important—but the fact the artist felt needed and felt like the community"— meaning the larger society—"was behind them. I think that was a wonderful period, where artists became more conscious of their place in society." Looking back, Jean Ames agreed. She believed the projects made an artist feel that "he had a place in our culture and there was a need for him. And the very fact that public buildings for the first time were extensively decorated I think gave everyone a feeling that the artist was a part of society."[79]

To a significant degree, then, the federal art programs in Los Angeles represented a magnification of the Edendale community networks. Their impact was larger: they spun networks that pulled artists together from across the city. And their funding was greater: they provided sustenance to hundreds of painters, sculptors, and ceramicists in the depths of the Depression. But their key officials and their framework drew from the men and women who had already made a community for themselves in the hills of Edendale. What is more, they made artistic expression seem like a socially and politically relevant endeavor.

ARTISTIC MEMORY

The emotional weight of the ties forged in Edendale in the 1920s and '30s remained cherished for years afterward. During the early and mid-1940s, when painter Sueo Serisawa and his wife, Mary, left Los Angeles to live elsewhere in the country, they wrote steadily to the Landacres. Their letters were filled with longing for the neighborhood and art community they had left behind. "Wish I could come over & talk to you people," Sueo wrote early in 1944, "then I might get some inspiration to work—The world is sick & only in the realm of art can I breath clean fresh air." From New York he wrote that he "miss[ed] the contact with nature," but even more, he said, "Wish I could come over & talk about paintings & things. Perhaps in couple of years we can, we hope."[80]

Ward Ritchie wrote with a similar longing about the Landacre estate, shortly after World War II and not long after leaving the Edendale hills himself. "Like a redwood dam," he wrote, the Landacre home

> lies on a steep slope backing up a few small areas of flat ground where flowers grow and where in the summertime they plant the tallest stand of corn in the West. A twisting dirt road encompasses their place around three sides . . . barely wide enough for a car to navigate. . . . When it rains people wonder if the Landacres will slide down into the valley below. And when, with summer, the spring grass has become brown and tangled beneath the oaks and eucalyptus trees and the lot cleaners begin to burn off the hills, people ask if the Landacres have survived. Only the initiate can ever get to their place. It even took the tax collector two years to find it. They don't

seem to live where they do, and according to the maps, the streets that should take you to them don't. . . .

And yet up there they are very close; the breezes bring nostalgic music from the trains in the valley below and the lights of the city make a varicolored pattern that the Landacres love and you would love.[81]

Ritchie's writing reverberates with nostalgia and love of those Edendale hills; of being up above and isolated in the rougher wilds, freed from the bustle of the dense city; of being somewhere where light and sound—the rawest tools of art—seemed to be sustaining; and of finding there that intimacy was "close" at hand, perhaps closer somehow. That was what the Edendale world and its community seemed to have. And the Landacre's position among those hills was perhaps higher, perhaps poorer, but not so unlike that of Ritchie himself, or Zeitlin, Grace Clements, the Disney staff, the Yateses, and so on.

The nostalgic music of those years was more than train sounds or even old songs: it was old songs sung by familiar voices that were familiar up and down the narrow, poorly designed roads and hilly passages. They were familiar from the Hill or the Club or even the Association. The intimate ties of shared creativity and the sustaining organizations they built pulled the Edendale artists together and created a communal structure for being artists. As a community, they strove to make their art into avenues for expressing intimate feelings and desires and for effecting change in the world. In so doing, they transformed Edendale into a place where self-expression itself could be the mark of identity and the potential basis of a community. They lay the groundwork for just the kind of expressive community that Mattachine would be. In fact, many of the Mattachine founders were active in the worlds of theater, film, and dance, and they grappled with questions of self-expression first and foremost as artists.

Mattachine, however, was more than a self-aware community organization. It was deeply and explicitly political, attentive to rights, laws, and police actions in a way the artists hardly became. And while the artists of Edendale hoped that their art might stir the social conscience of society, they could not foresee how politicized the very idea of emotional self-expression would become. During the 1930s, government officials outside Edendale transformed the bohemian project. They limited what they deemed acceptable expression and codified the unacceptable as politically dangerous. They infused the search for essence with previously unimagined political meaning.

THREE

1930s Containment

Identity by State Dictate

WHILE EDENDALE'S ARTS COMMUNITY focused on sustaining independent artistic expression, the involvement of the federal government politicized art-making dramatically and narrowed the range of acceptable art. Although the Federal Art Project set out to support creative aesthetic exploration, the coordinators increasingly pushed for artists to "speak a language which is directed to the people and comprehensible to them." Painter Herman Cherry, who settled into Edendale in the 1930s, insisted that as a result "there wasn't much experimentation" within the program. The earlier questions about modes of expression and unique artistic visions were drowned out by the demands of subject matter. Instead, project directors pushed artists toward work that the public wanted.[1]

Still more constrained was the power of art to itself be political and galvanize people in the way that Grace Clements had demanded. For instance, during Millard Sheets's tenure on the PWAP oversight committee

---

Clifford Clinton on the air in 1938, denouncing the presence of vice dens around the city as part of his regular radio program, *Civic News Forum.* This image was touched up by the newspaper to make his silhouette stand out even more dramatically. (HERALD EXAMINER COLLECTION/Los Angeles Public Library.)

with Merle Armitage, a group of muralists from New York began working on a local project. They "were damn good artists," Sheets recalled, but they insisted on doing what Armitage deemed "a Siqueiros type of mural where the workers were all being beaten down by the capitalists. . . . It was so obviously a left-wing group that was working on this thing." Armitage insisted that they change their mural, and when they resisted, he fired them. "We had them all come in one morning," Armitage remembered, "and I said to them, 'Now, there's a certain situation that you cure by giving pills, and . . . then there are other situations where you have to amputate, and you are being amputated.'"[2]

Further controversy erupted in the summer of 1935, when a group of artists finished a mural project for the Frank Wiggins Trade School. The Wiggins school was one of the preeminent trade schools in the city: Harold Burton had gone there to study dry cleaning, and Ward Ritchie had gone to learn printing. Under the auspices of the PWAP, the painters had set out to design a set of murals showing the history of tools, and continued working even after the PWAP closed down. When they finished, the three-wall mural in the school's lobby included a panel showing a strapping youth choosing between the tools of war and destruction, and peace and creativity. The Board of Education was outraged and demanded that the mural be modified. The head muralist, Leo Katz, insisted that it would be "spiritual murder" to alter his work and stated, "I would sooner risk my reputation as an honest artist than to change the mural." Although the mural was deemed "a distinguished and powerful work" by the *Times* art critic and loudly supported by Grace Clements, the American Arts Foundation, and a host of art teachers, the Board of Education overruled Katz: the offending mural, a year's work done for mostly no pay, was removed from the school walls. According to the *Times* critic, art that expressed "personal convictions" and was "based on a merely personal view of life"—meaning an ideological view—was now "unpalatable as public fare."[3]

Historians debate the impact of the 1930s Great Depression on the city of Los Angeles. Some suggest that L.A. was hit hard and struggled to come through, buoyed in the end only by the wartime military demands that brought work and prosperity to so much of the country. Others argue that Los Angeles suffered much less than other cities in the country, that its economic woes arrived later and departed sooner than San Francisco's, for instance, or New York's.[4] But beyond economic conditions, the impact of the Depression on Los Angeles residents is quite clear: the city experienced an unprecedented politicization of the search for the authentic self and the project of self-expression. In the broadest terms, governmental activity at the federal, state, and local levels expanded enormously. Yet quite specifically, politicians, bureaucrats, and police officers all reached their hands into the art studios, burlesque halls, and nightclubs of the city and gave a heightened political meaning to the search for essence. Their goal, superficially, was to aid and sustain Angelenos during a period of crisis and thus limit the impact the crisis might have. The results, though, were far more onerous. During the economic challenges of the 1930s, state support went hand in hand with state repression and control, and the development of a political culture that made those actions seem necessary.

Much as the federal government began to limit the intimate expression of artists, the local government began to control more determinedly the intimate sexual lives of the city's residents. For the homosexually active men and women of Los Angeles, the mid-1930s witnessed a dramatic expansion of governmental persecution. Early in the decade, Los Angeles "fairies" became objects of public fascination and celebration, often stealing the show as some of the hottest acts at local nightclubs. But as the decade wore on, government officials in Los Angeles embraced the "degenerate" or "desire" paradigm, slowly agreeing that homosexual desires constituted a fundamental but troubling essence. They began to read the fairies' gender play as a code, insisting that under the make-up lay a truer, more important fact of homosexual desire. And within the framework of a newly powerful political culture, they began to argue that those desires constituted a dangerous and disturbing essence or identity. As a result, during the early 1930s, the city, county, and state began an attack on fairies that eventually included all homosexually active men. Their efforts, incorporating new legal sanctions, arrests, imprisonments, and institutionalization, decisively transformed the meaning of homosexual desires and activity.

Importantly, these 1930s Los Angeles crackdowns against homosexuality were not a sideshow of Angeleno public life.[5] In fact, they took on increased importance because they were wrapped up in dramatic events at the heart of the city's political life. In the late 1930s, the city witnessed a massive campaign to recall its mayor. That campaign folded together concerns about homosexuality with broader anxieties about moralism and Communism. It made vivid a new cultural system that marked sexual perversion as a potentially dangerous and political identity. By the end of the decade, that cultural frame inscribed homosexual activity as the indicator of an essential criminal identity.

For a time in the early 1930s, the wider public embraced the city's "fairies," and female impersonators were celebrated in the city's nightlife. In fact, in the early 1930s, the city witnessed something akin to the "pansy craze" George Chauncey identified in New York City. Chauncey explained that in 1930 and 1931, the major nightclubs of New York were dominated by various styles of female impersonators. Some were fairies who dolled up with make-up and finery but were clearly men; others were men dressed completely as women. In some places they were the hosts, in others the star performers. As Chauncey explained, when New York City cracked down on the performers, some of them came to Los Angeles.[6]

In the fall of 1932, for instance, La Boheme in Hollywood hosted Karyl Norman, the "Creole Fashion Plate," fresh from New York City. La Boheme seated about 350 guests and, according to *Variety*, Norman was heading one of "the smartest and most entertaining floor shows seen in these parts in a long time." Norman's revue stood out, the paper said, even "with female impersonator shows flourishing in this neck of the woods." The show's style was hardly as discreet as an early Eltinge performance. Indeed the most exciting performer was Norman's protégé, Leon La Verde, whom *Variety* deemed "the last word in the impersonation art." Said the paper, "Boy has box-office qualities that could be cashed in with a New York revue. He does a mean rumba, and as nifty a snake hips as has been seen anywhere. Has grace in his walk, knows how to use his hands and gesturate, and is plenty of 'hot cha' when it comes to appearance."[7]

The same week, *Variety* praised Jean Malin's show at Club New Yorker. Malin, also newly arrived from New York, was one of the Big Apple's brightest stars. His "femme impersonations" took up half the show at the 250-person club. The other performers included dancing German twins, a young Betty Grable, and a Miss Eddie Adams, who performed alternately in male and female attire.[8]

Not all the performing fairies were New York imports, however. These were the days when Estelle Milmar's 808 Club, with its nightclub setting and steady stream of impersonators, was growing in popularity. In addition, the much smaller B.B.B.'s Cellar featured a "pansy revue" for some seven months in 1932. Hollywood folks dropped in at B.B.B.'s, according to *Variety*, but there was little effort to offer an elegant show or draw "class patronage." Instead the show was mostly comic, with many of the laughs garnered by the master of ceremonies who joked about the floor show.

An unknown female impersonator performs in a Hollywood nightclub. In the early 1930s, Los Angeles clubs featured a bevy of "pansy revues" that drew encouragement from the press and hostility from the police. (Los Angeles Daily News Collection, Department of Special Collections, Charles E. Young Research Library, University of California, Los Angeles.)

According to *Variety*, "there's no attempt to fool anyone on the revue's sex. Costumes are mostly made by the boys themselves. None wear wigs, probably due to being paid off in sandwiches." Nonetheless, wrote the paper, B.B.B.'s was "about the best after-theatre spot for the money in town."[9]

Explaining the allure of the impersonator revues is challenging: there are few records to indicate clearly the audiences' interest in them. Likely the combination of Eltinge-esque gender play and the suggestion that these men really did have "woman's blood" in them, as Macon Irby would have said, intrigued the cosmopolitan set. But as Marybeth Hamilton argued, these performers—much less mainstream than Eltinge—differed from him in that they "used the stage to flaunt an illicit offstage sexual self." The various expressions of desire, both feigned female desire and masked homosexual desire, would have titillated the audiences as well.[10]

Historian George Chauncey suggested that the "pansy craze" in New York fit within the underworld ambience that Prohibition generated in speakeasies and nightclubs—which were already criminal operations just by dint of serving liquor. "By driving middle-class men and women to break the law if they wanted to socialize where they could have a drink and bringing them in contact with 'low-life' figures, Prohibition encouraged them to transgress other social boundaries as well." Nightlife crowds cultivated a steady appetite for the new, the thrilling, and the outré. Much as a fascination with African American culture lured white New Yorkers up to Harlem in the 1920s and '30s, a similar curiosity about "perversity," he suggested, attracted nightclub denizens to the pansy shows. In addition, Chauncey explained, pansy performers may have comforted men whose unsteady position in the economic roller coaster of the 1920s and '30s generated anxieties about their masculinity. "The spectacle of the pansy," he wrote, "allowed men to confirm their manliness and solidarity with other men by distinguishing themselves from pansies." And it is equally possible, of course, that audience members found the fairies genuinely erotic, genuinely sexy. At least one pornographic film from the early 1930s suggested some men's obvious curiosity and enthusiasm for having sex with female impersonators.[11]

But whatever the interest, once club managers realized that fairies were a lure, they began competing to book their acts. In fact, according to film historian Vito Russo, the movie industry followed the clubs' lead, incorporating fairylike characters so much that during 1933, "the existence of homosexuality was alluded to more often than at any other time in film history before . . . the early 1960s." *Variety* newspaper noted the same development, commenting that "producers are going heavy on the panz stuff in current pix. . . . They are now apparently the stock comedy business easiest at hand."[12]

Ironically, though, just as *Variety* was writing up these movies and shows, the vice squad began cracking down on them. Indeed, the same issue of the paper that praised the "pansy revue" at B.B.B.'s Cellar, also noted a double raid on the Cellar and Jimmie's Back Yard. Jimmie's Back Yard was raided repeatedly in 1932 and 1933, and the initial liquor law violations gave way to charges of indecency. In November 1933, when the owner and various entertainers were arrested, the police said they were acting on neighbors' complaints and that the entertainment was "of a character scarcely suitable for parlor presentation." The owner, mistress of ceremonies, and piano player each ended up with ninety-day sentences.[13]

This 1932–33 burst of anti-impersonator activity was new for the city. While female and male impersonators previously had appeared in the city records, they were hardly ever treated so harshly. For instance, police approached Pablo Perez in the summer of 1928 when he was fumbling with a door while dressed as a woman. Perez ran but was pursued and apprehended by the police. Found guilty of masquerading, Perez was offered either a fine of twenty-five dollars or a sentence of ten days in jail. Similarly, when Harold Brown was arrested on suspicion of posing as a federal narcotics officer, he was discovered to be a woman. Brown pled guilty to two counts of masquerading and offered to leave the city within forty-eight hours; instead the judge imposed a suspended thirty-day sentence for obtaining a driver's license while posing as a man. Three men arrested as female impersonators in 1933, however, were each sentenced to six months' jail time—the maximum allowable penalty.[14] The club raids raised the ante on impersonation.

The 1932–33 raids were the flip side of the "pansy craze" in Los Angeles, and they distinguished Los Angeles from San Francisco, which, according to historian Nan Boyd, stayed as much of an "open town" during the 1930s as it had been under Prohibition. Similarly, according to David Johnson, fairies in 1930s Chicago seemed little worried about police oppression. But in Los Angeles the police regularly interfered with the nightclubs' business, although not enough to shut them down entirely. Clubs, in fact, were raided frequently but continued operating. The Big House, for instance, on Hollywood Boulevard, was raided in the fall of 1932. When the vice squad entered early in the morning, the patrons fought back, while a female impersonator tried to escape through a window; he was arrested nonetheless, along with the owner and two aggressive patrons. The resistance of the patrons suggests not only their refusal to see fairies condemned but also the scornful way they viewed police action. For the moment, their scorn was justified: the Big House, renamed Buddy's Rendezvous, continued to operate. Eight months later the police returned there. In addition to arresting the waiter for selling hard liquor and beer without a proper license, five men in women's clothes were arrested on vagrancy charges. Each received the maximum six-month jail sentence for masquerading, and this time the bar finally closed.[15]

Jimmie's Back Yard had incredible staying power. The bar was raided again the week after the second Big House raid, along with another bar, the Barn. According to the police, the Barn was featuring "a floor-show in which men masquerade as women and women pose as men." At Jimmie's, two men—one of whom worked at the Back Yard—were arrested on similar masquerading charges. Three months later, though, Jimmie's was still in business, seeking a dancing permit from the Police Commission. A police officer reported that female impersonators worked there, and the chief of police, James Davis, retorted, "Any place where that type congregates should not have a permit." The permit was denied, and in fact, the following month the Police Commission began to insist that all area café–dance halls "keep out female impersonators and their ilk." Applicants for permits were warned that "if any female impersonators were employed, or admitted, the permit would be voided." Nevertheless, Jimmie's continued to operate, and when the police returned a few months later, the impersonators were still at work.[16]

Thus while the vice squad dampened the business at these clubs *Variety* called "panze joints," they hardly quenched the interest in them.[17] In fact, the 1932 and 1933 back-and-forth combination of the pansy craze and the raids to contain it expressed an ongoing fascination—half positive, half condemning—with fairies. And while bar patrons may have celebrated the fairies for their gender play, their homosexual desires, or both, the raids marked a growing state-sponsored belief that the "panze joints" represented a serious danger.

THE WATERSHED MAYORAL RECALL

As the 1930s unfolded, Los Angeles, moving from the throes of the Depression into the economic revival of the New Deal and the war build-up, underwent a clear political and moral transformation. City officials shifted increasingly toward viewing fairies and other homosexually active men as possessing a fixed and dangerous fundamental essence. Their assessment of sexual perversion as dangerous was part of a wider cultural fabric that wove together a series of anxieties about sexuality and Communism and labeled them as interrelated dangers. That political culture leapt into sharp focus during the efforts to unseat Mayor Frank Shaw in 1937 and '38.[18]

The ultimately successful drive to recall Shaw remains one of the major political events in the city's history. Yet the recall accomplished more than the downfall of an allegedly corrupt administration. It pulled together a cultural framework that ascribed political significance and a sense of identity to sexual activities and desires. Indeed, the emergent political culture wove together three distinct worries: about moralism, Communism, and homosexuality. That cultural system and the fears it cultivated held much greater significance than the election's final outcome. It dominated Los Angeles—and American—political life well into the Cold War. Within a decade of the recall, those fears drove the purges of homosexuals and Communists from the federal government, left thousands of homosexual men institutionalized or imprisoned, and further laid the foundation for the nation's homosexual rights movement. The Los Angeles recall drive of 1937–38 demonstrated the dramatic power of that evolving cultural frame.

Recalls were one of the reforms instituted by Progressives in California and elsewhere, and the Shaw recall has been noted as one of the first—if not the first—successful recall of a major urban mayor. For most historians, the recall represented the finale to a long-running, dramatic, and at times dastardly political battle. At its heart lay a conflict between two men, Mayor Frank Shaw and Clifford Clinton, with Justice Fletcher Bowron as Clinton's key ally.[19] Shaw, the merchant son of immigrants, rose to political office after nearly two decades of work in the greater Los Angeles community. First elected mayor in 1933, he was an avid supporter of Franklin Roosevelt and, working with his brother Joseph as his secretary, led the city confidently through the depths of the Depression. Most citizens were satisfied enough with Shaw's performance that in the spring of 1937, they returned him to office.

Clifford Clinton did not share their assessment, however. Born to a pair of Salvation Army captains, Clinton worked principally as a restaurateur. A husband and father, he owned the much beloved Clifton's Cafeterias—fantastically decorated establishments where the Golden Rule was deemed the management philosophy and patrons were encouraged to pay only what they could afford. Clinton had traveled with his parents when they were missionaries in China and had developed a strong passion both for righteousness and for public affairs. Clinton's cafeterias—and later hotels—also made him quite wealthy, and, believing that Mayor Shaw lacked righteousness, Clinton spearheaded the drive for his removal. Clinton did not seek the mayor's office for himself: that position fell to Justice Bowron. Nevertheless, it was the formation of Clinton's CIVIC organization, the Citizens Independent Vice Investigating Committee, in mid-1937 that marked, according to most accounts, the final chapter in Shaw's mayoralty.[20]

The battling between these two men had begun earlier, at least as far back as 1934, when Progressive county supervisor John Anson Ford asked Clinton to join a four-person committee investigating food services at the county's General Hospital. Ford had been elected to office in 1934 and was a liberal progressive who advocated welfare reform and publicly supported cultural institutions. The hospital committee found that 25 percent of the budget was being mismanaged, and Ford and Clinton charged that the hospital was a " 'political playhouse' of patronage" for Shaw. Shaw refuted the allegations, and shortly after the hospital report, Clinton's business taxes were raised, numerous patrons filed suits over injuries or poisonings at his two cafeterias, and both cafeterias were deemed to be in massive violation of state sanitary codes. Shaw, it seemed, was exacting his revenge.[21]

Within a year, a grand jury, seated by Justice Bowron, began investigating the Shaw administration's ties to gambling and street-paving profiteering, but it issued no indictments. Then Bowron nominated Clinton to the 1937 grand jury, and Clinton urged that the jury address the ubiquity of vice in the city. Only a handful of jurors were intrigued, so that April, Clinton himself began compiling the names and addresses of brothels, gambling joints, and "vice dens," as well as taking pictures of prostitutes and police officers at the various establishments and publishing them in a partisan newspaper. Nevertheless, Shaw was reelected that very spring—defeating John Anson Ford—and so Clinton formed the Citizens' Independent Vice Investigating Committee (CIVIC) to press the vice issue further and make the case that the Shaw administration was deliberately allowing vice to prosper.[22]

Throughout the fall, Clinton tried to present his evidence to the grand jury, but they repeatedly rejected his offers. When the DA, a Shaw crony, demanded Clinton's evidence, though, he refused to turn it over. A pro-Clinton notary was beaten up by the DA's detectives, Clinton's home was bombed, and several grand jurors launched an investigation into CIVIC itself and the larger "reform racket." And then on January 14, 1938, Harry

Raymond, a CIVIC investigator, stepped on the starter of his car and detonated a bomb that destroyed his garage, tore the motor out of the car, and drove 150 wood and glass shards into his body. Miraculously, Raymond survived, but the police investigation and trial that spring ultimately implicated both Chief of Police James Davis and the mayor's brother, and resulted in the conviction of two men from a police detective squad. The city populace now began to embrace the prospect that Clinton and CIVIC suggested to them: it was time to recall Mayor Frank Shaw. A heated recall campaign unfolded in the summer of 1938, and by mid-September the deed was done: Shaw was removed from office and in his stead stood grand jury coordinator Fletcher Bowron.[23]

The battling among these men and the subsequent recall were plainly dramatic events.[24] Yet the mobilization that drew Angelenos into the recall drama involved much more than accounts of a long political rivalry. Clinton and CIVIC first captured Angelenos' attention with charges about vice, and those charges not only laid the cultural foundation of the recall but had a life well beyond the election. The campaign successfully linked multiple ideas about social and political dangers into a powerfully cogent world-view, one that marked as synonymous the threats of moralistic fervor and Communism, and tied them to deviant sexual and gender behavior. These multiple threads and figures that coalesced in the political culture made the recall campaign both riveting and powerful.

VICE AND THE RECALL

The foremost issue in the recall effort and the first key theme of the emergent political culture was the moralizing force of the anti-vice campaign.[25] The corruption of the Shaw administration had been widely discussed in the city. Even young William Mason, then growing up in Edendale, had the sense that graft was everywhere. Certainly, he recalled, "it was a foregone conclusion that the police were corrupt," but in addition, "everybody presumed the Shaw regime was corrupt." Part of the corruption meant that "a blind eye" had been turned toward prostitution, which flourished in 1936, '37, and '38. Main Street bars proudly offered B-girls and the Wilshire district just west of downtown—the Crown Hill area, where the 808 Night Club was located—became known as "Lysol Hill," rife with call girls and in-the-know taxi drivers. The *Hollywood Citizen-News,* in a July 1937 editorial, deemed Shaw, "an underworld-controlled Mayor." When the mayor insisted that he wanted information on organized vice in order for the police to "clean up the situation," the editorial called him "the city's biggest liar."[26]

From the beginning, as Clinton launched his efforts, he sought to publicize the immoral stains of inappropriate sexual and economic desires. The wealthy restaurateur hired investigators who photographed bookies at newsstands taking bets, even from police officers. They identified prostitution houses, raided them, and photographed the prostitutes. They found stores and saloons where pinball and slot machines were played, and these they also photographed. CIVIC and Clinton, in leaflets and radio programs, called on citizens to "face the facts." And for them, the facts were that despite the presence of law enforcement, there were 1,800 bookies, 342 houses of miscellaneous gambling, "some with liquor," 603 houses of prostitution, and 23,000 pinball and slot machine games in Los Angeles: Angelenos' improper desires were running rampant. Additionally, Clinton and CIVIC repeatedly asked local citizens to be their own investigative force. While he sought out citizens who could "spend some time unremunerated working with our Citizen's Intelligence Dept.," Clinton also asked them to write in about local hot spots. "CITIZENS NEED NOT have law violations in their communities if they do not wish. An accurate, timely report of conditions to CIVIC starts wheels in motion."[27]

The presence of just such moral conviction held many fast to the CIVIC cause over more than a year and a half. Offers of help poured into Clinton's home, on handwritten note cards and in typed-up letters, from people who had been moved by some event or radio broadcast and who saw clearly his moral purpose. "I marvel at," wrote Irene Dyer, "and glory in your strength and determination to prove that 'the truth can set you free.'" (First Clinton and then many of his supporters latched onto this phrase, seeking liberation in revelation.) T. Matthew Thompson declared, "Mr. Clinton I feel this is a great work and I want a part in it, I want to be in the drive." And Clinton wrote back to them, declaring, "Your devotion brings great courage," and signing the letters, "Your fellow soldier in the great crusade." They saw themselves as just such soldiers in salvation's army.[28]

Importantly, that sense of idealism and moral purity did not disappear when CIVIC's energies so clearly shifted from the anti-vice campaign to the recall of Shaw. That political project remained infused for supporters with the same exalted meaning and rhetoric. After the recall's success, an array of citizens, like E. Zacariah Croxall, wrote Clinton, praising "the courageous and wonderful work you have been carrying on under tremendous odds and with every possible obstacle that the adversary could place in your way, but this merely demonstrates that right always wins the right of way. . . . All I can say is that I am happy and rejoice with you over our outstanding victory and I know that 'the cause is right and the truth has made us free.' "[29] For Croxall and countless others, the seemingly narrow political question of the recall continued, in fact, to be about a "cause" that was "right" and that was sustained by "truth" and "courage." Even as the votes were tallied and the political implications of Clinton's efforts became apparent, the moral fervor remained, for the wider public, interwoven stitch by stitch with the political drama.

MORALISM AND COMMUNISM

Such moral rhetoric was compelling. Certainly a strong argument could be made that it was Clinton's very successful articulation of a rhetoric and framework of morality that caused the majority of Los Angeles voters to view Shaw as untenable as mayor. At the very least, moral probity came to be the dominant rhetorical currency of Los Angeles' political culture. Yet morality proved to be both a productive and a slippery language.

On the one hand, in the wary culture of 1930s L.A., the virtuous crusader role was not easy to retain. Clinton's moral integrity quickly became suspect, and questions about morality and morally appropriate behavior soon swirled ambiguously around him, CIVIC, and the recall itself. Many of Clinton's critics charged not only that he was wasting his and the city's time with his obsession with gambling and prostitution but also that his prurient fascination with these issues of excessive desire demonstrated his own despicable morality. Several residents decried Clinton for invading the secrets of people's private lives. He was lambasted for having "suddenly changed from a fine cultured gentleman to a cheap, petty sneaking night prowler." One angry Legionnaire, who feared that the anti-vice campaign would ruin the national American Legion convention scheduled for Los Angeles, wrote Clinton, "If you and your ministers can't stand to tend to your own business why don't you give up your places and move way out and have a community of your own."[30] The rhetoric of moralizing was turned against the moralizers.

At the same time, the language of moral anxiety provided traction for the articulation and manipulation of other anxieties. Indeed, various partisans tarred the candidates with a wide array of allegations throughout the recall campaign, ranging from secret Ku Klux Klan memberships to hidden anti-Semitic agendas.[31] Fundamentally, though, the anxiety about moralizing became reframed through two fears that were linked in the local culture: fear of Communism and of sexual perversion.

The Communist framing was hardly surprising. As historian Leonard Leader pointed out, most civic protesters or demonstrators in 1930s Los Angeles were labeled as Communists. The red-smear campaign that tailed Upton Sinclair's bid for governor in 1934—the *Los Angeles Times* said he represented a "threat to sovietize California"—is well documented.[32] And as *Liberty* magazine declared in its multipart analysis of the 1938 recall campaign: "Los Angeles has long been an open-shop town; Red-baiting long has been its popular sport. This is not to imply any criticism of either but to point out that some of Los Angeles' most incompetent politicians have managed to climb to office on a campaign that promised little more than that they would pull a bomb and an anarchist from beneath each worried citizen's bed." Indeed, as the summertime recall campaign opened, Joseph Fainer, the special prosecutor in the Raymond bombing, linked the police department's maligned detective squad to Communism. In his closing arguments, he compared the squad to the Soviet Union's secret police and shouted to the jury, "That's how Communism starts—with a secret political spy squad which owes no allegiance to the taxpayers, but owes allegiance only to a boss. . . . Talk about subversive interests, this squad contains the very kernel and basis of Communism!" The dangers of Communism provided an increasingly powerful rhetoric and framework for denouncing a host of public actions.[33]

The red smear was certainly applied doggedly to Clinton, Bowron, and the reform efforts of CIVIC over the course of the recall campaign. One sneering pre-election note to Clinton, for instance, asked if he were not "neglecting an important announcement? So far I haven't heard you announce the Communist Rally at the Olympic Auditorium, where Earl Browder [the general secretary of the national Communist Party] is to close the campaign in the interests of the folks with whom you have surrounded yourself." William Lewis chided Clinton for starting to "affiliate with radicals and communists"; after that, he "and many others that I personally know of, shook you off like a burning coal. Listening to your radio talk is like reading a Communist's literature, filled with disproved filth and damnations unfit for decent eyes and ears to absorb." Many citizens wrote to Clinton, fearing that while he himself was honest, he had "become a pawn of the radical communist element." Just as many, though, agreed with W. M. Bennett: "People do not like Mayor Shaw, but prefer him to these fake groups, camouflaged by psued-names *[sic]*. I know some of the members, and nobody could describe them, truthfully, as anything but Reds." And by election's end, once Bowron had taken office, folks like S. M. "Larry" Doyle, a past national commander of the American Legion, decried the new administration as a "vicious wheel of Communism. And I tell you this after due and mature consideration that the man from whom all of this stems is that peddler of Hate, Hypocrisy and Hash, Clifford E. Clinton."[34]

It would be hard to make a case for Clinton as pro-Communist. More apt would be the suggestion that Communists filled Clinton with a fair amount of concern. He kept two files devoted to clippings and publications on Communism, including such items as a *Life* magazine article by Arthur Schlesinger and a lengthy historical brochure from the Los Angeles County Communist Party. And his actions as an employer seemed hardly communistic: he refused to let his cafeteria workers join a union, and as one biographer noted, he was "concerned" about any radical presence on the campaign.[35]

It is true that Don Healey, who was very active in left-wing and Communist causes and head of both the Congress of Industrial Organizations (CIO) and the Labor Non-Partisan League, became a member of the executive committee coordinating the recall. Nevertheless, the American Federation of Labor (AFL)–affiliated Central Labor Council came out strongly against Judge Bowron because of his affiliation with Clinton. One campaign leaflet insisted "LABOR CONDEMNS CLIFFORD E. CLINTON" and listed their condemnations for his being an "open-shopper," running a company union, boasting about it, and firing employees who wanted to join the AFL. "Labor would strongly condemn any administration Clinton would control as reactionary and anti-social."[36]

Despite the facts of a clearly anti-radical record, though, Angelenos could still be convinced that Clinton was a Communist. The alleged dangers of Communism were so persistently woven into Los Angeles political life that such a charge was easy to imagine and easier to circulate. Perceiving that possibility, Clinton took to the airwaves to deny the red accusations. Noting that "certain writers in the *Times* give the impression that I am a communist," Clinton deemed it an accurate appellation only "if desiring honest, efficient administration in the interest of the public welfare is communism—then I am a communist. If, however, communism is as terrible as the officials would have me believe, I would not want such a system here." In fact, Clinton tried to turn the tide of the smears. "I stand—and will stand," he insisted, "for my country . . . when I know we are being robbed of everything dear to us by those who would lull us into apathy with stories of what might happen if we let reds come in. What do they mean— might happen? It is happening. I know!" Clinton vowed, "I'll fight reds— taking over our country—yes, even if they wear blue suits, with shiny gold badges—upon which are these letters: LAPD." Allegations of Communism were thus a principal and dangerous rhetorical weapon, constituting a pow- erful charge that needed to be refuted. And at the same time, Angelenos seemed to have an endless appetite for Communist charges and counter- charges, and a continuing willingness to believe them.[37]

Indeed, the power and danger of the red smear lay in the fact that the socially understood definition of who or what constituted a radical was ter- rifically loose and flexible—so loose that even a moralist such as Clinton could be identified as a radical. In 1938 Reverend Robert Shuler, himself a powerful figure in local politics, wrote Dr. A. M. Wilkinson, a friend and founding member of CIVIC, in order to counsel him and Clinton about the dangers of being associated with leftists. Shuler feared that there was "right much radical leadership" in the new Federation for Civic Better- ment, the organization formed to coordinate the specifics of the recall. He worried that they would sidetrack the campaign with strikes and talk of civil liberties. "Now I am definitely interested in justice for all classes," he wrote, "but we will never win a battle against vice and crime in this com- munity under radical leadership. When I say radical leadership, I simply mean a leadership that is more interested in liberal ideas on economics than it is in morality and public decency."[38]

According to the reverend, the danger of a radical presence lay in precisely how easily a red smear could be broadened within the city's Communist- wary political culture. Shuler reasoned that "when you get too close to these red radicals, they will smear you in spite of everything. At present Clinton has kept himself clean, so that Shaw and Davis and the Times, etc. could not accuse him of red activities, and I do hope that he will be very careful in his attitude in the future." Yet proximity, Reverend Shuler understood, was equivalent to identity. A moralist, by association, could be made to look like a Communist. When Wilkinson wrote back, he confirmed that Clin- ton understood this as well; he had "caught the idea you have expressed very fully I am sure as to the need of avoiding any entanglements with other groups, radical, pink, red, or otherwise."[39]

Obviously, though, the cultural entanglement of Clinton's moralism and Communism persisted in the minds of many Los Angeles citizens.

Placed there by smear or fact, in passing moments it somehow made sense to them. Moralism began to appear as if it were a form of Communism. Indeed, part of the power of this emergent political culture lay in how it made these various threats appear equivalent. In certain moments, it could seem that all that talk about vice and prostitution was really just a smoke screen for a hidden Communist agenda.

THE DANGERS OF SEXUAL DEVIANCE

In addition to moralism and Communism, the third fear woven into Los Angeles political culture focused on deviant sexuality. Clinton's questions about morality were reframed through the figure of the fairy, and through that reframing, "sex perverts" or "degenerates" began to appear increasingly dangerous, as if they possessed some kind of political power. Homosexual desires were tagged with political significance.

Raids of clubs like Jimmie's Back Yard and B.B.B.'s Cellar had surged again in 1936 and 1937. According to a local tabloid called *The Equalizer,* the district attorney, county sheriff, and state Board of Equalization had met in 1934 to discuss "curbing of Liquor permits where The Sex Perverts assembled to exhibit their wares." The paper stated that the state licensing board had shut down six bars as a result: three bars were closed in 1936, and three more in the spring and summer of 1937. For *The Equalizer,* "the very heart of Sex Perversion . . . was the entertainment of The Public by these Farries, with women dressed as men and men dressed as women before groups of liquor-crazed youths."[40] The gender play of the fairy no longer constituted light-hearted entertainment; for *The Equalizer* it quite clearly indicated that he was a "sex pervert." The degenerate paradigm, defined by an emphasis on consistent desires, was beginning to overcome the fairy framework.

The 808 Club had already been shut down in the new upsurge of activity. According to Estelle Milmar's memory, in 1935 or 1936 the police began to harass the club with increasing fervor. First they would not allow the impersonators to wear wigs, because "they didn't want them to make people think they're women." Then the police issued minor complaints. One night they closed the club down, claiming that the stage curtain was not fireproof, although the tags on it clearly marked it as within the code. Another night, they picked up Milmar's husband on a liquor charge violation, although the license had not been violated. After driving him around in handcuffs until three in the morning and jailing him, they released him the following day without filing charges. According to Milmar, though, "things finally got too hot." On Saturday nights when the club was full of patrons, plainclothes policemen would walk up and down the aisles, staring at the assembled audience. "Oh, we fancied ourselves daring at the time," said Milmar, "but not enough to stand up to that. They wouldn't touch anybody or say anything, but their presence was enough to frighten the customers away."[41] That fear locked the door on the 808.

Early in the winter of 1936, the police also declared a "War on Vagrants." According to the *Los Angeles Examiner*, the police swept into parks and loitering districts to hunt down the nighttime visitors. The police met first in Pershing Square, then moved out along the Run, some heading down Main Street, others heading as far west as the cruising area of Westlake Park.[42]

As Clinton's anti-vice and recall campaigns unfolded, however, officials began to target the sex pervert even more aggressively. During the summer of 1937, the first season of CIVIC's anti-vice activism, Mayor Shaw tried to quell the anti-administration furor that CIVIC was stirring by demonstrating his own leadership against moral turpitude. As a crucial piece of that effort, in August 1937 Shaw called for the establishment of a city "Sex Bureau" to control "sex degenerates." Acknowledging that the city had already "gone a long way toward establishing surveillance of known sex degenerates," Shaw called for "developing this police function to the utmost possible degree of efficiency." The "immediate need," as he saw it, was "to establish a board of psychiatrists to carry these examinations of perverts to the full limit of the law and accomplish commitments of psychopathic cases to suitable institutions in every possible instance before degeneracy leads to some tragic crime."[43]

Historians such as Estelle Freedman, George Chauncey, and Stephen Robertson have documented the widespread panic over "sexual psychopaths" that consumed the nation as a whole in the summer of 1937. A series of sex crimes in New York led to fast and furious media campaigns— the *New York Times* added a new index heading for the 143 sex crime stories it ran that year. The director of the FBI, J. Edgar Hoover, himself wrote a widely syndicated article entitled "War on the Sex Criminal!" that demanded, "The present apathy of the public toward known perverts, generally regarded as 'harmless,' should be changed to one of suspicious scrutiny. The 'harmless' pervert of today can be and often is the loathsome mutilator and murderer of tomorrow." As a result, several states passed laws directed against sexual psychopaths and, to a degree, Shaw was moving in step with other politicians around the country.[44]

But Shaw was also addressing the swirl of morality concerns that were churning specifically in Los Angeles. Importantly, Clinton was not spreading information about sexual degenerates: that was not the high moral path that so appealed to his supporters. Nevertheless, Shaw responded to CIVIC's allegations about vice by beginning an attack on "perverts." In a city swamped in the language of morality and teeming with the unemployed men of the Depression, the mayor could gain some political ground by arguing that rounding up perverts was the city's "immediate need." Responding to that "need" in 1937 made political sense, and as a result, moralists, radicals, and perverts all became interwoven figures in the city's political life. That CIVIC summer of 1937, politics was revealed to be in an intimate and inextricable embrace not only with moralism and Communism but with fears of sexual deviance as well.[45]

The effort to establish Mayor Shaw's Sex Bureau lasted several months. Various local officials, including the county sheriff, and the Hearst-owned *Los Angeles Examiner* joined the call for such a program. By the first of September a meeting was held in the district attorney's office to discuss the bureau, with the idea that such an office would assist the sheriffs, the DA, the police, the judges, and even the local PTAs. In an editorial, the *Examiner* staff asked that the operation have a wide jurisdiction. They called for it to handle not only people convicted of morals charges, "but all who are arrested on morals violations and persons suspected as *potential* offenders." Suspects and convicts alike were to be given "thorough mental and physical examination by these doctors."[46]

Officially, the Sex Bureau was not intended exclusively to contain homosexual activity. In fact, when Shaw pressed the case for the bureau with the Police Commission in October, he stressed the need to wage a "persistent campaign against criminals whose sexual aberrations make them a constant menace to women and children." Nevertheless, from *The Equalizer*, it seems particularly clear that Shaw's "sex degenerates" were understood as homosexually active men. It was his Sex Bureau proposal that prompted the *Equalizer* article about sex perverts and, while the paper did suggest that a pervert might be a child molester, its attention was much more devoted to "these Farries" and the "liquor-crazed youths." Much as in other cities, the sex pervert was principally the man who inverted the sex and gender code.[47]

Despite the perceived danger of the sex pervert, establishing the new police bureau still took some negotiating, which itself was revealing. After first approving funding for the mayor's panel of three psychiatrists, the city council changed its mind. Then, in the middle of spring 1938, while the Harry Raymond bombing trial gripped the rest of the city, the council reconsidered the proposal. During the discussion, one councilman, obviously cynical about additional police expenditures, substituted one request for another, asking if "the necessary appropriation would be for the purchase of a new automobile by the Police Department for Harry Raymond to replace the one that was blown up?" "No," teased a second councilman, "it's to furnish Raymond with a psychiatrist."[48]

The humor was flimsy, but to some degree the flimsy joke relied on the notion that the CIVIC investigator would be helped by psychiatric attention, especially from sex specialists. The joke suggested some vague cultural logic—what might be called the logic of the "lavender smear"—which made it easy to taint Raymond, the anti-vice sleuth, with some sex perversion. The strangeness of the joke was picked up by a newspaper reporter covering the council who wrote, "Perhaps Freud . . . could have solved the devious mental processes of the City Council yesterday when psychiatrists, sex and the Harry Raymond case became a jumble of discussion."[49] In part, the reporter's reference to Freud indicated the widening recognition of psychoanalytic theories and their significance in reinforcing a connection between public acts and private, perhaps perverted, sexual desires. At the same time, the reporter's and councilman's comments pointed to the contemporary logic in which the action of a moralizer could be easily read as a mark of perversion.

The conflation of moralism and reform with effeminacy was not a new political practice. According to historian Kevin Murphy, "mugwump" reformers of the late nineteenth century who set out to clean up the civil service system were often lampooned as effeminate, and twentieth-century liberal reformers were regularly criticized for their failure to acknowledge the competitive masculine nature of life. Charges about reformers' effeminacy did not mark them, however, as possessing "perverted" sexual desires; rather they were statements about their absent courage or their inability to live up to certain gender norms.[50]

In the 1930s, though, the celebrity of performing fairies gave credibility to the notion that male effeminacy was not simply troubling but was equivalent to same-sex desire. The fairies gave wider support to the reading of moralism—itself an effeminate posture—as a marker or sign of perversion. Not surprisingly in that context, the lavender smear was also applied to Clinton, who was tagged as a kind of unmanly pervert. One Beverly Hills housewife presented this analysis in a letter she wrote to Clinton on behalf of her women's club. The members, she said, suspected that he had been a "problem child." What is more, they were convinced that "you certainly couldn't be 'all man' other wise you'd have other interests besides being a snoopy old woman! Maybe a good Doctor for instance would tell you if you're suffering from delusions of grandeur."[51] That is, while it would take such a psychiatrist to explain it fully, Clinton plainly was a man interested in being a woman. His manhood was now in question.

Thus many of Clinton's initial concerns about immorality were recast and thrown back not just as questions about Communism but also as questions about gender and sexual deviance. Clinton's moralizing was reinterpreted as masculine anxiety. Mayor Shaw responded to CIVIC's high moral tone by joining a campaign against sexual and gender deviants. Just as moralist crusaders were recast as Communists, the conversations about moralism were also remade as conversations and concerns about deviant sexuality and gender identity. Moralists themselves could be marked as perverts.

THE POLITICAL LINKAGE OF COMMUNISM AND PERVERSION

But in this particular moment, likely because of the equal anxiety about Communism, the concerns about deviance became freighted with political significance and power. While notions of leftist danger and sexual anxiety have a complicated history in American and Angeleno political life, during the recall campaign, the Communist and the degenerate became understood as dangerously allied. The week before the actual recall election, for instance, the *Highland Park Post Dispatch* ran an advertisement on behalf of a businessmen's association that asked, "RECALL OR RECOVERY? Experiments vs Experience! Do you want to Keep Los Angeles the White Spot"—its oft-repeated moniker of moral purity and economic success— "or Invite the Red Menace of Radicalism?"[52] The threat of Communism went hand in hand with the sexual dangers that both CIVIC and the mayor's Sex Bureau were trying to address.

J. Nielsen-Lange, a wholesale feed broker who wrote Clinton about whom to nominate as Shaw's replacement, made similar ties between Communists and perversion. While Neilsen-Lange had no particular candidate in mind, he urged that Clinton select a "positive individual." "Your opposition would like nothing better than you would put in a man they could call 'A goody, goody' 'A sissy' or 'A long-hair.' You will be far better off by having a totally unknown man, who is positive, than to have a well-known one for whom you must make excuses."[53] A "long-hair," presumably, was an intellectual or a radical; the "goody, goody" was a moralist; and the "sissy," in Nielsen-Lange's language, would likely have been merely an effeminate "cake eater"—the kind of overcivilized, "unmanly" man Eltinge often defeated in his theatrical and cinematic productions. Given the context of the recall, however, his vocabulary begs the question of how easy it was to distinguish a "sissy"—or even a "long-hair"—from one of the *Equalizer*'s "farries," those "men dressed as women." Presumably they were different in fact, but hardly so in language; in rhetorical terms, they all seemed vaguely similar. So the worrisome options were a moralist, a Communist, or a man who was not really a man: these three were grouped together as the dangerous suspects. Neilsen-Lange recognized that in the wider culture, and certainly in the minds of CIVIC's opponents, moralism, Communism, and gender or sexual inversion were perceived as related threats.

This merger of the degenerate and Communist in the local political culture can be seen more graphically in a cartoon entitled "Black Reaction + Red Communism = Loathsome Fascism" that was published in the heat of the recall summer by the *Allied Democrat*. The drawing depicts a wedding. Judge Bowron, by then CIVIC's designated candidate, is the officiant. He sports a slanted halo and declares, "In the spirit that the end justifies the means—I bless this unholy alliance." The groom is Paul Cline, Communist Party county secretary, flanked, as best man, by "Communist Stooge Don Healey," organizer for the local CIO. Cline is holding a placard that cites a *People's World Daily* endorsement of Bowron, and Healey's card is signed, "Yours for a United Front, Jo. Stalin." The bride, of course, is none other than Clifford Clinton in a flowing gown and is identified as " 'Cliffie' Open Shop Clinton," with Reverend Shuler as his bridesmaid. According to the long caption below, this "unholy wedding"—truly a "marriage of political expediency"—filled "all decent minded citizens of this city with repugnance."[54]

Clearly the cartoon was not an article claiming that Clinton was a sex pervert. Nevertheless, its operative structure stated implicitly that the same men who posed as moral crusaders were men who dressed as women, men who married other men: they were "farries." What is more, allowing these fairies into politics meant opening the door to an expansive Communist network that stretched from the CIO local all the way back to Joseph Stalin. The fairy, via the elaborate and elusive structure of international Communism, was grasping at the political reins. And his ultimate goal was nothing short of "loathsome fascism."

An "unholy wedding," according to the *Allied Democrat,* brought together moralizer Clifford Clinton and Communist Paul Cline under the auspices of mayoral candidate Fletcher Bowron. The cartoonist wove together implications of radicalism and gender inversion in this image. (Courtesy Department of Special Collections, California State University at Long Beach.)

This was what many Angelenos saw when they looked at the recall literature or heard its radio broadcasts. Through the lens of the local political culture, they saw a political and social system under siege by a vast and potent network of dangerously radical deviates. The imaginary pervert and his radical allies were coming to possess powerful political agency. That was the danger lurking behind the recall.

The late 1930s were not the apogee of that cultural system, though they marked its strong debut. Fear of the radical deviate certainly shaped the campaign Clinton and Bowron had to wage in order to challenge and defeat Shaw, but they did succeed in overcoming it. While the evidence suggests the recall effort would likely have failed had not the Raymond bombing trial so explicitly implicated the Shaw administration, the cultural convergence of moralism, Communism, and perversion grew beyond electoral politics.[55] The fear of the radical deviate weighed heavily on the real "perverts" and "farries" who populated Southern California in these decades. Marked in the culture as a social and political threat, they became the subjects not merely of bar raids but of carefully orchestrated police investigations that landed them in state prisons for five, ten, and fifteen years.

After much delay on the part of the City Council, the Sex Bureau was finally established in midsummer 1938. The bureau was designed to operate, according to the press, "on the theory that each minor sex offender is a potential major sex criminal." Under its auspices, all sex offenders were to be classified by their "methods of operation," and that information was filed in a vast catalog that would then be made available to other law enforcement agencies in the county. In addition, each offender was given a psychiatric examination and recommended for particular punishments as well as possible rehabilitation. While previously sex criminals had received psychiatric examinations only under the orders of a judge, now all arrested offenders would be analyzed prior to appearing before a judge. According to the *Times,* "Under the new program each judge will have a copy of the bureau's report at the time the offender is first brought before him for plea, thus aiding prompt corrective measures." For a time, the bureau budget provided for a team of three psychiatrists working part-time for the city; quickly, though, the psychiatric work fell on the shoulders of a single man, Dr. J. Paul de River, a former brain surgeon with the Veterans Administration.[56]

The establishment of the Sex Bureau was only the first step, however. The police department also developed its own sex crimes detail. Egged on by the *Times,* which publicized the level of sex crimes, the chief of police moved to establish a new group of officers in April 1939 to round up sex criminals. The following year, the city council unanimously passed an ordinance establishing a registry for sex crime offenders. The ordinance, according to the *Examiner,* made it compulsory for all "convicted perverts"—whether they were convicted in California or any other state in the previous twenty years, and whether they were sentenced to jail or simply put on probation— to register with the city, giving their name, address, history, and fingerprints. Said Police Chief Arthur Hohmann, "Registration of individuals of this type would provide the Police Department with a reliable index to persons of degenerate tendencies when necessary to make an investigation of persons of this character when serious crimes have been committed and the identity of the perpetrators is unknown." By the late 1940s, there was a statewide registry as well.[57]

The new attention to sex criminals by the police resulted, not surprisingly, in an increase in arrests. Unfortunately, it is difficult to identify specific numbers of men arrested for homosexual activities from published police arrest reports. Few men in Los Angeles, for instance, were actually arrested and charged with sodomy—or the "infamous crime against nature," as it was also called. Instead, most homosexually active men who were arrested by the police were charged or convicted of a fairly loose and vague charge, like "lewd and lascivious conduct" or "lewd vagrancy." While such charges were regularly used against men cruising for other men or propositioning undercover officers, prostitutes and their customers, flashers, and others could also be arrested on the same charges. Nevertheless, a clear pattern in the history of arrests can be discerned.

The arrests of homosexually active men can be correlated most closely with arrests for "sex perversion." The law against sex perversion was written into the books in 1915, shortly after the Long Beach arrests, and it explicitly identified oral sex as a felony distinct from anal sex. In Los Angeles in the 1920s, '30s, and '40s, men constituted 90 to 95 percent of arrestees charged with sex perversion. While there are cases of men being charged for having performed oral sex on women, a sampling of the court records suggests that the majority involved men having oral sex with other men.[58] Across the 1920s and early 1930s, the numbers of men arrested for sex perversion remained relatively consistent, approximately half the number of people arrested for murder. While there were small rises in 1934

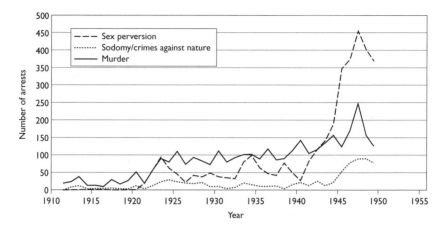

Arrests for sex perversion and sodomy compared to those for murder. SOURCE: Los Angeles Police Department, *Annual Report of the Police Department,* Arrest and Disposition tables, 1911–54 (Los Angeles: Police Department).

and 1938, from 1940 to 1948 the number of arrests increased steadily and dramatically. By contrast, the murder arrest rate rose much more evenly, and was much more in line with the general population growth. The new assessment of the dangers of homosexuality translated into more aggressive police actions.

The arrest rates on vagrancy charges tell a similar, if less precise, story. Vagrancy laws were used readily by the police to arrest drunks, prostitutes, unemployed men, and others, along with men prowling for sex. They indicate, therefore, a broader picture of police activity. Nonetheless, the numbers offer a similar account. While arrest rates on lewd and dissolute vagrancy charges were high in the early years of the Depression—when Police Chief Davis worked fervently to keep the unemployed of other states out of Los Angeles—they dropped significantly by the middle of the decade. Beginning in 1940, however, those arrests skyrocketed as well, peaking at the end of the decade.

This narrative of a 1930s decline in police hostility followed by late-1930s and 1940s increases is supported as well by a broad comparison of all possible same-sex sex crime arrests with other major crimes in the city. The figures for sex crimes are not exclusive to homosexual activity alone, although the compilation rests on those crimes for which homosexually active men were arrested. As such, they show a similar decline in police activity dur-

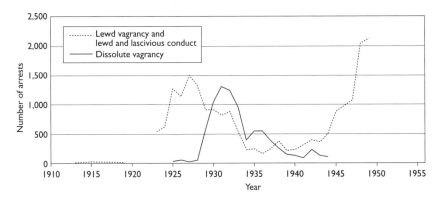

Vagrancy arrests. SOURCE: Los Angeles Police Department, *Annual Report of the Police Department,* Arrest and Disposition tables, 1911–54 (Los Angeles: Police Department).

ing the early 1930s. Indeed, compiled in this fashion, sex crime arrests declined fairly steadily from 1929 until 1936 and '37, falling well below the general growth rate for the city. That decline appears even more dramatic when contrasted with arrests for burglary and robbery, which rose steadily across the decade. Beginning in the late 1930s, however, sex crime arrests began a steady climb that, while dipping early in the war years, continued until the early 1950s. On the one hand, the increase in arrests put sex crime arrests in line with those of robbery and burglary: the police were treating sex crimes as seriously as other crimes in the 1940s. At the same time, however, this was a dramatic shift in the treatment and pursuit of sex criminals. Taken together, these sets of figures demonstrate how the political culture translated directly into arrests.

Being arrested had dramatic implications. The arrest alone often yielded a write-up in a local newspaper, offering the name and address of the arrested men. That kind of publicity broke apart careers and families. While punishment for a vagrancy arrest might be only three to six months in jail, a sex perversion conviction carried a possible sentence of fifteen years in state prison. And for many men, input from the Sex Bureau—like many of the "sexual psychopath" apparatuses set up around the country—could leave them committed in some psychiatric institution where their release remained contingent upon whether or not the mental health staff deemed them "cured." And cures themselves could involve electroshock therapy, castration, and lobotomy.[59]

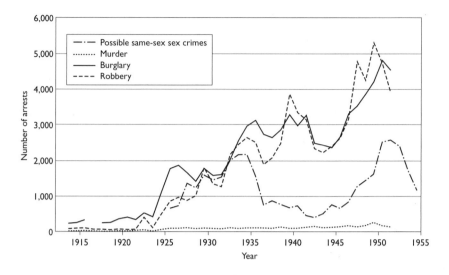

Arrests for possible same-sex crimes compared to those for other crimes. SOURCE: Los Angeles Police Department, *Annual Report of the Police Department,* Arrest and Disposition tables, 1911–54 (Los Angeles: Police Department).

These were drastic consequences, and the fear they evoked was sharply conveyed in an extortion case from 1937. In that case, three men extorted money from William Hayman by alleging they had stopped him while having sex in a café bathroom close to Westlake Park. While Hayman was using a toilet in a stall, one of the extortionists suddenly stepped inside his stall. The leader of the extortionists, Edward Jones, then rapped on the stall door, and when the first man stepped out, Jones shouted at him, "Oh, you are a pervert. We know you." Jones told a third man to "take him away" and then, claiming to be a constable, proceeded to "charge" Hayman with attempted sodomy. Jones next demanded money from Hayman to drop the charges, first taking the ten dollars he had with him that day and then coming to his home several days later to insist on another twenty-five hundred dollars. Hayman, who had apparently committed no crime that day, so feared a potential arrest that he nonetheless tried to raise fifteen hundred dollars before eventually turning to an attorney for assistance.[60] The emerging regimen of arrests and incarcerations created a climate of tremendous anxiety for homosexually active men in Los Angeles.

Yet these policing actions—like those elsewhere in the region and country—were fundamentally an expression of the wider fear generated by

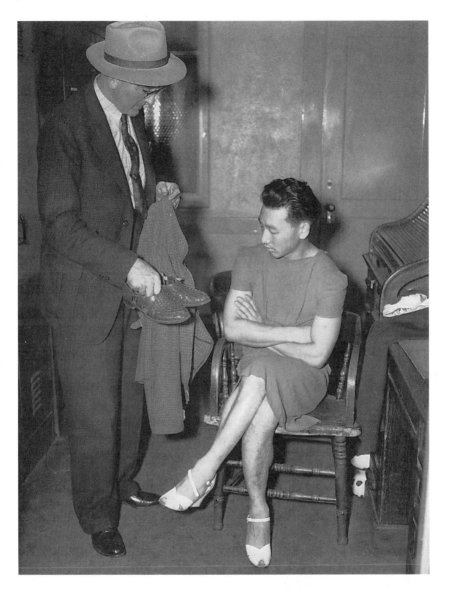

A man in a dress seems to look defiant as vice detective G. A. Hahn hands him a pair of men's shoes. This photograph, seemingly from inside a police office, was taken by a photographer for the *Los Angeles Daily News* around 1940. (Los Angeles Daily News Collection, Department of Special Collections, Charles E. Young Research Library, University of California, Los Angeles.)

the increasingly powerful culture that marked homosexuality as a significant threat to contemporary society. The level of that fear was demonstrated quite vividly in the arrest of Clifford Holm, a young army lieutenant stationed just outside the town of Riverside, some forty miles east of downtown Los Angeles. In the spring of 1937, Holm was twenty-four and working at March Air Field for the Army Air Corps. One Saturday, two soldiers invited him to a "stag party" at a cabin on the edge of Riverside. Holm went with about ten other men. The cabin was a simple two-bedroom wooden structure, but good enough for them: they drank, acted silly, and even danced. Two of the dozen men appeared "in drags" as the Countess and the Duchess. At one point the Duchess donned hula dance attire and put on a show for everyone, and at another point Holm tried dancing with one of the other soldiers but was "cast off to one side" because he did not know the steps. Then everyone went home with an explicit invitation from the host to come back the next Saturday and bring along anyone "who knew what the score was." The next Saturday, not only did Holm and seven of the original guests return, but they were joined by ten others.[61]

The guests, however, were not the only ones in attendance that second Saturday. In fact, even the first Saturday, four police officers, alerted by a suspicious landlord, sat outside the cabin, listening, waiting, and trying to make eyewitness identifications of what was going on inside. They did not succeed, but they heard the invitation to return the next week. Before they came back the second Saturday—joined by three more officers—they made sure they would have better luck. During the intervening week, they took a hammer and popped out knots to leave holes in the wooden walls. They squeezed apart slats in the wooden roof. They even built a wooden hideaway up on the roof, large enough for a mattress and two officers, who could then peer down between the slats into the bedrooms. They needed to see the criminals.[62]

The second party was louder: someone brought a radio and a guitar, and at one point all the guests sang "Let Me Call You Sweetheart." It was drunker as well: Holm was bartending, and he was mixing whiskey with ginger ale, lime rickey, and pineapple juice. And the seven police officers, who lay on the roof, in a drainage ditch behind the cabin, and in the bushes in front of it for six hours, watched intently. Over the course of their stakeout, they claimed, they witnessed twelve acts of oral sex and one act of sodomy. At one in the morning, sensing the party was going to break up, the police decided to move in and arrest the men.[63]

While the elaborate efforts of the local police force (assisted by military police) indicated the enormous amounts of energy expended on apprehending homosexually active men, their indictment and trial demonstrated still more clearly how dangerously they were viewed. All of the men were charged for each sex act that the police saw them commit. In addition, however, the very first count in their indictments was the charge of conspiracy—a crime that carried an extra five-year sentence. In planning the party, in inviting people, in setting the stage with music and a lewd poem, and in providing whiskey—one of the "necessary supplies," according to the district attorney's office—the men were viewed as acting in a conspiracy.[64] And while such accoutrements may have made these men's gathering little different than those at the "96 Clubs" that L. L. Rollins described in 1914, the Riverside men were now perceived as a distinct conspiratorial society. The police officers sat outside the cabin watching for six hours because this case was framed and understood as being about mainstream society at risk from the growth and expansion of a secret, perverted, and dangerous society within its midst.

The two DAs' remarks during the trial were rife with references to that conspiratorial society. One DA called it a "cancerous growth" within the mainstream body that needed to be removed before it could spread.[65] Over the course of the trial, the DAs especially latched onto the phrasing of the host who, that first Saturday, said to invite anyone who "knew what the score was." The lawyers liked that phrase because it indicated that there was indeed a score to know, a secret society to know. In fact, at one point the DA told the jury that normally "these men do not advertise this kind of a crime or this trait of character which they have," and therefore they are often hard for the police to track down. He pointed, though, to one of the defendants: Walter Epperson, a Fuller Brush salesman who lived in San Francisco and had been in the area little over a month. Epperson, he said, had easily found these men and attended both parties. Why? Because these men, he said, "are known to each other by some invisible token; whatever it is I don't know." Yet these men knew the score, he implied; they knew the code, the secret language. Like Masons or, more aptly, like Communists, their legibility to one another only further marked them as a hidden society and a threat.

A sixteen-year-old testified during the trial to having had oral sex with one of the men, though not at either party. On the one hand, his testimony indicated the legal acceptance of the "desire" paradigm. Whereas during the 1924 trial of Macon Irby the appellate court criticized the prosecution's effort to introduce his prior sexual activity into the record, by the late 1930s, the fact that the defendant had previously engaged in sex with a young man now proved he possessed a consistent desire to do so again. He possessed a homosexual essence. On the other hand, the young man also served as evidence of the cancerous society. "My heart goes out for that boy," one DA said in his closing argument, because "I think the boy is earnestly making an endeavor to come back to society and straighten himself out. . . . He has unburdened his soul and with that unburdening there is a chance for the boy to come out." The teenager had fallen not simply into degeneracy, as the Long Beach florist Herbert Lowe had, but into this other world, this place away from society, this cancerous world threatening to consume the rest.[66]

In 1937 Southern California, the pervert was not seen as a lone, if disturbing, figure. He was part of a social system that haunted and threatened mainstream society. Much like the cartoon depicting cross-dressing reformers as allies of Communists, these men were also perceived as possessing a social and political valence, a power that threatened an apparently fragile social order. And the threat was seemingly enormous.

Clearly, the attribution of political power to these men was merely the rhetorical spin of eager district attorneys. Yet such rhetoric, like the culture that sustained it, had a real-life impact. Most of the cabin conspirators— like hundreds of thousands of other local men—landed in prison, in San Quentin, with sentences ranging from six to twenty years.[67]

ELTINGE UNDONE

Even as the danger of the sex pervert required increased police vigilance, it also conjured a demand for silence and invisibility. In the mid-1930s, the major movie producers agreed to accept the dictates of a censoring film production code; in so doing, they also agreed to keep quiet about perversion. The code specifically banned the use of the words "fairy," "nance," "pansy," and "sissy." The guidelines for screenwriters further stipulated, "No hint of sex perversion may be introduced into a screen story. The characterization of a man as effeminate, or a woman as grossly masculine, would be absolutely forbidden for screen portrayal. This means, too, that no comedy character may be introduced into a screen play pantomiming a pervert."[68]

The censoring of sexual and gender deviance was more than a screen phenomenon. By January 1940 the police Sex Bureau had also applied a new set of regulations to female impersonators. The Police Commission determined that in order to receive an impersonation license, performers needed to submit to a "character analysis" and be interviewed by a department psychiatrist. This was how the *Photoplay* call for essence and the consistent desire paradigm of fixed sexual identity became official. State-sponsored psychiatrists would evaluate and label that "essence," and most likely, find the "degenerate" hidden behind the "superficial" gender play.[69]

Among the first to come up for review was, sadly, Julian Eltinge. Eltinge had been out of the public eye for several years. Already down on his luck, by the late 1930s he had seen his career and popular appeal wane. He had lost money, began drinking more heavily, and put on the weight that he had always struggled to keep off. Then in January 1940 Eltinge was booked for a return engagement at Hollywood's Café Rendezvous. When Eltinge arrived for the show, the police barred his entrance. According to news accounts, he then appeared before the Police Commission, requesting an impersonator license. The *Los Angeles Examiner* quoted him as insisting, "I am in desperate need of employment." Despite having made hundreds of thousands of dollars in his career, Eltinge was now worried about money. "I have invested more than $200 in new gowns with the expectation of taking the job offered me at the Rendezvous," he explained, adding, "Gentlemen, I have to eat."[70]

The press gave no indication that Eltinge submitted to a psychiatric evaluation, and the Police Commission yielded little ground. Eltinge did get to perform briefly at the Rendezvous, but the nature of the performance was forcibly altered. He could no longer appear in public as a man who played at being a woman. Instead, he appeared dressed in a tuxedo, while standing next to a mannequin that wore his $200 gowns. He sang the songs he had intended to sing, but introduced each with a comment such as "And for this number I would have worn this lovely dress."[71] The art of female impersonation—and the playfulness about gender that Eltinge had mastered to such success—had simply become untenable. Instead, the new paradigm quite explicitly divided the tuxedo-clad man from the gown-draped mannequin: gender play apparently pointed too clearly to an internal degenerate identity. Political action was reaching out to dictate how intimate life and personal identity were to be understood.

Importantly, who Eltinge was, what his performances were, was not a secret. The local press accounts of his appearance before the Police Commission were headlined with enormous familiarity. "Eltinge Can't Wear Dresses for Café Act" read one, while another said, even more familiarly,

" 'That stuff won't go here, Julian.' " Although Eltinge was being given the boot, the rejection was not exactly an attack on him personally or the spirit of his show. Even the president of the Police Commission, Henry G. Bodkin, reportedly told Eltinge, "I have seen your act many times, and I know that the entertainment you provide is clean and wholesome." The attack, instead, did two things. In part, it served to abort the display of gender as merely art. The fluidity and unnaturalness of gender roles could no longer be performed or recognized as a playful show. Only a performance adhering to strict gender roles could be allowed.[72] At the same time, the restriction and condemnation of Eltinge confirmed that the desire/degenerate paradigm had overtaken the fairy/gender framework. Female impersonation in particular and gender play in general were perceived now as markers of a deeper degenerate truth. They revealed a "character" or fixed identity that only a police psychiatrist could fully comprehend. Gender play pointed not just to a vice but to an identity that was socially and politically dangerous.

For Eltinge, living a life that divided gowns and tuxedos so sharply did not suit his needs. Within a year, he had moved back to New York, and although he was able to perform for a short time in a kind of "vaudeville old-timers" revue, he did not last long. Apparently, the corsets that had bustled his onstage figure for so many years had destroyed his kidneys, and he collapsed. By March 1941 he was dead, and the playful possibilities that he had represented died with him.

Eltinge's final banishment from the stage was, in a sense, an answer to *Photoplay* and the *Architectural Record*'s search for Eltinge's authentic self at Villa Capistrano. It was not Eltinge's answer: he would have refused to suggest that his performances said anything about who he fundamentally was. Instead, it was the Police Commission's answer, and it was by far a more powerful statement. It was based on the argument that a display of inverted gender was tantamount to a far more troubling display of inverted sexual desires and thus an inverted essence. In the Irby-Solovich case, that argument did not hold: the jurors did not believe that Solovich's feminine actions meant he was homosexually active, and the appellate judges did not believe that Irby's prior sodomy arrest meant he was predisposed to homosexual behavior. Less than two decades later, those arguments carried the day. By then, inverted desires were interpreted as constituting a fundamental essence, and that essence possessed a political valence. The interior life of emotions and desires was no longer simply a cultural concern; it now carried political and social significance.

The Depression years witnessed the construction of a new and wide-reaching political culture. In that culture of late 1930s Los Angeles, politics and emotion were pulled into a tight embrace. Public officials took the earlier multiple paradigms of sex, gender, and desire and collapsed them into a single one that politicized desire. They had accepted a version of the artists' claim that the interior life counted. However, city officials now evaluated what was expressed, categorizing some emotions and some inner lives as hazardous for an already troubled social order. Such threats, they insisted, would not be tolerated.

Long-haired radicals and long-haired "fairies" were now perceived as the same powerful enemy force. In the city leaders' eyes, this was the inner truth of the fairy, the answer to who Eltinge was. In the crucible of city politics, he—and those who shared his kind of interior life—had become identified as a danger. In a sense, these late 1930s developments marked the clear Althusserian moment for homosexually active Angelenos. Society shouted out to them with increasing menace, "Hey, you there!" as they stepped out of a bar or into a cabin. Those shouts and the accompanying arrests and prison terms made clear that the artistic project of emotional self-expression could be fraught with peril if those emotions and desires were deemed politically threatening.

The expanded policing of homosexuality did not shut down the Run, however, or the desires that sustained it. Instead, state policing further paved the way for the resistance that Mattachine represented. What is more, public officials did not offer the only model for how emotions might matter politically. In Edendale, a second community, of leftists, constructed a highly organized political life that was also infused with deep emotional significance. The Communists of Edendale mapped out a very clear alternative to the state formula of politicized emotion. In their version, affection, camaraderie, lust, and love constituted the sustaining fiber of political life, not its opposition.

The Brooks family gathers at Ocean Park Beach at Santa Monica a few years after
their move from New York state. From left to right, they are Eleanor, Isidor,
Miriam, Bessie, and Dorothy. (Courtesy Miriam Brooks Sherman.)

FOUR

Left of Edendale
The Deep Politics of Communist Community

WHEN MIRIAM BROOKS SHERMAN moved with her parents and two sisters into Edendale in 1931, they were at the leading edge of a Communist community that would soon take root in Edendale alongside the neighborhood artists. Isidor and Bessie Brooks had brought their three girls with them to Los Angeles from Albany, New York, in 1927. They had lived for four years in the vibrant, predominantly leftist Jewish community of Boyle Heights in East Los Angeles, and the whole family had been caught up in the life of the Communist Party. Isidor, who had been a Party member since 1919, devoted the bulk of his energy to running the Party's cooperative restaurant in the neighborhood, coordinating the activities of the Young Pioneers (the Party organization for young children), and organizing the educational efforts of the International Labor Defense (ILD)—an offshoot of the Party that organized legal defense and publicity campaigns for labor activists. Miriam, along with her two sisters, followed in Isidor's footsteps, joining the Young Pioneers and then the Young Communist League; soon she started coordinating the youth activities for the ILD.[1]

A passionate devotion to Communism transformed Sherman's life. As a teenager she delivered speeches and organized events around Southern California. At fifteen, she was arrested for the first time by the Los Angeles Police Department. At seventeen, she traveled to Moscow to participate in an international conference. And in her twenties, she helped make Edendale a center of Communist organizing in the city and a dynamic community in which leftist activists infused their politics with the deep feelings of intimate connection.

At the same time, the price of participation was high. Sherman was denied her high school diploma, crushing her dreams of a college education and a career as a music instructor. She and her husband and children were followed and harassed by the FBI. And her own father, Isidor, was beaten so badly about the head by the Los Angeles police that he suffered a stroke and eventually died from his injuries.

But the greater dream, of a better, more just world, always seemed worth the fight.

In mid- and late-1930s Los Angeles, fairies and degenerates became identified as dangerous, in part because they were allied in the political culture with leftists and radicals. That imagined convergence of deviant sexuality and deviant politics in the cultural imagination was transformative for homosexually active men and women because it attributed to them some of the political power—and hazard—that Communist activists were believed to possess. But underneath the red smears and the vocal hostility of city officials, police officers, and American Legionnaires, the relationship of Communists to mainstream Angeleno and American politics was a complicated one, not nearly so univocal or hate-filled as the violence and name-calling suggested. Certainly during the 1930s, as the economic hardships of the Great Depression swept across the country, millions of Americans considered anew the social contract—and particularly the economic structure—that governed the country. Most significantly, of course, Franklin Roosevelt's New Deal revised that contract to include publicly funded aid for the unemployed and the elderly, as well as millions of government-financed jobs in the arts, construction, and conservation. Yet the New Deal programs represented only a fraction of the ideas then circulating about how to handle the economic crisis, and many of the most popular alternatives came out of Southern California. In 1933 Dr. Francis Townsend of Long Beach suggested that seniors be paid a monthly pension in order to pump money into the economy, and set off a nationwide movement calling for such a program. The socialist journalist Upton Sinclair ran a nearly successful bid for governor of California in 1934, campaigning on a platform that included state-run factories, a graduated income tax, and the establishment of a barter economy. Although defeated in the final election, Sinclair handily won the Democratic primary. Such ideas for economic reform possessed real traction in 1930s California.[2]

The most vigilant agitators for economic change in those years were American Communists. Around the country, Communists coordinated rent strikes and Unemployed Councils, they pushed sharecroppers to unionize and farm workers to organize. Communists fought hard for their vision of economic justice and became lightning rods for both passionate support and violent repression. This was certainly true in Los Angeles, where leftist activism had deep roots in the city. The far left's most dramatic achievement there was the near election of socialist Job Harriman as mayor in 1911. During the Depression, as historian Mark Wild demonstrated, leftist activism surged in the city, and Communists in Los Angeles became among the most visible agitators on the city's streets, leading demonstrations, leafleting factories, and offering street corner oratories. Despite the denials of Bowron and Clinton's ties to Communists, the Los Angeles Communist Party did throw itself aggressively behind the effort to recall Shaw in 1938. And throughout California, Communists joined in a resurgence of liberal politics in the late 1930s that ushered Culbert Olson into office as governor and other liberal officials in his wake.[3]

To a degree, then, even though they never numbered more than a few thousand in the city, it is not entirely surprising that Communists became a cultural foil against which issues like sex and morality were measured and understood: at least from the 1930s forward, Communists around the region played a highly visible role in local politics as vocal mouthpieces of economic and political discontent.[4] Communism entailed much more than a cry for economic and political change, however. For families—like those of Miriam Brooks Sherman, Peggy Dennis, Harry Hay, Serril Gerber, and Barbara Kaplan—Communism was a deeply lived and richly experienced way of life. The state-led crackdowns against homosexual activity were not the only form that the politicization of emotion took. In Edendale, emotional bonds within individual relationships, across activist organizations, and through a shared culture sustained the dramatic political activism of Communists. Edendale Communists cultivated a dynamic relationship between individuals and society that further transformed and politicized the quest for essence.

At least as early as 1931, Communists began to move with purpose into the hills of Edendale and forge a community there. In the 1910s and '20s, socialist and Communist activists in Los Angeles were based largely in

Boyle Heights, east of downtown. In the 1930s, though, activists dispersed across the city, with a new center of activity emerging along and amongst the arts community of Edendale. Not all the activists there were officially Communists: in fact, as Michael Denning explained, the majority of 1930s American radicals were never Party members. "Many figures thought of themselves as generic 'communists,'" according to Denning, "using the term with a small *c,* the way earlier and later generations thought of themselves as generic 'socialists,' 'feminists,' or 'radicals.'"[5] Yet to become active in the circle of the party, and certainly to become a full-fledged Communist in Edendale, meant taking on an identity that organized and affected even the most intimate aspects of life.

Communists may seem unlikely protagonists in a narrative about the politicization of essence. Famously *not* introspective and even hostile to psychological thinking, they were first and foremost people who cared about the larger society—often before their own families and lovers—and who wanted to communicate directly with that society to enlist its support and engagement.[6] Rather than eschew personal passion, however, Communists and many sympathetic fellow travelers felt that their engagement with the wider world itself constituted the "essence" of who they were at their core. Their political activism was the truest, purest thing about them. Thus, the Communist lifestyle put politics and the self into a direct relationship that was the reverse of the neighborhood artists: the leftists' engagement with the public was the expression of their intimate emotions.

Historian Vivian Gornick discovered that for many Party members, political identity was not simply a matter of principle. Behind their carefully analyzed public positions, many Party members latched onto the organization because of the way it fulfilled a particular sense of themselves and provided emotional connections. The Party, as Gornick explained, "brought to astonishing life the kind of comradeship that makes swell in men and women the deepest sense of their own humanness, allowing them to love themselves through the act of loving each other." Within the American Communist Party, the notion of mid-century American political identity was reformulated by those powerful emotions.[7]

In Edendale, that remaking was the product of the complex and subtle ways in which Party members developed intense and often intimate relationships with one another. First, members of the Party and their supportive allies formed a tightly woven neighborhood community in Edendale. In so doing, they followed the lead set by the local artists in constructing community organizations to facilitate their goals—and further elaborated a model of organizing that Mattachine would follow.

Second, the depth of commitment and engagement demanded by the Party affected all reaches of its members' lives and created a powerful experience of an identity for its members—that of *being* a Communist. While that identity was reinforced by hostile opponents (especially the Los Angeles police), the experience was about more than political principle: it was a lived identity that affected every realm of members' lives—social, cultural, intimate. In fact, Party life made those distinctions between categories of experience moot. Social, cultural, personal—all of these were part and parcel of being a Communist. Fundamentally, to be a Communist was to possess a certain "essence," and joining the Party was an invitation into the deep experience of political identity. In many ways, Edendale leftists forged a personal-political identity not unlike what Mattachine would embrace.

COMMUNIST AGITATION

The history of the Communist Party in Los Angeles involves the efforts of a small cohort of agitators pushing to organize workers and the unemployed around Southern California. While one scholar has referred to the Communist Party of Los Angeles as one of the "largest and most influential" local branches in the country, others have been more measured in assessing their effectiveness. Yet all the tales of the local Party describe a determined organization meeting with limited success and violent opposition.[8]

From its start in 1919 and throughout much of the 1920s, the Communist Party of Los Angeles was based among the Jews of Boyle Heights. Community members worked in the needle trades or as store owners and focused their energies on the Cooperative Building, where Isidor Brooks worked. The building served as a multipurpose community center—meeting hall, bakery, barbershop, and restaurant all rolled into one. There at the Co-op, policies were debated, strategies were constructed, youth groups formed. Most energy focused on Boyle Heights itself or on the garment trades, with one of the most successful groups, the Women Consumers' Educational League, offering advice about food prices, encouraging the purchase of union goods, and actively assisting striking workers. While a new local organizer in the mid-1920s pushed for activists to work beyond the neighborhood and organize workers at the new heavy industries in the city—such as the Sampson, Goodyear, and Goodrich tire companies—his efforts, as well as efforts later in the decade to organize waterfront workers, met with only small success.[9]

Peggy Dennis's family was part of this community. Dennis and her sister moved with their parents—both cloak makers—to Boyle Heights in 1912. Both Dennis and her mother had some kind of respiratory ailment, and their doctors prescribed a move to the Southwest. The two girls grew up taking socialist classes at the Labor Temple and memorizing revolutionary Yiddish poems. Their parents kept them home from school on May Day and brought them to march on picket lines protesting meat and milk prices. And in 1922 the two sisters launched the first group for Communist children in Southern California. "We lived in isolated security amongst our own kinds," Dennis wrote years later. "The goals and hopes of our parents were ours. We rejected those of society around us; ours was the dream of the Future."[10]

During the late 1920s, Communists became increasingly visible in the city. They expanded their focus beyond the Boyle Heights neighborhood, and in response, the police department began making assiduous efforts to disrupt their activities. Officials assigned that task to Captain William Hynes and his Intelligence Bureau, known widely as the Red Squad, which meted out far harsher punishments than simple arrests. With boots, clubs, horse hoofs, and tear gas, they attacked left-wing assemblies, regularly beating protesters whether they arrested them or not. The city's economic elite had long worked to keep Los Angeles a largely union-free—or open-shop—town, and thus fully supported the police department's efforts to keep union organizers at bay. Hynes, who joined the LAPD in 1922, worked initially as an undercover agent in the Party before becoming head of the Red Squad. He devoted himself to learning everything about the workings of the local party, collecting and reading much of the Party literature and, through plants in the Party, keeping track not only of their organized efforts but their personal lives as well.[11]

Hynes's squad arrested activists under various statutes, including the state criminal syndicalism law, and used aggressive tactics to terrify Party members. In the summer of 1927, for instance, as despondent demonstrators gathered in the downtown Plaza to bear witness to the Boston execution of Sacco and Vanzetti, the Red Squad beat the protesters who moved anywhere beyond the Plaza proper. And by the fall of 1928, the Red Squad began with regularity to arrest party activists, young and old, wreaking havoc in the Co-op, raiding members' homes, and inflicting horrific beatings along the way.[12]

Party members focused broadly on the needs of regional workers. In January 1930, for example, key figures in the Los Angeles Party lent their assistance to farm workers in the nearby Imperial Valley who were threatening to go on strike. The farmhands worked in the most egregious of conditions, often side by side with their own children, and lived in dirt-floor shacks and tents, obtaining drinking water from the irrigation ditches. Working at night and in secret, three Angelenos helped leaders of the Mexican and Filipino workers to organize strike committees, and within a few days, some ten thousand workers walked out on the lettuce harvest, cutting the size of the harvest in half. While the three Party leaders were arrested and the strike quickly broken, they planted the seeds that in a few years yielded the largest agricultural strikes in the country's history, creating turmoil in what Carey McWilliams deemed California's "factories in the fields."[13]

During the Depression, Party activism also focused on the needs of the unemployed. Early in 1930, as part of the national Party's campaigns, the local Party organized two days of unemployment protests in downtown Los Angeles. The first day, which brought some two hundred Communists to the downtown Plaza—then designated as a free speech zone—was described on the front page of the *Times* as "one of the most stubborn riots in the city's history." Peggy Dennis sat with her parents the night before as they lined her husband Eugene's coat and hat with newspapers, to soften the blows from the police batons. The next day he and several other speakers chained themselves to lampposts so as to thwart police efforts to drag them away; with tear gas, billy clubs, and fists, the police nonetheless shut down the demonstration and arrested thirteen activists, including Eugene Dennis. The following week, when the Party staged a second demonstration at City Hall, the police aggressiveness provoked charges of brutality from the Southern California Civil Liberties Union. It was at a demonstration the following year commemorating these unemployment marches that Isidor Brooks was beaten into a stroke.[14]

Across the 1930s, the Party expanded its activities and encountered equally increasing violent opposition. Regularly, when Party members organized demonstrations, whether in Los Angeles or outside the city, Hynes's Red Squad arrived to break up their meetings and disband the activists with brutal violence. In fact, Hynes often hired out the Red Squad to work as private strikebreakers, and he shared his intelligence about radical activity with multiple organizations. After joining with a contingent of U.S. Marines and American Legionnaires to shut down one mass meeting and

Police officers move in against a Communist protester. The newspaper caption for the photograph read, "Police are shown in the thick of conflict, subduing one of the most belligerent of the Reds, while a cloud of tear gas, at left, forces other agitators back. Police squads, including reserves, rushed to the scene, emerged victorious, but with scars of conflict, and jailed several rioters. Whenever police tried to silence shouting orators the Reds attacked anew." January 22, 1931. (HERALD EXAMINER COLLECTION/Los Angeles Public Library.)

battle some fifteen hundred activists in Pershing Square, Hynes made clear to the press that his squad was not worried about "protecting any asserted rights of known enemies of our government." Hynes's indifference ran so high that after his men nearly killed Japanese American activist Karl Yoneda at an unemployment demonstration, Hynes himself casually called the local International Labor Defense office to say, "Come and pick up the Jap, he's dying anyway."[15]

Local citizens and public officials either sanctioned or ignored the police brutality. Elaine Black, for example, the daughter of Russian labor activists and Yoneda's future wife, was not interested in leftist politics in 1930; despite her family's labor background, she assumed that the police acted violently only when justifiably provoked. One police commissioner, responding to complaints about police violence at the 1930 unemployment demonstrations, declared that he would not "listen to any argument on behalf of Communists. The more the police beat them up and wreck their headquarters the better. Communists have no constitutional rights." Similarly, when the Civil Liberties Union tried to obtain an injunction against police interference in a 1932 campaign rally for William Z. Foster, the head of the national Communist Party and then a candidate for U.S. president, the judge who heard the case attacked the Party and "ridiculed its audacity in coming for aid to the government it seeks to destroy."[16] Among the powerful of the city, the Party was an unwelcome provocateur.

SETTLEMENT

These violent and highly public confrontations with the police distinctly shaped the image of the Party for the average Angeleno. Yet Party life was much more than these moments of conflict and action. Indeed, these turbulent encounters were only the most visible expression of a lifestyle dominated much more by quotidian tasks—planning meetings, newspaper sales, petition drives, theory classes, and leafleting—conducted within a handful of neighborhood communities around the city. The thousands of Angelenos who not only joined the Communist Party but stayed with it were pulled into the deep life of the Party by the culture of those very daily activities. Around that culture, they fashioned a clear community for themselves as distinct, rich, and tightly woven as any ethnic community of the time. During the 1930s, as Boyle Heights ceased to be the center point of area activism, Party members created one such community among the hills—and alongside the artists—of Edendale.[17]

The emergence of a sizable left community in Edendale followed patterns of chain migration, with Party families relying on each other to find way stations on their travels and permanent places to live. That seems true of much national left migration and settlement during the early twentieth century. Miriam Brooks Sherman was twelve years old when her father brought their family from Albany. En route, they traveled with another leftist family, and Sherman noted in her diary how they stayed with "comrades" in South Bend, Indiana, and were toured by union activists through coal mines in West Virginia. Once in Los Angeles, they settled among the leftists of Boyle Heights and moved to Edendale only after four years and largely in reaction to her father's beating. At that point they became the pioneers in a new leftist migration, but until then their journeying had carried them along a well-established national left network.[18]

Like Sherman's family, many leftist families moved to Los Angeles and Edendale because of the assistance and inspiration of friends, family, or comrades already living there. Max Hilberman moved to Edendale from Cleveland in 1935, when his money ran out and he had been forced to drop out of Case University; his older brother David lived in the neighborhood and worked as an animator for Walt Disney, so Hilberman followed him out west. Barbara Kaplan grew up in Harlem in the 1920s and, inspired by the Communist effort during the Spanish Civil War, joined the Party in the mid-1930s; she and her husband were lured out to Edendale in 1940 by a Party friend from New York who had become a film technician in Hollywood. Ten-year-old Stanley Schneider moved from New York with his parents in 1947. Initially, they moved in with Sherman's family because Schneider's father came from the same city in Russia as her husband and knew him from New York. Even Jeannette and Samuel Reisbord, never real Party members, moved to the area not long after the bombing of Pearl Harbor; having worked for several years in the Soviet Union during the 1930s, the young couple was drawn to Edendale by friends who were living on Micheltorrena Street.[19]

Beyond these comradely ties, the neighborhood attracted people for economic reasons as well. Harry Hay explained that he and his family moved into the neighborhood in 1942, not because they knew of its left or artistic reputation, but simply because it offered cheap housing. Additionally, to a certain degree, Edendale's hilly inaccessibility must have made it seem somehow safe and attractive. Given the bouts of virulent anti-Communism that regularly rocked the city, and the violence meted out by the boots and clubs of the Red Squad, a neighborhood that was off the Los Angeles grid must have felt more secure. Certainly Miriam Sherman's mother hoped that by leaving Boyle Heights, their family would be somewhat removed from the uproar.[20]

Given this assortment of reasons, Edendale became a magnet for leftist activists, some of whom were also involved in the arts. By the time the Hays settled in 1942, Luba Fuchs Perlin, a dancer with the Lester Horton Dance troupe and the Federal Theater Project, and her husband, Jared, a union grip in the movie industry, were already there. Max Hilberman lived not far from his animator brother, David, and worked as a machinist; the two men had married a pair of sisters, Molly and Libby Kirschner, from Cleveland.

Barbara Kaplan and her first husband had crowded into an apartment that Hack Mann, a film technician and Party literature director, lived in with his wife and another leftist couple—a cartoonist and his wife—but eventually found their own place nearby.[21] And the Hays' landlords, a German émigré couple named Fritz and Alma Meier, had quite consciously rented a number of units in the neighborhood to "progressive" tenants.

Because of all the Communist and Communist-inspired meetings and fund-raisers that were held among the hilltop homes, there were "well-worn paths [that] connected the houses scattered over the ridge of hilltops." Harry Hay and Barbara Kaplan both offered classes in Party theory and literature out of their homes. There were dances and dinners around the neighborhood each weekend. The events always involved fund-raising of some kind, but as Hay pointed out, money raised one week on one side of the neighborhood was often spent the following week on the other side; some of the funds simply circulated around the hills. Eventually, said Hay, he and his neighbors began referring to their hill, along Lake Shore Avenue, as "Mt. Moscow." Barbara Kaplan called the area the "Red Hills" and remembered that even as the three couples who had jammed into in a single apartment dispersed, "nobody moved out of the Red Hills."[22]

Maurice Isserman wrote that in the late 1930s and 1940s, Communists were "a highly concentrated minority" in the country. "They tended to live in the same neighborhoods, they spent most of their social life with other Communists, and their children played together." Edendale was recognized as one such pocket of concentration. While it is difficult to pinpoint the first leftist resident, these settlement patterns gave the neighborhood a new reputation. During the 1940s, more and more people referred to the area as Red Hill or Mt. Moscow or Lenin's Hill. Alice Greenfield McGrath moved to the neighborhood with her husband, the poet Tom McGrath, around 1940. Asked years later if they called the neighborhood Red Hill, McGrath said they did not. Instead, she said, "we *thought* of it as 'Red Hill.' . . . It was where we thought of as being the center of bohemian and radical life." In a sense, the juxtaposition of the artists and leftists gave the neighborhood a reputation that was itself a lure. Indeed, in describing the 1940s community, Jeannette Reisbord linked its "reputation of being a liberal area" with the fact that "it was filled with artists." This combination of politics and aesthetics marked the neighborhood, in her eyes, as an attractively bohemian community.[23]

Many Party members clearly desired to live in a world that was as expressive of their values as possible. Shared living along those values created a strong sense of community. Sophia Lewis, a shipbuilder who grew up in Boyle Heights near Miriam Sherman and began participating in Party events as a youth, explained the significance of living among like-minded people. "All the people I lived with had to be of my own thinking, otherwise I couldn't live with somebody. You sought out your own level . . . to associate with. . . . We had to have common goals and common ideology and common feelings about the things that were wrong in our society and how to change it."[24]

For Alice McGrath, the bonds of shared goals and feeling that she found in the local leftist community were rewarding and inspiring; they motivated her to move to Edendale. Born in 1917, McGrath grew up around Los Angeles and Long Beach and attended Los Angeles City College. While at college, she worked at a Japanese import store and stumbled into politics, learning about unions, discrimination, and the Spanish Civil War in conversations at the shop with a group of politically active individuals. She was captivated, and by 1938, during the height of the Popular Front, she threw herself into leftist activities. She was twenty-one years old and found a previously unknown sense of intimate commonality: "I do remember feeling good. . . . I felt as though I had found my community. It was a community not based on race, it was not based on ethnicity, it was not based on nonchosen ties. It was based on what I felt were principles and convictions and like-mindedness, and I thought that was a marvelous kind of community. There was a great deal of community feeling among the people that I encountered."[25] To be sure, this was a community whose apparent basis was political ideology—"principles and convictions"—and whose actions were, in theory, turned away from the "inner life" and toward the greater society. Yet it was a community that generated "a great deal of community feeling" and sustained McGrath emotionally. In framing her relationships this way, McGrath repeated sentiments echoed by full-fledged Party members who underscored the powerful friendships they found among fellow leftists.[26] Inspired by those feelings, McGrath and her first husband moved into Edendale in 1940.

In the hills of Edendale, the Party was a strong and well-organized presence. Eleanor Grossman described working closely with the local section organizer. "This guy believed in a functioning organization where people were required to take on the responsibilities of keeping the organization going." The organizer made certain "that the meetings were held, that branch officers were elected, that dues were collected, that censuses were taken, people were accounted for." In other words, he insured that the Party was active and functioned well in the area.[27]

Miriam Sherman's memories echoed Grossman's. By 1936 Sherman was married and had lived with her husband and daughter for two years near the port of San Pedro, doing labor organizing. The young family moved back to Los Angeles proper and settled in Edendale. Her mother and two younger sisters were living in a house on North Coronado (with dancer Luba Perlin as a boarder), and Sherman and her own family moved in next door. Within two or three years, they had moved ten or so blocks away to Micheltorrena Street and lived in the back house on a property where friends lived in the front house. Sherman spent a lot of time walking petitions in the neighborhood and selling copies of the *People's World,* the West Coast Communist newspaper. According to her memory, there were easily fifty official members on the local Party rolls and twenty or twenty-five in attendance at any given meeting. But beyond the members, hundreds more allied themselves with Party work and supported the causes that the Party emphasized. As much as the neighborhood bore the clear imprint of the many artists there pursuing emotional and creative expression, Edendale was becoming equally invigorated by what Sophia Lewis called "common goals" and "common feelings." It was a neighborhood of shared purposes.[28]

TIES INTERNATIONAL AND LOCAL

The 1930s and early 1940s were heady times for the Communist Party. During the years of the Popular and United fronts, as Communists around the country strove to work in unison with other political organizations, national party membership rose steadily, peaking at some 100,000 members by the end of the 1930s. The rising numbers represented a new generation of freshly minted activists, many of whom were the children of Jewish immigrants. Under their stewardship, the Party achieved demonstrable local success. The Cannery and Agricultural Workers Industrial Union, one of the few successful unions formed within the Party's Trade Union Unity League, made significant strides in organizing migrant farmworkers in California's nearby Imperial Valley. Similarly, a maritime strike in San Francisco in 1934 shut that city down and catapulted the left-allied Harry Bridges into a public leadership role. Within the Popular Front, Party members also built successful alliances. Party members held leadership positions in several CIO organizations, including Phil Connelly, the Los Angeles–based state president of the CIO, and Don Healey, head of Labor's Non-Partisan League in California. The New Deal provided sites for Party goals to be pursued, and the evolution of post-WPA arts groups—such as the League of American Writers and the American Artists' Congress—found important creative allies for the Party. In Hollywood the Communist-inspired Hollywood Anti-Nazi League led the local charge against fascism and racism, while Communist organizers moved into several film industry unions.[29]

The local political leadership also changed its attitudes. In 1938, shortly after his election, Mayor Bowron disbanded the Red Squad. That same year, Communists played a vital role in the election of liberal Democrat Culbert Olson as California governor. Olson, who had first been elected to the state legislature in 1934 on Upton Sinclair's socialist-leaning platform, was the first Democratic governor in the century, and Party members maintained strong ties within his administration. Olson also named Carey McWilliams to be chief of the Division of Immigration and Housing. McWilliams was not only an Edendale resident and a close friend of bookstore owner Jake Zeitlin but also a long-standing left-wing writer and attorney. His blistering 1939 critique of farmers' treatment of migrant workers, *Factories in the Field,* established him as a powerful advocate of change; he continued those efforts from within the administration. Most dramatically of all, shortly after Olson's inauguration, the governor pardoned Tom Mooney, the union and Industrial Workers of the World (IWW) activist imprisoned since 1916 for allegedly bombing the San Francisco Preparedness Day Parade and killing ten people. His release, more than thirty years later, made clear that these years were, as many scholars have noted, the "heyday" of American Communism both nationally and in California.[30]

During these heyday years, the Party was terrifically active in Edendale. Sustained by this new generation of activists like Sherman, Kaplan, and Hay, the Party became the structural base from which the Edendale left built an extensive network of neighborhood organizations, not unlike the networks of the local artists. Some of these organizations sought to transform the Party's principled vision of society into reality. They tackled a host of issues, including housing reform, inter-race relations, police brutality, and labor and Party organizing. Some days, five or six members would take a soapbox and a banner and go stand on a street corner near Echo Park to deliver speeches they hoped would heighten awareness in the neighborhood. Miriam Sherman's first husband, Jack Moore, ran for state assembly in 1940 on the Communist ticket as a representative of the neighborhood. Although he lost, Sherman said he never expected to win, only raise issues.

The neighborhood groups also focused on the needs of the members themselves, constructing cooperative housing arrangements and child day care programs. In addition, all the groups, some more copiously than others, drew members together for social and cultural events—dances, songfests, concerts, and lectures. As a whole, the left in Edendale became a vibrant and powerful subculture.[31]

These various groups and activities had a powerful impact. They forged a set of multiple connections between Party members and the world around them and gave them a sense of community and identity. Members felt that they were participating in a worldwide struggle that profoundly tied them to one another. Thus, in addition to galvanizing and expressing their members' senses of social justice, these groups also reached deeply into the nonpolitical aspects of their members' lives. What Paul Lyons wrote of Communists in Philadelphia was also true in Edendale: their "social networks of aid, comfort, and warmth were the core strength of the local Party." Indeed, as a whole, the groups organized where people lived, how they spent their days and nights, and most significantly, what interpersonal emotional attachments they developed. They structured what a Communist essence entailed.[32]

At its broadest, the sense of Communist community stretched around the world. The Party tied people's lives—both ideologically and in reality— to a wide international movement. Miriam Sherman's life demonstrated this dramatically; her ties to the larger world were profound. Very active as a teenager both in the Young Communist League (for youth ages sixteen and up) and the youth section of the International Labor Defense, Sherman experienced firsthand the dangerous significance of being a Communist in 1930s L.A. Not only was she arrested as a teenager, but the principal of her high school encouraged the school's football team members to join a "Junior Red Squad" and violently break up the meetings of the youth groups. The same principal also withheld diplomas from several radical students— Sherman included—thus preventing Sherman from attending college and becoming a music teacher in the public school system, as she had hoped.[33]

At the same time, Sherman increasingly traveled a network that took her steadily farther from her parents' home. Even as a Young Pioneer (the younger children's group), she ventured down to Long Beach to distribute leaflets at the naval base. As a teen, she delivered fund-raising speeches in parks all over Southern California with the Blue Blouses, an agitprop theater troupe then performing a play called *The Scottsboro Boys Shall Not Die*. In fact, Sherman organized a ten-city tour for the players that generated

Miriam Sherman (center), as youth coordinator for the International Labor Defense, organized a "wheel parade" of children to demonstrate against the unfair convictions of the Scottsboro defendants. (Courtesy Miriam Brooks Sherman.)

crowds of twenty-five to five hundred spectators. She also joined with other young activists to speak in black churches around the city about the Scottsboro case. The Scottsboro Boys were nine young African American men who had been falsely accused of raping two white women in 1931 on a train in Alabama; the youths were quickly convicted and sentenced to death. Their plight was taken up by the ILD, which coordinated legal support and mass rallies to protest their convictions. The fact that Los Angeles youth, on the other side of the country, were putting on plays on their behalf suggests the sense of connectedness that was a vital piece of the Communist experience.

In 1932 Sherman was elected to be a youth delegate to a Moscow congress for the ILD's international umbrella organization and, on her way back, to tour the East Coast and parts of the Southwest, giving speeches with Ada Wright, the mother of two of the Scottsboro defendants. Sherman traveled to Moscow with the mother of Tom Mooney (who was then still in prison), and listened to reports on Red Aid work in places like Poland, China, Mexico, and Germany. She later recalled that the Congress "gave me the feeling that this was really a worldwide movement." Her diary attested to the weightiness of what she heard. Her notes from the Polish report, for instance, stated, "strikes spreading . . . Growth of white terror . . . State of siege—forbidden to walk in streets in evening. Any manifestation of nat'l liberation movement suppressed. Fascist prison regime. Barbarous treatment in prisons." She then proceeded to list that already that year, twenty thousand people had been placed under arrest, eighty-three had been killed, and twelve thousand remained political prisoners. Plainly, this was heady stuff for a seventeen-year-old, giving her both a sense of a larger worldwide endeavor and her own responsibility in it. In fact, during the conference's last discussion, which focused a fair amount of criticism on American organizing efforts among African Americans, Sherman wrote down a quote from the day: "Must be worthy of the tremendous tasks which face us at the present time!" She felt involved and accountable. As she later framed it, "Everything you did, you sort of felt that your life was at stake. Everything was a revolutionary act."[34]

Organizers frequently found themselves being moved around the country and the world to pursue goals the Party mapped out. One Los Angeles activist was so effective at organizing students in the local peace movement that he was called first to New York and then Detroit to do similar work at higher organizational levels. In order to escape the pursuit of Southern California law enforcement, Eugene Dennis, Peggy Dennis's husband, was sent first to Moscow and then on research trips to the Philippines, South Africa, and China. Many other foreign-born activists, if sentenced to deportation, sought refuge in the Soviet Union instead.[35]

Perhaps the most striking international connection that Party members experienced lay with warfare abroad. Sherman's papers contain a handful of letters, dated 1938, from Jack Eggan and Virgil Rhetta, two local men fighting in the Spanish Civil War. They described the darkest reality of the international struggle within which Sherman saw herself. As Eggan wrote, "The fascists are busy attacking our lines every day hoping they'll be able to smash through." In one letter he portrayed the villages they passed through, saying, "When you have seen these little places bombed, and the general effects of two years of war, as I now have, you know the real meaning of the fight in our own countries to give all possible help to Spain." Nothing could have placed the Los Angeles battles in a starker, more invigorating context. The battle on the streets of the city was the same war waged in the hills of Spain. In fact, Sherman's husband had recruited young people to go to Spain, and Rhetta sang with a leftist chorus in which

Sherman was active and served as accompanist: these men were their peers. "We took it all as a matter of course," she said much later. "We were convinced that this was what had to be done." Both Eggan and Rhetta were killed in the Spanish war.[36]

And it was not only the direct conflict of the Spanish Civil War that riveted Angeleno Communists; the broad rise of fascism around the world and the threat of American combat galvanized them as well. Serril Gerber moved to Los Angeles in 1929 at the age of sixteen. He and a few friends came west from South Dakota "to make our way in the world." After working for a few years, Gerber enrolled in Manual Arts High School, where "I had my eye-opening experience." A variety of progressive teachers, including an economics instructor who used the *New Republic* as the class textbook, began to change how Gerber viewed the world. From participation in the peace movement, challenging Hitler's rise and the threat of fascism, Gerber became "a Communist Party activist." As a student at Los Angeles Junior College (now Los Angeles City College), Gerber became a key organizer of the Communist-led National Student League, organizing student peace strikes and all-day conferences on war and fascism. Student strikers faced police clubs and fire department hoses, but for Gerber the prospect of war was simply "not reasonable, not comprehensible." That threat of a global conflict implicated him, demanded that he act.[37]

At the same time that the Party called members to see their lives in relationship to worldwide events, life in the left also tied people very much to their local experience. As the patterns of chain migration suggest, membership in the Party determined in large part where and with whom people lived. Perhaps the most vivid example of this was the 1948 design and construction of a complex of cooperative housing units on Avenel Street, just north of the Silver Lake Reservoir. Modernist architect Gregory Ain, a disciple of the Viennese architect Richard Neutra who had built his own home and studio on the eastern shore of the reservoir, worked with ten leftist families to build the hillside structures. Ain, who was politically progressive and something of a "social activist," according to architectural historian Michael Webb, had become very interested in designing group housing for low- and middle-income families. Although it was fairly difficult to obtain financing for group projects, Ain worked steadily to "refine and dignify the low-cost house." On Avenel, as elsewhere, Ain incorporated simple lines, moveable walls, and patios to create as much flexible and usable space as possible. The final co-op design consisted of ten nearly identical two-bedroom units arranged in two tiers along a slope; both tiers opened onto panoramic views across the city, with the units in the upper row looking across the rooftops of the lower level.[38]

Serril Gerber, his wife, Lillian, and their two children formed one of the ten families. Asked years later if the idea for the cooperative was political, Gerber replied, "Well, I'd say everybody in the group was what we called a left person or a left sympathizer. Were they activists? No, I wouldn't say that. But there was a tenor to the meetings that indicated . . . that there was that commonality among us. . . . The idea of a co-op suggested right away people who really believed in this kind of togetherness—living together—instead of individualism."[39]

The co-op members also chose builders who shared their political view. According to Gerber, they received two serious bids from contractors to create Ain's design: one, a fixed price, came from an experienced builder who "had no political outlook," and the other, somewhat lower, came from two young men "just starting out in the world as builders, and very sympathetic to our whole philosophy." Not surprisingly, the co-op members chose the progressive young men, but "this was their first project and they knew nothing. As a result of which, it took them over a year to build it and the price kept going up, up, up."[40]

But eventually the co-op was built, ten families moved in, and then the challenging and stimulating work of living as a community began. Of the breadwinners in the families, there were schoolteachers, an attorney, professional musicians, a union business agent, an actor, and a dental assistant. In the days before condominiums, the co-op members organized a shared mortgage, common water bills, clean-up days, and gardening days. There was talk of building a swimming pool in back of the units and of hiring a cook for the entire co-op—talk that never amounted to anything. But members owned shares in the property, not their unit per se, and when, for instance, one owner wanted to rent out her unit, there was a discussion as to whether she could keep the income or whether it belonged to the co-op as a whole. Esther Asimow, who through her children became good friends with several of the co-op residents, jokingly suggested that "the meetings would take up all your life." Gerber's wife, Lillian, kept a pot of coffee warm all day, and people would regularly drop in for a visit or discussion. "Our house was sort of the center of social life, and people would come down here," Gerber recalled. "It was a good feeling of comradeship." While it may have been the shared principles and ideology that drew leftists like the Mc-Graths, Perlins, and Shermans to Edendale, they went on to create a full neighborhood community there.[41]

This photograph of the Avenel co-op shows the intimacy between families that the buildings were designed to promote. Playtime outside one tier of the units brought together children from multiple families. Rose Brant (standing, in the plaid skirt) watches while her mother, Dorothy, guides her brother, David, on his tricycle at the far end of the walk. A child from a different co-op family races along on her own tricycle while a youngster from a third family looks on. (© J. Paul Getty Trust. Used with permission. Julius Shulman Photography Archive. Research Library, The Getty Research Institute, Los Angeles.)

While only a handful of Edendale leftists lived as intimately as the Avenel co-op did, many more were drawn together through the construction and sharing of common institutions.[42] As with the neighborhood's artists, the left in Edendale built a network of organizations—educational, cultural, and social—that drew the residents together not just for ideological purposes but also for communal living.

A pair of cooperative nursery schools started by neighborhood leftists represented the kind of community-focused efforts that were typical. Harry Hay and his wife, Anita, joined with Max Hilberman and his wife, Molly, and a few other families to set up a cooperative nursery school—the first in the city—at Echo Park Playground. They began the school during the war as a way to help people working in the defense industries care for their children. Volunteers from the participating families ran the school, Hay recalled, and they began with just five families. Soon enough, fifty were involved, and the parents managed to hire a neighborhood resident, Rose Scharlin, to direct the program. Scharlin was also a leftist émigré to Edendale, having come from the same area in Cleveland as Max and David Hilberman; in fact, her family came from the same shtetl in Europe as the Hilberman family. Soon after the war ended, conflict erupted over various political issues between Scharlin and some of the parents, so Scharlin joined with several parents, including Esther and Nate Asimow, to coordinate a second cooperative school.[43]

The two schools survived on a mixture of parental payments, theater parties, rummage sales, and even fund-raising concerts from Harry Hay's record collection. Principally, though, they relied on the labor of the parents. "Everyone had a job," recalled Esther Asimow, whose two daughters attended the second school. At both schools, parents met frequently to discuss and coordinate the school's activities, and they took on different responsibilities: building benches and cots for the kids, installing plumbing, or working in the classrooms and helping with the teaching. Scharlin even required that parents at the second school attend a night class in childhood development. According to Asimow, as the economy improved and more parents found employment, the cooperative nature of the school was "argued about: if someone couldn't participate, would they be able to be a member? I felt, if they could pay for a surrogate, why should their child be denied this experience?" Eventually, Asimow recalled, the school began to allow parents to buy out of their share of work, but the school—like Scharlin herself—retained a strong leftist bent.[44]

A leftist school for adults was also established in Hollywood during the 1940s, just a few miles west of the Silver Lake Reservoir. The People's Educational Center (PEC), where Hay eventually taught folk song history, offered a host of low-priced classes and lectures, often at night, many of which were taught by Hollywood-area professionals. A course on film directing boasted sections led by director Herbert Biberman (brother of Edendale painter Edward Biberman and later one of the Hollywood Ten), Kenneth Macgowan, Hume Cronyn (on acting), and Frank Tuttle. There were courses in trade union organizing and political economy, as well as classes in foreign languages, bodybuilding, modern Jewish history, and current events. In 1946, 553 students attended, paying six dollars per class unless they were union members, students, or military personnel. Clearly, while not all the classes at the PEC were focused narrowly on leftist topics, the school cultivated the sense of an intellectual and vocational left community.[45]

These organizations had fairly nonideological goals. They did not set out to change the class dynamics in the neighborhood, per se, nor alter race relations. Their attention focused on the members and their families, and through their programs and projects, they pulled the neighborhood into a tighter community. Indeed, these organizations structured a broad neighborhood community, based not simply on principle but on day-to-day living.

CREATING A CULTURE

Beyond these institutions, local activists shared a host of more informally presented social and cultural events in their own homes. In Miriam Sherman's household, for instance, there could be two or three meetings a week, and sometimes two or three in one night. "An active Party person," she said, "never had time for anything else except Party work." Saturday nights featured regular fund-raising parties, somewhere in the area, generating cash to keep the Communist newspaper going or to send in support of Republican Spain. At the parties, the events varied. There might be a musical, a lecture, or a book review. Lee Wintner, a singer and instructor at Los Angeles City College, often performed. There might be a birthday party, for which a donation was requested. Sunday mornings often consisted of group breakfasts that dispersed into paper-selling afternoons.[46]

The Party and its affiliated organizations created, especially during and after the Popular Front years, a rich subculture of activity that stretched

A number of progressives, including Harry Hay (center) and Anita Hay (right, in the striped blouse), spend an afternoon with other leftist families. (Courtesy *Hope along the Wind.*)

from small events in people's homes to massive hootenannies with Woody Guthrie leading the singing. Party leaders Dorothy Healey and Miriam Sherman saw these social events principally as fund-raisers. That must have been their explicit goal, and often enough, the invitation or leaflet about the event made that relatively clear. But their achievement was more complex. Vacuum salesman Morris Markoff, on first arriving in Los Angeles in 1936, became active in local party activities by attending a dance for the Young Communist League that took place in someone's home in the neighborhood. "Naturally," he said, it was "the place I went to try to get some friends."[47] These events folded the social, cultural, and political all together and forged a deep sense of connection and community.

During the late 1940s and '50s, for instance, the local chapters of the Party-affiliated Civil Rights Congress offered a bevy of activities well beyond demonstrations and letter-writing campaigns. The CRC took up the work of the ILD after World War II and also battled against racial discrimination. But as part of that work, the congress hosted a steady stream of birthday, anniversary, and housewarming parties, in addition to "jamborees," Thanksgiving dinners, and performances by local chapter singing groups. Leaflets for these events encouraged people to come "enjoy the good fun," "join good friends," and "partake of good food under the stars." One even detailed the food offerings to be had, including "delicious spareribs, tempting french fries, tasty cheesecake (both varieties), coffee, etc." Even as late as 1952, when the political climate was quite restrictive, CRC events still featured this combination of social and political. In May 1952, for example, the local chapter hosted a typical multi-task evening with a flyer that announced "3 Good Reasons . . . to Get Together": the first reason involved important legislative work, but in addition, participants needed to "Celebrate Paulette's Birthday—our chairman" and "Have Fun!!!" The event itself featured a talk by a leading Party organizer and a song session with a Party song leader. While such leaflets do not document how the actual events unfolded, they indicate how regularly the political and cultural, intellectual and experiential were intertwined.[48]

Cultural activities in particular came to be seen as essential. The creative life of Edendale artists was mirrored in the cultural events of the Party. According to Sherman, the local Party never had a big public meeting without performers. Sherman herself was a talented pianist and had been an accompanist with Lester Horton and in the WPA theater program, before taking a job in the physical education department at UCLA. Her sister Eleanor was a dancer, and she danced both with the WPA and Horton's company before joining the UCLA faculty as well. Eventually, it became Sherman's responsibility to find performers for Party events. The performers were seen as an alternate means of communication. "Through drama and song and dance," explained Sherman, "there would be a greater dramatization of what our goals were." The performances made those goals more explicit, while also entertaining and broadening the cultural horizons of the audience. Thus while some Edendale artists continued to focus on individual self-expression, some interested in art that engaged directly with society were pulled into the Party's orbit.[49]

During the 1930s, left-leaning writers and artists formed and joined a wide variety of cultural organizations. As historian Michael Denning noted, they established "literary clubs, workers theaters, camera clubs, film and photo leagues, composers collectives, Red dance troupes, and revolutionary choruses." The organizations, like the national John Reed Clubs for artists, offered a variety of lectures, workshops, performances, and exhibits of different kinds of art; they served as genuine cultural centers. The Los Angeles John Reed Club, for instance, of which Grace Clements became a member, presented lectures by Mexican muralist David Siqueiros, an exhibition of the paintings of several African American artists, and a production of Langston Hughes's show *Scottsboro Limited*. In some ways, Lester Horton's dance company also operated in a similar fashion, presenting pieces like *Dictator* in 1935 that expressed Horton's convictions about the dangers of fascism. When Sherman's sister Eleanor danced with the Horton company in the mid-1930s, she enjoyed the confluence of politics and culture and spent hours at the company studio rehearsing and taking classes. "The Horton Dance Group fully satisfies my craving for a cooperative, revolutionary group," she wrote relatives in a letter. "Technically, choreographically and revolutionarily (if there be such a word) we are progressing by leaps and bounds." Through these institutions and organizations, artists and audiences alike expanded their cultural horizons and contemplated the political significance of cultural activity.[50]

Historians have focused a great deal of attention on the debates among leftists about whether or not culture could or should be a "weapon" of the revolutionary movement. Many writers and artists reported that participating in the cultural life of the far left was comparable to being an artist in the WPA: you were told what the political message of your work should be. While testifying before the House Committee on Un-American Activities, for instance, Los Angeles screenwriter Bernard Schoenfeld described frequent Party discussions on the role of the "cultural worker." What quickly became clear, he said, was that "the role of the cultural worker was to obey whatever the Party told you to do as a writer. You were supposed to have no creative thoughts of your own." If there was a strike, he said, you were told to write something in support of the Party position at the time. "The individuality of the creative writer was to be stamped on." Screenwriter Roy Huggins echoed this description, noting that in his group, "there was a good deal of propaganda . . . to get all the members to write proletarian novels, and this seemed to be the line."[51] As their own testimony indicated, many artists resisted this line.

Focusing narrowly on these debates about cultural production obscures the role that artistry in fact held within the Party. Cultural performances were not intended exclusively as a means to articulate Party ideology. Sherman, for instance, was pleased that the musicians often simply exposed the audience to abstract and unfamiliar pieces. For her, the cultural works served a wider goal of enlightening and enriching the audience. They were essential, Sherman said, because "it was an all-encompassing life, because we were building a new society." Healey agreed, arguing that music and theater contributed to the members' "spiritual life." There existed "no separation between explicitly political and implicitly nonpolitical" activities. Instead, there was a sense of fluidity among these characteristics. "There was a recognition," she recalled, "that the cultural expressions in life were as essential as the political treatises." The cultural realm, while not free from ideology or politics, was significant in and of itself. It represented the wider reaches of Party life.[52]

Fundamentally, the Edendale left developed a rich culture of participation. Significant organizational energy focused on creating participatory experiences, especially through singing. At least since the late 1930s, big Party meetings always started with shared singing, according to Dorothy Healey's memory. The singing, she sensed, was "very powerful" and "created bonding" among the attendees. The cultural elements were more than just entertainment or another form of expressing goals, she thought; like Sherman, she saw a broader vision.

Perhaps the most famous participatory experiences in the Angeleno left centered on the career of folksinger and songwriter Woody Guthrie. Guthrie was born in Oklahoma in 1912, but his professional proletarian musical roots lay in Southern California, and in good part in Edendale, in these years. Guthrie arrived in Los Angeles in 1937, carried from the dusty fields of Texas to settle with cousins in Glendale. Not long after Guthrie got established on a downtown radio station as a "singing cowboy," performing first with his cousin Jack and then "Lefty Lou," he began singing "hillbilly" songs and Dust Bowl ballads on the air and offering snippets of his own philosophy—a combination that became increasingly popular. Steadily he began mixing social commentary with his art. His song criticizing the Los Angeles police, "Do Re Mi," became a hit, with its refrain about how those lacking in "dough," or cash, were treated. "California's a Garden of Eden," sang Guthrie, "a paradise to live in or see / But believe it or not, you won't find it so hot / If you ain't got the do re mi." Guthrie's eyes became steadily turned toward local politics and the struggles of migrant laborers.[53]

Guthrie's involvement in local politics increased, and he was soon pulled into the Party's orbit by Ed Robbin, an Edendale leftist who delivered news commentary at the same radio station where Guthrie had his show. One night in 1938, on impulse, Robbin convinced Guthrie to sing at a Communist rally celebrating Governor Olson's pardon and release of Tom Mooney. When Guthrie sang, Robbin wrote, "the house came down." The rally, with Mooney present, launched Guthrie's career performing in left and Party organizations. While clearly an attraction himself, a Guthrie show was as much a song session as a concert. Many of his songs were written with a simple and recurring refrain that encouraged audiences to join in. Also, many of his songs became familiar to left audiences who sang along with Guthrie. He led them through an experience rather than simply show them one.[54]

For a time, Guthrie and his wife lived next door to the Robbins in Edendale and attended the Workers' School in Los Angeles. Guthrie also began writing a daily brief column for *People's World* entitled "Woody Sez." Robbin introduced Guthrie to Will Geer, a leftist agitprop actor who had been involved in efforts to create a workers theater. Geer was then coordinating a traveling troupe of four performers, Folksay, that performed across California's vast agricultural valley, offering skits and songs to migrant workers and picketers; Guthrie joined the troupe. Then, when Geer began performing on Broadway in *Tobacco Road,* he convinced Guthrie to head east, where he eventually began to work with another group called People's Song.[55]

People's Song was founded after World War II to generate music for activists and organizations in the left and labor movements. Its goal was to create a kind of Guthrie sing-along without Guthrie there. As folksinger Pete Seeger outlined the idea to Guthrie, it was "to organize all of us that write songs for the labor movement, to put all our collections of songs into one big cabinet, and to send any union local any kind of song, any kind of historical material about any thing they might need, to shoot it out poco pronto, in today out tonight."[56]

Starting in 1946, People's Song set out to amass old songs and write new ones (ultimately twenty thousand, by one estimate). They began teaching the songs at a handful of schools around the country, and they began organizing hootenannies. "Hoots" were participatory singing festivals that were viewed as an opportunity to enliven an audience, offer political commentary, introduce new performers, and communicate "music, ideas, and a sense of the real America." As the principal historian of the organization has suggested, the Songsters saw themselves as recuperating and extending a folk tradition of "the people." In so doing, they felt they were pursuing a "counter-hegemonic" goal, challenging "what they saw as a corrupt, mindless popular culture."[57]

Outside of New York City, Los Angeles was the other great center of People's Song activity. The executive secretary was Mario Casetta, a left-leaning disc jockey who had been in the army with Pete Seeger, and he was joined by Earl Robinson, the progressive composer of "Joe Hill" and other songs. Harry Hay threw himself into the organization, as well, and by 1948 the group's finances were also being handled by an Edendale resident named Cesar Goldstein. The group maintained an index card catalogue of songs that could be called upon for a given event or demonstration. Each card had an activist topic on the top, like "Anti–Jim Crow," "Seamen," or "Auto Workers." Listed beneath the subject were the songs that would work for that kind of a protest. The "Anti–Jim Crow" card, for instance, listed songs like "What's Your Freedom Worth?" "Black, Brown and White Blues," and "Mr. K.K.K." The "Political" card listed tunes like "Election Day," "I'm A-Lookin' for the New Deal Now," "The Guy That I Send to Congress," and "I'm the Man That Broke That Egg." These were the songs that could energize protesters.[58]

Hay felt that songs were practical and yet powerful. In simplest terms, singing picketers could put in more hours than those who were not singing. What's more, said Hay, the organization often drew new members from picket lines. Hay took on the role of being the music history instructor within the group. He began offering a class about folk music at the People's Educational Center, and the Hays' house on Cove Avenue became a monthly meeting spot. Meetings often included singing and sometimes an out-of-town guest like Seeger. In fact, Seeger stayed with the Hays for several months.[59]

Importantly, People's Song was relatively free of the ideological debates about culture as a political weapon. As historian Robbie Lieberman noted, the Songsters "did not participate in the debate, did not follow the Party intellectuals' dogmatic stand about how to measure the quality of a work of art, did not narrow their range of songs, and did not abandon their broad, populist approach to cultural work." To a degree, they believed that songs could be used as a weapon. Even more, though, they felt that singing was a powerful appeal to people's emotions that drew them into a participatory activity. That activity itself created a sense of unity and strengthened morale.[60]

Healey affirmed that goal, stressing the role of participation in the singing. In a recent interview she criticized passive spectator events. As a listener, she said, "you're giving to the performer what you should have yourself." By contrast, at Party events, she said, "everybody participated. . . . And it wasn't just meetings—parades, demonstrations, whatever took place, picket lines, there was always singing. And it produced a closeness, an affinity among people. . . . I thought it was very important." Indeed, at the near-monthly Los Angeles hoots, organizer Casetta reported, "people used to go crazy for these things. It was just fantastic."[61]

Singing was much more widespread than People's Song. Music and performance was at the heart of the activities for the Young Pioneers, the Communist children's group. As a teenager, Peggy Dennis was one of the main coordinators of the L.A. group, and she viewed the little *Red Song Book* as the essential educational tool for the children. "Those songs and the discussions we stimulated around them expanded the children's horizons. . . . The struggles of miners and textile workers, of Wobbly jailbirds in faraway places—all became part of the child's world in L.A.'s Jewish Boyle Heights. The 'Internationale,' the songs of the Italian, German, Russian movements—these made us part of a worldwide movement and the single barricade of battle."[62]

Some seventy years later, Lillian Carlson still remembered the first revolutionary song she learned as a Young Pioneer:

We are the builders; we build the future.
The future world is in our hands.
We swing our hammers, we use our weapons
Against the foe in every land.
And we, the workers, who are the builders,
We fight; we do not fear to die.[63]

Certainly Guthrie's songs and others' had political-ideological messages in them. "Do Re Mi" was plainly a critique of the Los Angeles police and their obvious corruption. To this degree, art within the Party served Clements's call for engagement with social issues. But learning "Do Re Mi" and singing along did more than just teach a message. Like the housewarming parties and birthday celebrations, singing together joined and empowered the audience. It gave them the experience of their own shared voice. These social-cultural activities were at least as important as the policy meetings or activist campaigns. They forged a connection among the participants that was built on more than intellect or shared principle. It was a potent social and emotional bond.[64]

THE PARTY AT HEART

In each of these ways—with its cultural, social, and principled campaigns—the Party became a powerful influence. It, and the groups around it, created a deep organizational structure within people's lives. It shaped where they lived, determined how and with whom they spent time, and led them to forge bonds with the people with whom they worked, played, and sang.

At a still deeper level, the Party affected members' core emotional lives. Perhaps that is not altogether surprising. As a group of sociologists recently wrote, the networks of the left were important not simply for connecting people with shared beliefs but also for forging "affective bonds." The Party shaped participants' friendships and intimate affairs. It facilitated relationships and it destroyed relationships. Party membership became deeply entangled with people's emotional lives. Harry Hay explained that for a member, the Party was supposed to be "your first love," and for many it plainly was.[65] It profoundly affected whom they attached themselves to and what kind of attachments they made.

Miriam Sherman remembered how emotionally central Party issues were in her family when she was a child. When Lenin died, she wept. Similarly, when her father left Albany for Los Angeles, he wrote to his wife that he thought only about "you, my dear, and our loving little angels from whom that big, roaring monster [the train] was separating me brutally; and Sacco and Vanzetti whose doom, I thought, was only a question of time." His emotional life rested equally between his family and the martyrs to the cause. These were his "first loves."[66]

The year after Sherman's father died, friends saw their attachment to his memory as a motive for donations to the Party. In fact, on the first anniversary of his death, Sherman's mother and sisters wrote a letter to the *Daily Worker,* explicitly urging Party members to funnel their emotions toward the good of the Party. "We, the four members of his family," they wrote, "commemorate his life's activities by subscribing to the *Daily Worker.* We think that this is one of the best ways of building a monument to the memory of our dear Comrade who died as a result of injuries sustained four years ago when he was arrested and beaten by Hynes and his Red Squad. We call upon all the friends and relatives of Isidor Brooks to do likewise and help build a strong revolutionary mouthpiece, something Comrade Brooks worked very hard for."[67] Celebrating the life of their husband and father entailed supporting the Party causes for which he had worked. Personal grief could be expressed through political action.

Yet the Party engaged and entangled members' emotions at a still deeper level. Vivian Gornick's collected interviews with former Communist Party members reveal some of that depth. They show the degree to which the

Party was sustained by interpersonal emotional bonds at least as much as by principle. As the title of Gornick's volume—*The Romance of American Communism*—attests, the Party was often driven by private passion for and about people.

One man told Gornick, with an acid bitterness, that "Communism was a response to the loneliness of the universe." He meant his comment to have grand theoretical implications, but on a more banal level, it was a sentiment he shared with others in the Party: the men and women of the Party, seeking connection, found within the Party a great sense of companionship. Alice McGrath's comments about friendships among leftists, like those of many Party members, attested to that. Sophia Lewis spoke of the need to be with people who shared her views, and Miriam Sherman echoed that perspective, noting that in her youth all her friends were either Young Pioneers, Young Communists, or musicians (her other passion).[68]

But the attachments the Party generated between people were often stronger than mere friendship suggests. Dick Nikowsski, a "lifelong Communist Party functionary," described for Gornick the consuming excitement of discovering Marxism and being "on fire with politics." But equal to the intellectual excitement was the sense that Nikowsski "loved everybody! . . . When we were in the middle of some intense analysis of the Russian Revolution at three in the morning and we all had to be up on our feet and at work at seven, I'd look around the room at these guys, and they were my comrades, and I loved them so hard I thought I'd burst with it."[69] Comradeship inspired a greater passion, a greater attachment.

Similarly, Kansas-born organizer Tim Kelley thrived on the drunken festival of union organizing and told Gornick that he grew especially attached to a friend and comrade named Johnny McWilliams. "Johnny was like nothing I'd ever known before. He was everything I was, only a thousand times more than I could ever be it. . . . When you were with Johnny, I don't know how to put it, you felt more alive than with anyone else, more like you could do or be *anything*. . . . Ah, I loved him, I loved him fiercely." Unfortunately for Kelley, McWilliams was more devoted to the union than the Party, and in 1946 he wanted to challenge the Party on a union issue. Kelley protested that doing so would get him expelled from the Party and thus break their friendship. McWilliams made his challenge nonetheless, and Kelley, following Party doctrine, broke off their friendship. Such broken relationships over Party politics were not entirely unusual. What is striking, however, is that thirty years later, recounting the story to Gornick, Kelley burst into uncontrollable sobs. When Gornick asked why he felt so bad, what exactly he regretted, Kelley replied, "It was the particular quality of that particular friendship. There's been nothing else like it in my life. Not before, not since." And then he added, "I thought I couldn't have both the Party and Johnny . . . and I couldn't give up the Party. . . . I regret it all, I regret it now, I'll regret it till I die."[70]

For both Kelley and Nikowsski, interpersonal love was at the core of their Party life: it was the very essence of their politics. Theirs were the intimate passions that often tied people to the Party, brought them to live in its community, and kept them active in its events. Their emotional lives were wrapped up in their political lives.

The significance of that comradely passion was not always clear. For some, like Betty and Morris Markoff or Esther and Nate Asimow, that passion provided entrée into deeply romantic relationships and marriages. According to Serril Gerber, he and his wife, Lillian, shared many of the same ideals. In fact, while he had learned his leftist values as a young man, she had grown up with a mother who was a socialist and so had "a real background in leftist politics." Those shared values were vital for them. In later years, when Gerber was persecuted for his political views, Lillian never raised "any questions whether this was worthwhile or not, whether she'd cooperate or not cooperate. No. . . . Her background gave her more strength than mine did. So she just didn't question what you should do."[71]

For other people, though, political passion—without great romance—became the sole basis of their marriages. Peggy Dennis, for instance, was very active in the Los Angeles Party as a girl and teenager in the 1920s. During those years, she met and married her first husband, Bill. "We had been active together in our radical movement in Los Angeles, and we had gotten married. We were comrades among other comrades, involved in movement activity together, but not deeply, irrevocably involved with each other." Looking back at that marriage after meeting her second husband, Dennis saw its limitations, its romantic shallowness. "I might not have known the difference if I had not stumbled on what Gene and I now had."[72]

Paul Levinson, a Party member from age fifteen to thirty and one of Gornick's interviewees, had a similar experience. Talking about his marriage, Levinson criticized how easily "political excitement" and the "mad wild joy of revolutionary expectation" got confused with "romantic love." He clearly believed that political passion and interpersonal passion should be separate affairs. At the same time, though, Levinson made clear that his earlier political life had reverberated with "private" intimacy. Despite the later presence of truly "personal relationships" in his life, he insisted that he did not "feel intimate with any of these people. And I know I never will. And with the people from the Party, I felt intimate. I couldn't tell them anything about what we call my 'personal life,' but I felt an intimacy with them I also know I'll never feel again with anyone else." The Party created just such complex kinds of attachment between its members.[73]

To the degree that Levinson's marriage was more about ideological similarity than traditional romantic passion, he was hardly unique. Among Los Angeles Party marriages, Dorothy Healey said, "for most of the people that was a given. They shared a common political goal that was greater than anything else." Around Edendale, political enthusiasm often became the foundation for marriages or relationships. Sherman said she saw several affairs and marriages born in the Party, and while many were explicitly romantic or sexual, not all were. Simply being in the Party was "an exciting life," she explained, so that people may have been content with less exciting marriages. "There was so much passion and excitement and devotion within the Party and in the Party work that that could certainly fulfill your needs and your dreams." In fact, when Harry Hay married a female Party member, he and his wife, Anita Platky, determined that they would be good spouses in spite of Hay's history of sexual activity with men; their comradely passion would be greater than his sexual desires.[74]

Of course, Party passion and personal romance also came into conflict. Sherman reported, "There were a lot of divorces, there were a lot of separations. Yes, there were a lot of families broken up in the Party. It took a lot." Sometimes the comradely passion dulled to reveal emotionally empty marriages, but often the Party strained relationships simply because it demanded so much time and energy of its members. Barbara Kaplan remembered, "You were at a lot of meetings, a lot of distributions of material, a lot of street corner speaking." And members juggled family life as best they could. For instance, she said, "we took the kids to most of everything. All the picket lines, the Rosenberg picket line, the Willie McGee picket line—we took them, in their strollers, whatever, all of us did. And it was just part of life, that's all. . . . Everybody was doing the same thing." True enough, said Sherman, whose first husband ran for state assembly when her daughter was just a toddler, and so she accompanied her on their door-to-door campaigning: "Whatever political work I did I had her with me."[75]

In Sherman's memory, that juggling could be difficult. "Party work," she recalled, "was so engrossing. It took up much more time than a meeting once a week, or once every two weeks. In order to be a Party member you had to assume responsibilities. It was so engrossing that it was bound to create friction and problems at home." Those problems were painful and significant. Elaine Black, who had blithely assumed that police brutality was justified, changed her mind when she saw the police beat unemployment demonstrators in 1930. She soon began working full-time for the ILD, but in large part because of the demands the movement placed on her, her first marriage collapsed: her ILD work, according to her biographer, "often took precedence over her family life." Peggy Dennis wrote sorrowfully in her memoirs about the absence of her husband, organizer Eugene Dennis, when their first child was born and the fact that "Gene and I saw little of each other" in those years of their marriage. And the memoirs of "red diaper babies"—the children of many of these activists—are replete with feelings of abandonment and the sense of being a "Party orphan" whose existence was overshadowed by the greater causes to which their parents devoted themselves.[76]

For Sherman, accepting these constraints was one of the practical reasons that so many Party people married other members. Sherman's marriages—like Healey's, Luba and Jared Perlin's, Serril and Lillian Gerber's, even the Hays' marriage—attest to the regularity with which Party members built their intimate lives with other members. In fact, Sherman explained, in the case where someone married a person not in the Party, that person either joined the Party or the marriage usually collapsed. But many marriages also suffered predictably under husbands' expectation that their wives would be both revolutionary partners and traditional housewives. Their revolutionary fervor did not often alter their ideas about family sex roles, and they carried a set of expectations that was far too demanding.[77]

When those strains surfaced, the Edendale Party often joined the effort to keep marriages together. If a marriage was known to be in trouble, Sherman said, it would not "be unusual at all for the Party to intervene and have a discussion. 'Let's have a discussion and see what's happening.'" She recalled Party members meeting with her and her first husband to try to preserve their marriage, and she recalled meeting herself with Eleanor Grossman and her first husband during the break-up of their marriage. "Sometimes that went over," she said, "and sometimes it didn't go over. Sometimes it helped. Other times men would become angry and irate and it would result in problems." Sherman explained that the interventions represented a recognition of how demanding the Party could be. Helping solve marital disputes "made it possible for people to function better, both within the Party and outside as individuals. And the Party was always concerned about keeping the family together."[78] Stable marriages made for stable members.

At the most intimate level, principle and love overran each other within the Party. Barbara Kaplan recalled taking care of a Party member who had had a miscarriage—bathing her, cleaning her home, arranging for a doctor. Dorothy Healey remembered essentially asking the state and county organizers whether it would be all right for her to have a baby. And Peggy Dennis wrote about how closely her colleagues studied her after the birth of her first child: "Could a woman's independence and revolutionary activity be combined with motherhood?" they all wondered. Party members shared life at an extremely personal level.[79]

Kaplan said being active in the Party "was like having a great big family—everybody who cared about everybody." Yet Boris Edel's comments to Vivian Gornick were perhaps more direct: "It's as though people are *real* to me only in a political engagement," he said. "Our political life is so deeply intertwined with our personal life, always has been. It *is* our personal life. I mean, I'm not sure what else there is. I'm not sure what else there is *apart* from politics."[80]

THE POLITICIZED ESSENCE

That was life in and around the Communist Party. Certainly some experienced it more deeply than others, but that was its potential. Unlike their contemporary counterpoints in more mainstream American political parties, Edendale Party members allowed the "essence" of their lives to be stamped by public politics. Party activism was hardly a nine-to-five job. Life in the Party was a full life that shaped, directed, and organized members' time and activities. It affected where they lived and with whom they lived. It forged affinities with singing partners and love among classmates in Marxist theory. It constructed a deep identity and provided a full community for its members.

As Edel said, the Party blurred any distinctions between personal life and political life. It demanded a political attention that burned like personal passion. And every intimate interaction was touched by its political implications. Party living made political activism a profoundly personal and emotional experience just as much as it gave every emotional experience a political significance.

In this way, Party living fused the inner life or emotional world of artistic expression with the public actions of the political arena. Like their artist neighbors, the public life and political action of Edendale Communists had real emotional content. They lived out a relationship between their inner world and the public one. In the case of the artists, the emphasis lay on their effort to communicate their inner lives and make public statements out of it; in a sense the bridge from private to public ran mostly in one direction. For the Communists, that relationship was two-way. Through their public actions, meetings, and demonstrations, Communists and fellow travelers found people with whom they bonded and shared deep connections: their public lives led them into rich emotional connections. At the same time, those interpersonal bonds only deepened the activists' commitments to each other once they were out amidst the hostility and potential violence of the wider public.

Communist living, then, drove further forward the politicization of emotional lives and individual essence. Like Grace Clements, who pushed artists to speak about their inner lives in a way that addressed the issues of a wider public, and like the city and police officials who marked homosexual desire as the telling indicator of socially dangerous degenerates, Communists also infused the emotional richness of their community with tremendous—even international—political significance. To be a Communist or a fellow-traveling leftist was to possess a full identity—an identity imbued with multilayered private and public meanings—that profoundly shaped one's life. That identity marked Communists as separate and distinct: they were recognizable to one another as members in a beloved community, and they were well known to the police and politicians who pursued Communists and leftist agitators aggressively.

Harry Hay and several of Mattachine's cofounders participated actively in the Communist Party and the left, both in Los Angeles and elsewhere. As a result, they took away several lessons from their experiences. Most profound was this possibility of an emotionally rich, politically significant identity that rested on the deep bonds of community. While the crackdowns of the late 1930s politicized the emotional self by labeling homosexual desires as a major societal threat, the Communists of the 1930s and '40s offered an alternative positive model of how personal passion and political action could be meaningfully intertwined to inspire action. They demonstrated vividly one way that the personal could become political.

The Mattachine members did not see themselves, however, simply as loving political activists. They also understood themselves as members of an oppressed social minority. That was a notion that they had to learn, and they learned it in the crucible of the racial conflicts of World War II. In fact, they adopted a minority framework both from the Communist Party and from the city as a whole, as Angelenos struggled to make sense of the unprecedented racial upheavals that engulfed the city during and after the war.

Young Mexicans and Mexican Americans were arrested by the hundreds during World War II in the wake of the death of José Díaz, a local youth, and again during riots provoked by white sailors. (HERALD EXAMINER COLLECTION/ Los Angeles Public Library.)

FIVE

The United Nations in a City

Racial Ideas in Edendale, on the Left,
and in Wartime Los Angeles

WHEN MIRIAM SHERMAN, DOROTHY HEALEY, and others spoke across forty and fifty years of memory to reflect on their lives in the Los Angeles Communist Party, many of the predictable details slipped in and out of their grasp: names, dates, locations. Nevertheless, on one aspect of their experiences, they were keenly verbose and exceedingly clear: the power of the Party to focus their and their contemporaries' attention on issues of race. In Miriam Sherman's recollection, race was the "paramount issue" for the Party, at least as important as its focus on workers. Dorothy Healey concurred, reporting that for her, racial discrimination was the galvanizing force that pushed her into Party activities as an adolescent; the first public speech she gave was about the injustice faced by the Scottsboro Boys. "That was just the beginning," said Healey; fighting racial injustice "lasted all through the Party."[1]

Even as Edendale Communists elaborated and deepened their own sense of community and their own distinct politicized identity, they also became more and more concerned with the identities of others. In particular, these white Angelenos paid increasing attention to racial identities and the treatment of racial minorities in the city. Across the 1930s and '40s, the white Communists and leftists of Edendale—like Communists around the country—became steadily focused on addressing racial discrimination and injustice. In fact, for many Edendale leftists, what drew them to the Party and its related organizations was the priority placed on racial issues. Beyond cultivating a community, culture, and identity of their own, therefore, they also examined identities broadly as a matter of political principle and practice.

Bringing political attention to issues of discrimination had long been a goal of Mexican American, African American, and Japanese American activists in the city, albeit one they pursued fairly independently from one another. Leftists joined their efforts and also helped formulate a unifying argument for viewing oppressed racial groups broadly as entities meriting respect and power in the larger political arena. Racial groups in general, they came to argue, constituted distinct social minorities—akin to colonized nations—whose rights needed protecting. Leftists maintained, therefore, that racism was politically significant and demanded political action. At the same time though, Communists began to treat multiple Angeleno ethnic, racial, and even political identities as fairly analogous, laying the framework for an argument that the oppression of any group of people—racial or otherwise—made them a distinct political unit with legitimate political demands. Fundamentally, they suggested that racial group politics constituted a model for all politicized identities.

During and after World War II, however, white leftists were not the only white Angelenos who finally began to pay attention to racial issues: race relations became a citywide issue as the war unfolded, and remained so during the early years of the Cold War. While leftists began thinking about race earlier and more deeply than many of their white neighbors, the war made racial concerns—something they had largely managed to ignore prior to then—a central issue for many white Angelenos. Local events brought forward a dramatic and previously unrecognized level of racial discord within the city. Those divisions made the city seem less of a unified and homogeneous entity and more like a racial coalition, at best, or a racial war zone, at worst. As Edendale leftist Carey McWilliams wrote to returning veterans in 1946, "Great changes have taken place in race relations in America since the beginning of the war." Each incident and the concerns of each group were no longer seen as separate and minor concerns. "Since the war, the various aspects of the race problem, seldom correlated in the past, have been drawn together so that all phases of the matter, involving Negroes, Mexicans, Orientals, Indians, Filipinos, etc. have come to be regarded as a single national problem."[2]

The stories of Los Angeles' wartime racial struggles—whether the Japanese internment or the Zoot Suit Riots—have been told before. They are well-established elements of the city's World War II history, and many other historians continue to work hard to deepen our understanding of the racial history of the city.[3] Yet this familiar sequence of race battles did not occur in isolation from the other political and cultural changes then occurring in the city. The conflicts over race during the war and postwar years injected a vital conceptual framework into the evolving thinking about the political meaning of individual essence: the broad notion of oppressed social minorities with valid political claims. Indeed as essence was being politicized in the 1920s and '30s—by heraldic artists, "degenerate"-hunting DAs, and impassioned Communist activists—the racial battles of the 1940s promoted a clear and increasingly powerful model of oppression-driven group-based political power. That model rooted the quest for essence in an explicitly political framework of group action.

Importantly, as Michael Omi and Howard Winant have argued, the meaning of racial groups—who has belonged to them and with what consequences—has been a product of ongoing struggles and negotiations. Racial identities, rather than being fixed, have been steadily remade and altered, often in negotiation among individual group members and between them and the larger society. During and after the war, those negotiations captured the attention of white Los Angeles residents in a way they never had before. White Angelenos awakened to racial conflict during the war years much as white Americans had in countless other cities several decades before. That awakening—provoked by violence, state brutality, and political action—transformed their understandings of the city and how other minority groups, Mattachine included, came to see themselves.[4]

RACE AND THE CITY OF ANGELS

Nonwhite racial groups had long been part of the city's social fabric, but dramatic geographic segregation and West coast demographics combined to keep the perception of their presence at a low level. In fact, when Los Angeles' political and social elite called the city a "white spot," that term pointed not only toward the city's bright economic future and its moral probity but toward its perceived monoracial identity as well.[5]

Unlike major urban centers elsewhere in the country, Los Angeles had a small and highly segregated African American population. While other cities had struggled for decades with often violent black-white relations, Los Angeles had avoided much visible turbulence. Just prior to the war, the black population of the city was not quite sixty-four thousand, or barely

2 percent of a citywide population of one and a half million. At the same time, the small black population was highly constrained by housing covenants and employment discrimination. Blacks lived in nonwhite neighborhoods (though ones that were shared with other racial minorities) and were largely excluded from white jobs as well. For white Los Angeles, according to historian Josh Sides, the black community was "small and isolated enough to be virtually invisible."[6]

Within those confines, black Angelenos developed vibrant communal organizations, churches, newspapers, and sense of neighborhood, and for some, cultivated what Douglas Flamming deemed "community consciousness." Nonetheless, as Sides explained, for the city as a whole, "African Americans remained essentially out of sight and out of mind" prior to World War II. Unlike New York or Chicago, Los Angeles had no black local elected officials, and in terms of the national black-white racial paradigm, the city appeared surprisingly free of racial concerns.[7]

Although Japanese and Japanese Americans numbered less than fifty thousand, they were a more distinct presence in the city. They dominated the city's produce markets, which placed them in regular interaction with the white majority. Nevertheless, Japanese and Japanese Americans were also severely segregated, residing only in three distinct districts of the county. Within those districts, Japanese Americans developed a rich subculture, but as historian John Modell argued, "indifference, rather than either contempt or hatred usually characterized Los Angeles public opinion toward the Japanese Americans."[8] While Los Angeles County did have a large Mexican and Mexican American population—at least two hundred thousand in 1940, and likely more—they were similarly excluded from much of the city, living predominantly in unincorporated portions of Los Angeles County, not the city itself. And though Mexican American activists concerned themselves with social uplift, the white majority again remained largely "indifferent" to the Mexican population. Captivated much more by the city's mythic "Spanish" past, they ignored the violence of that past and present, much as they ignored the city's complex racial composition as a whole.[9]

Los Angeles Communists, however, white and nonwhite, were far from indifferent to racial issues in the city. Since nearly the beginning of the Communist Party, various figures had identified black oppression as a vital feature of American capitalism. "Capital," as historian Mark Solomon paraphrased, "was not divided by prejudice or by nationality, but was united in pursuing its own interests at the expense of workers of both races";

therefore, both races merited attention. In part, Party doctrine treated racism as a tool of the bourgeoisie to divide the working masses and turn them against one another, white versus black, thus stalling their unified class action. By 1928, however, the Comintern—the leadership body of the world Communist movement—began to distinguish racial oppression from economic concerns and issued a resolution defining blacks as a separate nation trapped under capitalist American rule. The Comintern called for self-determination—and possible secession—for African Americans in the Black Belt, a stretch of the southern states with a black majority, and urged the American Party to organize African Americans. Despite the potential tension between the simultaneous ideals of separatist "nationalism" and working-class solidarity, self-determination for blacks soon became a key strategy for Party organizers in the South and elsewhere. The Party also began a campaign to abolish racism—what it called "white chauvinism"— from its largely white ranks.[10]

During the 1930s, the Party throughout the country began to address issues of race. In 1931 the national Party's position on racial issues became the focus of several public actions, including the trial and expulsion of a New York Communist from the Party for "white chauvinism" and a series of campaigns on behalf of a black activist convicted in Georgia for inciting insurrection. Perhaps most significant that year, the Party took on the fight to vindicate the Scottsboro Boys from their rape and assault convictions in Alabama. The Party, through the efforts of the International Labor Defense, became the major organizational supporters of the young African Americans, surpassing even the NAACP in its efforts. The ILD campaign featured rallies around the country and the globe. Saving the young men was the cause that galvanized Miriam Brooks Sherman in her early activist years.[11]

The Party's position on racial issues was quite explicit. In 1932, for instance, the Party nominated James Ford, an African American man from Alabama, as its candidate for vice president and running mate to William Foster, the white head of the Party in the United States. When Ford's name was put forward at the Party's convention, the speaker insisted, "The Communist Party stands squarely for *complete* and *unconditional* equality for the Negro people. We do not propose equality in some narrow and limited sense. We do not say that the Negro is all right 'in his place.' We say that any place open to the whites must be opened for the Negroes. We stand unequivocally for *full* political, economic, and especially—we emphasize— *social* equality." Similarly, a list of popular publications put out by the

Workers Library in 1933 indicated the continuous commitment to what was called "the Negro Question," with titles like "Smash the Scottsboro Lynch Verdict," "Lynching," "On the Chain Gang," and "Race Hatred on Trial."[12] For the national party, racial injustice became a steady call for action.

In Los Angeles, beginning in the late 1920s, Communist agitators began to focus explicitly on racial justice. Activists became a regular presence along Central Avenue, the main thoroughfare in the city's largest black neighborhood. They picketed businesses that operated with Jim Crow policies and, as the national party took up the plight of the Scottsboro Boys, they tried to draw Los Angeles blacks into that fight. They succeeded only to a small degree, although several Japanese residents did join the Party. Importantly, the Edendale left was very much in step with, if not at the forefront of, this movement. As Sherman and Healey pointed out, work on racial discrimination was the key issue—and the key attraction—for many local members. Healey, who rose in Party ranks to become the organizational secretary of the Los Angeles Party, noted that "there was never anything in the Party that compared with the attention that was given to the question of African Americans." Race, for them, was primary.[13]

The war, however, accelerated the degree to which nonleftists in Los Angeles began to share some portion of the Communists' concern with race relations. In part, that racial awakening came about because of the labor demands of the war industries and the changing demographics they produced. War work certainly made Los Angeles a magnet for African Americans, who flooded the city so dramatically that during the summer of 1943, they arrived at a rate of ten or twelve thousand a month and constituted half of the city's arrivals. As Josh Sides wrote, "The city's black population grew so fast that even the most determined could not ignore it."[14]

At the same time, the tie between racism and warfare was a product of the war's ideological framework. American propaganda portrayed the war as more than a battle among nations. It was also framed as a conflict over political ideology, one between fascism and democracy, and the propagandists emphasized the racist features of Japan and Germany's fascist ideologies; the effort to defeat fascism was portrayed, in part, as a fight against racism. The broader propaganda campaigns echoed the left in highlighting racist Nazi attitudes and framing battles against fascism as a kind of anti-racism. For instance, when the Hollywood Anti-Nazi League, a Communist-led Popular Front organization, formed in the winter of 1936, it declared that "racial tolerance, one of the main tenets of democracy, is vitally threatened by Nazism and its wide-spread propaganda in this country." The official propaganda campaigns followed this same line, arguing that the rise of Nazism was dangerous because it threatened to unleash racial intolerance. Implicit in these formulations was an evocation of American racial tolerance. While that evocation may have exaggerated the truth of American racial attitudes, it demanded that Americans reject racism.[15]

The ideological evocation of American racial tolerance, as opposed to the reality of harsh discrimination, jarred many racial minorities in the country. As Kevin Leonard wrote about Los Angeles, the "war made many black, Mexican, and Japanese Americans acutely aware of the pervasive discrimination that they faced." The language of racial equality, however, also provided leverage to launch stronger campaigns against discrimination, and the same groups that were "passive and subdued" in 1940, according to historian Gerald Nash, were "actively striving for equal rights" by 1945. By the end of the war, the left and others also began to speak of American nonracism as "inter-racialism." As a term, "inter-racialism" marked a shift away from a "melting pot" ideal. Rather than suggesting that racial differences would fade as different groups assimilated into the majority culture and society, inter-racialism was intended to acknowledge the unyielding differences between racial groups and to advocate that these groups could harmoniously interact.[16]

Finally, if the ideological framing of the war made racism suspect, the war also raised the question of the relationship between American racial groups and foreign nations. In the 1930s, for instance, the ethnic descendants from different nations were often understood as being of different races. Thus Japanese, Koreans, and Chinese were all considered separate races: such racial categories were conceptualized as the lingering residue of national origins. The war raised the question, however, of what those origins meant in the context of inter-national conflict. Should racial groups be seen as loyal first to their nation of ethnic origin, or was that original tie less important than their tie to the United States? Was a racial identity subsidiary, ultimately, to an American national identity? These questions were fought over on the streets of Los Angeles during the Second World War, and also prompted a reconsideration of race and race relations in the city.

Driven by these multiple factors, this elevated focus on race among Angelenos in general and among white Angeleno elites in particular marked a key transition in the politicization of identity. In part, racial politics paralleled the politicization of emotional and sexual behavior by artists and the police, as well as the intense emotionalization of politics by the Communists: another quality of personhood became politicized. At the same time, though, the politics of racial identities were much better established. Minority groups, even in Los Angeles, had already been pushing, with varying degrees of assertiveness, to limit discriminatory practices in the city. And white Angeleno elites had successfully instituted employment and residential segregation to limit their presence in the city. Racial minorities, even if largely ignored, already held places in the public imagination. What shifted in the war years, as Carey McWilliams articulated, was the coalescing of these separate racial groups into a single "national problem": interracial relations. That "problem" pushed forward a notion of political life as defined by competing racial groups and their demands. Unlike the "degenerates"—and despite many Angelenos' racist attitudes—minority racial groups were not dangers that could be eradicated: instead they became grudgingly recognized as constituent if competing participants in the body politic. As a result, in 1940s Los Angeles, the politics of personal identities began to signify group politics.

PREWAR UNITY AND DIFFERENCE

In June of 1939, nearly ten thousand young Angelenos gathered in the seats of the Hollywood Bowl to participate in the nation's first ever "I Am an American" panegyric. The Bowl, an outdoor amphitheater nestled in the foothills above Hollywood, had been serving as a cultural performance center for over twenty years. Since 1916 it had been used for productions ranging from *Julius Caesar* and Los Angeles Philharmonic Orchestra concerts to Easter sunrise services. Increasingly, though, the Bowl had been used for political rallies.[17]

The celebration that June was a rally of American unity that had been designed in part by Los Angeles County supervisor John Anson Ford, and it was soon repeated in cities across the country. Ford was the progressive county supervisor who had been vital in the long battle to defeat Mayor Frank Shaw, and he was an avid booster of Los Angeles and its cultural affairs. The ten thousand Angelenos were new voters, just turned twenty-one that year, and they were called to the Bowl to listen to exhortations from Mayor Bowron on what it meant to be a good citizen and to declare their allegiance to the shared project of America. In a special oath, the young men and women repeated lines that were read to them from the stage. "I am an American!" they shouted back from the bleacher seats. "The Golden Rule is my rule!" "Problems of interest to my country," they promised, "shall be of interest to me! . . . My heart is in America and America is in my heart! I am an American!"[18]

Within such declarations of national unity and shared identity, there was room for limited ethnoracial difference. Indeed, such differences could be celebrated to the degree that they did not carry significant political implications. At the start of 1939, for instance, the state of California demonstrated what was allowable in designating the first week of February "Negro History Week." Mayor Bowron opened his arms to such an idea, acknowledging that "the Negro has helped and is helping to build our country; and it is fitting and proper that we are all given the opportunity, through study and research, to learn of his contributions and his services to our American Democracy."[19] What African Americans had contributed to a *shared* American society—this was what could be embraced.

Similarly, on the same day as the Bowl rally, Bowron appeared on a new radio program called *The Jewish International Broadcasting Hour*. During his segment, he encouraged listeners to note the cultural contributions American Jews had made to America and Americanism. At the same time, he wanted to specifically limit the embrace of difference to something celebratory and cultural. He insisted that he had "no desire whatever and no intent whatever to accentuate any line of cleavage or point of difference which, unfortunately, may have been developed in the United States as between Jewish and non-Jewish citizens. On the contrary, I feel that it is to the best interests of all concerned that such lines of demarcation in the political, social and economic realms should be obliterated as speedily and completely as possible." Bowron tried to strike a balance between appreciating cultural difference as an addition to the richness of American life and refusing to see those differences as representing some kind of unbreachable political or cultural division. Public officials like Bowron advocated a position akin to what historian Peggy Pascoe called "racial non-recognition," opposing any deeply politicized acknowledgment of racial difference. At the same time, they regularly extolled the cultural virtues of a particular ethnic or racial group.[20]

As the war drew closer, both the Nazis' politicized racism and the far left's critique of it gained prominence in the city. The combination of the two forced Angelenos to consider their racial attitudes in a political context. Supervisor John Anson Ford, for instance, explicitly reframed his thinking about race as the war unfolded. A politician whose career on the county council ran from 1934 to 1958, Ford had long been attentive to ethnic and racial identity and prejudice as cultural issues. In the mid-1930s, much like Mayor Bowron, he had encouraged various Japanese groups in their cultural efforts, prodding one to "continue to preserve the festival spirit of Old Japan" and another to start a theater group. Ford himself had treated prejudice as a concern principally in the realm of private, personal relationships. In 1940 he wrote a constituent, insisting that

> proof of my lack of racial prejudice and of my defense of minority groups is my personal history of steadfast opposition to any manifestation of prejudice against Jews, Japanese, Greeks or any other group. . . . I am particularly proud of the friendship of such fine people as Adolph Levy, attorney, Max Strasburg, Hollywood jeweler, Clarence Nuse, Negro concert singer and cinema star, Kay Sugahara, Japanese importer, and others.
>
> Both myself and Mrs. Ford have been honored to have people of all these races as guests in our home and around our table.

For Ford, combating racism meant building friendships and inviting guests for dinner. He seemed to view racism as principally a problem of individual attitudes.[21]

As war clouds loomed, Ford's thinking shifted. He began to see racial issues as political, in addition to being personal or cultural. "Hitler's racial superiority idea," he wrote, is "a blessing in disguise. It is forcing a great many of us to think democracy through." By 1942 that thinking made Ford begin to see the political implications of racial attitudes. It was much clearer to Ford then that "the way we of the white race treat the colored people, the Mexicans in our midst and the other minorities hinders or helps Hirohito and Hitler. Whether we like it or not, we're up against the necessity of clear courageous thinking about the far flung implications of democracy." Fundamentally, political democracy at home was coming to mean an egalitarian racial democracy of some kind. And if the war abroad was making that clear, events on the home front solidified that belief.[22]

WARTIME BATTLEGROUND

As the violent tidal wave of war cast its shadow across Southern California, fear about the vulnerability of the city began to pervade Los Angeles. As early as 1939, more than two hundred local business leaders, with Bowron at their head, formed the Defense Committee of Southern California to strengthen the city and protect it from attack. But in the wake of the assault on Pearl Harbor on December 7, 1941, that anxiety magnified enormously.

According to Arthur Verge's study of Los Angeles during the war, "Fear began to sweep though the Los Angeles basin. Many citizens worried that the city itself would soon be the target of Japanese military attack." The local press played up the proximity of the Hawaiian Islands and the disloyalty of the local Japanese, and danger felt imminent. Defense plants were camouflaged and blackout procedures introduced. The coast guard and army began to patrol the beaches, while bunkers of machine guns and artillery were constructed along the coast. Antiaircraft guns were placed throughout the city, as were large balloons to entangle low-flying aircraft. The city took on a defensive stance.[23]

On Christmas Eve 1941, as witnesses watched from the San Pedro harbor, a Japanese submarine torpedoed an American lumber carrier in the Catalina Channel just off the coast. Two months later, a Japanese submarine fired on an oil storage area less than one hundred miles north of the city, near Santa Barbara, and sent a wave of panic through the city. The *Times* headline the next morning read, "Submarine Shells Southland Oil Field," and rumors quickly spread that the submarine had flashed signal lights to subversive insurgents on the shore. A few days later in the middle of the night, military units thought they saw enemy aircraft over Los Angeles and for an hour fired hundreds of shells into the night sky as searchlights scanned for the planes.[24] Southern California seemed under siege.

That perception inspired a mass mobilization of the population. Nearly a tenth of the Los Angeles population—165,000 volunteers—signed up for a civil defense program. Defense workers arrived as well, as the city became the second largest industrial center in the country: by one estimate, Los Angeles' population grew by an unprecedented 17 percent between 1940 and 1943, and a noticeable number of the new arrivals were African Americans, whose citywide presence easily tripled during the war. Almost everyone from the West who enlisted in the navy passed through Los Angeles, as did many of the nation's combatants in the Pacific Theater. In fact, during the war, California housed so many military programs that "millions of young men and women [were] trained, staged, shipped, or returned in one way or another to, from, in, or through California."[25]

The war footing heightened the politicization of racial categories in Los Angeles. The association of different racial groups with their country of origin—ally or enemy—framed and sustained the very public battles that soon ensued over the presence of ethnic Japanese and Mexican residents in the city. The transposition of national hostilities onto the domestic front was sharpest in the tragic story of the Japanese internment. In the wake of Pearl Harbor, a cohort of West Coast officials and military leaders pressured the War Department and President Roosevelt to remove all Japanese and Japanese Americans from the Far West. The president yielded, issuing Executive Order 9066 in February 1942, authorizing their evacuation. Soon after, 40,000 local Japanese residents and Japanese American citizens—out of a national total of close to 120,000—were deported from Los Angeles and sent to internment camps as far away as Wyoming and Arkansas.[26]

For Edendale artists, the evacuation orders struck close to home. Sueo and Mary Serisawa, the Japanese-born artists who were close friends of Paul and Margaret Landacre and active in their Edendale network, fled Los Angeles to avoid the internment. They moved steadily during the war, living for several years in Colorado, Chicago, and New York City, and returned to Los Angeles only in 1948. The Landacres preserved much of the Serisawas' correspondence from those absent years in their personal files. The Serisawas' letters reverberated with their longing to return to Edendale. When a mutual friend, the art dealer Fillmore Phipps, visited them in Chicago, Mary wrote ecstatically about how wonderful he looked, "& I *mean wonderful!* It was so nice to see him again. We talked of old times & of the good ole days & asked about everyone and who lived where & what were they doing & etc, etc, & how much we missed you all & that California was the *only* place to live!" Sueo's letters to Paul, which underscored the importance of their arts community, also revealed the pain of his enforced banishment. When Sueo wrote that he wished that "I could come over & talk about paintings & things. Perhaps in a couple of years we can," his wish was as much about the value of their community as a repudiation of the federal government. When the Serisawas returned to Los Angeles in 1948, they returned transformed by their years in exile.[27]

In the days immediately following Pearl Harbor, it was far from predictable that Japanese and Japanese Americans would be removed from the city. Both Mayor Bowron and the far more progressive Supervisor Ford had long been supporters of a cultural Japanese presence in the city. In August 1941, for instance, Bowron had spoken at the annual Japanese American cultural celebration, reassuring the Nisei—the American-born citizens—that "we know you are loyal." In fact, Bowron repeated that declaration late on December 8—the day after Pearl Harbor was bombed—at a nighttime meeting of the Japanese American Citizens League (JACL). The largest Nisei cultural and political action group, the league had steadily worked to promote a positive impression of Japanese Americans in white Angeleno society; that night its members had gathered to pledge war bonds to the American cause. Bowron arrived at 10 P.M. and, according to the JACL minutes, "expressed that he didn't doubt the Niseis' sincerity and patriotism and that Niseis did stand for American ideals and assured us that local Administration and local government will give us all the knowledge and protection accorded any other citizen."[28]

Such vows did not last long. Before January ended, Bowron and the city council voted to suspend all ethnic Japanese employees, and the county supervisors, with Ford's approval, did the same. In fact, the county supervisors went a step further and endorsed a resolution calling for the removal of all Japanese aliens inland. Within a week of the firings, Bowron went on the radio, complaining that Angelenos were "impatiently waiting" for a federal decision "as to what to do with the Japanese in California." Unless an evacuation occurred, he insisted, "each of our little Japanese friends will know his part in the event of any possible attempted invasion or air raid. . . . We are the ones who will be human sacrifices." In the framework of warfare, Bowron's view of Japanese Americans as an interesting cultural minority had collapsed. He now saw them only as the domestic representatives of an international political threat.[29]

It was not new for Japanese and Japanese Americans in California to be viewed as threatening. In some ways, as historian Kevin Starr argued, "California had been at war with the Japanese, foreign and domestic," for forty years. San Francisco laborers had all but forced Theodore Roosevelt to negotiate a limit on Japanese immigration in 1907, and the state legislature in 1913 had made it essentially impossible for Japanese immigrants to own land in the state. In 1922 the U.S. Supreme Court confirmed that Japanese immigrants were ineligible for citizenship, and by 1924 Congress banned nearly all Asian immigration. But the war magnified that hostility throughout the state and gave it a heightened political slant. Both the fighting and the internment crystallized the notion that the local ethnic Japanese were part of and representatives of the enemy nation Japan.[30]

Wartime anti-Japanese sentiments drew on the belief that local Japanese and Japanese Americans possessed the warring traits of Japan itself. In contrast to other minorities, the scorn that was heaped on them did not rely on stereotypes about individual qualities such as lustiness or greed. Instead, as historian Modell explained, "the competence, diplomatic skill, ambition, and pride of the Japanese nation were attributed to her citizens in America and to her progeny, while the political power of the mother country was thought to be at the immigrants' disposal." For 1940s Angelenos, every Japanese person possessed the power of the Japanese emperor.[31]

Few voiced disapproval of the internment. Bowron, Ford, the liberal Governor Culbert Olson, state attorney general Earl Warren, the entire California membership of the U.S. House of Representatives—all supported the evacuation. Carey McWilliams, an Edendale resident and one of the country's leading liberals, had hoped to limit the scope of the internment, but he too eventually gave a "muted endorsement" to the internment camps, writing positively about them in what historian Chris Gantner described as "summer camp brochure prose."[32]

Even the Communists did not raise their voices against the evacuation, although many Japanese activists worked within their movement. Miriam Brooks Sherman was quite close with Elaine Black and her husband, Karl Yoneda. Yoneda had been born in California but spent his youth in Japan before returning to the States in 1926. Although he was nearly killed by the police in an unemployment demonstration, he was also very active as a Party organizer and became friends with Sherman's parents, often eating meals at their home in the late 1920s. Black, who had been the politically indifferent daughter of labor activists, joined the ILD after witnessing police brutality firsthand, and she and Sherman became friends through their work there together. When Yoneda was interned and their son's internment was scheduled, Black—who was not Japanese—insisted that she be taken to the camp as well. "The Party didn't say anything," Sherman recalled. "I remember saying good-bye to them at the railroad station. It was very sad. We all cried. But we never thought of it in terms of it being incorrect. . . . I think we were all taken in with the war danger and the possibility of infiltration on the West coast particularly. It seemed like it was necessary for security. Now we know better about everything."[33]

Two former Japanese American constituents wrote Ford from the camps soon after internment, describing their experiences and how they interpreted them in terms of local politics. One, Fred Tayama, a restaurateur and chair of the local JACL, wanted to believe that the internment was a reasonable security measure, not motivated by racism or by the identification of Japanese Americans with the Japanese nation. Yet he found it difficult to sustain that view. Many of the first-generation immigrants in the camps were wagging their fingers at the American-born Nisei, saying, " 'You see, we were right; no matter what you say you are not going to be accepted as full fledged Americans.' It's a tough job we're going to have ahead of us, Mr. Ford, trying to convince these people that this was not a problem of racial discrimination; that America affords equal chances to all mankind." The internment seemed to argue against racial equality, against a notion of minor cultural differences outweighed by fundamental political unity.[34]

The second constituent, Keiichi "Kay" Sugahara, the millionaire graduate of UCLA and first president of the Los Angeles JACL of whose friendship Ford had boasted, insisted that a line had been crossed and "certain democratic rights have been infringed." He predicted that all racial and ethnic minority groups—Jews, African Americans, Germans, or Italians—would be equally vulnerable. "Is there not a possibility, that this may lead to wider types of discrimination after the war in which the fever of hatred would not have yet cooled?" He saw the internments as predicting a very different notion of race relations than dinner party guests sharing their different cultural contributions. In some ways his prediction was right.[35]

ANTI-MEXICAN VIOLENCE

In the year following the Japanese evacuation, racial identity was further politicized through the tumult of the Sleepy Lagoon trials and the violence of the Zoot Suit Riots. These anti-Mexican actions did not only demonstrate the growing racial tensions in the city. They were also interpreted as involving American foreign policy and gave further credence to the notion that Los Angeles was a city of warring nations.[36]

A cohort of poor and disenfranchised Mexican American youths made their presence more visible in the city streets in the late 1930s and early 1940s by dressing in the baggy pants, oversized jackets, and wide-rimmed hats of zoot suit fashion. Their outfits marked their rebellion against mainstream Los Angeles, and white Angelenos moved to respond. First, in the spring of 1942, Los Angeles newspapers began a recurring drumbeat of stories about Mexican American criminals and juvenile delinquents that labeled Mexican Americans as a dangerous internal enemy.[37] Then on August 2, 1942, when a young man named José Díaz was discovered unconscious near an East Los Angeles swimming hole (he died shortly thereafter), the police went into overdrive. They began aggressive assaults against Mexican American youths, including slicing their zoot suit pants with razors as they came out of dance halls. In a massive three-day sweep the weekend after Díaz's death, the police hauled in more than six hundred Mexican American youths. When Díaz died—and it was hardly clear that he had been killed—murder charges were filed against twenty-four of the arrested youths in what became known as the Sleepy Lagoon murder.

The proceedings that fall were a sham. There was no evidence connecting Díaz's death to the young men, nor even that he was murdered. Nevertheless, the prosecution pushed ahead. Witnesses were not instructed of their rights. The judge mocked the defense attorneys. Two of the defendants filed successfully to have separate trials—and saw their charges dropped—but the remaining twenty-two defendants were tried en masse, and prevented from sitting with their attorneys. The young men were not even allowed to cut their hair or clean themselves up for the trial: the prosecuting attorney wanted them to appear guilty in their filth, and the judge concurred. Mexican Americans and leftists led by Edendale residents formed a defense committee on their behalf, but only five of the twenty-two group defendants were acquitted. Three were convicted of first-degree murder, nine of second-degree murder, and five of assault: the twelve convicted of murder were sent to San Quentin.[38]

That August and October—immediately following the arrests and then the trial—the county grand jury held special sessions to investigate the issue of Mexican American juvenile delinquency. The police generally suggested that Mexican delinquency was—like Japanese nationalism—biologically rooted. Captain Edward Ayres of the county sheriff's department epitomized this view, explaining that Mexicans were descendants from local Indians and that a "total disregard for human life has always been universal throughout the Americas among the Indian population." Ayres insisted that the only thing a Mexican "knows and feels is a desire to use a knife or some lethal weapon. In other words, his desire is to kill, or at least let blood." Although academics and liberals like Carey McWilliams testified that the "problem" of ethnic Mexican youth should be understood as "a problem of cultural conflict," they all shared the view that crime among Mexican youths constituted a serious danger for the city.[39]

The following spring, the local press heightened the aura of danger surrounding Mexican American youth with a stream of articles that increasingly portrayed them with warlike language. Headlines like ". . . Zoot Suit Revolution," "Zoot Network over L.A.," and "Zoot Arsenal" generated unjustified fears that young Mexican Americans constituted a kind of rebel army. In May 1943 a *Los Angeles Times* article went so far as to say that "in a veritable reign of terror, four separate gangs of zoot-suiters yesterday launched attacks on peaceful citizens at widely scattered points"; the story all but demanded that the "rebel" forces be stopped. Soon thereafter, when a group of zoot-suiters did pick a fight with some white sailors, the sailors coordinated a massive retaliation. Beginning on June 3, servicemen launched several days of citywide rioting. Sailors rode a convoy of taxicabs from their base near downtown into East Los Angeles to "punish" Mexican American youths, who, they said, were avoiding military service and—more ominously—assaulting white women. The soldiers pulled random men from streetcars, movie houses, and sidewalks and beat and stripped them of their clothes. On June 7, perhaps the worst day of rioting, civilians and servicemen together swarmed into downtown, converging on a spot where the press said zoot-suiters were planning an attack, and began "bursting into restaurants, bars, penny arcades, pool halls, and theaters, dragging out unsuspecting Mexican American boys, beating them, and leaving them lying naked in the gutters." The police did little to stop the violence, often following the servicemen at a distance; when they finally began making arrests, they mostly arrested Mexican American youths—the victims, in this case. In the end, as many as six hundred young Mexican Americans were arrested and hundreds more injured and humiliated.[40]

The level of physical destruction from the Zoot Suit Riots may not have been dramatic, but the political impact was tremendous. The story of the rioting circulated widely, both in the country and abroad. To some, it looked as if the war had come home, and they analyzed the riots as part of the war. State senator Jack Tenney, for instance, insisted that the zoot-suiters were "Axis sponsored." By contrast, Rudy Sanchez, a Mexican American youth, wanted to know, "Whose side is the Navy on anyway, Uncle Sam or Hitler?" The riots felt like an echo of the war, and as in the case of the Japanese internment, they again blurred the connection between race.and nation. In the press, and among diplomats, the riots were treated as having an international significance. Bowron complained bitterly about the news accounts, saying that "irreparable damage to the city of Los Angeles has been done and probably some misunderstanding created on the part of Mexican officials by reason of these news dispatches." His worries were well placed: not only were Latin American governments alarmed by the riots, but also the Mexican government filed a formal complaint to Washington. The pro-Axis political party in Mexico even argued that the riots demonstrated that Mexico had chosen the wrong allies in the war. Alarmed by the responses, both Nelson Rockefeller, the State Department coordinator of inter-American affairs, and the War Manpower Commission delivered stern warnings to Los Angeles officials.[41]

Bowron's complaints were revealing. Contrary to his handling of the Japanese internment, Bowron now feared an analysis that linked the treatment of Mexican Americans to the nation of Mexico. Because of Mexico's status as an ally, he did not want ethnic Mexicans to be understood as having an identity that was essentially a nationalist loyalty. In fact, he did not want the riots to be interpreted in racial terms at all. "This is in no sense a racial problem," he argued, "and would have no possible international implications if the busybodies and a few organizations composed of radicals had not made it so by rushing to the defense of the young hoodlums when they were arrested and raising a hue and cry about racial discrimination and minority groups."

While he had been outspoken in his analysis of Japanese and Japanese Americans as a racial-national group, Bowron now resisted applying the same equation. The internment of the Japanese was justifiable because an assault on them as a race was an assault on the enemy nation. If the Zoot Suit Riots were also interpreted as an assault on the Mexican race, then surely they would be read as an assault on the Mexican nation as well. Only "radicals," Bowron suggested, would want to make such a claim and disrupt the American-Mexican alliance.[42]

VIEWING RACES AS EQUIVALENT NATIONS

The international race-nation analysis, however, was not exclusively a "radical" one, as Bowron implied: it became more widespread. Alan Cranston, then an official with the Office of War Information, rushed out to Los Angeles to "handle" the situation. Simply the fact that a staff member of the national war propaganda office was sent to address an arguably domestic incident underscored how quickly the riots became framed through the war's international lens. One of Cranston's ideas was to photograph a parade of zoot-suiters at a blood bank. He believed this would demonstrate their decency and, more important, their American patriotism. When the Red Cross refused, Cranston sought Bowron's support, but Bowron resisted as well, convinced that the idea was "wrong in principle." In direct opposition to what he had said about the Japanese and Japanese Americans, Bowron said, "[We are] striving to make those of Mexican blood in this community realize that they are Americans, rather than Mexicans. We do not feel that the people of Mexican parentage need to redeem themselves because of the acts of a few young hoodlums who have violated the law."[43]

Unlike Bowron, though, Los Angeles leftists did embrace the internationalist framework wholeheartedly. That framework spoke to Party members because they did view minority races as oppressed nations within the

United States' colonial empire. As nations, minority racial groups possessed the right of self-determination: equal rights and social treatment were only steps along the way to the option of self-governance. Party theorizing, which focused principally on African Americans, was transmitted to members through classes and discussions. Even discussion programs designed after the war promoted the analysis of race in national terms. In February 1946, for instance, the Party's California education committee circulated discussion guidelines entitled "The Search for Freedom for the Negro People." The guidelines offered a sequence of questions for analysis: "What is the Marxist definition of a nation? Does this apply to the Negro people in the United States? What is meant in general by the right to self-determination? (for any nation) How would this apply to the Negro people?" Similarly, in 1950 the Los Angeles Education Department circulated a ten-unit curriculum on "Negro Liberation" to be taught around the city. The seventh unit was devoted to exploring how African Americans in the United States fulfilled the Marxist qualities of a nation—"a historically evolved stable community of language, territory, economic life, and psychological make-up manifested in a community of culture." Because the Party viewed blacks as meeting these standards, it assumed that they also had the right to self-determination—let alone to equal civil rights. The heart of such an analysis was that blacks possessed a distinct identity and independent authority by virtue of their race: this was the most clearly theorized argument for what could be called "race-nationhood."[44]

Although Party theoreticians emphasized the "Negro Question," in application, Party members treated multiple racial groups as oppressed nations and viewed them as occupying analogous positions in society. This analogizing of races as equivalently oppressed was a fairly new idea; it was just beginning to gain traction among the city's racial minorities themselves, pushed in large part by leftist activists within these communities. As Kevin Leonard noted, for instance, while local African Americans had celebrated the interning of Japanese Americans in 1942, by 1943, after the Zoot Suit Riots, the NAACP called for federal action, and the Urban League tried to open up its local "round table" to all minority group leaders: these African American leaders now began to argue for a sense of common cause. For white leftists, the idea of analogous racial groups proved extremely productive. First, discrimination against African Americans or Mexican Americans as race-nations could be equated to that against Jews, a race-nation with which many Party members identified. This helped Party members bring a sense of personal understanding and identification to the question of racial discrimination. Second, they linked racist violence in Los Angeles to similar events around the country, as part of a wider system of oppression. Third, the leftist framework allowed activists to frame the struggle to defeat racism in the United States within the context of national liberation struggles worldwide. Thus, a framework of equivalency attributed national and international importance to otherwise small-seeming, local events and also drew Party members into the fight against racism through personal motivation.[45]

For Edendale leftists in particular, their concern about racism was heightened by the fact that they were living in a neighborhood that was steadily becoming more racially mixed. As early as 1920, there were numerous Mexican and Mexican American families scattered around the northern and western edges of the neighborhood. By 1930, they were joined as well by several Japanese Americans and a cluster of African American families gathered in a few blocks in the western part of Edendale. That area was described in 1939 by the Home Owners Loan Corporation—a federal agency that organized mortgages in the wake of the Depression and determined which neighborhoods constituted safe investments—as "highly heterogeneous with more than a sprinkling of subversive racial elements." In fact, HOLC tagged many parts of the neighborhood with red flags for their racial composition, and by 1940, while Edendale remained predominantly white, the streets along its perimeter contained relatively high numbers of African Americans, Japanese Americans, and Mexican Americans.[46] The local Party, though, possessed a membership that was almost entirely white and easily half Jewish, which was typical of national party trends. Yet especially because of the small pockets of black population in the area, local members shared the continuing goal of recruiting black residents into the branch. During the 1940s there was a small percentage of black members, as well as one or two Japanese and Mexican members, but never a sizable number, and black recruitment was a perennial topic of discussion and focus of action.[47]

The demographics of the neighborhood carried multiple connotations for the white residents. Jeannette and Sam Reisbord's daughter, Susan, remembered growing up in Edendale in the late 1940s and 1950s. Her family lived on Cove Avenue, the same street as Harry Hay and his family, on a block where the street dissolved into a stairwell. Her home, she recalled, sat in the middle of the stairway, 98 stairs from the top of the hill and 108 from the bottom. The stretch of the stairwell incorporated a wide swath of the city's racial and economic mix. A Mexican family lived at the bottom of the steps and had a dirt yard with chickens. A Slavic man living with his mother, a white widow, and a white newlywed couple filled out the bottom half. The top half of the block was occupied by an older white actor (who was a friend of Carey McWilliams), a pair of white "old maids," two Hispanic families that shared a duplex and were the poorest residents on the block, two white men who shared a home hidden along an access road, and a white leftist couple who owned a beautiful home at the top. This was a highly variegated slice of the neighborhood, certainly with more Mexican families than elsewhere, and according to Susan's childhood memories, a tone of "tolerance" dominated. "At the least, it was 'God bless you' and go your own way." While their block was more diverse than elsewhere in the neighborhood, the Reisbords' attitude of tolerance echoed the Party goal of inter-racialist harmony.[48]

Stanley Schneider lived, as a ten-, eleven-, and twelve-year-old, closer to Echo Park than the Reisbords, but his part of the neighborhood was demographically similar to theirs in the late 1940s. He recalled that Mexican families lived on his block—including the world lightweight boxing champion—and that a Mexican family of seven or eight children lived next door to Schneider, his parents, and grandmother. At the same time, while his classmates were predominantly white, there were several Japanese American and Mexican American children at his junior high and high school and many of his close friends—and baseball teammates—were Japanese American boys who lived on the other side of the neighborhood in one of the pockets of Japanese American and African American residents. The white families, many of whom were Jewish, were largely working-class. His own father was a furrier, and his mother a seamstress in the garment trades.[49]

Despite the Reisbords' message of tolerance, inter-racial harmony was not always maintained in the neighborhood. Schneider remembered Mexican gangs in Echo Park that, though their members might have lived in the neighborhood, seemed to him of another socioeconomic level; he was mugged by one such group in the park. Additionally, he and his friends referred to the neighboring poor Mexican area of Chavez Ravine as "Dog Town" and saw it as an other-worldly place. "It felt like you were stepping into part of Mexico." Morris Markoff, the vacuum salesman who moved to the area in the mid-1930s, also pointed out that racial housing covenants remained rampant in the neighborhood throughout the 1940s, restricting African Americans and ethnic Japanese from living in much of the area. Asked about the black population in the area, Markoff's wife, Betty, replied, "Oh, heaven, what's a black?" and Markoff himself insisted, "I

The Thomas Starr King Junior High School A–9 baseball team posing for a team photo. Stan Schneider is in the bottom row, third from the right. The team expressed the growing racial diversity in the neighborhood. (Courtesy Stanley Schneider.)

never saw one. I can't remember any neighbors, or anybody on the streets, or anybody." So while "tolerance was part of the upbringing" for Susan Reisbord or Stan Schneider—the heroes in Schneider's childhood home were Paul Robeson, Joe Louis, and Franklin Roosevelt—it also had its limits in the neighborhood.[50]

In a sense, then, Edendale leftists were living in a community that was beginning to reflect their values, yet still had some distance to go. They worked, therefore, to accelerate the rate of change. Much of the local activists' efforts focused in and around the neighborhood, with agenda items ranging from restrictive covenant cases to segregation at the Bimini Baths. Indeed, Miriam Sherman remembered the goal of desegregating the pools there as an important struggle, initiated by the local Party section, with picket lines and neighborhood petitions, that ultimately succeeded.[51]

Perhaps more dramatic was the defense of the young Mexican Americans convicted in the 1942 Sleepy Lagoon case. Their plight, especially once they were convicted, became a vital cause in the city, referred to by historian Michael Denning as the Scottsboro case of California. The campaign to overturn their convictions was led in large part by the Edendale left. Local leftists joined with Mexican American activists to form a Citizens' Committee for the Defense of Mexican-American Youth (later renamed the Sleepy Lagoon Defense Committee, or SLDC). In the model of the ILD, the committee raised funds for the young men's legal expenses and promoted awareness of the case. The committee successfully drew support from the labor and entertainment worlds and quickly came under the leadership of Edendale locals Carey McWilliams and Alice McGrath; he became chair and she, executive secretary.[52]

For two years following the arrests, the SLDC worked steadily on behalf of the jailed young men, raising funds to stage a court appeal. McGrath emerged as a central public figure for the organization and a key liaison to the imprisoned men. She wrote to them regularly, first individually and then later sending them a newsletter; visited them; and generally tried to explain why so many people had taken up their cause. She also sought out supporters of the SLDC's effort, raising money and convincing high-profile individuals to add their names to the committee's masthead. The group drew on Party frameworks to mobilize supporters, and the case illuminated the way those frameworks functioned. One early pamphlet criticized the prosecution and trial as "grimy with prejudice" and argued that it fit within the context of "an ancient campaign of bigotry and persecution of an entire people, the Mexican-Americans of California, a half million decent citizens long leased in 'second-class' status by profiteers of labor and an indifferent public." Thus the trial and convictions, according to the committee, represented the persecution of a "people," a race-nation.[53]

Such persecution, the SLDC further insisted, constituted fascistic behavior. A 1943 pamphlet, for instance, quoted at length from the claims of Captain Ayres of the sheriff's office that Mexicans had a biological desire to kill. The committee argued that Ayres's racism was no different from Hitler's. Indeed, they presented the case as a threat to the international alliances that were sustaining the war drive. "We are at war," they wrote, "not only with the armies of the Axis powers, but with the poison-gas of their doctrine, with the 'biological basis' of Hitler, and with his theories of race supremacy." Ayres and the Sleepy Lagoon prosecution represented international fascism at home. Pardoning the defendants, they claimed in a 1944 pamphlet, would mark a defeat for Hitler's racist theories.[54]

The Sleepy Lagoon Defense Committee did not succeed in obtaining pardons for the convicted men. However, two years of fund-raising drives,

Alice McGrath (standing second from right) visits with some of the young men—and their girlfriends—whom she fought to have pardoned during her work on the Sleepy Lagoon Defense Committee. (Courtesy Alice McGrath/Department of Special Collections, Charles E. Young Research Library, University of California, Los Angeles.)

petitions to the governor and attorney general, and legal wrangling in the state court system paid off when the Second District Court of Appeals unanimously overturned all seventeen convictions, agreeing that there was no evidence of murder. In addition to helping to free the young men, though, the committee and the publicity that it generated transformed the shape of local racial politics. As historian Edward Escobar wrote, the work of the SLDC "catapulted Mexican Americans to the forefront of the civil rights debate in California and helped define them at the national level as an oppressed minority group." It focused city attention on their needs and demands. What is more, for a brief moment, the committee forged an inter-racial coalition within the city, with support for the Sleepy Lagoon defendants coming in from various Jewish groups, the largest African American paper, and a group of Japanese and Japanese Americans interned at Manzanar. The success of the Sleepy Lagoon Defense Committee suggested that inter-racialism might yet guide the city once the war drew to a close, and for a little while it seemed to do just that.[55]

WAR'S END AND THE LIMITED SUCCESS OF INTER-RACIALISM

On the Fourth of July, 1945, Bowron returned to the Hollywood Bowl stage. The occasion was yet another Americanism rally, but one framed differently than those of 1938. It was called a "Declaration of Inter-Dependence" celebration, and Bowron's remarks made explicit the new attitude. "Our country," he explained,

> is, in a sense, composed of minorities; it is the United Nations on a continent; it knows first hand those problems of racial tensions which agitate Europe; and like that devastated region it has come to understand that our civilization can be saved only when groups, as well as nations, learn cooperation in inter-dependence. . . .
>
> We still retain our national, group, and individual freedom. There is no intention here to change the meaning of this sacred Independence Day; only the hope of tying-in the idea of human cooperation with the idea of human liberty. We must learn to be free *with* others, rather than merely free *from* others.[56]

This was "inter-racialism." America and Los Angeles were the United Nations, composed of race-nations that could as easily make war as peace. Only cooperation and a positive attitude would keep that possible war at bay.

Fifteen thousand citizens joined Bowron at the Bowl that day, even more than at the first 1938 "I Am an American" panegyric. They also heard from U.S. Supreme Court associate justice Frank Murphy. Murphy spoke about the necessity and reality of "inter-dependence." "Our boys have not offered up their lives to provide safe haven at home to intolerance and persecution," he said. "Ours is now the spiritual battle, the battle against all the manifestations of the Nazi disease we may find among our own people." He called on Angelenos to be on the watch for "the symptoms of moral decay," which included "the exaltation of any race, or nationality as superior to all others" and "the denial of the right of minority groups to compete in any way with the privileged groups." Racial concerns were not the whole of Murphy's list of symptoms: those signs of moral decay also included disparaging freedom of the press and religion, glorification of war, and contempt for parliamentary institutions. The linchpin of Murphy's agenda, however, was the encouragement of racial tolerance and acceptance. "The melting-pot philosophy," Murphy said, "with its implications of reduction to a grey uniformity has given way to a new emphasis. American civilization encourages and embodies the contributions of the various cooperating national and cultural groups in the United States in the way that a symphony orchestra creates a rich and complex harmony through the contribution of each instrument with its specific qualities of tonality and timbre. In this way we achieve cultural variety within the larger unity provided by our common language, economy, and political institutions." Racial differences would not disappear. They were to be embraced—albeit as "national and cultural groups"—but embraced nonetheless. Yet by embracing those differences, Murphy told the gathered throng, a "larger unity," that of "American civilization," could be achieved. It was a new vision of America and Los Angeles: not simple and efficient, nor stunningly unified, but complex and divided and making harmony together.[57]

The violent treatment of the Japanese and Japanese Americans and Mexicans and Mexican Americans were powerful lessons for the city and its white residents. Particularly for the elite, the ugly racial conflicts during the war clarified a new possible way of seeing Los Angeles—as a city of distinct, conceivably warring racial groups each of which, like a nation, represented a potentially significant political power. In the case of the Japanese and Japanese Americans, that potential power was squelched by their removal; the internment was designed to prevent them from exerting their strength. Likely because of the United States' alliance with Mexico, in the case of the Mexicans and Mexican Americans, that power was recognized.

As County Supervisor Ford wrote, the international context of the war made him view the domestic scene with new eyes. When "the whole of Latin America became acutely sensitive to the disparity between our professed democratic ideals and some of our practices," Ford indicated, ". . . we [began] discovering the folly of racial discrimination."[58]

Following the Zoot Suit Riots, the city government began a series of reforms to address the Mexican American "situation." "For the first time in the twentieth century," historian Escobar noted, "the city's elite focused on the issue of race relations, providing forums in which Mexican Americans and other minority groups could air their grievances." In 1944 the city established a Human Rights Commission to formalize the handling of racial issues, and in 1949 Edward Roybal was elected to the city council as the first councilperson of Mexican descent. While Escobar indicated that the commission and Roybal's election did not suddenly transform the treatment of Mexican Americans in the city, they represented "an understanding by local political leaders that they needed to respond to [the Mexican American] community."[59]

The aftermath of the war also proved a watershed for Japanese Americans. Bowron admitted the internment had been "a great error and injustice" and apologized to the internees for having doubted their allegiances. Furthermore, leading black, Filipino, Jewish, and Korean figures joined the effort to help facilitate their return. Shortly after the war, when a group of Californians put a proposition on the ballot to reinscribe the laws preventing Japanese landholding, the Japanese American Citizens League led a successful effort to defeat the initiative, and within a decade, all major laws and court decisions against ethnic Japanese were revoked. As historian Ronald Takaki pointed out, the war marked a definitive turning point in the struggle for Japanese American civil rights.[60]

While nothing as vivid as the riots or internment framed the war for African Americans in Los Angeles, the new ideas of inter-dependence also changed their experience in the city. In the wake of those events Bowron and other officials worked hard to address the needs of blacks in the city, particularly in terms of housing. During the war, the city was flooded with a mass arrival of African American migrants. They crowded into the old black neighborhood along Central Avenue and took over the former Japanese neighborhood in downtown Los Angeles: the blocks that were once known as Little Tokyo now were renamed Bronzeville. None of the housing was adequate for the enlarged population. Bowron created a housing committee, to which he appointed a leading black businessman as chair, and he fought to get federal funds to create public housing. (By 1944 he had also created the Committee on Home Front Unity, for which half of the members were African American.)[61]

The war also transformed the goals and strategies of African Americans themselves. During the war, local leaders used the ideological framework of the war to challenge successfully discriminatory hiring practices at the local United States Employment Service and the streetcar company. Following the war, blacks in the city demonstrated "a new assertiveness," according to historian Josh Sides. In particular, they launched "unprecedented challenges to the racial boundaries of the city's public spaces." These long, often ugly battles involved wide-ranging efforts to integrate residential neighborhoods and workplaces, as well as beaches, theaters, and restaurants. The war's impact on those battles was perhaps most explicit in the fights about integrating residential neighborhoods. Supervisor Ford, for instance, referred to the war in advocating integration. In the spring of 1944, when a neighbor and constituent of Ford's sent him a petition to exclude "non-Caucasians" from their neighborhood, Ford wrote back that "somehow when our boys are fighting Hitler so heroically, I cannot bring myself to take the step you ask because it certainly is walking on the same path of racial intolerance that his bloody feet have trod."[62] Hitler's fascism illuminated restrictive covenants as race hatred.

At the same time, Ford also argued that segregation dangerously provoked the potential violent power of racial groups. In 1946, when Ford joined his fellow county supervisors in passing a resolution to support the lifting of race-restrictive residential covenants, he received angry letters from irate constituents. Ford wrote back and described the danger of blocking the "normal expansion" of "colored people" by covenants. "This makes for a social condition which some day may explode because any group of individuals, minority or majority, will only stand suppression and 'compression' so long."[63] Geographic containment could create a situation of potential war—race war or race-nation war—and that was just the thing to be avoided.

To be clear, it was not simply that race relations were now a new political issue. It was that racial groups—understood in multiple contexts as race-nations—were beginning to be recognized, even if only grudgingly, as political players or forces themselves; their needs demanded attention. Los Angeles politicians who had managed to avoid the ethnic politics so dominant in other cities were now forced to acknowledge a very different situation: their "white spot" of a city constituted an aggregation of racial groups that required mediation. Inter-dependence was the answer to the emergence of race-nationhood. As the world war drew to a close, racial groups were taking and being accorded new political power, and the notion of a citizenry composed in part of multiple minority groups took deeper root.

RACE ON THE LEFT:
THE CIVIL RIGHTS CONGRESS AND
EMPATHIC ANALOGIES OF RACE

As the world war faded in memory, however, and the Cold War expanded, the wide support for inter-racialism fractured. Political equality was not conferred upon the city's racial minorities. Nonetheless, or perhaps because of that, the left in Edendale continued to fight aggressively for racial equality and the ideal of inter-racial interdependence. In 1946, in one of the first postwar electoral struggles that focused on race, neighborhood activists coordinated a successful recall of the local city councilman, Meade McClanahan, for his support of Gerald L. K. Smith. Smith had inherited the leadership of Louisiana senator Huey Long's populist movement of the 1930s after Long was assassinated. But beyond the Share the Wealth ethic he helped promote, Smith also emerged as a leading anti-Semitic, anti-black, and anti-Communist demagogue. Smith appeared repeatedly in Los Angeles in the waning days of World War II and seemed to receive shelter from Councilman McClanahan. McClanahan, who had defeated the left-leaning Joseph Aidlin for the council seat, organized several Smith events, appeared on the platform with him, and was rumored to have tried to give him the key to the city.[64]

A citywide campaign—led by the Mobilization for Democracy—quickly formed to oppose Smith and block him from speaking in the city. With Olson's liberal attorney general, Robert Kenny, as honorary chair and Carey McWilliams the designated treasurer, the organization coordinated protests against Smith. Activists gathered at mass meetings and in enormous pickets outside his speaking engagements. In Edendale the left quickly began to publicize both Smith's positions and McClanahan's support. One local "action letter" published a double-column "Special Gerald L. K. Smith Exposé," which ran quotations from Hitler down one column, with parallel remarks from Smith in the adjoining column. Because of his embrace of Smith, neighborhood activists set their sights on removing McClanahan from office. Within a year, they succeeded, organizing a recall drive

Mobilization for Democracy moved aggressively against Gerald L. K. Smith whenever he appeared in the city and against his supporter on the city council, Meade McClanahan. The Mobilization linked racism with fascism, continuing the wartime argument that Americans must necessarily be anti-racist. (Los Angeles Daily News Collection, Department of Special Collections, Charles E. Young Research Library, University of California, Los Angeles.)

that convinced nearly 60 percent of district voters to choose someone new. In McClanahan's place, the district elected a leftist-backed twenty-eight-year-old war veteran named John Roden, who had a brief tenure on the council.[65]

Beyond such a high-profile campaign, however, the more significant and typical battles against racism in the area were waged under the auspices of the Civil Rights Congress, or CRC. Within the CRC, the Party's set of equivalent analogies for explaining racial issues remained in continual operation but were applied to much lower profile situations. Formed in 1946, the CRC was a Communist-led organization whose membership extended beyond Party members. The organization grew out of the merger of the National Negro Congress, the International Labor Defense, and the National Federation for Constitutional Liberties, and therefore combined broad concerns on racial equality, labor rights, and civil liberties. Often focused on criminal cases that involved false charges, excessive punishments, and sloppy trials, the CRC fought for its goals for ten years, both through court cases and mass actions, such as picket lines, demonstrations, letter-writing campaigns, and petition drives. Its reliance on mass movement activities distinguished the CRC from the NAACP and American Civil Liberties Union, with whom it frequently shared its battles. The organization was a loud voice in the fight for civil liberties, even though it was often smeared for its ties to the Communist Party.[66]

In Los Angeles, the local chapter drew from the ranks of the anti-Smith Mobilization for Democracy. Like the national chapters, the local one strove to defend labor activists, leftists, blacks, and Mexican Americans, and framed these goals as analogous. The CRC caseload was thus wide and varied. The group's files included people arrested for speaking in Pershing Square, black youths framed with marijuana, people arrested from their homes for robberies they denied committing, individuals being deported to Canada, and people who were beaten or threatened by the police. In Gerald Horne's history of the organization, he explained that the Los Angeles office was consistently cited as one of the most active and successful branches in the nation. In 1952 the national secretary, Aubrey Grossman, noted the strength of the Los Angeles organization and its successful recruitment of some two hundred people per month. Similarly the Los Angeles CRC lawyers' panel had one of the strongest records: in 1950, fifty-three lawyers tackled ninety-eight cases, and by April they had already successfully concluded thirty-five with only three resulting in unfavorable conclusions. Tellingly, the bulk of the cases involved racial discrimination and police brutality against minorities: the activists were leaders in the fight against racism.[67]

The Los Angeles chapter grew steadily and federalized into smaller branches around the city. An Echo Park chapter began in 1948, and in 1951 an East Hollywood chapter formed, both of which covered portions of Edendale. These smaller chapters relied heavily on the Party framework in its treatment of racial groups as equivalent race-nations and in its view of racism as part of a wide system of colonial oppression. The first six months of 1952 were representative. The previous year had ended with racist and religious bombings and murders in Florida, including the killing of Harry Moore, state secretary of the NAACP, in Mims, Florida. The Echo Park CRC felt both outraged by and implicated in these events, and in reaction they sent protest telegrams from their public meetings to the Florida governor, President Truman, and Secretary of State Dean Acheson. The East Hollywood chapter issued a leaflet that ran headlines across the top linking the Christmas killing of Moore and the shooting of a handcuffed prisoner by a sheriff in Florida with a local guilty verdict against a man in neighboring Riverside. "These acts of violence cannot be separated from 11 other bombings in Florida of Jewish Synagogues and of a Catholic Church. The implications involve us all. We are all responsible for what happens to our fellow citizens and our first defense is to fight back with all who are attacked." Clearly, the CRC leaders perceived and articulated a wide web of involvement and implication: persecution on one side of the country three thousand miles away troubled them and called them into action. Additionally the persecution of an array of groups—in this case, blacks, Jews, and Catholics—was all the same, each analogous to the others, each linked to the others. The CRC leaders saw Jewish and black persecution as related struggles that marked out the contours of a joint cause and a need for a joint reaction.[68]

The activists responded in a similar fashion that same March when two bombs rocked West Adams, nearly killing two families on Dunsmuir Avenue. West Adams, once one of the wealthiest white neighborhoods in Los Angeles, was several miles south of Edendale and was becoming integrated. Within a ten-second interval at four o'clock on a Sunday morning, two bombs exploded across the street from each other on residential Dunsmuir. On one side lived William Bailey, an African American science teacher and recent war veteran, along with his wife and child; they had moved into the neighborhood in January after purchasing a small bungalow home. Their front room, where their child usually slept, was destroyed. On the other side lived the Hartsteins, a Jewish family living in a duplex recently sold to another black family.[69]

These bomb blasts reverberated among the Edendale activists. Through the lens of analogies, they perceived and explained the events as yet another part of a series of attacks on black, Jewish, Mexican, and Japanese families that had begun the prior year and were inspired, they felt, by the speeches of Gerald L. K. Smith. On the one hand, the activists pointed to analogous local practices, noting that "the Los Angeles police have taken no steps to halt these bombings. How can they be expected to do so when they themselves have participated in physical attacks on the Negro and Mexican people?" On the other hand, they saw the events in a national framework. As one leaflet read, "Yesterday, Mims, Florida. Today, Dunsmuir Avenue, LA. Tomorrow, It will be YOUR street."[70]

One of the regular analogies the CRC made was between Jews and blacks or Mexicans. A leaflet announcing a meeting about the Dunsmuir bombings declared, for instance, "Such attacks have a special meaning for the Jewish people in our community as well as the Mexican people and other minorities. To permit this example of growing Southern terrorism to go unchallenged and unpunished is to encourage its spread by Ku-Kluxers and white supremacists." Similarly, when the CRC spoke of anti-black and anti-Mexican police harassment, it often used the word "genocide," a term coined late in the Second World War largely in reaction to Hitler's campaign against European Jews. In this way, not only did the organization make the multiple discriminations seem analogous, but it also tapped into many of the members' sense of themselves as Jews. Party members have typically been described as secular Jews, oriented much more to the Party than to Judaism. Edendale members do not seem to be an exception. In her family, Miriam Sherman recalled, May Day was treated with more reverence than the Jewish High Holy Days. Nevertheless, in analogizing the persecution of Mexicans, blacks, and Jews, the CRC was articulating a framework that allowed a large portion of their membership to see themselves in the people for whom they were fighting. The analogy was thus personal as well as conceptual.[71]

These analogies demanded empathy and identification from white leftists, and thus, racism—or "white chauvinism"—within Party organizations themselves constituted a crucial obstacle to the effective empathic application of these analogies. As a result, white chauvinism received serious group attention in the Los Angeles CRC in the early 1950s. One Sunday in the summer of 1952, the Echo Park CRC organized a ten-hour full-day workshop on "White Chauvinism and Genocide." The invitation to the workshop made several familiar connections. First, it set up a framework of the "rising tide of war and fascism" in which the work of defending rights and liberties was becoming increasingly important. Second, it argued that

> to effectively fight the possible annihilation of the world, we must develop a greater sensitivity and alertness to the abuses of civil rights on national and political minorities. We must be particularly aware of the genocidal attacks

against the Negro and Mexican people who are the first to be hit by reaction in its attack on the rights of the people as a whole.

The key to progress in fighting reaction is Negro-white unity, but we have found from experience that one of the main stumbling blocks to this unity is a disease which has been bred into us by the ruler of our country—white chauvinism.

"White chauvinism" marked the limit of the empathic analogies.[72]

As Paulette Frishkoff, the chapter chair, explained at the start of the workshop, in order to achieve "real unity between all peoples, white chauvinism must be eradicated." Elizabeth Porter, a black neighborhood resident, was the keynote speaker. Porter explained that she experienced "white chauvinism" in her life every day, and that peace and democracy could not be achieved until she too had freedom, peace, and democracy. She emphasized the international analogies, connecting the domestic goal of racial equality with global battles for colonial liberation.[73]

A discussion following Porter's remarks shifted the focus from the conceptual to the personal and practical. Participants revealed their own personal experiences of "white chauvinism," and a questionnaire was circulated. It insisted that the fight against "white chauvinism" needed to be constant, and it asked, "Are you making a real fight against white chauvinism, 24 hours a day, every day?" It then listed forty-two questions that probed steadily into personal details of daily living, ranging from "Are you a member of the NAACP?" to a sequence of queries asking, "What have you done about—Restrictive covenants and lily-white neighborhoods?" or "—Seeing that your market hires a Negro checker?" or "—Bringing your Negro friends into social contact with your white friends, with your non-progressive white friends?"[74]

The group finally agreed that their failure to organize blacks or to convince them to picket or sign petitions was ultimately due to their own "white chauvinism." They themselves were the obstacles. According to the workshop minutes, the group set out not only to build "personal friendships with the Negro people" but also "to identify ourselves with what is happening to our Negro brothers and sisters" and "to realize the life and death struggle not only for the Negro people but also for the white people."[75] The CRC was demanding greater identification and deeper empathy—a stronger belief in the equivalences of the analogies—from its members. They needed to recognize that fundamentally their social and political oppressions were the same. These individual changes were necessary to create political change.

According to Horne's history of the CRC, this workshop and other efforts placed the East Hollywood chapter far ahead of the rest of the national organization on the "Negro Question." The workshop's final list of practical goals—building black-white friendships, expanding the efforts to fight housing discrimination in the neighborhood, pressing for the hiring of black schoolteachers and librarians, and placing black women on executive boards—marked the chapter as the CRC avant-garde. Around the country, other chapters were much slower to link race issues with nonracial political goals. In Edendale, however, making the case for the existence of systemic racism and connecting that racism to wider political practices was a vital motivating principle. This was the ideology that the Party articulated and that drew neighborhood people into left organizations like the CRC.[76]

In Edendale, this ideology was widely expressed and acted upon. Particularly the sequences of empathic analogies—blacks and Mexicans to Jews, blacks and Mexicans to Communists, blacks and Mexicans to nations, and blacks and Mexicans to whites—established a framework that correlated communities and their attached group identities. Fundamentally, the system of analogies divided up local society into a series of comparable categories. The CRC framework suggested, in a sense, that everybody was in some kind of equivalent category. That was the analysis of society that the CRC promulgated.

LIMITS OF DEMOCRATIC TOLERANCE

Despite the left's ongoing work and the expanding notion of racial tolerance, inter-racialism inspired great hostility. Even though the mayor declared the city to be a United Nations of races before a Hollywood Bowl crowd of thousands, the notion of society as divided among multiple analogous social groups did not sit easily with many white Los Angeles residents. They adamantly rejected the ideals of inter-racial interdependence and the CRC's program of change.

The tenor of that hostility surfaced, for instance, in the correspondence between Supervisor Ford and one constituent, attorney Kemper Campbell. Campbell gave voice to the threat that inter-racialism and Ford's notions of democratic tolerance implied. In such a climate, he feared, "the danger now is not that minorities will not be afforded equal opportunity but that we may be ruled by minorities. It will mean viciously bad government for us if we get into the frame of mind to which minorities are endeavoring to persuade us that all races are the same, that there are no differences, in the hope that we will ignore their deficiencies and differences and permit them to attain positions of power and oppression over the majority."[77]

Campbell was hardly unique in resisting the equivalencies that the left and the CRC promoted. In fact, despite his speech making, Mayor Bowron grew increasingly conflicted about the broad implications of "interdependence." While he himself had articulated the United Nations vision of America and insisted to a group of Japanese American war veterans that they were "again citizens of our city. . . . There are no longer any lines of demarcation," he also bemoaned what he felt was a heightened level of group conflicts. In the fall of 1946 Bowron spoke to a local Kiwanis club, complaining about the lack of unity in the city. He attributed its source to "parlor pinks." "We have conflicts in races, colors, religions. We have all of those problems that are indigenous to those who form themselves in organizations and submit to leadership, generally on the part of persons who call themselves liberal but who for the most part are radicals and talk about minority groups." Bowron wanted a milder inter-racialism, one in which conflicts between races did not exist.[78]

Opponents of inter-racialism consistently criticized it as a Communist-inspired ideal, and leftists were taken to task for advocating too drastic a change in the city's racial structure. In fact, Bowron turned quickly against the left-leaning Mobilization for Democracy, which had spearheaded the campaign to keep Gerald L. K. Smith from speaking in the city. Although Bowron had initially supported their efforts against Smith, when the organization began rallying and leafleting in the fall of 1946 to protest a rise in Ku Klux Klan activity, Bowron called on the county grand jury to investigate this "Communist-inspired group . . . [whose] main objective is to stir up the local population, particularly Negroes and Jews, and cause as much distrust of established government as possible." He even encouraged the editor of *Readers' Digest* to investigate the Los Angeles situation, because he was so convinced that Communists, "under the pretext of elimination of racial prejudice, are glorifying these Negroes and turning their heads." Communists were encouraging a dangerous racial pride among blacks. With their agenda, they were not merely "attempting to break down deed restrictions or restrictive covenants so that Negroes may live in all residential sections of the city, all of which is bad enough"—all of which, that is, threatened the delicate détente among the city's racial groups. In addition, he complained, "they are frightening Negroes with the Ku Klux Klan bogey and making communists out of them."[79] In Bowron's eyes, too much racial tolerance was now viewed as a signal of Communist infiltration.

Pushing too hard for racial interdependence was one of the central criticisms that were heaped on Los Angeles Communists in the early years of the Cold War, but hardly the only one. While the wartime alliance with the Soviet Union had led to a diminishment of anti-Communist activity, the war's conclusion had brought back the old refrains. Soon enough, as fears of domestic Communism were generated throughout American society, the California legislature considered bills for registering Communists, requiring oaths of allegiance, and outlawing the Communist Party. Locally the city council pushed the housing authority to evict a Communist family from a public housing project in Griffith Park, on the northern edge of Edendale. The council also adopted a resolution urging Congress and the state to outlaw the Communist Party, and initially, County Supervisor Ford himself said that he was "in full sympathy with the spirit of it." In 1947 the county Board of Supervisors established its own employee loyalty oath: it was the first in the country, and a wave of loyalty legislation and investigations followed, sweeping the city, county, state, and nation.[80]

The resurgence of anti-Communism had a wide reach in the city, destroying careers and personal lives alike. Bowron himself was ultimately voted out of office—after nearly fifteen years—because he advocated public housing for the city, a program that was cast as Communist by its opponents.[81] Anti-Communist persecution also reached directly into Edendale. FBI agents began asking residents about the activities of their neighbors. Boy Scout leaders drove a leftist family from their troop. School children taunted their classmates who were red diaper babies.

In Edendale anti-Communist persecution most dramatically reshaped the lives of Serril Gerber and Miriam Brooks Sherman. Gerber, who had moved from South Dakota at age sixteen, was one of the original residents of the Avenel co-op and had been very active in the Party and the peace movement. After the war, he finished college at UCLA and, in 1948, began teaching in the Los Angeles school system. In 1953 he was teaching sixth grade at Evergreen Elementary School when he was summoned to the principal's office, handed a subpoena to appear before the House Un-American Activities Committee, and suspended. Two years earlier Gerber had denounced the loyalty oath programs while testifying before a Senate committee investigating Communism in the public schools, saying, "Few Communists ever will be discovered through the fact that they do or do not sign a loyalty oath. At the same time, the enforcing of the oath might keep some able professional people from entering the teaching field." When called before HUAC, he refused to state whether or not he was a Communist, and was fired. Gerber's name was in the paper, and his home on Avenel came "under fire. People began throwing things at the house." The neighbors down the street would not let their son play with Gerber's son, and his daughter was devastated, frightened about "what everyone must think of her." "A part of me was feeling I was heroic, I did the right thing," Gerber later recalled. "But that only lasts a few minutes. Every day the family has to eat; you don't have any money." It was two or three years before Gerber landed work as a teacher again, at a private school. In the meantime, he took odd jobs at markets, and the family lived off the retirement money that he had accumulated. "It was painful and it was desperate."[82]

For Miriam Brooks Sherman, the rise of postwar anti-Communism was equally dramatic. Sherman, whose father had died from police-inflicted injuries in 1934, remained ardent in her activism after the war, fighting vehemently for the integration of the Bimini Baths and becoming the Party's membership secretary for all of Los Angeles. In October 1948 Sherman was subpoenaed and then detained by the county grand jury for refusing to give information about the Party. The jury also detained Dorothy Healey and eight other activists, and the ten defendants, who became known as the Los Angeles Ten, were the first Communists to use the Fifth Amendment strategically as a courtroom shield. While Sherman and another young mother in the group were allowed to return home, the other eight were held in jail for a week and then all ten were formally charged with contempt and sentenced to a year's imprisonment. Sherman's conviction was overturned on appeal, and she survived the case, although for much of that time FBI officers trailed her and her family.[83] Then, however, she was caught in the storm of loyalty oaths.

The wave of enforced oaths and affidavits reached up into all academic echelons, affecting universities like Harvard, Yale, the University of Washington, and the University of California. Both Sherman and her sister Eleanor were employed in the Physical Education Department at UCLA; her sister, who had danced with the Lester Horton Company in the 1930s, began teaching dance there in 1944, and Sherman, who played the piano, joined the department as an accompanist two years later. The University of

California tried to establish a loyalty oath for its employees in 1949, but faced heated opposition from the faculty through much of that year and into 1950. During the contretemps in March 1950, state senator Jack Tenney, who had fought with Sherman in his own days as a songwriter and musicians' union leader and had subsequently become the state's leading anti-Communist figure, named Sherman as a Communist to the university president, Dr. Robert Sproul. Tenney also shared his information with the press, which published excerpts of his letter to Sproul and copies of Sherman's voter registration forms indicating her Communist declaration.[84]

For four weeks, the university investigated Sherman's Communist activities. Outraged, Sherman issued a public statement decrying Tenney's efforts to be "finger-man" for the university and to "dictate the cultural and educational standards of our community." She also made clear that she would sue the university if it fired her, insisting that "a person's political beliefs are a private matter." She did not have the chance to test that argument, however. The university sidestepped the Communist issue altogether and fired Sherman in mid-April 1950, under a rule guarding against nepotism. The fact that she and her sister worked in the same department violated a previously overlooked personnel policy. She had no grounds to challenge them.[85]

Sherman, like Serril Gerber, lost her job but avoided jail and was physically unharmed. Nevertheless, the state had stepped in to define the implications of her being a Communist. Clearly she had already organized much of her life around that label—fighting for racial equality, marrying Party members, and organizing hundreds of events. Now, however, while the wider public followed her case under banner headlines on the front pages of the city's daily papers, the state stepped in to alter the meaning of Sherman's self-made label. Being a Communist, they said, meant that Sherman could not participate in the wider public sphere.

Home-front Los Angeles during World War II and the early Cold War carried the question of identity quite explicitly to the level of groups and communities. The wartime conflicts enacted the power and significance of group identities, of essences writ large. Those battles, in a sense, gave shape to inter-racialism not merely as a contentious ideology but as a lived reality. As both an ideal and a lived experience, inter-racialism suggested that Los Angeles did not contain an easily unified population, but rather a fragile United Nations of social groups interdependent on one another. The strongest and clearest proponents of inter-racialism as ideology were the

Communists, who articulated a notion of racial groups as possessing the rights and powers of nations. Yet that notion of racial groups' power was also put into practice, albeit less self-consciously, by the political leaders of the city. Their embrace of such a notion of racial powers led, on the one hand, to the internment of Japanese residents and Japanese American citizens during the war and, on the other hand, to the first political recognition of Mexicans and Mexican Americans in the city. Inter-racialism as an ideology and an approach to city politics had a significant impact. Nonetheless, inter-racialism won at least as many enemies as friends and its loudest proponents soon came under heated attack. As the country developed strategies to contain Communism abroad, American Communists found themselves and their ideas once again under siege.

Yet inter-racialism, as pressed by the Communists and dramatized by the race riots and internment, ultimately addressed more than racial concerns.[86] It offered a clear and powerful model of group politics rooted in identity. Those identities, honed by state-sponsored oppression, provided the foundation for political action either by group members themselves or by others on their behalf. As equivalent oppressed social minorities, African Americans, Mexican Americans, Jews, Japanese Americans, and even Communists themselves had the right to resist discrimination and demand some version of self-rule. That model of analogous oppressions and analogous political rights created a central framework for identity-driven political action and opened the possibility for groups other than racial groups to lay claim to a similar equivalent position. Indeed, this notion of analogous oppressions and equivalent minorities proved crucial in the conception of homosexuals—individuals identified by their innermost emotions and desires—as an oppressed social minority. That notion of analogous minorities further paved the way for the birth of Mattachine.

Mattachine members, photographed by Jim Gruber, meeting at Harry Hay's house on Cove Avenue. Hay was so concerned about secrecy that Gruber had to convince him that there was no film in the camera when he took the picture: he revealed the truth only years later. Top: Harry Hay; bottom from left to right: Dale Jennings, Rudi Gernreich, Stan Witt, Bob Hull, Chuck Rowland (in glasses), and Paul Bernard. (Courtesy John Gruber.)

SIX

Getting Some Identity

Mattachine and the Politics of Sexual Identity Construction

IN THE WINTER OF 1952, early in the Cold War, five Mexican American boys in Echo Park—toward the southern end of Edendale—got into a fight with the police. One of the boys was shot, two were beaten, and all five were arrested. The case came to the attention of the neighborhood leftists. Under the auspices of the Edendale Civil Rights Congress, they launched a defense campaign for the boys. The CRC framed its case in an open letter to the community. In now familiar language, they argued that the violence and arrests "fit into the pattern of the increasing crime of genocide being committed against Mexican and Negro people." This was a case about racial groups or race-nations under siege. The CRC also insisted that "if police entrapment and outrage can happen to these youths without community protest and action, then it can happen to anyone." Everyone was vulnerable to police harassment, they suggested, and thus everyone could belong to equivalently oppressed social groups.[1]

Another local organization joined the CRC efforts that winter. Called the Citizens' Committee to Outlaw Entrapment (CCOE), this second group wrote the civil rights group repeatedly and attended a public hearing about the police action. It presented itself as being in full sympathy with the Mexican American cause, contending that speaking out on entrapment then would "cover all minorities."

But the list of minorities that the CCOE had in mind was larger than the one even the CRC had been focused on for the previous several years. Beyond the Jews, the Communists, the blacks, and the Mexicans, the CCOE now wanted the civil rights group to pay attention to homosexuals. And to convince them to do so, the Citizen's Committee began to articulate the claim that homosexuals were an equivalent oppressed social minority, analogous to all the others. Homosexuals shared an equivalent identity to racial groups, and an analogous political position in society. The CCOE proposal marked the first claim of a new, broader emotion-centered politics of identity.

In truth, the CCOE existed only on letterhead. It was the adoptive name of an organization born in Edendale during the winter of 1950–51. That organization, the Mattachine Society, was tentatively stepping into the world of politics under the guise of the CCOE. In doing so, Mattachine members both continued the legacy of their Edendale neighbors and built upon it. Like the artists, they worked to find a medium for expressing their innermost dreams and desires and to make those desires socially relevant. Like the Communists, they focused their attention on aiding and defending an oppressed minority within the local society. And like both groups, they self-consciously built a community and set of organizations to support these efforts. But they also expanded the leftist mandate. The minority they focused on was not oppressed because of their economic or racial status—the more familiar forms of American social oppression. This minority—which they referred to as homosexuals or homophiles—was oppressed for their sexual desires and actions.

That oppression was widespread and growing. The war mobilization laid the groundwork for a national effort to eliminate homosexuals from public life. During the war itself, a host of psychologists and psychiatrists had convinced military leaders that they could help limit the number of soldiers suffering from psychological ailments as a result of the fighting. One of their principal strategies was to prevent homosexually active men and women from serving, and they began questioning recruits about their sex lives in order to weed out the homosexually active as mentally unfit.[2]

In the wake of the war, the systematic persecution of such men and women expanded exponentially, moving well beyond the military. As historians like John D'Emilio, Robert Dean, and David Johnson have demonstrated, the early Cold War years witnessed the elaboration of a culture of hyper-masculinity as part of the American defense against Communism. Horrified by the success of Communism in places like China and by the expansion of Soviet dominance in Poland and Czechoslovakia, federal officials began to view homosexuality as a threat that was linked to Communism and equivalent to it in danger. Their fears were heightened when, in 1948, Alfred Kinsey shocked the nation with research indicating that more than one-third of American men had participated in some kind of homosexual behavior and that up to 10 percent did so relatively exclusively for several years. Provoked by growing anxieties, officials moved aggressively to expand and invigorate the political culture of the late 1930s. Homosexuality, suddenly seen as rampant, was widely deemed a sign of moral weakness; those who engaged in it were considered vulnerable to Communist brainwashing and blackmail. Even more, they were seen as infectious.[3]

While the pockets of American life that came under scrutiny for harboring political subversives were legion, both the executive and legislative branches also organized consistent attacks on "perverts" as indicative of the hard line they were taking to protect the United States from the moral weakness that could undermine the nation. Indeed, while the Red Scare of the McCarthy era has dominated historical memory, it occurred in conjunction with and was entangled with a Lavender Scare during which federal officers developed stringent policies to remove "homosexuals" from the civil service, particularly the State Department. From Congress and the Federal Employee Review Board all the way down to local police bureaus, homosexuals along with Communists were hunted with vigor, fired from their jobs, and banned from public positions. So dramatic was the Lavender Scare that within nine months of Senator Joseph McCarthy's infamous speech announcing 205 known Communists in the federal government, nearly 600 civil servants were fired or forced to resign. But the bulk of them were pushed out on charges of homosexuality, not Communism.[4]

The war years had expanded visible homosexual activity in cities around the country, and Los Angeles was no exception. The rapid growth in population that the war produced—and particularly the increase of single service men and women—led to an expansion of arenas for homosexually active men and women to meet one another. These years were the heyday of "The Run," the group of bars and cruising spots that crept through downtown Los Angeles from the dives along Main Street to the bushes and trees of Pershing Square. Sailors and soldiers flocked to Pershing Square, known to be a pick-up area, and many more poured into the bar of the Biltmore, the elegant hotel facing the square. Burt Miller, then twenty-one and stationed outside Los Angeles, told historian Allan Bérubé that one night after dinner he wandered through the Biltmore bar. "About 75 percent of the men were in uniform—and I asked myself, 'Can what I think is going on here *be* going on?' I stopped to find out, and sure enough it was! I was in that bar every night."[5]

But the bar and club scene expanded well beyond downtown during the 1940s and 1950s. Bars sprang up repeatedly around Hollywood, there were female impersonators at the V Club, the If Club on La Brea catered especially to women, and there were several popular bars out at the beaches. A servicemen's guide to the city even recommended The International, a bar out on the Sunset Strip—a stretch of restaurants and clubs that sat between Hollywood and Beverly Hills on a swath of land just outside the city perimeter and thus just beyond the reach of the Los Angeles Police Department. During the 1940s the nightclubs along the Strip—like the Trocadero, Ciro's, and the Mocambo—made the area famous for the wealth and glamour of its clientele. The International, though, run by a woman named Tess who wore make-up and pearls and greeted her guests by the door, catered to what the guidebook described as a "a crowd following theories from the Isle of Lesbos." Servicemen apparently were intrigued by such places.[6]

The Café Gala nightclub also sat just off the Sunset Strip and was one of the most celebrated clubs of the postwar era. Run by a baroness, Catherine d'Erlanger, and Johnny Walsh—a combination manager, doorman, and performer—the Gala was more Hollywood than homosexual, with Venetian decor, white-gloved waiters, performers like Dorothy Dandridge and Bobby Short, and a steady stream of celebrity clientele. Although the club welcomed homosexually active men—even catering to men willing to pay for sex—Walsh also insisted on a dress code, and according to one recollection, he "enforced standards of behavior inside. At the bar, which was often crowded with people—mostly men—two or three deep, Johnny would tell someone to sit facing forward. The inference was obvious: no groping on the premises, which in effect meant, 'Don't provoke the Vice.' " Because behavior was under control and because the bar was along the Strip, the Gala had a long life throughout the 1940s and into the 1950s.[7]

Much like the bars of earlier decades, these bars were rarely exclusively homosexual in their clientele. Even the If Club, much loved as a women's bar, also had many men—not homosexual—in the bar. The police knew about these bars, and as the public life of homosexual activity expanded, the police worked to keep it in check, if not to stamp it out. They were on the lookout for people propositioning each other, touching, dancing together, or even dressing inappropriately. For that reason, a great deal of social activity also occurred in people's homes, and for individuals for whom fears of public attention became too great, homes were the safest places to be. Tom Gibbons and Bob Clark, a couple since the start of the 1950s, felt that private parties were the only place they could let their guard down, particularly in terms of physical affection. Parks were far too dangerous, they thought, and they remained wary whenever they were out at clubs or restaurants. They feared being seen by a coworker while in some kind of compromising position—which might be merely sitting with a loud or outrageous friend. While the men did go out, Gibbons and Clark invested their social energies much more in developing their own peer group of homosexually active men and women.[8]

Gibbons and Clark's fears were legitimate. In Los Angeles, arrests for sex crimes rose sharply in the years following the war and stayed at a high level in the late 1940s and early 1950s, so much so that sections of the Lincoln Heights jail—called the sex tank or fruit tank—were set aside for homosexual arrests. One man, in a letter to a member of Alfred Kinsey's research staff, described being arrested on New Year's Eve 1951–52 and, after pleading guilty to a misdemeanor charge, spending thirty days in a Lincoln Heights cell block with some thirty men convicted of similar sex crimes. The nature of their crimes were well known, and when they were led at meal times past other jail cells, " 'cat-calls' and various and sundry remarks concerning our sex (such as 'get ready for the floor show, here come the girls' . . . 'how about a date' . . . 'get a load of that ass') greet[ed] us."[9]

The stories of his fellow inmates indicate the scope of the effort the Los Angeles police force was then exerting to find, sometimes entrap, and arrest homosexually active men. A young Mexican man who could barely speak English was propositioned by a vice officer on Hollywood Boulevard and then arrested; on the stand, the officer reversed their roles, stating that the non-English-speaking Mexican man had propositioned him—that alone was grounds for arrest. A waiter reported that while he was at a downtown movie house, a man sat next to him and began to touch him; the waiter pushed him off, but a vice officer, working undercover inside the theater and watching the men in the audience, arrested them both. A third man was arrested while looking at another man at a public urinal: they were seen by vice officers who were hiding in the ceiling of the bathroom. A fourth man was arrested in the restroom of the downtown Pacific Electric train station because he watched while a vice officer masturbated at a urinal. Police officers themselves, in multiple contemporary court cases, offered similar accounts of carving peepholes in bathroom walls and lurking in the semi-dark of bathhouse steam rooms. The police poured enormous amounts of energy into stopping men from interacting sexually.[10]

The men in the county jail were frequently not there for engaging explicitly in sex; their arrests more often were for propositioning, showing interest, expressing desire. The punishment for sexual activity could be more dire. Under California law, arrest for one act of oral sex could easily land a man in prison for a term of five years, with a ten-year sentence for sodomy. If more than one act was demonstrated, that sentence could multiply, and in 1950 the California legislature doubled the prison term for a sodomy conviction to twenty years. At the same time, at the end of the 1940s, California moved forward aggressively to establish facilities for hospitalizing "sexual psychopaths." In December 1949, following a conference on sex crimes organized by Governor Earl Warren, the state finalized plans for a thousand-bed maximum-security hospital for sexual psychopaths and the criminally insane two hundred miles north of Los Angeles, as a well as a smaller temporary facility in San Pedro, Los Angeles' harbor community. Calls circulated widely for institutions where "the curable may be rehabilitated"—perhaps through shock treatments or surgery—and "the incurable may be forever confined."[11]

The tactics used against homosexual men were so aggressive that even local Communists, already under siege in the new wave of anti-Communism that culminated in the McCarthy witch hunts, turned against their homosexually active members, fearing that they represented security risks for the Party. Barbara Kaplan, who became an organizational secretary for one of the major Los Angeles districts and was very active in Edendale, remembered there being many such men "in our chapter up in the hills." "And we had to say to them, which killed us because they were wonderful guys, 'They are going to pick you up and they are going to do all kinds of things to you to make you tell who's in the Party. We want to suggest to you that you leave now while you're still OK, before they can identify you.' And they said, 'We don't want to.' I said, 'I know, and we don't want you to. But to protect you, and to protect us, you better do it.' And they left." The Edendale treatment may have been fairly gentle; elsewhere in the country, homosexually active men were vigorously interrogated by Party officials and expelled. Homosexuals were under siege, even from potential allies.[12]

Against this backdrop of state-sanctioned oppression, Mattachine organized a widespread effort to define who homosexuals were and what homosexuality was from the perspective of the men and women who lived it themselves. It would be a mistake, however, to view Mattachine simply as a response to the state-led tactics against homosexually active men and women. Oppression alone did not call homosexual politics into being. Much more fundamentally, Mattachine activists followed in the steps of their neighborhood forebears—the artists and Communists who surrounded them. First and foremost, like the artists, Mattachine members set out to create a medium in which they could express and discuss their inner lives and desires; Mattachine created a forum where sexuality, rather than simply being acted upon, could be talked about and given a public, nonsexual hearing. Once those desires could be expressed and recognized as shared, Mattachine could and did, then, launch a group project of self-definition. Similar to the artists and leftists, Mattachine members made it possible for emotions to become the basis of some other social, cultural, or political formation. At the same time, they drew directly from the leftist analogies that linked Los Angeles racial groups to other groups, locally, nationally, and internationally. Evidenced throughout Los Angeles during the 1940s, the model of distinct, politically identified, and active racial groups became a key model for the Mattachine founders.[13]

Fundamentally, what Mattachine shared with both its neighboring communities was the determination to make a relationship between "essence" and the wider society, between the inner self and politics. Mattachine members took their most intimate feelings and sought to construct a public life around them. That possibility allowed homosexually active men and women to define the significance of their lusts and affections not only for themselves as individuals but also from within an organized community working to challenge the state definitions of homosexuality.

By including a sexual minority in the list of analogous oppressed "nations," Mattachine transformed the meaning of all these groups. They created a new framework for thinking about them that has come to be called identity politics. This was Mattachine's achievement.

IMAGINING A FUTURE

The Mattachine Society was the undeniable offspring of Harry Hay, a friend and Party coworker with Miriam Sherman; its roots lay in his roots. Yet Mattachine was equally the child of Edendale, where Hay lived and where he experienced the same conjunction of artistry and leftist politics that defined the neighborhood. Born in England in 1912, Hay settled with his parents in Los Angeles in the fall of 1919. As Hay's biographer Stuart Timmons wrote, he was a bright and precocious boy, always a year or two younger than his classmates, and he completed high school when he was sixteen. He was also ever eager about sexual experience: at age six he was caught masturbating by his parents, and they forced him to sleep for a year and a half with his hands tied to his bed. As an eleven-year-old in his high school's military training program, he stood naked with his cohort for the semiannual physical, staring at the genitals of two or three attractive boys. "I knew that there was something wonderful and sacred and beautiful, and something that I wanted to do," he later recalled, "but I didn't quite know what it was. Maybe I wanted to touch it, maybe I want to hold it against my cheek. . . . And I'm also aware I'm getting a terrific erection just by watching."[14]

Hay's first sustaining sexual relationship began in February 1930 with a man named Champ whom Hay, just shy of his eighteenth birthday, had encountered in Pershing Square. (He had enjoyed one previous liaison with a man.) It was a wonderful experience, he later reported: "I don't suppose I need to go into the details, but I got beautifully laid." He continued to have sex with men regularly for the next seven or eight years, two of which he spent at Stanford University, before entering the Los Angeles theater world and then the leftist subculture.[15]

At Stanford in the early 1930s, Hay toyed uncertainly with the desire paradigm and the notion that he might possess a consistent and defining sexual identity. In the fall of his sophomore year, he decided to disclose his sexual activities to his friends. "I don't know what it means to be a 'homosexual,' but I think I'm going to tell all my friends and all the people I know that this is what I am." Unlike the florist Herbert Lowe, who fifteen years earlier had fought not only his arrest in Long Beach but also the notion that his sexual activities represented anything more than a vice or a degenerated state that he could fall into or out of, Hay pondered the possibility that his sexual activities did indeed reveal something "essential" about him. In a sense, he took up the lead of L. L. Rollins and even New York City's fairies in suggesting that his sexual desires *did* define the essence of who he was. For the time being, he set aside the fairy paradigm and the notion that gender was a central part of the mix. The possibility that he was imagining was one in which appearances, as *Photoplay* magazine had suggested, were indeed set aside. Instead, like Grace Clements, he sought out his defining "personal landscape." Perhaps sexual desires constituted that inner essence.[16]

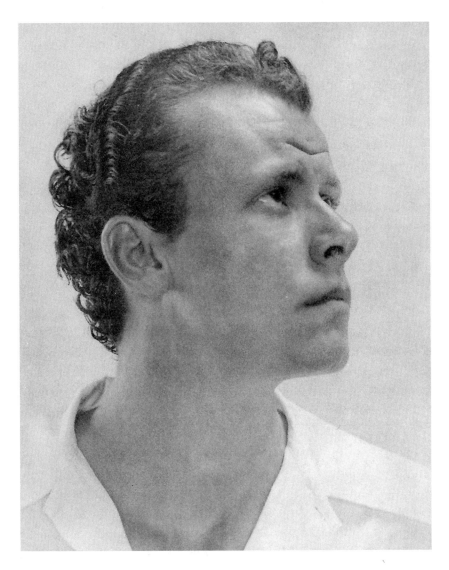

Harry Hay, in a headshot from his early acting days. His experiences in the theater led him, through a relationship with Will Geer, into the world of the Communist Party. (Photograph by Hazel Harvey. Courtesy *Hope along the Wind* and Stuart Timmons.)

Hay's notion, however, was hardly as formulated as all that. He also had in the back of his mind some vague idea that this potential identity might be a shared one. His first lover, a merchant seaman, had told him that they were part of a global "silent brotherhood." He might be traveling in the most foreign place, the seaman explained, lock eyes "across the square" with another man, and realize "you are *home* and you are *safe!*" More a vision of sexual possibility than community solidarity, it was nevertheless elaborated by Champ when, four years later, he described for Hay the efforts of a few Chicago men to form a homosexual social group in the 1920s. That group collapsed in a rash of arrests, and Champ insisted that no one he knew in Los Angeles would be involved in such an endeavor. "But this is the revelation," said Hay: "There aren't just two or three of us in any city, there are lots. And it's heart-warming, and it's wonderful."[17]

Both the seaman's "brotherhood" and Champ's Chicago history spoke to an end to solitude. It would be two decades before Hay articulated an idea of transforming that potential into some kind of active and supportive community. In 1930s Los Angeles there were several possible versions of homosexual identity afoot for Hay to choose from. Nevertheless, even the long affair with Champ did not frame for Hay a clear sense of his "sexual identity" or what might now be called his "gayness." When asked more than once by historian John D'Emilio in 1976 about the process of "discovering your gayness" or even how he had moved "from fantasy to . . . mature homosexual experiences," Hay resisted those codifications. "In our period it's not that easy. It doesn't work that way. I had no words yet." Hay had no way to articulate "gayness" because the idea itself did not exist. "You guys in this generation," he told D'Emilio, "now have many things to put together and you can give them words. In our time, we don't have words, we just have feelings." Hay did not have the conceptual constructs, just desires.[18]

The particular version of identity and community that Hay ultimately adopted was a product of his own involvement with leftist politics and theater. As a youth, Hay fell in love with the world of theater and performance, ushering at and attending as many shows as he could. When he returned to Los Angeles from Stanford, he floated around for a while, hanging out and performing with composer John Cage (of the Ritchie Roadhouse coterie) and eventually acting in local theater. His theater company staged plays such as Clifford Odets's *Waiting for Lefty*, and one show found him acting opposite Will Geer. Geer, the actor, had yet to become friends with Woody Guthrie at this point, but he was already very active in left-wing politics. As a teenager Hay had spent summers working on a relative's ranch, imbibing lessons from other ranch hands about the Industrial Workers of the World, and was thus predisposed to share Geer's leftist ideas. From discussions about politics and theater, the men became lovers. They went to demonstrations together and even once handcuffed themselves to the gates of the old UCLA campus. Soon, the two began performing agitprop street theater around town—putting their art to political purpose, much as Miriam Brooks Sherman did with the Blue Blouses—and ultimately, Geer introduced Hay into the Communist Party.[19]

It was a few years before Hay began to understand the theoretical discussions within the Party, but he was immediately captivated by the action. "I liked the demonstrations. I liked the theater work that we were doing. And I *felt* lots of things, and I felt my way into a relationship with people, because I didn't *understand* anything particularly much." His closest ties were with dancers and other theater folks, especially people who were involved in the Hollywood Theater League and, later, the Hollywood Anti-Nazi League. His connection to the Party always remained very emotional, even when he could later articulate Party goals in terms of principle. Like Sophia Lewis and Dick Nikowskski, who needed to and did love their comrades, Hay felt a strong emotional connection to the men and women who shared the cause. Indeed, in remembering various actions in San Francisco when striking maritime workers shut the city down in May 1934, he recalled that he and Geer traveled north together and that they were present when workers were shot and a funeral procession marched up the central boulevard. "And I was committed from then on, man," Hay later said. "The commitment was not an intellectual one to start with, it was pure emotion. It was a gut thing. You couldn't have been a part of that and not have your life completely changed."[20] Increasingly, political activism did begin to define Hay's life. He participated in Upton Sinclair's 1934 gubernatorial campaign and the recall campaign against Mayor Frank Shaw. Later he joined a Marxist study group through which he began to understand the theory; he found it very exciting.

When Hay's relationship with Geer ended, he continued to envision his ideal partner, or "golden boy," as a similar comrade in arms: "The golden boy has to be one who sees as I see; he has to be somebody who is not afraid of the strike line; he has to be somebody where we can walk shoulder to shoulder and hand in hand and he's not afraid to be beaten up. And if I'm beaten, he won't be worried about me; he'll carry on. He won't be someone that will stop with me: he's got to finish the job." None of his other lovers fit that ambitious description. While Hay was filling with political fervor about social justice, his sexual intimates balked at the idea of action. He did not lack lovers, Hay later explained, "but what I did lack for was lovers with guts. They were people who were hanging back, people who were frightened, people who said, 'Well, there is no way to make social change; we have to relate the best we can.'" Hay's involvement in the left and the Party gave him the capacity to envision and enact change, not around questions of homosexuality yet, but simply in the larger society. When he sought that in a male lover, he instead found political apathy and passivity.[21]

Years later Hay described that apathy to John D'Emilio. In explaining the fear and unwillingness to seek change, Hay insisted, "This is not exactly a closet position, but it's damn close to one." Hay was not seeking a lover who would fight for homosexual freedom; his own thinking had not moved to that point. But his use of the closet metaphor—a phrase emphasized by 1970s gay liberation activists to describe people who kept their homosexual desires and activities a secret—suggested that the notion of a life half-lived or lived in shadows and fear was a rubric familiar to Hay well before he applied himself to changing homosexual life. That is, for Hay, before "the closet" was a gay closet, it was a political closet, and public political action was the thing that people hid from, not being public about their "sexuality."[22] So that when he later called on people to step out of the sexual shadows, that was a trope he knew well.

Meanwhile, Hay was convinced by a psychiatrist to try heterosexual relationships. Apparently still uncertain about whether or not he had a fixed "sexual identity," Hay set out in 1938 to woo a woman, Anita Platky, whom he knew from leftist activities, shows, and demonstrations. His wooing succeeded, even though he told Platky about his sexual history. Together, they imagined a working relationship very much like the other Party marriages. As Platky put it in one letter, "I do want to be with you, work with you, and live with you—start our job of building together, and I can build without attaching paramount importance to sex. I'm pretty sure I can, and you can too." Thus, even though Platky could not be Hay's golden boy, she would very well attempt to be his golden comrade. The same month they married, Hay formally became a Party member. He was twenty-six.[23]

OTHER PATHS

Leftist politics proved a crucial background for starting a homosexual movement. Three of the five Mattachine founders were, like Hay, active

Communist Party members, the other two were fellow travelers, and those that joined their leadership rank were invested in leftist causes. Life on the left schooled Hay and the others both in a vision of a society divided into analogous social groups and in a belief and capacity for enacting social change.

Formally, by 1950 the Party had taken a position against homosexuality. According to Ted Rolfs, who was a few years older than Hay and active in the Marine Cooks and Stewards Union, the earlier Party had no such position, and he remembered a number of Communists who were homosexually active as well. They were "drawn to the Party, to Marxism, simply because it was a rebellious group working for recognition and acceptance. And that, fundamentally, was the same thing that a homosexual, as we used that term in those days, as a gay person was working for: acceptance."[24]

The left, however, was not the only school for imagining social change. Jim Kepner, who joined Mattachine in 1952, participated in the Party from 1945 to 1948. Even prior to that, though, in the early 1940s, he often had conversations with intellectual homosexually active men who were imagining a changed future, "looking toward the day when . . ." In their thoughts, said Kepner, the men projected a kind of classic "science fictional progression": there would be a link between a hope to "get back to like it was with the ancient Greeks" and a plan to "build a better society where we can be freer." For whatever reasons, these men had the imagination to construct something different.[25]

The science fiction paradigm was particularly meaningful for Kepner because science fiction and the science fiction clubs of San Francisco and Los Angeles served as the schools where he learned to imagine a different future. Kepner felt that for those whom the social "straight jacket" does not fit, "we are more likely to dream about or desire worlds that are different; that is, to be science fiction fans or revolutionaries." In fact, Kepner said, "the science fiction clubs were mostly big closets with a few heterosexuals in them."[26]

Kepner felt that there was a significant cultural connection between science fiction and homosexuality. Certainly science fiction, as a literary phenomenon, received treatment similar to that of homosexuality. "It was being written of with embarrassment . . . with contempt," he remembered. "If they talked about science fiction, they would quote a psychoanalyst" who would talk about rockets and ray guns as penis symbols designed to aid in the "escape of heterosexuality." For a time, Kepner toyed with the idea of starting a homosexually themed science fiction magazine, feeling that both issues were "on the cutting edge of the future, that both were critical of the present society, that both were interested in changing things, and that an awful lot of science fiction fans were gays who hadn't come out yet." Ultimately, the magazine that Kepner did devote his energies to, *ONE,* was a spin-off from Mattachine and exclusively a homosexual magazine. Yet the impetus to work on it ran to older roots than Kepner's involvement in the politicization of sexual identity.[27]

Kepner found no way to move from imaginings to action in the 1940s, however. Occasionally, he would say to a lover, "When are we going to organize? We've got to do something about this situation." But the inevitable reaction he received was "The last thing in the world I want to do is get into a room with a bunch of screaming queens." Even Kepner himself was inconsistent in his imaginings. Having witnessed a police raid when he first attempted to enter a gay bar, he had felt a mixture of fear and outrage. Because he had read two or three novels that described bar raids, he had come to feel that they were "something that was taken for granted. If you were in the gay life, then you were playing Russian roulette, and you were relieved if you didn't get caught. . . . That was your chief concern about the affair. After it happened, you weren't particularly angry or anything." In his experience, a bar could be raided regularly, sometimes twice a night, and the crowd would be back in a few minutes, not even really discussing the events. Kepner was among those who returned with little protest.[28]

By contrast, the left provided Hay with the intellectual and organizational tools to transform imaginings into action.

DRAFTING POLITICS

From 1939 to 1942 Hay and Platky lived in New York and were very active in the Party there. Upon hearing about the Japanese submarine attacks off the California coast, however, they decided to return to Los Angeles and participate in the local war effort. They moved first onto Lake Shore Avenue, the area that Hay called Mt. Moscow, with its web of footpaths worn down by activists shuttling between various meetings and events. Eventually they moved into a house atop Cove Avenue, the same street the Reisbords lived on, where Susan knew her neighbors up and down the stairs. They settled onto the same hill where Julian Eltinge had built his mansion twenty-five years earlier, though they found little appeal in Silver Lake Reservoir, which Hay recalled as dirty and full of junk. Soon enough Hay began teaching courses out of his house on political economy, imperialism, and revolution. Additionally, shortly after returning to Los Angeles, the couple, who had discovered that Hay was sterile, adopted first one daughter, and then a second.[29]

Hay and Platky were deeply involved in Edendale's leftist network; its culture and activities filled their lives. Hay's classes were quite successful, and as the war wore on, he helped the Edendale Communists set up the cooperative nursery school. The neighborhood Party club met regularly, working on grocery prices and rent control. Members also took up the issues of restrictive housing covenants, which persisted in the area; labor rights; and ongoing struggles with racial discrimination, particularly at the Bimini Baths. By the fall of 1945, Hay joined Dorothy Healy as a local representative to a Southern California Party conference, and soon thereafter Hay was named education director for their area.[30]

Significantly, during these years Hay's political activity was also artistic. Although no longer working in the theater world, he became involved with People's Song, the organization that developed the musical repertoire that served both as entertainment at many Party functions and as solidarity builder. One local Party member remembered club meetings where they simply stood around the piano and sang songs. During Henry Wallace's 1948 campaign for president, People's Song members went to various meetings and Wallace functions as the entertainment, teaching people rounds and getting them to add their own lines. By 1947 Hay not only was teaching Party dogma but had also begun teaching a folk music class at the People's Education Center.[31]

In many ways, Hay's life embodied the convergence that was Edendale: he was merging his expressive artistic inclinations and political attitudes, and soon enough, his sexual ones as well. Although he and Platky remained married, he began cruising again, looking for sexual liaisons in city parks, including the neighborhood Echo Park. Hay did not participate avidly in the bar scene. Rather, from roughly 1946 on, he increasingly engaged in the world of musicians and writers, and through them he also began dealing with homosexually active men again in a nonsexual way. "And all of a sudden I recognized how comfortable it is, and what a relief it is. And yet we don't have a language and we're not communicating as gay people but we are communicating as sort of people who understand each other because we're all in the Party or all in the left or in the Progressive [Party]; we're all moving in that direction. We sort of sense that there is something with each other."[32]

While researching for his folk music class, Hay stumbled upon the story of the Mattachine Society—a French medieval society of men who always appeared masked, with a leader who wore women's dress. The Mattachines offered themselves up as fools, using satire and improvisation to protest oppression against local peasants. They were also involved in great fertility rituals. Somehow, Hay began to feel that "I know who these people are. They're my antecedents. And wouldn't it be wonderful if we were able to do this again?" In other words, Hay began to think about the possibility of organizing as the French group had. "But we've got to know who we are," he felt. "We really have to understand who we are now."[33]

In the summer of 1948 Hay was invited to a beer party near the University of Southern California, in the neighborhood of the Dunsmuir bombings. The host, who worked at a music shop, wanted Hay to meet a seminarian to discuss musicology. Some two dozen people attended the party, and they all seemed to be, in Hay's terminology, "of the persuasion"—that is, active homosexually. Rather than discussing music, though, Hay started discussing politics, particularly Wallace's presidential bid and the new Progressive Party. In a manner half joking and half serious, people began toying with the idea of starting their own support club and calling it Bachelors for Wallace or Bachelors Anonymous. They imagined they might get a plank on the Progressive platform enforcing privacy in the home or ensuring that homosexual activity would no longer cause people to be hounded out of the State Department.

Hay left the party bubbling with enthusiasm: this was the first time that the vague prospect of the "secret brotherhood" shifted into the realm of real potential. Hardly a bachelor himself, Hay nevertheless borrowed the Party's intellectual style and wrote up a draft plan for the "International Bachelors' Fraternal Order for Peace and Social Dignity." He began by mapping out the threats facing homosexually active men and women. Hay felt that there was a growing trend toward fascism in the federal government, even more dangerous than the McCarthy attacks and purges from the State Department; he thought the government would likely seek out a scapegoat to rally the public. Sensing that neither Jews nor blacks could be easy targets anymore, Hay argued that "homosexuals" were the likeliest candidates. "So it behooved us at this point to begin drawing ourselves together, find out who we were," he later said. "We would then negotiate our position with the parent society as a group, not singly as individuals, but as a group."[34]

Hay's prospectus for the Bachelors' order was elaborate, mapping out aims, activities, membership rules, and organizational structure. Fundamentally, the overall goal was, in spite of "our physiological and psychological handicaps, . . . [to achieve] socially, economically, politically, and morally, the integration of the best interests of the Androgynous minority with the common good of the community in which we live." In part the group would facilitate that integration by working on society itself. They would engage experts and professionals to "eradicate the vicious myths and taboos" and to develop "positive, scientifically predicated, and morale building legislation." At the same time, the organization would work on the membership. Following the model of Alcoholics Anonymous (itself founded in the mid-1930s), the group as a whole would strive to curb "exhibitionism, indiscriminate profligacy, violations of public decency" among its members. Members would not be cured of their homosexual desires, merely the socially disturbing displays of them.[35]

Not surprisingly, Hay also imagined an organization that would be interested in "the constructive social progress of mankind" and thus would join campaigns for peace or make "common cause with other minorities," helping "to supplement community campaigns for minority rights."[36] Like the Party-led, largely white Civil Rights Congress, the Bachelors' society would work on behalf of those whose oppression was analogous to their own.

The Bachelors would achieve all their goals through various committees—educational, public relations, legislative—as well as various therapy and study groups, including "First Aid squads" that would help "members in emotional and psychological distress." Membership would be explicitly open to all races, creeds, and political perspectives, but be offered only on the basis of recommendation. The membership would remain strictly secret, but the members would wear insignia to designate their level of commitment to the organization. Fundamentally, Hay envisioned an organization that would provide "a collective outlet for political, cultural, and social expression to some 10%"—echoing Kinsey's count of American homosexual men—"of the world's population."[37]

Hay's proposal was complex and, in its aspirations, vast. It would change before it became the Mattachine Society, adding in two crucial issues about cultural activities and a sense of self-awareness or identity. Several things are clear, though, about the Bachelors' society. First and foremost, it arrived trailing clouds of politics. Not only did Hay conceive an organization that could carve out a plank in the Progressive Party platform—and then go on to achieve legislative reform—but he was also responding to the political oppression, potential and predicted, of the state. Even though Hay would say his vision had been "fermenting" for years, the politics of the moment provided the fundamental arena in which it suddenly made sense and could be expressed.[38]

Second, while Hay had a vague notion of an "Androgynous minority," it was a distinctly leftist formulation. He referred several times to "Minorities everywhere" and "other minorities" and once made mention of "Jews and Negroes." In this way, his proposal read like a leaflet from the Civil Rights Congress. He was clearly beginning to think in terms of the Party's analogies. The "Androgynous minority" would simply join the list of blacks, Jews, Mexican Americans, and Communists as equally labeled, equally targeted, and equally in need of liberation. Yet Hay offered no definition of who belonged to this minority, nor of what, it might be said, their common "essence" was. In fact, in suggesting that the group might follow the model of the "well-known and respected 'Alcoholics Anonymous,'" Hay opened up the possibility that the androgynes were not as fixed a category as the racial model might suggest. Hay's language, at least, was ambivalent.

Third, the Bachelors group was built around secrecy. Hay stated explicitly in the text that the structure would follow the Masons in many ways. His own inspiration, he later said, though, was also the secret cell system of the Party.[39] Thus he intended to adopt not only some form of the Party's notion of racial groups but its organizational structure as well. Mattachine could be, in a sense, the conspiratorial society that the Riverside DAs had feared.

The Bachelors for Wallace idea, though, did not succeed. When Hay contacted various people from the beer bust to tell them about his plan, they told him that he was out of his mind, that no one would be caught dead in such a thing, that they had all drunk far too much the previous night and had simply been joking around. Their response was not unlike the one Kepner received when he suggested organizing to the men he met. "I suddenly discover," said Hay, "that here I am holding a perfectly good idea, but I'm the only one."[40]

Two years later, in 1950, however, Hay took his eldest daughter to her dance class at Lester Horton's studio on Melrose Avenue. Horton was the leading modern dancer of the West Coast who, like Hay, applied his cultural talents to progressive causes. Not only did his dances portray political subjects, but his programs were often the entertainment at Party functions. Like Hay, Horton also sought out the affections of other men, and in the mid-1930s, he and Hay had "intimate relations a few times." One of the dancers, a German refugee named Rudi Gernreich, was disposed in a similar fashion both sexually and politically. Hay caught his eye at the studio; they started talking. Hay mentioned his proposal and Gernreich responded enthusiastically. He was ready to go to work, and soon enough, they were in love: Hay at last had found a "golden boy."[41]

Gernreich began to circulate the proposal among his friends, and the two men even ventured out to the beach that attracted homosexually active men, chatting up the Bachelors idea while collecting signatures in opposition to the war in Korea. Nobody they spoke with seemed ready to be an active supporter, however. Finally, Gernreich suggested that they should look explicitly for another leftist, perhaps one of Hay's students at the People's Education Center. Hay suspected that one of his music students, who often brought a male friend to class, was homosexual. On a Thursday in November 1950, after class, Hay gave the student and his friend a copy of the proposal. That weekend, one of the men, Bob Hull, called to see if Hay was at home and if he and a couple of friends could come over to discuss what they had read. Hay also invited Gernreich to come to his and Platky's Edendale home. Hull and Chuck Rowland, the students, arrived, bringing a third friend (Hull's then lover), Dale Jennings. Rowland came running up the driveway, waving the prospectus like a flag, saying, "I could have written it myself: where do we begin?" Mattachine was born.[42]

CREATIVE CONVERSATION

Mattachine grew dramatically. From the five at that November gathering, the organization engaged between two thousand and five thousand Californians over the next two and a half years. After that, the leadership and direction changed, and the membership fell off. A few years later, though, the internal politics changed again, and the numbers began to grow once more. As an organization, Mattachine lasted into the 1970s and, together with a handful of other organizations, provided the foundation for gay liberation politics.

Over the first six months, the founders drafted an official mission statement that revealed traces of Hay's earlier prospectus, though it was much simpler. The statement now identified three goals: unity, education, and leadership. The unity goal represented a much more systemic understanding of the persecution that had motivated Hay's prospectus. Rather than prioritizing the explicit state-led harassment, the founders instead claimed that "thousands of homosexuals live out their lives bewildered, unhappy, alone—isolated from their own kind and unable to adjust to the dominant culture." The fundamental injury that society inflicted was one of isolation, and rather than saying vaguely that they were cut off from an "Androgynous minority," the organizers identified "their own kind" as "homosexuals." That was the rather scientific term that, for the time, they claimed. Against that isolation, Mattachine aimed to offer "a consensus of principle around which all of our people can rally and from which they can derive a feeling of 'belonging.' " That is, Mattachine would offer a path out of the isolation of experience into the solidarity of community. Importantly, deeming that community "our people" smacked of Party language used to describe the "Negro people" or the "Jewish people." Mattachine offered the possibility of joining an analogous group.[43]

That analogy appeared more explicitly in their second goal. Mattachine aimed not only to dispel myths about homosexuality but also to develop a "highly ethical homosexual culture . . . paralleling the emerging cultures of our fellow-minorities—the Negro, Mexican, and Jewish Peoples." Here, Mattachine lay still more direct claim to the racial model that Hay had hinted at in his own proposal: they could form a community because they were an equivalent and distinct social minority. As such, they needed to bring forward what Hay and others were convinced was both a long history and vibrant present of homosexual cultural activity. That would prove their "fellow-minority" status as well as create a shared participatory life for their members. Third, Mattachine promised to offer the necessary "enlightened leadership"—the only means to "rouse the homosexuals . . . one of the largest minorities in America today . . . to take the actions necessary to elevate themselves from the social ostracism an unsympathetic culture has perpetrated upon them." Mattachine would be the revolutionary cadre. They were determined to make change.[44]

This three-part model in many ways drew on the Communist constructs of races, nations, or peoples. At the same time, whereas Communist Party membership in Edendale became an "essence" because of how deeply it seeped into the intimate corners of members' lives, Mattachine members set out to construct social and political support for an emotional essence they felt they already shared. Hoping to express safely their intimate feelings, the organizers, like the Edendale artists, aimed to create social organizations to support that effort. Like some artists, they believed their inner lives held political relevance, and they envisioned a politics similar to those of the Party that would be infused with deep passion. They followed their Edendale peers in seeking to forge a relationship between their inner essence and the outer world.

As historian John D'Emilio has vividly documented, for the first year of Mattachine, all these ambitious goals were attacked principally in a single yet powerful manner: through conversation. Initially, those conversations were shared among the original five men—soon supplemented by a young couple, Konrad Stevens and Jim Gruber, and then three others, including for a time photographer Ruth Bernhard (whose first show had been in Jake Zeitlin's shop in 1936). They met regularly, at least weekly, and discussed, revealed, fought, made plans, sometimes sang, even danced. They always drew the blinds, placed a pillow over the phone (a likely site for a bug, they thought), and if guests came, they met them elsewhere and drove in circles before arriving. They protected themselves from the law and infiltration, but within their cocoon, they indulged in intimate life-changing conversations.[45]

Within several months, the expanded founding group, which became known as the Fifth Order Guild and later the Mattachine Foundation, began to carry their conversational work beyond the confines of their inner circle. They started more public discussion groups about homosexuality. These public groups met in people's homes and apartments, and while officially no one acted as a leader, a Fifth Order member quietly led each group. The groups were deliberately isolated from each other so that if anyone was arrested or interrogated, only their individual group would be in danger, not the organization as a whole.[46] These public groups met regularly, dividing in two when they grew too large for a given living room. By late 1952 there were some fifty to one hundred groups meeting in and around Southern California, stretching from Edendale and Hollywood to San Pedro, Laguna Beach, and San Diego. Discussion groups also formed in Central and Northern California, as far away as Fresno, Monterey, and Berkeley. And while the group numbers were supposed to stay small, many individuals recall attending meetings of one hundred–plus people.

The discussions, both among the founders and among the semipublic, moved across a variety of topics. In the early conversations, Hay recalled talking about "what it means to be a homosexual, what it means to be gay. We talk about whether it's possible for us to have a consummated relationship. We're trying to find out what is the nature of our relationship, and we don't have words for it at this time. . . . So we're working in intangibles, we're working in cotton wool." One early Mattachine document offered a list of questions as potential discussion topics: "Why are there so few successful homosexual 'marriages'?" "What causes swishing?" and "Is there a homosexual culture?" Other nights were devoted to how to address homophobia, what members should call themselves, and whether they might include straight transvestites in the group.[47]

In addition to these abstract conversations, the members also discussed their complaints about the police. Both Jim Gruber and Dorr Legg, an Edendale resident who went to his first meeting in 1951 and was soon invited to join the Fifth Order Guild, said they felt that some meetings were like anti-police protest meetings. Legg believed that many attendees sensed that the police were being stricter in their patrols than they had been in previous years, and so came with a sense of outrage. Gruber himself felt that addressing "vulnerability" in the face of the police "was certainly what we were selling."[48]

This combination of theory and reality proved an attractive one, as the numbers alone attested. Jim Kepner was brought to his first Mattachine meeting in late 1952 or early 1953 and found 140 people. "I was fantastically turned on at the meeting," he said. It was "a beautiful thing." He felt as though the idea he had argued about with various people for the past decade was actually coming into existence. At the earliest meetings, according to Hay, people were timid about identifying themselves as having had a homosexual experience. "Nobody in our group ever seemed to know Gay people in California, let alone L.A. . . . It was always somebody else, not present, who'd had this homosexual experience, or who knew someone somewhere else who had." By the time Kepner attended, however, the tone sounded more like the Alcoholics Anonymous meetings of Hay's earlier proposal. Each meeting was charged with personal declarations, Kepner recalled, such as " 'I just did not believe that this could happen.' 'This is the most wonderful thing in my life.' 'I can suddenly feel proud.' 'I thought I was the only one in the world.' " Said Gruber, the youngest founder, discussions possessed an "electric feeling" as people let their guard down and spoke with candor. Not unlike the young people sitting around the bonfire with Paul and Margaret Landacre, the Mattachine members spoke about their inner lives. And while they did not mimic the artists of the Landacres' circle who then expressed those "personal landscapes" in some other medium, simply discussing their romantic and sexual desires in these conversations proved a tremendous step.[49]

Clearly, these discussions were powerful, but it is important to qualify that power carefully. It is easy enough from our contemporary moment to view them as consciousness-raising groups. That is, in those groups these men and occasional women shed their false consciousness and came to recognize something about themselves that had always been true, if not acknowledged: that they were a group or a class with a particular societal or political position.

Yet rather than revealing something that had been hidden, what seems clearer is how much these meetings fundamentally served as arenas for construction. What was being constructed in them was a shared notion of what it was to be a "homosexual." Many of the members described the kind of solidarity—the first of the Mattachine aims—that emerged in the discussion groups. Hay himself said, "We get this sense of a brotherhood, we get this sense of a belonging, this sense of a being together, which is so different from cruising." Cruising in a park or bar was the very epitome of isolation for which Mattachine was the antidote. Gruber described the "camaraderie" that resulted as a "family feeling" of "nonsexual intimacy." Among these men, he said, that "was a very new idea. And just that was what kept the organization afloat." He emphasized how exciting it was for new people who "all of a sudden . . . realize, 'Well, gee, this is me. They're me, and I'm one of them.' That's why it grew so very quickly."[50] Indeed, that is how they ended up with meetings, such as Kepner described, where people were declaring, "I just did not believe that this could happen," and "I thought I was the only one in the world."

This sense of "nonsexual intimacy," of a "brotherhood" or "family," was decisively new for the many men who had expressed their desires exclusively in a sexual world and moved through it fundamentally as individuals. Many historians have argued that bars provided a valuable arena for creating homosexual solidarity and launching political activism. Elizabeth Kennedy and Madeline Davis, for instance, argued that during the 1940s, women in Buffalo, New York, developed a "common culture, community, and consciousness" through their bar-based relationships. With those friendships they "explored what it meant to be a lesbian, talked about the difficulties they faced as well as the fun, and supported one another." Nan Boyd also wrote that San Francisco's bars and taverns proved a more vital source for "less organized (but numerically stronger) pockets of queer association and camaraderie" than did early political groups. In addition, these scholars have argued that simply entering a bar like

Maxwell's or the International or cruising in Pershing Square constituted what Marc Stein deemed "everyday strategies of resistance . . . which challenged those who opposed the public pursuits and pleasures of lesbians and gay men." Bars where homosexually active men and women could congregate, they have explained, provided a "seedbed" for political community formation.[51]

While the possibility of bar scene solidarity is undeniable, the comments of Mattachine participants speak loudly to their own sense of isolation prior to joining Mattachine. Many apparently had moved through the world of bars without feeling that they had joined a community, let alone gained a shared identity. Either the camaraderie along the Run did not include them—and thus was hardly widespread among all bar patrons—or it paled in comparison to the camaraderie of Mattachine meetings. Certainly Fred Frisbie's descriptions of speakeasies in the 1920s pointed toward a sense of solidarity among the patrons that did not constitute an identity or sense of community. Similarly, Jim Kepner knew his way quite well around the bars of the Run, but the homophile movement offered him something more dramatic.

What Mattachine offered was a different kind of camaraderie: "non-sexual" "family" camaraderie, in Gruber's words, that was well organized and increasingly more defined. This was camaraderie *about* sexual desires that was not constituted by those desires. The repeated and shared non-sexual expression of desires was the bedrock of Mattachine meetings, and it was new and transformative; it was how a communal identity—a shared self-perception—was constructed. The shifting of common desire into something beyond the circuits of desire and within some other kind of public or shared venue was a distinctively new thing at mid-century.

Ken Burns, who helped lead Mattachine in the mid-1950s, suggested that these discussion groups—focusing on why people were "gay," what "gayness" was, how to achieve self-acceptance—ultimately allowed people to "get some identity." It is a telling phrase because it underscores the creative work of the groups. It does not suggest that these men and occasional women were not living similar experiences, prior to their meeting. But in discussing those common experiences, they began to codify who and what they were "as homosexuals" or "as gay men and women." They were bringing their "essence" to the surface and defining it for the first time as a broadly shared identity. Kennedy and Davis argued that pre-political bar-based consciousness proved "central" in the later success of gay politics in Buffalo, and undoubtedly it did. But homophile consciousness was of a different order, and it succeeded in galvanizing those uninspired by life on the Run.[52]

Nobody, ultimately, knew in advance what exactly that shared identity was or what it could be. Frequently in describing those Mattachine years, Hay noted the challenge of describing something for which there was no language. He sounded like an abstract painter or Post-Surrealist struggling to find a visual language for the "private landscape." "We are fumbling for ideas, for concepts," he later told D'Emilio. "We are beginning . . . to try to find ways to communicate what we now talk about as 'gay consciousness,' twenty-five years ago, before you have the word, before you even have the phrases that are going to be able to [convey] that idea." Importantly, he acknowledged, "it's an educational job on ourselves before we can reach out to our discussion groups."[53] Nobody had the answer already.

Fractious questions about what this common identity meant abounded and ultimately divided Mattachine, sending it off into a new direction in 1953, and sending its founders out of the movement. Yet the fact that Mattachine helped everyone to "get some identity" was its uncontested and unprecedented achievement. The organization carved out a space for a shared public identity to be explored, constructed, and reinforced out of private emotions. In that achievement, the group represented one more step in the creation of passionate public identities that were the mainstay of Edendale.

THE PARTY LEGACY

Increasingly central to Hay's vision of that identity was the notion of homosexuals being an oppressed social minority. For Hay, that position was the crux of their identity and the thing that needed to be understood. Although not explicitly present in Hay's initial draft of the Bachelor society's prospectus, Hay felt that this idea was the fundamental Party legacy that he carried with him into Mattachine. With it, Hay imagined homosexuals to be like a race and a revolutionary class, needing to overcome their false consciousness and see themselves for what they really were: a distinct group with a distinct identity shaped in large part by their place in society.

Hay's comments at the first public discussion group spoke to the "heroic objective of liberating one of our largest minorities from the solitary confinement of social persecution and civil insecurity." The isolation homosexuals experienced was a product of state-led oppression. Instead, Hay wanted to do for homosexuals what the Civil Rights Congress did for racial groups and Communists, "guaranteeing them the basic and protected right to enter the front ranks of self-respecting citizenship, recognized and honored as socially contributive individuals." A key piece of that liberation, Hay felt, was self-awareness. Hay explained that because the homosexual is "largely unaware that . . . [he is] a member of a social minority imprisoned within a dominant culture," he fails to recognize his own unique culture. Homosexuals, he felt, recognized neither their shared identity nor the shared culture they were producing. That culture, in his view, needed to be developed. Fundamentally, Hay urged, "our people should refuse any longer to be stampeded into the inertia of not being able to see the forest for the trees." Enough time as isolated individuals: recognize your unanimity! Act politically and culturally as a unit![54]

Hay was certainly raising a call to arms. Despite the familiarity and relative acceptance of that framework today, it was fundamentally a new and challenging idea, even for those with a progressive past like Hay. Of the early core members, Rowland and Hull had been active Party members, and Jennings was considered "one hell of a fellow traveler." And while Gernreich had been more culturally leftist than politically so, the young couple Stevens and Gruber had both been very active in political causes. Still, while Hay felt that homosexuals fit directly into the system of Party analogies, he was by far the most convinced. He had to work hard to explain and convince others of the oppressed-minority position. In his own later recollections, Hay described the challenge of getting "people to thoroughly consider the possibility that homosexuals were a social minority. This is a concept that has not been as yet really approached." While Chuck Rowland recalled immediately embracing the idea, Hay remembered rather that he had "violently opposed the idea of homosexuals as a minority of any sort. Rudi [Gernreich] didn't. . . . Dale [Jennings] was opposed. Bob [Hull] probably wasn't. Jim [Gruber] and Steve [Konrad Stevens] were confused." Clearly, even with a Marxist background, even with Party experience, the "oppressed social minority" theory was not an easy or natural fit. Stevens recalled that the fights about the minority position were "one of the biggest arguments we had."[55]

Hay lobbied hard for his view. At one of Mattachine's first mini-conferences in the fall of 1951, Hay presented the idea to the twelve or fifteen participants. Several people responded that they would at least consider the notion and try it out. Gruber, for one, felt that the shared identity experiences of the discussion groups fed into the notion of being a minority. By his thinking, "if you considered yourself a member of the homosexual minority, that gave you an identity, and therefore, a place in the race, so to speak. And to deny that content would be crumbling our whole superstructure." Yet clearly, even if participants accepted what the discussion groups were revealing—that there were many shared experiences—that did not mean that they bought the idea of a homosexual minority or of a community. In fact Dorr Legg said that Hay's push for the minority position was "the cause of endless debate . . . just pitched fights." Not unlike the constituents of John Anson Ford who, in the 1940s, resisted the elevation of racial groups to political constituencies of distinct significance, Mattachine members similarly resisted treating homosexuals as a group at the same level.[56]

One of the keys to making Hay's theory fit lay in analogizing homosexuals to racial or ethnic groups. Both the city debates over racial discord and especially the local Communist Party's efforts to mobilize activists around a race-nation framework had made the language of racial groups and "minorities" very prevalent in Edendale. This meant that while Gruber and Stevens may not have grasped all the theory behind Hay's model, they understood it at some more implicit level. In fact, in explaining why he did not react to Mattachine with the same fear that many of his friends and acquaintances did, Stevens suggested that he and Gruber already saw the analogy. "We had been very progressive in our thinking: the Negro question, discrimination—we had been in tune with that sort of thing. And this went right along our line of thinking. We thought, 'Well, it's the same thing, only we hadn't really thought of it before.' "[57] For Stevens, the racial model worked: it already existed in his mental framework.

Later on, when he tried to convince newer members of the utility of the minority model, Stevens himself made analogies to African Americans. Stevens said that people would challenge the minority idea by saying that homosexuals were rich, poor, Republicans, and Democrats. "We're such a wide variety of things," they would say, "how can you call us a minority?" Stevens would respond, "Well, all of those things you can say about a black person, too. They are all of these things and yet they're black, and our homosexuality is all it takes to make us a minority." At the same time, Stevens would emphasize the place of oppression in making homosexuals into a minority. "We wouldn't be a minority if we were accepted and had equal rights. We would no longer be a minority any more than the Irish are a minority. They're a minority numerically, but they're not discriminated against, so they're not a minority. We are, so we are a minority."[58]

Even beyond the racial analogy, the organization was also marked by contention over the shape and meaning of "homosexual identity." At the fall 1951 conference, for instance, when Hay proposed his minority framework to the larger group, he also proposed that their minority include drag queens and "screaming queens"—the "obvious" homosexuals who displayed feminine gender traits; Mattachine, he said, should reach out to include them. That proposal, however, received none of the consideration of the linked minority idea. Instead, feeling "quite provoked," the attendees refused it. Much like Harold Burton, who distinguished himself and his boyfriend from the "sissyish faggots," and like Julian Eltinge, who roared at the "prim gentles," Mattachine members were not yet ready to stretch the boundaries of their community to include men who did not conform to traditional gender roles. They did not want inverted desires to be understood as attached to inverted gender.[59]

In addition, the group's members fought over Hay's idea that a minority status carried explicit political implications. It was not that the early years of Mattachine were devoid of nonpolitical elements. In fact, Mattachine did begin to develop its own culture, creating rituals of induction and organizing various social events. To raise money, Mattachine sponsored a night of performance from the Lester Horton dance troupe and a big dance party out at the beach.[60] Yet at least these last two events were culture put to work for politics, and politics remained the official emphasis of Hay's Mattachine.

Nevertheless, for some, politics were not what drew them into Mattachine nor where they hoped to focus their energies. They were, in truth, more eager to develop a homosexual culture than to lay claim to certain "civil rights." Gerard Brissette, a young Berkeley lab technician, had heard about Mattachine while at an orgy. He wrote to Rowland and spent some time visiting with the group in Los Angeles before returning to the Bay Area to start a chapter. But even as the organization evolved, Brissette was turned off increasingly by the political emphasis. "More and more," he recalled with criticism, "the political, or social action kind of things, seemed to be the growing consensus, the mobilizing thing. 'Well, what do we do about the cops?' . . . The thing began to become far too politicized." Brissette, who had gotten poet friends of his to attend discussions, envisioned a group that would both trace the historical roots of homosexual culture and work to expand it in the present. If he saw homosexuals as a minority, he saw them the way John Anson Ford saw the Japanese American theater group or Fletcher Bowron viewed American Jews before the war: they were a cultural minority without political implications. By the fall of 1953, he said, "those of us who had come in more from the artistic, creative, church, spiritual, scholarly . . . we got turned off, because we began to see more and more [that it was] a kind of political thing."[61]

Jim Gruber, one of the earliest members, was also put off by the overt political tone of the organization. His partner, Konrad Stevens, described Gruber as frightened of how "scary" things could get, "because there was definitely a political atmosphere to all of this." In addition, some newer members objected to the confrontational tone and forthright tactics that Hay advocated. Jim Kepner found his discussion group to be "politically conservative and closety." Their notion of political action, he sneered, was hoping that someone had the "key to the governor's bedchamber." The attitude implied, "Don't make waves, don't make a public campaign, just find someone who knows the Chief Justice of the Supreme Court or the governor personally . . . and everything can be taken care of quietly."[62] They wanted legal discrimination to be resolved by discreet actions of the political elite.

Perhaps because of these opposing views, Hay worked steadily to build support for the minority position and its political implications. Two court cases in 1952 provided the necessary fuel. In the first, Hay made a connection with the rising tide of Mexican American activism. In Southeast Los Angeles, a series of police raids against Mexican American organizations, spanning the fall of 1951 and the spring of 1952, provoked a growing furor in the Mexican American community. Hay sensed a heightened identification among young Mexican Americans of themselves as a minority.[63] Then, in January 1952, little more than a year after the earliest meetings of Mattachine, five Mexican American boys in Echo Park fought with the police. One was shot in the chest, two were badly beaten, and all five were arrested and taken to jail. The case galvanized the neighborhood leftists. When the Civil Rights Congress wrote that police entrapment "can happen to anyone" and that the arrests constituted part of a genocidal campaign, the Mattachine founders—spurred by Hay—felt they understood: they were an analogous group of people, and they offered themselves as allies to the Civil Rights Congress, using the name "Citizens Committee to Outlaw Entrapment."

Mattachine's interest in the case was not purely altruistic, however. Although the civil rights group did not dwell on this issue, the police and the boys they fought with had been hanging around Echo Park because it was a homosexual cruising area. The boys confessed to CRC staff that they had robbed a "queer" there earlier in the day, and the police had a "cop's roost" above the park's bathroom to watch the men inside. The fight broke out when one boy went into the bathroom and encountered an undercover police officer who was trying to entrap homosexuals at the urinal. The young man resisted the officer's entreaties and shouted for his friends, screaming, "Help! Help! A queer!" in Spanish and English. His friends came running, as did the officer's partner, and the fight, shooting, and arrests ensued. In this case, racial issues were embedded directly in a conflict about homosexual activity.[64]

Because of that overlap, the Mattachine members were explicitly able to draw on the leftist framework about racial identity and social minorities, and use it to enter public politics for the first time. They made the case that speaking out on entrapment would "cover all minorities," including, implicitly, the homosexual one. To present an argument about the social and political needs of homosexuals, the Mattachine members argued in their correspondence with the civil rights group that homosexuals constituted a minority just like any social minority. Indeed, they went so far as to cite "a fairly generally-established definition of a nation" as possessing a common territory, language, economy, and "psychological make-up manifest in a community of culture." Women, they noted, "are spoken of today as a minority because they qualify under points 2 and 4. So also do the Homosexuals. Indeed, perhaps even more so than women because their deviant culture encompasses the characteristic double-entendres of all groups who are economically, socially, and politically oppressed."[65]

Additionally, the Mattachine members affirmed the leftist idea that entrapment or infringement of the rights of any one group hurt all others. In an "Anonymous Call to Arms" leaflet that its members circulated around the city, Mattachine (in the guise of the CCOE) argued that

> so long as there is one group whose members, *as citizens,* are prey to blackmail, intimidations both social and physical in nature, shakedown, entrapments, search and seizure without warrant, incarceration without charge, denial of right to summon counsel or bail, and even subject to arraignments without being informed of the specific charges,—SO LONG AS ONE MINORITY GROUP (regardless of the justice or the injustice of the prejudice against them)—IS THUS HARRIED AND HOUNDED,—NO MINORITY GROUP OR COMMUNITY GROUP IS SAFE. . . . [W]e urge you to realize that if the Homosexual does NOT have equal citizenship guarantees, privileges, and dignities, under the law,—THEN NEITHER DO YOU.

The false arrests of homosexuals differed "not one iota" from the trumped-up charges used against Mexican Americans or African Americans throughout the city. Echoing artist Grace Clements's call to public engagement, Mattachine determined to stand up as homophiles on behalf of these Mexican American youths as an allied minority. And at the same time, the CCOE urgently demanded that the civil rights organization fight on behalf of the homosexual minority as well.[66]

The Mattachine members did not convince the Civil Rights Congress to act on their behalf. Nevertheless, their plea must have been comprehensible to them. It must have made sense whether or not you agreed with it, and whether you were inside Mattachine or outside. The framework of politicized identity that Mattachine put forward was already the shared framework of their leftist neighbors.

At the same time, Mattachine began actively to defend one of their own. Two months after the Echo Park confrontation, founder Dale Jennings, a writer and Edendale resident who led the area's public discussion group, was followed home by a man he had met in Westlake Park. Jennings allowed the man into his house, and the man suddenly revealed himself to be a police officer and arrested Jennings for soliciting him. Although Jennings was not inclined to challenge the arrest—the typical reaction at the time—Hay pushed hard for him to fight the charges and do so publicly. Hay saw the Jennings defense as another important opportunity to tie Mattachine to other "fellow-minorities" who were harassed by the police and thus to the emerging notion of minority politics. Mattachine even hired George Shibley, the lead attorney who had defended the youths in the Sleepy Lagoon case, to defend Jennings: entrapped homosexuals could use the same strategies as entrapped Mexican Americans. Jennings, in a first-ever court strategy, admitted to being homosexual but insisted that he was entrapped.[67] Mattachine issued leaflets seeking financial support for the Jennings case that made explicit that "THE ISSUE IS CIVIL RIGHTS! The issue is the restoration of basic citizenship guarantees, rights, and privileges, EQUALLY FOR EVERYBODY. . . . [D]eny the Homosexual his basic protections as a citizen,—and you'll have set up the very machinery which will deny yourselves [these rights]. The moment you establish second class citizenship categories . . . you too are headed for that class. *We're all in the same boat!*"[68] Echoing the analogies of the Communists, Mattachine argued that the homosexual minority was just like any other minority: it was in the same political position.

Jennings's court battle against his entrapment did not inspire uniform support among Mattachine attendees. Many members doubted Jennings's claims of innocence, and fewer decried the laws under which he had been

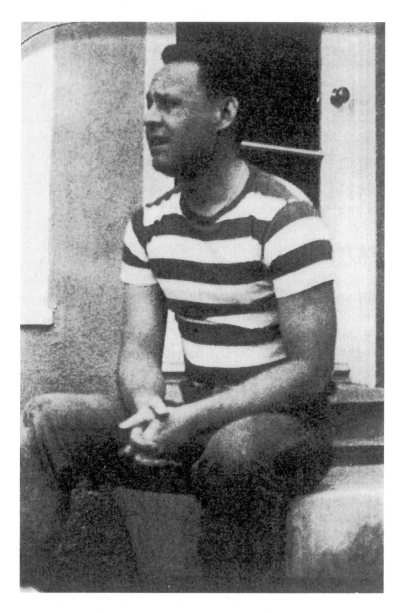

Dale Jennings. His arrest and successful court challenge made him a hero to many of the Mattachine leaders, though some of the rank and file scorned him for getting arrested in the first place. (Photograph by Chuck Rowland. Courtesy *Hope along the Wind* and Stuart Timmons.)

accused. The following year, Jennings wrote of the "peculiar agony" that came from being "innocent and yet not be able to convince your own firm constituents." Many of these, he said, "would have nothing to do with the case of a person who was so foolish as to let himself get arrested."[69]

But Jennings's entrapment defense in court essentially succeeded: the jury deadlocked and the charges were dismissed. The case received no media coverage, but news of the victory circulated widely among homosexually active men. Hundreds of people now began to flock to Mattachine meetings.[70] Mattachine was not only building on the left's system of analogies to explain the political significance of their oppression. It also demonstrated that its members were developing the muscle to take care of their own.

Emboldened by the Jennings court victory, the Mattachine leaders carried their political activism one step further. They sent out a set of questionnaires, first in the fall of 1952 and then again in the winter of 1953, to candidates for the city council, school board, and state legislature, asking their views on homosexuality. They began to engage directly, that is, with political decision makers. Only a single candidate replied to the questionnaires: Mattachine's political muscles had plenty of room to grow. But one of the letters made its way to the desk of Paul Coates, a syndicated *Los Angeles Daily Mirror* columnist, and he devoted a column to discussing Mattachine. His column, which set off a firestorm of controversy within the organization, stands as a testament to what Mattachine had so quickly achieved.[71]

Entitled "Well, Medium and Rare," Coates's article noted that "a strange new pressure group" claiming "to represent the homosexual voters of Los Angeles is vigorously shopping for campaign promises." Coates apparently pursued the postal box listed on the candidates' questionnaire and found it registered to Mrs. Henry Hay, Hay's mother. When Coates contacted her, she told him about the thousands of members and the group's incorporation. As he pressed her for more information—particularly about the structure and financing of the group—Hay's mother explained that someone else would call him back. Someone else did, likely Hay himself, who presumably told Coates about the name of the group and the medieval Mattachines. Coates supposed that "this modern, American version could be many things. Perhaps it's just another weird outcropping of election time. Or, it might be a group of responsible citizens, seriously concerned with a tragic social problem." But the political possibilities were clear to him. Mattachine, he wrote, "could be a device for gathering a strong bloc of votes." Endorsing Mattachine's estimate that there might be between 150,000 and 200,000 homosexuals in the city, Coates speculated that potentially they "might swing tremendous political power."[72]

According to Mattachine founder Konrad Stevens's recollection, some city residents were "just infuriated that things had gotten that decadent that homosexuals would want politicians to tell them what their stand was on homosexuality." And Coates only added to that furor by suggesting that the political power of homosexuals could easily be co-opted by a "well-trained subversive." What is more, the publicity and the reaction it inspired "scared the hell out of a lot of our members." For some members, the wider hostility that the questionnaires generated reaffirmed their conviction that politics was not the right public framework for addressing homosexuality. And other members latched onto Coates's suggestion about the group's vulnerability to subversives and called for a constitutional convention to alter the organization's secretive structure.[73]

Yet it is easy to imagine the excitement Harry Hay must have felt when he spoke with Coates and read his column. The oppressed minority, which had not even existed fifty years earlier, was now being acknowledged as possessing real political muscle. At the very least they were a "pressure group," but they could equally represent a "strong bloc of votes." Homosexuals had landed, albeit tentatively, on the political map.

And from that early perch, their presence continued to grow. Mattachine branches took root up and down California, and by 1955 there were small chapters in New York and Chicago, with groups soon to form in Boston, Philadelphia, Detroit, and Washington, D.C. At the same time, Mattachine was simply the first of a cohort of homophile organizations that quickly emerged after Mattachine. ONE, Inc., spun off from Mattachine in 1952 to become an independent organization, and the Daughters of Bilitis formed in San Francisco in 1955 to advocate on behalf of lesbians.[74] These groups—and more emerged in the 1960s—built upon the foundation of personal politics and shared identity that marked Mattachine.

This was identity politics: this embrace of an essential identity built on emotion and desire, this call for political rights based on that identity, this advocating on their own behalf. Mattachine stood as the culmination of the steadily unfolding politicization of essence in Angeleno and American life. Like the artists of Edendale, Mattachine members explored their inner lives and gave value to their emotions. As the constant focus on conversation and sharing experience suggested, Mattachine carried forward the artists' search for the "essence" of the "personal landscape." The Mattachine meetings looked as much like conversations around the Landacres' bonfire or style meetings with Lorser Feitelson at the Federal Art Project as they did the Civil Rights Congress workshop on "white chauvinism." Instead of painters standing up to explain, "Here's how I express my private landscape," there were newly self-labeled "homosexual" men and women explaining how they negotiated their own landscapes of desire. Their organization carved out a space for homosexually active men and women to begin to "get some identity."

The artists of Edendale attempted to communicate their personal landscapes to a wider public, believing that they held larger social and political importance. To a degree, they were sustained in that view by the support and control of the New Deal's public works programs. Even more, though, local politicians, judges, and police officers heightened that attribution of political significance to the inner life by arguing increasingly during the 1930s that deviant sexual desires were the mark of a dangerous and perverted identity that could threaten political and social stability: desire, they insisted, had perilous political implications. Nonetheless, as the Communists of Edendale demonstrated, intimate passion and desire could also form the very foundation of political activism. Contrary to what local police and district attorneys argued, leftists made evident that desire could mobilize united political action, not merely threaten it. Intimate passion could form the basis of political community. As the city descended into the racial conflicts of the Second World War, the leftists also provided a vital framework for thinking broadly about group-based oppression and identity-driven political activism. Their organizations, which articulated the plight of oppressed social minorities and aided them in the political struggle of eliminating that oppression, made plain that state harassment was the very mark of minority identity and should galvanize people into resistance. The left clarified that oppression itself defined a minority.

Mattachine rode the crest of this broad cultural and political momentum. They embraced the artists' call to express the inner self, and when that expression provoked oppression, they demonstrated the great mobilizing power in the racial model that they lifted from their leftist peers. Their conception of what homosexuality could mean, both in terms of building an organization for homosexuals and in terms of changing the response to homosexuality in the larger society, reverberated with Party notions and the tactics of the CRC. Like Party members, they constructed a political and organizational life infused with emotional intimacy. At the same time, drawing on Party language, the Mattachine founders mapped out a very political vision of what it might *mean* to be a "homosexual" and to accept one's homosexual desires and actions as the central defining feature of one's life. Hay in particular did not think of the homosexual as someone who may or may not be implicated in political questions, depending on his or her own will. The homosexual existed as a minority because of societal oppression, and was not separate from that oppression. "Rights" and "citizenship," therefore, were not secondary questions. To the contrary, the homosexual was, in a fundamental sense, a political category. And as Mattachine stepped out into the world beyond their group meetings—contacting legislators, condemning the police, and seeking allies—they did so as political actors. The politics of essence, broadened by the racial politics of the 1940s, yielded identity politics.

The hill where Hay's and Eltinge's houses are located, as it looks today.
(Photograph by the author.)

Conclusion
The Struggle of Identity Politics

HARRY HAY AND JULIAN ELTINGE framed a moment of transition in American life. In some ways, they had a great deal in common. They both lived on the slope of a small ridge in a corner of Los Angeles. They both loved the theater. They both shared a predilection for sexual activity with men. And, for a time, neither man let that fact define his public life. For Eltinge, that public life occurred onstage, and when anyone dared suggest that his dressing as a woman made him anything like the "prim gentles" who waited at the stage door, he let his fists be his answer. For Hay, public life meant politics and the Communist Party, and he married and raised children with another party member in order to live that life more fully. For both of these men, their sexual activities did not, at least for a time, constitute some essential part of themselves, some fundamental defining feature of their identities.

And then, in the wake of growing attention to self-expression and the political significance of certain emotions, in the wake of a new language about racial groups and racial interaction, and in the wake of expanding persecution of homosexually active men and women, that shifted. Born a generation after Eltinge, Harry Hay and his founding colleagues at Mattachine made the argument that their sexual lives were indeed a fundamental—if not *the* fundamental—piece of who they were. And they insisted that sexual essence had the sort of political implications that made homosexuals

269

equivalent to Jews or blacks or Mexicans. As such, Harry Hay and Mattachine brought to a firm close the world that Eltinge had occupied, in which gender predominated over sexuality and in which emotion, desire, and identification were the bailiwick of culture, not politics.

As emotion and self-understanding took on increasing political meaning, American politics changed. Even long-standing arguments about competing group interests and social discrimination now came to rest on claims about the inner life. The trajectory of the black civil rights movement is telling. The 1954 majority opinion in *Brown v. Board of Education* that segregated schools gave African American children "a feeling of inferiority"—an opinion, as one supportive critic put it, that "insisted on equality of the mind and heart rather than equality of school facilities"—signaled the new emphasis.[1] Kenneth Clark, the sociologist whose research was crucial to the case, underscored that emphasis: "The *Brown* decision made it possible for blacks to defy and remove the traditional signs of social *humiliation* and *cruelties,* and to educate white Americans on the importance of concern for the humanity of their fellow human beings without regard to color or race."[2] That focus on humiliation and inferiority soon shared the spotlight with arguments about esteem and pride. This was a political project that now began to focus on the inner life and the emotional content of identity.

As activists for black separatism and nationalism became dominant in the late 1960s, in part they borrowed a framework that had been developing among African Americans since at least the middle of the nineteenth century. Nonetheless, the nationalism of "Black Power" represented what Richard King deemed a new effort to "create or make evident a new sense of individual and collective identity, even self-respect," and "for the first time—or for the first time in a long time—such ideas took on a new collective, political meaning."[3] Among the challengers to Martin Luther King, Jr., a cohort of black activists from Carlos Cooks to Malcolm X and Huey Newton drew attention to the significant difference between a Negro identity and a black one and underscored the need for African American pride and esteem. It is not surprising that they drew inspiration, in part, from Frantz Fanon, the revolutionary psychiatrist whose writing emphasized the importance of recognition and prestige. And well after the militancy of Black Power had subsided, educators in the 1980s were still advocating "Afrocentric" curricula as a means to address the sense of lingering stigma among black students. The inner life of African Americans remained central in their political demands.[4]

A similar dynamic characterized the new women's movement, as feminists in the 1960s and '70s reworked the older social movement for women's equality. They remade a movement that had relied on very traditional notions of womanhood and politics in light of the new personally oriented politics. Radical feminists argued for the vital project of self-fashioning, insisting that "we need a new premise for society: that the most basic right of an individual is to create the terms of its own definition." They called on women to investigate the particularity of their experience and emotion of being women, with feminist scholars like Nancy Chodorow and Carole Gilligan arguing that women were fundamentally different from men, unique in their ways of thinking, feeling, and relating to the world. Famously, these new feminists insisted on the political importance of women's experience of their private and emotional lives—even their sexual lives—and called for "destroying the high walls erected between public and private."[5]

These new movements of identity politics shifted the emphasis within American political life. To paraphrase one critic, the principal political question ceased to be simply "What is to be done?" and now also involved questions like "Who am I?" and "What does it mean to be that person?" This transformation of American politics might well be viewed as marking the heyday of the psychological, as inner lives garnered the attention of American society. Certainly this is part of what Christopher Lasch was describing in his 1979 portrait of the United States, *The Culture of Narcissism*. Some have blamed the emphasis on the psychological in American culture for allowing important societal dilemmas to be viewed as merely individual in nature. This focus, critics wrote, helped "to remove the problem of the individual from the broader social sphere, to substitute judgments about apparently isolated monads for a broader social analysis of the roots of individual problems." The heyday of psychology and the inner life, they suggested, represented a deflation of political action and its power.[6]

Identity politics, however, constituted a challenge to that view, and it was a challenge that began at least as early as the 1920s if not earlier. Even as artists embraced the importance of the inner life and its exploration, they also insisted on its expression and, to a large degree, the public importance of that expression. That is, they fought to keep the psychological from being bound within a narrow private sphere, instead attempting to have it speak to the larger social sphere. These broad identity politics constituted a countermovement to the isolation of the psychological within a private realm, a refusal not of psychology's prioritization of emotional issues, but of leaving those issues outside of the public sphere.

Homophile politics, as practiced by Harry Hay and the early founders of Mattachine, stood as a clear expression of this project to infuse political life with questions and language that elsewhere were being deemed personal. Typically, the emphasis on the personal and self-esteem in American politics is narrated as a product of the New Left and the feminists of the 1960s and '70s. A recent study by Elizabeth Armstrong, for instance, argued both that 1970s gay liberation activists were starkly different from their homophile forebears because of their emphasis on self-esteem, and that such an emphasis demonstrated the influence of the new left. But an argument like Armstrong's marks as new something that had a much longer and deeper history. In truth, the emotional self—esteemed, expressed, or vilified—had been moving steadily toward the heart of American politics for several decades before that. And while the long roots of black nationalism—the prehistory of Black Power—clearly indicate that such questions were to some degree already being folded into other social movements, the homophile movement—because of its unique emphasis on desire and sexuality as the starting place of identity—marked in many ways the purest demonstration of this politicization of the personal and personalization of the political.[7]

The placing of personal identity toward the center of American politics, however, did not amount to the *acceptance* of shared notions of personal identities. Hay and Mattachine represented the opening of a new chapter in gay history and American political history, in which the very ideas of identification and minority group definition became the subject of heated controversy—which is to say, the subject of politics. In many ways, American identity politics have not been marked by agreement about which identities matter: quite to the contrary, American identity politics have been defined precisely by ongoing battles over who counts as a minority and what the politics of minority groups should be. Certainly notions of "gay identity" and "gay community" were never—and never have been—self-evident and well agreed upon: gay identity politics did not expand easily from 1950 forward, riding high on the growing acceptance of the early Mattachine vision. Much like inter-racialism or racial civil rights, conceptualizing homosexuals as possessing an identity and as being socially oppressed became the focus of political conflict. Mattachine and Hay launched a now decades-long battle about the significance of homosexuality to notions of self and identity and to the construction of a community, a battle that has been fought vociferously by homosexually active men and women themselves. Indeed, the very notion of a homosexual identity and minority has remained heavily contested even among those who have led homosexually active lives.

MATTACHINE IN CONFLICT

While Paul Coates's column identifying homosexuals as a potentially powerful new political bloc suggested that Hay's vision could gain a wider acceptance, its publication did not mark an embrace of that view or the easy application of that power. Instead, it sparked a battle among Mattachine members over whether they wanted to be such a political bloc. The column, "Well, Medium and Rare," heightened the simmering tensions within Mattachine. Not only was there ongoing disagreement about Hay's minoritizing view, but there were also divisions about the group's political goals. As Hay later recalled, there were "real dichotomies, real splits in political outlook. Because after all, we [the founders] are all radical and it's conservative for us to think Democratic. And we've got a whole flock of people coming in from Laguna, San Juan Capistrano, San Diego, who are Nixon-Eisenhower people."[8]

When Coates published his column, he hinted that there could be a connection between Mattachine and Communists. That same suspicion guided the federal government's civil service purges of homosexuals, and many Mattachine members' own suspicions had already begun to spin in that direction; some imagined (correctly) that the hidden leaders of the group might be Communists or (incorrectly) that the organization might in fact be directed from Moscow. In that early Cold War climate, said one member of Mattachine, "we didn't want to have ourselves made pawns by some secret group whose identity we didn't know." Within a month of Coates's column, various members moved for a constitutional convention in order to undo Mattachine's secret structure.[9]

Originally slated for a single weekend in April 1953, the convention spread into a second. Drafting the constitution provoked manifold conflicts. While the attendees did not question their shared "personal landscape" nor the "camaraderie" that had developed as a result of their discussions, they battled heatedly over whether their similar desires truly constituted their "essence" and, even more, whether those desires made them a social minority. Additionally, the secret structure of the organization came up for challenge as well. At the end of the process—one replete with red-baitings and ultimatums—Harry Hay and the other founders had stepped down from their positions of leadership, and a new contingent had taken charge.[10]

Founder Chuck Rowland delivered an opening keynote address at the conference that offered a politicized-minority vision and stirred the fires of controversy. In Jim Kepner's recollection, Rowland spoke about feeling for the first time that he could stand with pride and say, "I am a homosexual and I am here among my own people." He also offered a vision of "the day when we could all march down the street, arm in arm, heads upraised, eight or ten abreast, fists upraised." According to Kepner, most people around him found the speech "shocking" and "totally improper." Even Kepner at the time found the vision of marching down the street like that—a vision that gay liberationists and gay pride activists both later incorporated—to be "the last thing we wanted. To my thinking then . . . we didn't want that kind of militant or regimented organization." To someone like Hal Call, a San Francisco member who was already suspicious about Communists in the organization, Rowland's remarks smacked of the red menace. Call blew up at Rowland during one of the caucuses and threatened to have Rowland and his cohort "read out of the roll-call" of the organization.[11]

The greatest attention focused on Hay's oppressed-social-minority framework. Marilyn Rieger, an Edendale resident who eventually joined with Call to oust Hay and his cofounders, spoke passionately to the question. Playing with a line from *The Merchant of Venice*—"Hath not a homosexual eyes?"—Rieger made the case for non-minority status. Though her statement was hardly as theoretical as Hay's extensive analyses, she argued for homosexuals to see themselves as widely woven into the larger society and not a distinct faction within it. "We are first and foremost people," she urged repeatedly. "We know we are the same . . . no different than anyone else. Our only difference is an unimportant one to the heterosexual society, unless we make it important." Making it important—arguing, that is, that homosexual desires constituted a fundamental identity-defining "essence"—was a mistake.

> We protest when we are recognized by society for only one characteristic . . . that we are homosexual, and we strongly contend that we should be judged by our character and deeds alone. . . . Yet it is we who are establishing ourselves as being primarily homosexual. We are organizing a minority

which is emphasizing the fact that we are homosexual and pointing out our differences rather than our similarities. [That's what we are doing] by limiting our integration only with the homosexual population and by moving underground, in secrecy and with fear.[12]

A secret structure yielded the same results as highlighting "differences" and "essence"; it drove a wedge between homosexuals and mainstream society.

Significantly, even as Rieger opposed the formation of a secret organization and the construction of a social minority model, she did not advocate lives of hiding and quiet isolation. Quite to the contrary, she stated, "It is only by coming out into the open . . . by declaring ourselves, by integrating . . . not as homosexuals, but as people, as men and women whose homosexuality is irrelevant to our ideals, our principles, our hopes and aspirations, that we will rid the world of its misconcepts of homosexuality and homosexuals." Homosexuality need not be a secret any more than homosexuals need organize and define themselves as a minority. Rieger envisioned neither a world of fear and secrecy nor a separatist world of cultural isolation. She imagined a homosexual presence that was widely dispersed and integrated into larger society.[13]

Hay, of course, was wildly opposed to relinquishing the minority framework. Even before the conference, Hay maintained that the key goal must remain "integration of our minority *as a group.*" The people who were pushing for change, he wrote Rowland, "don't give a shit about [the homosexual minority]—and want assimilating (passing, by Christ!) made respectable. . . . No, Chuck! This move isn't radical, it's betrayal. . . . You can't build a democratic society on a bunch of diversified 'individualists' going nowhere."[14]

Yet Rieger's vision carried the day at the convention, and she and Call and others eventually assumed leadership of Mattachine. They did not perceive themselves as having relinquished an agenda that engaged with the wider public. In fact, when Call recalled the convention twenty-five years later, he remembered that the great divide was about "subcultures," not even politics. On one side were those who had "a strong feeling and desire to help create a homosexual subculture within the total society," and on the other were those, like himself and Rieger, who "didn't buy the homosexual subculture concept. We wanted to see homosexuals made a part of total society." When asked if he had accepted the idea of being a minority group at the time of the convention, Call said his memory was not clear. "We certainly were concerned with the things that minority groups are concerned with and that's that they're on the outside and they want to get into the mainstream." The goals of engagement were not being removed in total from the agenda, just Hay and Rowland's framework for articulating them as a minority group.[15]

In the wake of the convention, the non-minority vision of the political quickly took hold at Mattachine. In the fall of 1953, when three assembly and two congressional seats opened up in Southern California, Mattachine's Southern Area Council rejected the previous year's tactics of engagement. Rather than again ask the candidates for their views on homosexuality, the Legal Committee decided that "until the organization becomes larger and solves its internal problems, . . . we should not sponsor any questionnaire to political candidates." The 1954 brochure "The Mattachine Society Today—An Information Digest" made explicit its new stand on legislative action: "ORGANIZED PRESSURE WON'T WORK. Any organized pressure on lawmakers by members of the Mattachine Society as a group would only serve to prejudice the position of the Society in the opinion of those sociologists and law enforcement officials with whom the matter has been discussed. . . . The burden of activity must rest upon the individual and their friends, who upon being advised of legislation inimical to the minority, individually write to their legislative representatives, expressing their feeling in the matter." These were the new quiet politics of individuals and friends, not group action.[16]

Gay historians have argued about the meaning of this shift in Mattachine's political strategies and attitudes. Many have stressed that the post-1953 Mattachine was a cowardly shadow of its former self, unwilling to embrace a truly liberationist perspective. Certainly this move away from united political action dissipated the momentum that Mattachine had been building and was plainly devastating for several of the founders. Harry Hay sank into a deep depression. For two and a half years, he had thrown himself into Mattachine while cutting himself off from his prior life. When Hay informed his wife, Anita, of Mattachine's efforts, she asked him first to seek therapy, and then eventually for a divorce: Hay moved out. Soon thereafter, knowing that his homosexual activities made him a security risk to the Communist Party, Hay asked his longtime friend and the organizer of his section of the Party, Miriam Brooks Sherman, to remove him from its ranks. As rumors about his divorce, resignation, and sexual life circulated among Edendale leftists, Hay found himself quickly ostracized, with people crossing streets to avoid him. To lessen the pain, he simply cut himself off from his old circles. After all of that, to be shunted from Mattachine—the organization he had so long envisioned—just a year and a half later was crushing. He contemplated suicide.[17]

Dale Jennings went to work for *ONE Magazine,* the creation of one Los Angeles Mattachine chapter, but he grew increasingly bitter, regretting his actions and the public role he had taken. Chuck Rowland joined Jennings at *ONE,* but then left as well. For a time he tried starting a gay church, but he quickly gave up on that and moved away. Founder Bob Hull took his own life.[18] These men were passionate in their vision, and they viewed the transition within Mattachine as catastrophic. Because the politics of Mattachine were also a deeply intimate project, the rejection of their perspective was a personal tragedy.

Nevertheless, the turn in Mattachine was not in fact the end of homosexual political action or the debate about it. The structure that they created for men and women to talk about their sexual lives continued. It remained the foundation for building not just one organization but a complex host of them that became a movement. And at the heart of that movement was not a single idea about homosexuality and identity, but an evolving set of questions and debates about the centrality of desire and sexuality for constructing personal and political identity.

Those evolving debates within the homophile movement were echoed by comparable fights in other movements. The divide, for several years, between Martin Luther King and Malcolm X—between the integrationist vision of King's "beloved community" and Malcolm X's much more separatist language—echoed the conflict between Marilyn Rieger and Harry Hay.[19] Similarly, the movement to defeat the feminist Equal Rights Amendment in the 1970s—mobilized in large part by activist women—constituted a direct and successful challenge to the elevation of gender as just the kind of identity feature around which political action should be mobilized. For at least the last thirty years—even during what might be deemed the heyday of American identity politics—every group's definition of its minority status and demand for minority protections have been vociferously challenged from both without and within.

Plainly, over the past fifty years, Hay's notion of homosexuals as an oppressed social minority has gained significant ground. The gay neighborhoods, commercial districts, and community centers in cities around the country all attest to the wide acceptance of that notion. Edendale—now known more commonly as Silver Lake and Echo Park—became something of a gay mecca in the 1970s, and while it is far from exclusively gay, it continues to have a strong gay presence. Yet even given such acceptance—even given the widespread appearance of gay characters on national television—achieving equal rights for gay men and women and their families remains a challenging project.[20]

These years of identity politics can be perhaps best characterized as a two-step dance in which a politicized-minority view of American society has made gains in our political culture but has also inspired hard-fought challenges against what some view as a balkanization of American political and social life. A series of legal and political battles around the turn of the twenty-first century revealed that back-and-forth dance and indicated how divisive the notion of a gay minority still remained. In 1992, for instance, in response to the legal protections homosexual men and women had gained against discrimination, Colorado residents voted to rescind all those safeguards. Such protections designated homosexuals as an oppressed minority, and Colorado voters refused to grant them such a status, deeming those protections "special rights." While their vote was undone by the United States Supreme Court, which deemed the revocation unconstitutional, it nonetheless indicated the powerful lingering antipathy against recognizing homosexuals as a distinct social minority.

Similarly, in 2003, when the Massachusetts Judicial Supreme Court ruled that it was unconstitutional for the state to deny marriage licenses to same-sex couples—pushing forward the protection of homosexual men and women—the country erupted into a political battle. More than a dozen states quickly passed constitutional amendments deeming marriage to be legal only between a man and a woman, and President George W. Bush announced his own support for a federal constitutional amendment to secure the exclusion of homosexuals from the institution of marriage against so-called "activist judges." While the campaign for gay marriage could be seen as expressing both Harry Hay's demand for equal rights and Marilyn Rieger's hope for integration, it is nonetheless a vision that has not been universally accepted.

These challenges to gay rights must also be seen in the context of the simultaneous drive to end affirmative action programs at universities and public agencies around the country. That effort, which many would argue began as soon as affirmative action programs did, also underscores the powerful resistance to accepting even racial groups as oppressed social minorities. The fights about gay marriage express the same impulse as the fights over affirmative action: the very notion of minority rights and minority protections rooted in valorization of the inner self is not securely and universally embraced in this country. Sexuality, race, and gender, even as they have been framed and to a large degree accepted as the vital features of personal identity, have just as steadily and jointly been challenged as identities without political significance or relevance. The achievement of identity politics has not been the unquestioned securing of full rights for oppressed American minorities. Rather, what identity politics have forged is a political terrain in which the importance of such identities—racial, sexual, gender—can be the focus of determined political action.

Thus, what emerged in Harry Hay's moment of lasting significance was not an absolute agreement that homosexuals constitute an oppressed social minority. What emerged, instead, was a new political culture that attributed genuine importance to individual essence and group identity. In such a context, it became possible to imagine that a homosexual minority could have a real political valence and power—that if homosexuality was acknowledged as a fundamental human essence and source of identity, then around that identity a community and political movement could be built. Comparably, the broader emergence of identity politics—what John Skrentny has called the "minority rights revolution"—represented an expansion of American politics to incorporate an arena in which the significance of essential identities could be debated. The rise of identity politics constituted the rising significance of those very debates, not their resolution.[21]

When Mattachine for a time turned away from a leftist conception of homosexuals as a social minority, they were hardly turning away from the many forces that had brought them there. Indeed, fundamentally, by being rocked and shifted by these debates about "essences" and their political implications, Mattachine remained very much in the tradition of both its artist and Communist forebears. Edendale was indeed the place where various relationships between individual "essence" and the wider public were self-consciously fought over, modified, and lived out. That was the neighborhood tradition that Mattachine continued to embrace. That was what was made in Edendale.

EPILOGUE

When I interviewed the artist Sueo Serisawa at his home in Idyllwild, California, he was ninety years old. He still painted, but he had recently had a serious fall and his movements were slow. When I showed him copies of the letters he had written to Paul and Margaret Landacre sixty years earlier, he was jarred, made uncomfortable. When I asked him how he felt, he said, "It's like I'm dead and they're collecting." And then he added, "It's like looking at something that's gone."

Dorothy Healey was living in the basement apartment of her daughter's home when I interviewed her. The former defiant leader of the American Communist Party sat in an armchair near the door, her catalogs and correspondence on the floor in front of her. Her arm was bandaged from a recent fall she had had as well, this one in her own apartment. When I asked her questions for which she thought she had once known the answers, she looked them up in an indexed edition of previous interviews. When I thanked her for her time, she suggested that our conversation was a last effort at immortality.

On a windy autumn afternoon, Harry Hay lay propped up in a hospital bed. I watched his breath fog a respirator mask, while he lay too tired to speak. I knew that this was a man who had raced through the streets of Los Angeles doing agitprop theater, who had confronted segregationists and anti-Communists, who had launched transformative social movements. And yet here he lay, frail and weakened, holding my hand.

The present is deceptive: it erases its past, its formative beginnings. The sheer force of it—confronting us, surrounding us—all too quickly fools and diverts us. We hold weak hands, hear soft speech—the evidence of a long life journey—and all too easily forget that those hands and heart were ever strong.

To a degree, we can guard against that deception in the physical world. We can remind ourselves that old buildings and old bodies were once younger, shinier, fleeter. Occasionally we even succeed, in our mind's eye, at erasing wrinkles and renovations in order to catch glimpses of the past.

More difficult to perceive—more difficult to believe—is how much perception itself is equally age-able and historical. In particular, people's perceptions of themselves and their humanity are subject to radical alteration. Individual growth, communal effort, and new societal conclusions powerfully transform how people understand themselves. Akin to changing notions of masculinity and femininity, individuals and societies can and do consistently change the shared conceptions of personhood. What is the essence of the self? What combination of ethics, emotions, sexuality, political power? The culture of each era has offered different answers. Though contemporary notions of selfhood seem organic and eternal in the powerful moment of the present, they too are the accretions of time.

The task at the heart of this project has been to peel back the most recent set of additions to American conceptions of selfhood, in particular the conception of a politicized essential identity. In our own cultural moment, when notions of personal identity seem to lie at the center of American social and political life, it is difficult to see those beliefs as anything but natural and necessary. The American idea of a self simultaneously private and political seems fundamental and unchanging. And yet those beliefs are the legacy we carry with us, here at the start of the twenty-first century, from the cultural negotiations of the century now past. Indeed, the clear evidence of the arduous and unpredictable construction of those ideas—so apparent in Sueo Serisawa's letters to the Landacres, in Dorothy Healey's stories of Party song sessions, in Harry Hay's battles with the Mattachine membership—is the "something that's gone" from the present.

Eli Zaretsky deemed modernity as marked by the rise of "subjectivity," or what he called "an ethic of personal fulfillment."[22] The men and women at the center of this narrative took that ethic to heart and built their lives around it. Their lives demonstrate the powerful changes that occurred as the private self became public. Not only did Edendale artists like the Landacres and their "Clan" sit around the bonfire "sorting themselves out emotionally," but, like Grace Clements and Sueo Serisawa, they also tried to convey their emotional lives on their canvases and in their sculptures. They made the subjective self an object for public scrutiny, moving it into the social and political arena. Conversely, their Communist neighbors like Serril Gerber and Miriam Brooks Sherman moved their political vision directly into their social, cultural, and intimate lives. They too intertwined their politics and "subjectivity."

Mattachine moved in both directions. Like the artists, the founders tried to make lusts and desires into a foundation for public and political action. They framed their emotional lives as the basis for action and an identity. At the same time, the defining of that identity was not simply an individual or personal process. It was a political one, fought over and debated, and shaped very much by forces outside each individual.

The key players in this account, men and women like Harry Hay, Miriam Brooks Sherman, Dorothy Healey, Paul Landacre, Jake Zeitlin, and Sueo Serisawa, are now aging or even dead. Some of them I was lucky enough to meet, and I heard their stories directly from them; with others, like Grace Clements or Ward Ritchie, I learned about their lives from their journals or a newspaper article or a generous nephew. These stories came from a time before their frailty set in and took hold. Indeed, the narrative that has unfolded here is a testament to the power they wielded in their lives, unwittingly or not. Through their efforts, both individually and communally, and because of the responses they provoked, they altered American culture and changed precisely the perceptions people had of their own lives. We live with that legacy and those perceptions still.

NOTES

ABBREVIATIONS OF LIBRARIES, ARCHIVES, AND SOURCES

AAA   Archives of American Art, Smithsonian Institution at Huntington Library, San Marino, CA

CCP   Clifford Clinton Papers (Collection 2018), Department of Special Collections, Charles E. Young Research Library, University of California, Los Angeles

CRC   Civil Rights Congress Los Angeles Chapter Records, Southern California Library for Social Studies and Research, Los Angeles, CA

CVF   California Vertical Files, Los Angeles Public Library, Los Angeles

DHP   Dorothy Healey Papers, Special Collections, California State University, Long Beach

FBP   Fletcher Bowron Papers, reproduced by permission of The Huntington Library, San Marino, CA

FLP   Lorser Feitelson and Helen Lundeberg Papers, Archives of American Art, Smithsonian Institution

FWP   Federal Writers' Project of California Records (Collection 306), Department of Special Collections, Charles E. Young Research Library, University of California, Los Angeles

IGIC   International Gay Information Center Collection—Audiovisual Materials, Manuscripts and Archives Division, The New York Public Library, Astor, Lenox and Tilden Foundations

JAF   John Anson Ford Papers, reprinted by permission of The Huntington Library, San Marino, CA

JSP   Joseph Edward Shaw Papers (Collection 840), Department of Special Collections, Charles E. Young Research Library, University of California, Los Angeles

JZP   Jake Zeitlin Papers (Collection 334), Department of Special Collections, Charles E. Young Research Library, University of California, Los Angeles

KI   Library of the Kinsey Institute for Research in Sex, Gender, and Reproduction, University of Indiana, Bloomington

LAE   *Los Angeles Examiner*

LAT   *Los Angeles Times*

Locke   Robinson Locke Collection of Dramatic Scrapbooks, New York Public Library of the Performing Arts

MBS   Miriam Brooks Sherman Papers, Southern California Library for Social Studies and Research, Los Angeles, CA

MCK   Folder "McClatchy, C. K.: Homosexual Issue, 1910–1915," in History and Science Division, Sacramento Archives and Museum Collection Center

NYT   *New York Times*

OHP   Oral History Program, Department of Special Collections, Charles E. Young Research Library, University of California, Los Angeles

ONE   ONE Institute and Archives, University of Southern California, Los Angeles

PLP   Paul Landacre Papers, William Andrews Clark Memorial Library, University of California, Los Angeles

SCL   Southern California Library for Social Studies and Research, Los Angeles

WMC   Reverend Wendell L. Miller Collection 1926–1988, Urban Archives, California State University, Northridge

INTRODUCTION

1. Lanier Bartlett and Virginia Stivers Bartlett, *Los Angeles in 7 Days, Including Southern California* (New York: Robert M. McBride & Company, 1932), 199; Bartlett, "Movie Memories" (ms, 1938), 324, in WPA box 195, FWP.

2. John Holusha, "A Theater's Muses, Rescued," *NYT,* 24 March 2000, and "Commercial Property: A 1912 Playhouse on 42d Street," *NYT,* 30 November 1997; Michael Whitlatch, "The Empire (Eltinge) Theater," Virtual 42nd Street,

web.bvu.edu/faculty/whitlatch/42nd/index.html; New 42nd Street, "Empire Theater," www.new42.org/about_history_empire.cfm.

3. Historians remember Eltinge, however. While Sharon Ullman perhaps gave the most published space to him, Eltinge was also a focus of a few graduate student projects and noted by theater scholars. See Sharon Ullman, *Sex Seen: The Emergence of Modern Sexuality in America* (Berkeley and Los Angeles: University of California, 1997); Tamara Lee Gebelt, "Julian Eltinge and the Female Impersonators" (M.A. thesis, University of South Carolina, 1984); Joan Vale, "Tintype Ambitions: Three Vaudevillians in Search of Hollywood Fame" (M.A. thesis, University of San Diego, 1986); Jay Wilson Dorff IV, "Gender and Performance: An Introduction to Female Impersonation in the West Which Includes an Analysis of the Performances of Julian Eltinge and Charles Ludlam" (M.A. thesis, Brown University, 1986); Thomas Bolze, "Female Impersonation in the United States" (Ph.D. diss., State University of New York, Buffalo, 1994); and F. Michael Moore, *Drag! Male and Female Impersonators on Stage, Screen and Television: An Illustrated History* (Jefferson, NC: McFarland & Company, 1994).

4. William Taube, interview with author, Los Angeles, December 1996.

5. Charles Taylor, "The Politics of Recognition," in *Multiculturalism: Examining the Politics of Recognition,* ed. Amy Gutmann (Princeton: Princeton University Press, 1994), 30; Doug Rossinow, *The Politics of Authenticity: Liberalism, Christianity, and the New Left in America* (New York: Columbia University Press, 1998), 340; Jeffrey Weeks, *Invented Moralities: Sexual Values in an Age of Uncertainty* (Cambridge: Polity Press, 1995), 90.

6. Weeks, *Invented Moralities,* 90; Michel Foucault, *The History of Sexuality,* vol. 1, *An Introduction,* trans. Robert Hurley (London: Allen Lane, 1979), as cited in Weeks, *Sexuality,* 2nd ed. (New York: Routledge, 2003), 3. Weeks's claim also echoed Havelock Ellis's from early in the century that "a man is what his sex is"; the difference between them is telling. Ellis quoted in John D'Emilio and Estelle Freedman, *Intimate Matters: A History of Sexuality in America* (New York: Harper & Row, 1988), 226.

7. Taylor, "Politics," 28–29. Taylor traced the emergence and evolution of these ideas in his masterwork, *Sources of the Self: The Making of the Modern Identity* (Cambridge, MA: Harvard University Press, 1989), and encapsulated them in *The Ethics of Authenticity* (Cambridge, MA: Harvard University Press, 1991).

8. See Norbert Wiley, "The Politics of Identity in American History," in *Social Theory and the Politics of Identity,* ed. Craig Calhoun (Cambridge, MA: Blackwell, 1994), 131–49.

9. L. A. Kauffman, "The Anti-Politics of Identity," in *Identity Politics in the Women's Movement,* ed. Barbara Ryan (New York: New York University Press, 2001), 24, 23, 25–29; Shane Phelan, *Identity Politics: Lesbian Feminism and the Limits of Community* (Philadelphia: Temple University Press, 1989), 43; *Brown v. Board of Education* 347 U.S. 494 (1954), emphasis added. Taylor deemed iden-

tity politics a "politics of recognition" whose "thesis is that our identity is partly shaped by recognition or its absence, often by the *mis*recognition of others, and so a person or group can suffer real damage, real distortion, if the people or society around them mirror back to them a confining or demeaning or contemptible picture of themselves. Nonrecognition or misrecognition can inflict harm, can be a form of oppression, imprisoning someone in a false, distorted, and reduced mode of being." As one example, Taylor pointed to Frantz Fanon's insistence that in order for colonized people to be free, they must "purge themselves of these depreciating self-images" imposed by their colonizers (Taylor, "Politics," 25, 65).

10. The literature theorizing identity politics is rich and varied, but my thinking has been most influenced by Taylor, "Politics," *Ethics,* and *Sources; David A. Hollinger, Postethnic America: Beyond Multiculturalism* (New York: Basic Books, 1995); Calhoun, *Social Theory;* Phelan, *Identity Politics;* Robert Bailey, *Gay Politics, Urban Politics: Identity and Economics in the Urban Setting* (New York: Columbia University Press, 1998); Craig Rimmerman, *From Identity to Politics: The Lesbian and Gay Movements in the United States* (Philadelphia: Temple University Press, 2002); and Susan Hekman, *Private Selves, Public Identities: Reconsidering Identity Politics* (University Park: Pennsylvania State Press, 2004).

11. For various accounts of identity politics as a distinctly late-twentieth-century phenomenon, see Michael Kenny, *The Politics of Identity* (Cambridge: Polity Press, 2004); Todd Gitlin, "From Universality to Difference: Notes on the Fragmentation of the Idea of the Left," in *Social Theory,* ed. Calhoun, 150–74; Phelan, *Identity Politics;* Murray Friedman, "The Tribal Basis of American Life," in *The Tribal Basis of American Life: Racial, Religious, and Ethnic Groups in Conflict,* ed. Murray Friedman and Nancy Isserman (Westport, CT: Praeger, 1998), 3–18. Scholars who offer an earlier start include Rossinow, who argues that only after World War II did "the quest for authenticity . . . become a widespread preoccupation" (Rossinow, *Politics of Authenticity,* 4); John D. Skrentny, *The Minority Rights Revolution* (Cambridge, MA: Belknap Press, 2002), who begins his account with federal racial policies during World War II; and Craig Calhoun, who resists the notion of identity politics as exclusive to the twentieth century (Calhoun, "Social Theory and the Politics of Identity," in *Social Theory,* ed. Calhoun, 9–36).

12. I use the phrase "homosexually active" to distinguish behavior from identity and keep open the space between them. Even today, men and women who participate in homosexual activity do not necessarily perceive themselves as "gay" or "homosexual," identity labels that presume that sexual activity fundamentally defines who people are. (For a recent popular account of this practice among some African American men, for instance, see Benoit Denizet-Lewis, "Double Lives on the Down Low," *NYT Magazine,* 3 August 2003.)

The standout work on early-twentieth-century subcultures that facilitated homosexual activity while sustaining non-homosexual identities remains George Chauncey, *Gay New York: Gender, Urban Culture, and the Making of the Gay Male World, 1890–1940* (New York: Basic Books, 1994). Some of those claims were prefaced by Chauncey, "Christian Brotherhood or Sexual Perversion? Homosexual Identities and the Construction of Sexual Boundaries in the World War I Era," in *Hidden from History: Reclaiming the Gay and Lesbian Past*, ed. Martin Duberman, Martha Vicinus, and George Chauncey (New York: Meridian, 1990); and have been well supplemented by Peter Boag, *Same-Sex Affairs: Constructing and Controlling Homosexuality in the Pacific Northwest* (Berkeley and Los Angeles: University of California Press, 2003); Nan Boyd, *Wide-Open Town: San Francisco's Lesbian and Gay History, 1933–61* (Berkeley and Los Angeles: University of California, 2003); and David Johnson, "The Kids of Fairytown: Gay Male Culture on Chicago's Near North Side in the 1930s," in *Creating a Place for Ourselves: Lesbian, Gay, and Bisexual Community Histories*, ed. Brett Beemyn (New York: Routledge, 1997).

13. John D'Emilio, *Sexual Politics, Sexual Communities: The Making of a Homosexual Minority in the United States, 1940–1970* (Chicago: University of Chicago, 1983), 11. D'Emilio developed a more extended version of the argument, in D'Emilio, "Capitalism and Gay Identity" [1983], in *Making Trouble: Essays on Gay History, Politics, and the University* (New York: Routledge, 1992), 3–16. In so doing, he echoed related arguments put forward by Jeffrey Weeks, Michel Foucault, and Dennis Altman about the social and economic conditions that produced "the homosexual." Weeks, *Coming Out: Homosexual Politics in Britain from the 19th Century to the Present* (New York: Quartet, 1977); Foucault, *History of Sexuality*, vol. 1; Altman, *Homosexual: Oppression and Liberation* (New York: Outerbridge & Dienstfrey, 1971). More recent applications and modification of the economic thesis appear in Lawrence Knopp, "Sexuality and the Spatial Dynamics of Capitalism," *Environment and Planning D: Society and Space* 10 (1992); Jeffrey Escoffier, "The Political Economy of the Closet: Notes toward an Economic History of Gay and Lesbian Life before Stonewall," in *Homo Economics: Capitalism, Community, and Lesbian and Gay Life*, ed. Amy Gluckman and Betsy Reed (New York: Routledge, 1997); and Boag, *Same-Sex Affairs*.

Beyond D'Emilio and scholars of sexuality, a host of historians argued that the industrial revolution and the rise of capitalism fundamentally altered how people understood themselves more broadly, from their sense of their bodies and personalities to the importance they attached to family and sexuality. See, for instance, Francis Barker, *The Tremulous Private Body: Essays on Subjection* (New York: Methuen, 1984); Dorinda Outram, *The Body and the French Revolution: Sex, Class, and Political Culture* (New Haven: Yale University Press, 1989); Jacques Donzelot, *The Policing of Families* (New York: Pantheon, 1979); John Gillis, *A World of Their Own Making: Myth, Ritual, and the Quest for Family Val-*

ues (New York: Basic Books, 1996); Eli Zaretsky, *Capitalism, the Family, and Personal Life* (New York: Harper Colophon, 1976) (originally published in *Socialist Revolution,* nos. 13–15, Jan.–June 1973), esp. chap. 4.

14. The combination of demographic growth and oppression can be seen in a host of important studies, including, to a limited degree, D'Emilio, *Sexual Politics;* Chauncey, *Gay New York;* and Allan Bérubé, *Coming Out Under Fire: The History of Gay Men and Women in World War Two* (New York: Free Press, 1990). A second cohort of historians has examined specifically how the oppression within bars cultivated political action, particularly Elizabeth Lapovsky Kennedy and Madeline D. Davis, *Boots of Leather, Slippers of Gold: The History of a Lesbian Community* (New York: Penguin Books, 1994); Marc Stein, *City of Sisterly and Brotherly Loves: The Making of Lesbian and Gay Communities in Greater Philadelphia, 1945–76* (Chicago: University of Chicago Press, 2000); and Boyd, *Wide-Open Town.*

15. In some ways, this book can be viewed as joining Karen Krahulik's recent and dynamic study of Provincetown, in that both books fold the history of gay community formation into a study of multiple interrelated communities. See Krahulik, *Provincetown: From Pilgrim Landing to Gay Resort* (New York: New York University Press, 2005).

16. Moira Kenney, *Mapping Gay L.A.: The Intersection of Place and Politics* (Philadelphia: Temple University Press, 2001), 7.

17. Jeb Brighouse, telephone interview with author, Los Angeles, 11 February 1997; William Mason, telephone interview with author, Los Angeles, April 1997.

18. Ivanhoe advertisement, *Los Angeles Times,* 14 October 1887; "Silver Lake Terrace," Bihr & White, Los Angeles, n.d.; both in file "Los Angeles—Silver Lake," CVF. See also advertisement in *LAT,* 27 March 1927, and additional advertisement and clipping ("Paving of Important Silver Lake Boulevard Link Reported") in *Los Angeles Evening Express,* 22 May 1926.

19. Edward Soja, *Thirdspace: Journeys to Los Angeles and Other Real-and-Imagined Places* (Malden, MA: Blackwell, 1996), 3, 77, 97–98, 110.

20. Jerrold Seigel, *Bohemian Paris: Culture, Politics, and the Boundaries of Bourgeois Life, 1830–1930* (Baltimore: Johns Hopkins University Press, 1986), 25, 10–11; Ross Wetzsteon, *Republic of Dreams: Greenwich Village, The American Bohemia, 1910–1960* (New York: Simon & Schuster, 2002), 8. See also Christine Stansell, *American Moderns: Bohemian New York and the Creation of a New Century* (New York: Metropolitan Books, 2000); Leslie Fishbein, *Rebels in Bohemia: The Radicals of* The Masses, *1911–1917* (Chapel Hill: University of North Carolina Press, 1982); Robert Humphrey, *Children of Fantasy: The First Rebels of Greenwich Village* (New York: Wiley, 1978).

21. Tarrow offers the intriguing thought that movements succeed only when leaders tap into "more deep-rooted feelings of solidarity or identity." Taking

the broader approach that this book does, however, suggests how identities can be constructed within movements (Sidney Tarrow, *Power in Movement: Social Movements and Contentious Politics,* 2d ed. [New York: Cambridge University Press, 1998], 3, 6).

22. Louis Althusser, "Ideology and the State," in *Lenin and Philosophy and Other Essays,* trans. Ben Brewster (New York: Monthly Review Press, 1971), 174. Althusser explained this as the moment when "ideology hails or interpellates concrete individuals as concrete subjects" (173). See also Althusser, "Freud and Lacan," in *Lenin and Philosophy.*

23. D'Emilio and Freedman explain the period in terms of the "continuing salience of gender in shaping an individual's sense of sexual meaning" (*Intimate Matters,* 228).

24. Miriam Brooks Sherman, interview with author, Los Angeles, 4 October 2000, and Ventura, CA, 7 July 2005.

25. Bérubé, *Coming Out;* D'Emilio, *Sexual Politics.*

PROLOGUE

1. Campbell Gibson, "Population of the 100 Largest Cities and Other Urban Places in the United States: 1790 to 1990," Population Division, U.S. Bureau of the Census, Washington, DC, 1998, www.census.gov/population/www/documentation/twps0027.html; Boyd, *Wide-Open Town,* 45; Robert M. Fogelson, *The Fragmented Metropolis: Los Angeles, 1850–1930* (1967; reprint, Berkeley and Los Angeles: University of California Press, 1993), 78; Kevin Starr, *Material Dreams: Southern California through the 1920s* (New York: Oxford University Press, 1990), 69. The foreign-born constituted less than 20 percent of Angelenos from 1890 through 1930, whereas in New York foreign immigrants were more than 40 percent of the population (Janet Abu-Lughod, *New York, Chicago, Los Angeles: America's Global Cities* [Minneapolis: University of Minnesota Press, 1999], 138, 141).

2. On the start of this health migration, see John Baur, "A Health Rush Begins," in *Los Angeles: Biography of a City,* ed. John and LaRee Caughey (Berkeley and Los Angeles: University of California Press, 1977), 184–87.

3. Peggy Dennis, *The Autobiography of an American Communist: A Personal View of a Political Life, 1925–1975* (Berkeley: Creative Arts Book Company, 1977), 19–20.

4. Miriam Brooks Sherman, email to author, 30 September 2005.

5. Stuart Timmons, *The Trouble with Harry Hay: Founder of the Modern Gay Movement* (Boston: Alyson Books, 1990), 12–20.

6. Adamic and Garland quoted in Starr, *Material Dreams,* 132; Carey McWilliams, "Los Angeles," *Overland Monthly* and *Out West Magazine* 85 (May 1927): 136, as quoted in Donald Christopher Gantner, "Regional Imagination

and Radical Conscience: Carey McWilliams in the West" (Ph.D. diss., University of California, Los Angeles, 2001), 74.

7. Abu-Lughod, *New York, Chicago,* 151–52.

8. Jake Zeitlin, *Books and the Imagination: Fifty Years of Rare Books—Jake Zeitlin,* interviewed by Joel Gardner (OHP, 1980), 21–23. Anthony L. Lehman, *Paul Landacre: A Life and a Legacy* (Los Angeles: Dawson's Book Shop, 1983), 32–36.

9. Serril Gerber, interview with author, Los Angeles, 30 November 2002.

10. Charles G. Clarke, *Early Film Making in Los Angeles* (Los Angeles: Dawson's Book Shop, 1976), 10–22.

11. Lincoln Haynes, "Edendale—Where Stars Were Born," *LAT,* 26 December 1983; "City's New Reservoir, Now Near Completion, Will Connect with Mains to Cost $150,000," *LAE,* 20 May 1906; Ursula Vils, "Folk History of a Neighborhood: Altivo Way Residents Chronicle a Changing Cityscape," *LAT,* 2 November 1983; Norman Klein, *The History of Forgetting: Los Angeles and the Erasure of Memory* (New York: Verso Books, 1997), 127, 143; "Fact Sheet: Silver Lake Reservoir," CVF; "His Record Is Clear," *LAT,* 23 November 1900; "Silver Lake Reservoir," *LAT,* 26 November 1906.

12. Bartlett, "Movie Memories" (ms., 1938), 323–24, 332, box 195, FWP; Remi Nadeau, "Enter the Moviemakers," in *Los Angeles,* ed. Caughey; Clarke, *Early Film Making,* 29.

13. Bartlett, "Movie Memories," 330–31.

14. Bartlett, "Movie Memories," 324–25. See also Klein, *History of Forgetting,* 126, 144.

15. A chronological account of Eltinge's life appears in Moore, *Drag!* More detail appears in Gebelt, "Julian Eltinge"; Vale, "Tintype Ambitions"; Dorff, "Gender and Performance"; and Ullman, *Sex Seen.*

16. Harry Hay, *We Are a Separate People,* interviewed by Mitch Tuchman (OHP, 1987), 370; Robert Toll, *On with the Show: The First Century of Show Business in America* (New York: Oxford University Press, 1976), 239, cited in Marybeth Hamilton, " 'I'm the Queen of the Bitches': Female Impersonation and Mae West's *Pleasure Man,*" in *Crossing the Stage: Controversies on Cross-Dressing,* ed. Lesley Ferris (New York: Routledge, 1993), 110–11. Hamilton also linked Eltinge and Houdini.

17. Hamilton, " 'I'm the Queen,' " 107. For a fascinating portrait of the late 1960s and early 1970s drag queen milieu, see Esther Newton, *Mother Camp: Female Impersonators in America* (Englewood Cliffs, NJ: Prentice-Hall, 1972).

18. Otto Hauerbach and Karl Hoschna, "If Only Some One Would Teach Me" (New York: Witmark & Sons, 1910). Similar jokes appeared in "Mother, May I Go Out to Swim?" and "Don't Take Your Beau to the Seashore."

19. "A Tribute to Art," *Vanity Fair,* 6 July 1912, in Locke 160: 101; "Girls and More Girls 'Cut' Work to Form Waiting Line," *Cincinnati Times,* 7 March 1912,

in Locke 431: 19. A 1908 note declared, "When Julian Eltinge appeared in his female characterizations half a dozen near-sighted gentlemen retired to order flowers. One late arrival, who was unblessed with a program, refused to be disillusioned on the ground that ignorance is bliss" ("English's—Cohan's Minstrels," *Indianapolis News*, 30 September 1908, in Locke 182: 25).

20. "Jealous Husband Asks Mayor to Keep Julian Eltinge Away," *New York Telegraph*, 25 December 1914, in Locke 431: 157; "Bill Dalton," *Cincinnati Commercial*, 28 February 1912, in Locke 431: 10.

21. Hamilton makes a similar argument (" 'I'm the Queen,' " 109–11).

22. "Secret of Julian Eltinge's Grace," *Cleveland Leader*, 23 March 1913, in Locke 160: 105; "How a Man Makes Himself a Beautiful Woman," *Chicago Tribune*, 27 September 1908, in Locke 182: 26–28. A briefer but similar photo spread appeared in *Green Book*, December 1909, in Locke 182: 50. Also, by 1912 cartoonists had taken up the transformation, with versions of Eltinge's backstage efforts appearing in both the *Philadelphia Enquirer*, 9 April 1912, and the *Toledo Blade*, 24 February 1912, in Locke 431: 25, 39.

23. William Sage, "Eltinge Really a Manly Chap, in Fact His Name's Bill Dalton," *Boston Traveler*, 18 May 1912, in Locke 160: 91; italics added. A woman reporter from Cleveland cited a similar experience: "It's very trying, not to say unnerving, to talk to Eltinge back stage, when half of him, the skirt half, is a woman, and the head half of him, wig off, is a man. You feel dizzy, somehow, and lost in speculation as to just what to say to him" (Marjorie Daws, *Cleveland Plain Dealer* [1919?], in Locke 432: 186).

24. Leon Cass Baer, "Helig," *Seattle Star*, 30 June 1919, in Locke 432: 188; "The Man Who Plays the Part of Woman," *Pittsburgh Gazette*, 29 January 1911, in Locke 182: 81.

25. Toll, *On with the Show*, 237; Dorff, "Gender and Performance," 52. Dorff estimated Eltinge's salary between 1906 and 1912 as ranging from $250 to more than $1,000 each week, noting that some reports put it at $2,000 a week for his vaudeville routines.

26. "Boston: Julian Eltinge," *Boston Transcript*, 30 April 1912, in Locke 431: 27. An earlier article warned, "He could disguise himself and escape his creditors, he could gain admission to a Sorosis meeting or he could coquettishly delude some kind gentleman in blowing him off to a swell meal, with a quart or so on the side" ("This Fair Creature Is a *Man!* Now, What Do You Think of That!!" *The Standard and Vanity Fair*, September 1904, in Locke 182: 4). Also see Polly Pry, "Julian Eltinge," *Denver Times*, 14 December 1912, in Locke 431: 51. Lesley Ferris echoes this theme, suggesting that impersonators in general invite audiences to watch their performances in at least two ways—viewing them as men and as women—and that this double reading could itself be exciting (Ferris, "Introduction: Current Crossings," in *Crossing the Stage*, ed. Ferris, 8–9).

27. Ten years after *The Fascinating Widow,* in the Eltinge film *"Madame, Behave!"* one enamored suitor pursued Eltinge while wearing a false beard. Once alone with Eltinge, though, he lent Eltinge the beard. Eltinge again made the artifice of gender explicit by donning the disguise and becoming a man dressed as a woman wearing a most masculine beard (Al Christie [producer], *"Madame, Behave!"* [Los Angeles: Christie Films, 1925]).

28. "Woman Is Only Ten Percent Nature," *LAE,* 12 April 1914, in Locke 431: 113.

29. Harry Hay, telephone interview with author, Los Angeles, March 1997. Vale confirmed Eltinge's romantic liaisons with other men from a handful of sources, including a performer in his 1923 touring show (Vale, *Tintype Ambitions,* chap. 2, nn. 11 and 76). Norman Cohen, emeritus professor of American history at Occidental College, worked on a project involving Eltinge for several years and also confirmed his homosexual relationships (Cohen, telephone interview with author, Los Angeles, March 1997).

30. Newton, *Mother Camp,* 3. This old etiological framework dates back, at least in the more scientific literature, to Karl Heinrich Ulrichs, who in 1864 published his idea of the "third sex" as a person with male genitals but a female sex drive. As Jennifer Terry traced its evolution, Ulrich's idea was widely accepted by later European scholars like Richard von Krafft-Ebing and embraced in the United States as well (Terry, *An American Obsession: Science, Medicine, and Homosexuality in Modern Society* [Chicago: University of Chicago Press, 1999], 41–45, chap. 2, and chap. 7, on how analysts included cross-dressing within the framework).

31. Julian Eltinge clippings file, Billy Rose Theater Collection, New York Public Library of the Performing Arts, as quoted in Hamilton, " 'I'm the Queen,' " 117; Mme. Qui Vive, "College Boy as Chorus Girl," *Chicago Record Herald,* 7 July 1907, in Locke 182: 14–15; Sage, "Gossip of the Stage," *Cleveland Leader,* 21 March 1906, in Locke 182: 7; "HE Wears a Corset: This Man's Enormous Earning Power Is Furthered by His Grace of Figure and Supported by Public Who Revel in Clever Feminine Imitation," unmarked clipping [1912?], in Locke 160: 87. See also "Actor 'Buys a Hill,' " *Cleveland Leader,* 7 July 1918, in Locke 160: 127.

32. "Bill Dalton," *Cincinnati Commercial,* 28 February 1912, in Locke 431: 10. See the widely published batch of Long Island photos in the summer of 1911: "Noted Actor at His Summer Home," *New York Dramatic News,* 12 August 1911; *Vanity Fair,* 26 August 1911; *Cleveland Leader,* 20 August 1911; *New York Mirror,* 23 August 1911; all in Locke, 182: 94–95. See "Julian Eltinge Boxing with James T. Corbett," in *Julian Eltinge Magazine,* n.d., 21, in Locke 432: 23; "Julian Handy with Mitts," *St. Paul Dispatch* [October 1916?], in Locke 432: 128; "Eltinge at the Valentine," *Toledo Blade,* 24.

33. *Variety,* 23 December 1911, cited in Bolze, "Female Impersonation," 55; Bolze, "Female Impersonation," 57; "Girls and More Girls," in Locke 431: 19;

Joseph Schenck (producer), *Seven Chances* (Los Angeles: Metro-Goldwyn, 1925).

34. Vale, *Tintype Ambitions,* 11, 45, and 51 n. 11.

35. On Progressive Era masculinity, see Gail Bederman, *Manliness and Civilization: A Cultural History of Gender and Race in the United States, 1880–1917* (Chicago: University of Chicago Press, 1995); Michael Kimmel, *Manhood in America: A Cultural History* (New York: Free Press, 1996); J. A. Managan and James Walvin, eds., *Manliness and Morality: Middle-Class Masculinity in Britain and America, 1800–1940* (New York: St. Martin's Press, 1987); and Anthony E. Rotundo, *American Manhood: Transformations in Masculinity from the Revolution to the Modern Era* (New York: Basic Books, 1993). On tour, see Bolze, "Female Impersonation," 50.

36. Christie, *Madame, Behave!* Vito Russo read "sissy" film characters as *always* indicative of homosexuality. While highly feminized "fairies" clearly did make the case that effeminacy meant homosexuality, anxiety about masculinity ran both more broadly and deeply. See Russo, "Who's a Sissy?" *Celluloid Closet: Homosexuality in the Movies* (New York: Harper, 1987), esp. 31, where he lumps anti-intellectualism as anti-gay, and 35, where he denies Erik Rhodes's suggestion that feminine men were not simply gay.

37. Chauncey, *Gay New York,* 12–23, on terms; 50, 61, 65, and chap. 2 on the elaboration of the "fairy" as gendered. It is striking that in his efforts to construct a sexual identity, the "fairy" used gender identity as the necessary stepping stone. While Mattachine and later gay activists conceived and constructed sexuality as an independent identity code, "fairies" folded it into the larger gender system. See also Chauncey, "Christian Brotherhood"; D'Emilio and Freedman, *Intimate Matters,* 226–27; Leila Rupp, *A Desired Past: A Short History of Same-Sex Love in America* (Chicago: University of Chicago, 1999), 79.

38. A musician-dancer from a 1923 revue that Eltinge organized recounted to Vale how Eltinge punched a man in the face in a New Orleans nightclub "after he made a remark about Eltinge being a fairy." While at the beginning of the twenty-first century it would be hard to hear that remark as being about anything but sexuality, it is equally likely that Eltinge was fighting off the "sissy" part of fairy (Vale, *Tintype Ambitions,* chap. 2, n. 55). See also Hamilton, " 'I'm the Queen,' " on the distinction between Eltinge and the subculture of "underworld" performers.

39. Amy Leslie, "The Chorus Man," *Detroit News,* 10 September 1913, reprint of article from *Chicago Daily News,* in Locke 431: 88. To be certain, Leslie said nothing explicit about the "prim gentles' " sexual desires. Nonetheless, she made clear how much they, as "fairies," had indeed carved out a place for themselves within the gender code, regardless of a connection to desire.

40. By contrast, historian Ullman read Leslie's column as a clear attack on the "male homosexual subculture circling the entertainment industry" and in-

sisted that discussions of "manliness" were merely code for "sexual perversity" and that the "prim gentles" were homosexuals. Most telling, she felt, was the final story, "revealing a 'camp' sensibility among the 'prim gentles' who refer to Eltinge with a sisterly 'she.' Obviously, the men running from the roaring Eltinge saw him as one of their own" (Ullman, *Sex Seen,* 59–61).

41. "Julian Eltinge Refuses to Pose for Pictures," *Cincinnati Commercial Tribune,* 12 April 1913, in Locke 431: 79; "Eltinge an Actors' Colony Founder," *NYT,* 26 June 1915.

42. On Chaplin and Hollywood friendships, see Gerith Von Ulm, *Charlie Chaplin: King of Tragedy* (Caldwell, ID: Caxton Printers, 1940), 82–86.

I. "A MOST LASCIVIOUS PICTURE OF IMPATIENT DESIRE"

1. G. P. von Harleman, "Motion Picture Studios of California: A Review of the Wonderful Development of the Film Producing Industry on the Pacific Coast—Recent News of Some of the Big Plants," *Moving Picture World,* 10 March 1917, 1608; Pearl Gaddis, "He, She, or It," *Motion Picture Magazine,* July 1917, 27–33, as quoted in Anthony Slide, "The Silent Closet: Homosexuality in Silent Films," *Film Quarterly* 52 (Summer 1999), 30.

2. Louella Parsons, "Is Julian Eltinge Going to Wed? New California Home, All Complete Except for a Woman at the Other End of the Table, and Man with 64 Gowns Has a Wise Smile," n.p., 16 December 1917, in Locke 160: 121; Kenneth McGaffey, "Clothes Do Not Make the Woman," *Photoplay,* January 1918, 86, in Locke 160: 141.

3. While Hollywood joined the city of Los Angeles in 1910, both Burbank and Culver City remained independent of the growing metropolis. For more on the freedom these towns afforded the film companies, see Neal Gabler's *An Empire of Their Own: How the Jews Invented Hollywood* (New York: Crown, 1988).

4. The *Los Angeles Examiner* noted the prior fall that Eltinge was "building himself an Italian villa on the high shores of Silver Lake" and discussed the construction materials (*LAE,* 30 September 1917, in Locke 432: 139). Louella Parsons also wrote about the construction in "Is Julian Eltinge Going to Wed?"

5. "Julian Eltinge's Italian Castle in California," *Photoplay,* November 1918, 6; Elmer Grey, "The Residence of Julian Eltinge, Esq.," *Architectural Record,* February 1921, 2, 99. A precompletion visit to the house appeared in Archie Bell, "Actor 'Buys a Hill,'" Cleveland *Leader,* 17 July 1918, in Locke 160: 127. See also Parsons, "Eltinge Going to Wed?"; McGaffey, "Clothes Do Not Make the Woman"; "Julian Eltinge," *Dramatic Mirror,* 22 July 1919, in Locke 160: 145; "Villa Capistrano: The Palatial Residence of Julian Eltinge at Los Angeles, Cal.," *Theatre Magazine,* April 1919, in Locke 160: 146.

6. "Eltinge's Italian Castle," 6; Parsons, "Eltinge Going to Wed?"; Grey, "The Residence," 2, 99.

7. "The Melting Pot," *Photoplay,* November 1918, italics added.

8. Starr, *Material Dreams,* 84–87.

9. Peter Boag commented that middle-class same-sex subcultures in the Northwest favored "oral eroticism" as a sexual practice. While the information about the Long Beach men is limited, the few men whose professions are known were decidedly middle-class (Boag, *Same-Sex Affairs,* 5).

10. "Long Beach Uncovers 'Social Vagrant' Clan," *Los Angeles Times,* 14 November 1914. Sharon Ullman uncovered the original cases through a file of correspondence between the *Sacramento Bee* editor, C. K. McClatchy, and the reporter, Eugene Fisher. See Ullman, *Sex Seen,* 63–71; and MCK. Notes in the folder speak to the suicides. The preparations are mentioned in "Takes His Life through Shame," *LAT,* 15 November 1914. On the newspaper battle, see *E. T. Earl et al., Respondents, v. The Times-Mirror Company (a Corporation), et al., Appellants,* 185 Cal. 165, 1921 Cal. Lexis 534, 25 February 1921. I am grateful to Paul Herman for sharing his research on the cases with me.

A comparable contemporaneous case is discussed in Boag, *Same-Sex Affairs,* in which he documented a series of 1912 and 1913 arrests in Portland, Oregon, that exposed a "multifaceted homosexual underworld" (2) for the first time in the Northwest; those arrests sparked a much more reform-oriented response, however.

11. Although Ullman describes Lamb as a pharmacist, the newspaper obituaries described him as a banker and "prominent churchman" ("Takes His Life").

12. Eugene Fisher, report typescript, apparently a draft of a proposed article, MCK. Interestingly, a 1949 underground publication defined "ninety-six" as a "California term for reciprocal anal intercourse." See Swasarnt Nerf, Peter Asti, and Daphne Dilldock, "The Gay Girl's Guide: A Primer for Novices, A Review for Roues" (n.p.: Phallus Press Publication, 1949), 13, KI.

13. Fisher, report typescript.

14. Ibid.

15. Ibid. Leonard Pitt and Dale Pitt, *Los Angeles A to Z: An Encyclopedia of the City and County* (Los Angeles: University of California Press, 1997), 403.

16. Ullman, *Sex Seen,* 63; "Long Beach Recital," *LAT,* 19 November 1914. Leila Rupp recapitulated this account in *A Desired Past,* 94–96.

17. Fisher, report typescript. Types of arrests from author's survey of contemporaneous trial records, Los Angeles Superior Court. One of the first recorded twentieth-century accounts was the 1906 trial of John Erwin, who was found having sex in the Los Angeles River bed; *People v. John Erwin,* Crim. 4496 (1906). Bathhouse arrest in *People v. R. B. Harrison,* SC 6330 (1910); car arrest in *People v. Chris Jensen,* SC 25123 (1925); staged bathroom arrest in *People v. Edward Jones et al.,* Crim. 3048, 2d Dist. (1938). This general range applied in the 1940s and '50s as well. See, for instance, alley arrest in *People v. Von Benson,* DCA 2d Dist., Div. 1, Crim. 3278 (1940); alleyway arrest in *People v. Michael Kalpakoff,*

Crim. 3381, 2d Appellate Dist., Div. 1 (1940); roadside arrest in *People v. Henry Joseph Milo*, Crim. 4239, 2d Appellate Dist. (1947); hotel arrest opposite West-lake Park in *People v. Young*, Crim. 3964, 2d Appellate Dist., SC 101225 (1945); car arrest in *People v. Tommy Barney Estes*, Crim. 4467, SC 128233 (1949); public bathroom arrest in *People v. Russell L. Sellers*, SC 133566 (1950); hotel arrest in *People v. Sisto Ramos*, SC 154040 (1953); car arrest in *People v. Grayson Willard Massie and Jerry Hudson Williams*, Crim. 5076, SC 155095 (1953); bathroom arrest in *People v. Alfred John Mason and Rodney C. Owens*, Crim. 5230, 130 Cal. App. 2d 533 (1955).

18. Don Herndon Greenfield, interview with author, Glendale, CA, 3 April 2000; Jack Gard, interview with author, Los Angeles, March 2000; Harold Burton (pseudonym), interview with author, Los Angeles, 25 November 2002; James Kepner, interview with author, Los Angeles, 19 and 21 January 1997.

19. Kepner, author interview. In a separate interview, Kepner said that there was high traffic between the public library and the square, at the Pacific Electric streetcar depot, and at the Greyhound bus depot, as well as along 3rd, 5th, and 6th streets (James Kepner, *An Interview with Gay Historian Jim Kepner: On the History of Gay Men in Los Angeles in the 1940s and Early 1950s*, interviewed by John Mauceri [University of California, Santa Cruz, n.d.], file "Los Angeles History," ONE).

20. John Howard, *Men Like That: A Southern Queer History* (Chicago: University of Chicago, 1997), 14–15. Male same-sex sexual networks are a feature of most gay urban histories. See Boyd, *Wide-Open Town;* Chauncey, *Gay New York;* Stein, *City of Sisterly and Brotherly Loves;* Howard, *Men Like That;* Tim Retzloff, "Cars and Bars: Assembling Gay Men in Postwar Flint, Michigan," and David Johnson, "The Kids of Fairytown: Gay Male Culture on Chicago's Near North Side in the 1930s," in *Creating a Place for Ourselves: Lesbian, Gay, and Bisexual Community Histories,* ed. Brett Beemyn (New York: Routledge, 1997); Gayle Rubin, "The Miracle Mile: South of Market and Gay Male Leather, 1962–1997," in *Reclaiming San Francisco: History, Politics, Culture,* ed. James Brook, Chris Carlsson, and Nancy Peters (San Francisco: City Lights Books, 1997); Alvaro Sanchez-Crispin and Alvaro Lopez-Lopez, "Gay Male Places of Mexico City," and James Polchin, "Having Something to Wear: The Landscape of Identity on Christopher Street," in *Queers in Space: Communities, Public Places, Sites of Resistance,* ed. Gordon Brent Ingram, Anne-Marie Bouthillette, and Yolanda Retter (Seattle: Bay Press, 1997); and Randolph Trumbach, "London," in *Queer Sites: Gay Urban Histories since 1600,* ed. David Higgs (New York: Routledge, 2000).

21. Dale Jennings, interview with author, Los Angeles, 21 February 2000; Harry Hay, *We Are a Separate People,* interviewed by Mitch Tuchman (OHP, 1987), 273–74; Eugene Fisher notes, MCK; Jim Kepner, "Goodbye to Pershing Square," ms., file "Pershing Square," ONE; Kepner, *An Interview.* The sexual ac-

tivity in the square compares interestingly to Boag's description of Lownsdale Park in central Portland, as well as Stein's portraits of Rittenhouse and Washington squares in Philadelphia (Boag, *Same-Sex Affairs*, 113–15; Stein, *City of Sisterly and Brotherly Loves*, chap. 3).

For more general Pershing Square history, see Steve Fader, "Pershing Square Landmarks" (Los Angeles: Los Angeles Conservancy, 1993); Pitt and Pitt, *Los Angeles*, 389; William Deverell, "My America or Yours? Americanization and the Battle for the Youth of Los Angeles," in *Metropolis in the Making: Los Angeles in the 1920s*, ed. Tom Sitton and William Deverell (Berkeley and Los Angeles: University of California Press, 2001), 288.

22. Fred Frisbie, "Talk about Gay Los Angeles" (video recording), 1 March 1987, ONE; Merrill Leonard Harrod, "A Study of Deviate Personalities as Found in Main Street of Los Angeles" (M.A. thesis, University of Southern California, 1939), 25–26. Jim Kepner, "Angel's Flight," in *Loves of a Long-Time Activist: A Suite for Lovers, Tricks, Fascinations & Near Misses* (Los Angeles: self-published, 1996), 37. Compare the overlapping subcultures with Boyd, *Wide-Open Town*, 5, and Boag, *Same-Sex Affairs*, 6.

23. Jennings, interview. Hay confirmed the activity in Echo Park, having discovered it in the early 1930s and remained a regular for several years (Hay, author interview; Timmons, *Trouble*, 62).

24. Edward Weston, *The Daybooks of Edward Weston*, ed. Nancy Newhall (New York: Aperture, 1961, 1973), 1:10.

25. Weston, *Daybooks*, 1:10. See also Weston J. Naef, "Edward Weston: The Home Spirit and Beyond," in *Edward Weston in Los Angeles: A Catalogue for Exhibitions at the Huntington Library, November 25, 1986–March 29, 1987, and the J. Paul Getty Museum, November 25, 1986–February 1, 1987*, ed. Susan Danly and Weston J. Naef (San Marino, CA: Huntington Library, 1986).

26. Harrod, "Study of Deviate Personalities," 20–21. On bathhouses, see Suellen Hoy, *Chasing Dirt: The American Pursuit of Cleanliness* (New York: Oxford University Press, 1995), 15, 116, 126.

27. Harry Otis, "Some Southern Californiana, from the Reminiscences of Harry Otis," file "Baths," ONE; Greenfield, author interview. Eugene Fisher's notes also mention a Turkish Baths on Spring Street; the proprietor of that bathhouse was arrested and killed himself in the city jail (Fisher, notes, MCK).

28. Hay, *Separate People*, 187; "Reporter's Transcript," *The People v. R. B. Harrison*, Superior Court 6330, trial 10, June 1910, 128, 135, 138, 139; transcript in file for *The People, Respondent, v. R. B. Harrison, Appellant*, Court of Appeal of California, 2d Appellate Dist., Div. 2, 14 Cal. App. 545; 112 P. 733; 1910 Cal. App. LEXIS 71, Court of Appeal Records, California State Archives, Sacramento.

29. Kepner, *An Interview;* Kepner, author interview; Walter Williams, "Baths in Los Angeles County," ts., ONE (text combines notes of Williams's interviews of Kepner with Kepner's interviews of Harry Otis, Ted de Leigh, and Fred

Frisbie). Kepner said that the clerk would sometimes warn against "entering enemy territory," but even in the early 1950s, the Crystal Baths were thought of as "a great place for cruising" (W. E. "Bill" Houston, correspondence interview with Jim Duggins, December–March 1995, tape 2, in Gay Lesbian Bisexual Transgender Historical Society Library and Archives, San Francisco).

30. Frisbie, "Talk."

31. Basil Woon, *Incredible Land: A Jaunty Baedeker to Hollywood and the Great Southwest* (New York: Liveright Publishing, 1933), 10–11; Richard Halliburton, "Half Mile of History," *Reader's Digest,* October 1937, 73, as quoted in Harrod, "Study of Deviate Personalities," 11; Ted de Leigh, "1930s Bars Interview," ms. notes, ONE; Frisbie, "Talk."

32. Frisbie, "Talk."

33. Kepner, *An Interview,* 1, 5; Kepner, author interview; Harry Hay, interview with author, San Francisco, 6 April 2001. The official Waldorf liquor license was denied in 1936 on grounds that the business ran "contrary to public welfare and morals" ("Night Clubs Lose Liquor Sales Rights," *LAT,* 22 January 1936).

34. Nerf, Asti, and Dilldock, "Gay Girl's Guide"; Hay, *Separate People,* 393–95.

35. Brian Lee, "Everybody's Baby Estelle," *News West,* 3–17 February 1977, 14, folder "Los Angeles Bars," ONE. Estelle Milmar, interview with author, West Hollywood, CA, 21 December 1998.

36. Hay, *Separate People,* 488–89; Jerome Kern and Oscar Hammerstein II, "Bill," from *Showboat,* 1927.

37. Burton, author interview; Frisbie, "Talk."

38. Timmons, *Trouble,* 46; Harry Hay, interviewed by John D'Emilio, San Juan Pueblo, NM, 16–17 October 1976, tape 00403, side one, IGIC; Hay, telephone interview.

39. Gary Atkins, *Gay Seattle: Stories of Exile and Belonging* (Seattle: University of Washington Press, 2003); Kennedy and Davis, *Boots,* 35; Johnson, "Kids," 99.

40. Greenfield, author interview; Gard, author interview.

41. Ross Higgins, "Baths, Bushes, and Belonging: Public Sex and Gay Community in Pre-Stonewall Montreal," in *Public Sex/Gay Space,* ed. William Leap (New York: Columbia University Press, 1999), 190; Boyd, *Wide-Open Town,* 5.

42. Laud Humphreys, "Tearoom Trade: Impersonal Sex in Public Places," in *Public Sex,* ed. Leap, 32–35; Burton, author interview.

43. On handling the limited evidence of trials and press coverage, see Boag, *Same-Sex Affairs,* 9, and Howard, *Men Like That,* 127–73.

44. Fisher, report typescript.

45. Ibid.

46. Ibid.

47. See Boag, *Same-Sex Affairs,* 128–35, 137–39. For a richer context of degeneration, see Nancy Stepan, "Biological Degeneration: Races and Proper Places," and Sander L. Gilman, "Sexology, Psychoanalysis, and Degeneration: From a Theory of Race to a Race to Theory," in *Degeneration,* ed. J. E. Chamberlin and S. L. Gilman (New York: Columbia University Press, 1995).

48. "Pay for Seats; Trial Delayed," 17 November 1914; "Police Guard at the Door," 16 November 1914; "Attorney Aims Blow at Detective Witness," 11 December 1914, all in *LAT.* While the city did have a long record of occasional sodomy arrests and trials, the mass arrests seem to have been unprecedented.

49. "Long Beach Recital of Shameless Men," 19 November 1914; "Long Beach Uncovers 'Social Vagrant' Clan," 14 November 1914, both in *LAT.*

50. C. K. McClatchy, "Publicity Is Needed and Then More Publicity," *Sacramento Bee,* 23 November 1914, reprinted in *LAT,* 25 November 1914.

51. "Cleaning Up Long Beach," 21 November 1914; "Holy Bible on the Sodomites," 26 November 1914, both in *LAT.*

52. A variety of problems surfaced with the jury, including that one of the first jurors was discovered to have had a criminal record and to have been declared insane. "Long Beach Recital," 19 November 1914; "Eight to Four for Acquittal," 21 November 1914; "Week's Delay for Decision," 25 November 1914, all in *LAT.* On the acquittal, see Ullman, *Sex Seen,* 69.

53. "Week's Delay."

54. "Journalism That Is So Brutal That It Kills," *Los Angeles Tribune,* 19 November 1914; "The Brute," *Los Angeles Tribune,* 2 December 1914; "Defense of Degenerates," *LAT,* 3 December 1914; " 'Brutal Journalism,' " *LAT,* 27 November 1914; all as cited in "Reporter's Transcript," 36, 142, 106–7, in *Earl, Respondents v. Times-Mirror, Appellants,* L.A. no. 5498, Supreme Court of California, 185 Cal. 165. On Earl's grounds, see Earl testimony in "Reporter's Transcript," 105.

55. Opinion, *Earl v. Times-Mirror,* section "The Nature of the Newspaper Controversy."

56. "Jury Acquits in Six-O-Six," *LAT,* 12 December 1914. See Boag on Wilde's trial as a framework for understanding a similar homosexual scandal (*Same-Sex Affairs,* 127–35).

57. Information from "Clerk's Transcript" and "Reporter's Transcript," *People v. Macon F. Irby,"* Los Angeles Superior Court, Crim. 20595; "Reporter's Transcript on Appeal," *People, Respondent v. Macon F. Irby, Appellant,* Court of Appeal of California, 2d Appellate Dist., Div. 2, 67 Cal. App. 520; and additional appellate briefs; all contained in Court of Appeal Records, California State Archives, Sacramento.

58. Copy of "Arrest Report," in "Clerk's Transcript," *People v. Irby,* 61–62; "Reporter's Transcript," *People v. Irby,* 6, 136. Also see "Respondent's Brief on Appeal," *People, Respondent v. Irby, Appellant,* 2–3.

59. See Howard, *Men Like That*, 129–42, on a comparable case. See also Eve Sedgwick, *Epistemology of the Closet* (Berkeley and Los Angeles: University of California Press, 1990), 19–21.

60. "Reporter's Transcript," *People v. Irby,* 101–2.

61. Irby apparently told the arresting officer that once Solovich's advances were known, his actions would seem justifiable. Testimony of Officer John A. W. Stelzriede, partial transcript of first mistrial, cited in "Reporter's Transcript on Appeal," *People, Respondent v. Irby, Appellant,* 8, 48.

62. "Reporter's Transcript," *People v. Irby,* 98.

63. Ibid., 160.

64. Ibid., 136–37.

65. On the divergence between changing medical concepts and popular notions, see Rupp, *Desired Past,* 80–81; Chauncey, "From Sexual Inversion to Homosexuality: Medicine and the Changing Conceptualization of Female Deviance," *Salmagundi,* nos. 58–59 (Fall 1982–Winter 1983): 114–46.

66. "Clerk's Transcript," *People v. Irby,* 61.

67. Opinion, *People, Respondent v. Irby, Appellant.* This framework of not seeking a disposition was apparently in flux at the time. For an example of a contemporary case where the court did allow evidence that showed a sexual disposition, see *People v. Troutman* (1921), 187 Cal. 313. Similarly, see Boag, *Same-Sex Affairs,* 139–41, for 1912 Portland trials where such evidence was allowed by the lower court and disallowed by the Oregon Supreme Court.

68. Boag, *Same-Sex Affairs,* 24–25; D'Emilio and Freedman, *Intimate Matters,* 226–29.

69. Thomas Waugh, *Hard to Imagine: Gay Male Eroticism in Photography and Film from Their Beginnings to Stonewall* (New York: Columbia University Press, 1996), 319, 321; Bernard Natan (director), *The Exclusive Sailor,* circa 1923–25. The film, while French-made, had English title cards and circulated in the United States. *Monkey Business,* 1935. A much less staged film, *Piccolo Pete,* from the same year, also featured three-way activity, although the sexual activity between the men was exclusively oral and occurred only briefly at the film's end (Waugh, *Hard,* 312). All three films in Film Collections, KI.

70. Burton, author interview. Interestingly, Burton remained fairly disdainful of drag queens and female impersonators even late in life. "I don't need a make-believe woman," he stated in 2002. "If I were interested in women, I'd go after the real stuff." At the same time, he emphasized that gender inversion was not tied to homosexuality. "But you must understand," he stressed, "that's a separate thing entirely. That's a certain cliché. And if they wish to be women and are making a living as a woman, that's a whole different thing, and it has nothing to do with homosexuality."

71. Film quote and *Variety* (10 March 1926) cited in Slide, "Silent Closet," 30. On more such films, see Russo, *Celluloid Closet,* chap. 1.

72. Slide, "Silent Closet," 31.

2. TOGETHER AGAINST THE WORLD

1. Lehman, *Paul Landacre,* 19, 33, 39–40.

2. Margaret Landacre, "A Roof over Our Heads," n.d., n.p., 1–2, file 1, box 13, PLP.

3. Ward Ritchie, "The Forgotten Street of Books," in *A Garland for Jake Zeitlin,* ed. J. M. Edelstein (Los Angeles: Grant Dahlstrom & Saul Marks, 1967), 50–51.

4. Lehman, *Paul Landacre,* 42, 57.

5. To a degree, they were behind the curve of that change even in this country, where the artists of New York's Greenwich Village had begun pursuing similar goals in the 1910s.

6. According to art scholars, these poles of social relevance and individualist expression remained central guideposts for artists from the mid-nineteenth century forward. See Annette Cox, *Art-as-Politics: The Abstract Expressionist Avant Garde and Society* (Ann Arbor, MI: UMI Research Press, 1982), 6–33. In his thoughtful analysis of the mid-twentieth-century California avant-garde, historian Richard Cándida Smith argued that these artists disseminated their aesthetic and ideological goals easily into the wider popular culture after the Second World War. By contrast, my argument is that artists disseminated their ideology earlier than the war and did so within the context of other social actors pursuing a similar goal (Smith, *Utopia and Dissent: Art, Poetry, and Politics in California* [Berkeley and Los Angeles: University of California Press, 1995], xx–xxi).

7. Lawrence Clark Powell, "Mr. Bookseller," *Westways,* July 1974, 27, 28. Kevin Starr wrote that Zeitlin and his extensive circle of friends and contacts exuded "a sense of moment and place, of things happening or about to happen in literature, architecture, the fine and performing arts, and scholarship"—all of it "within the Zeitlin radius." In addition to those named above, the radius stretched from Will Connell, the Hollywood photographer, to Leon Yankwich, a superior court judge; from Joseph Pijoan, an art history professor at Pomona College, to furniture designer Kem Weber; from Lloyd Wright, heir to his famous father's name and architectural talent and designer of two of Zeitlin's shops, to Lawrence Tibbett, an aspiring opera singer from Riverside, scion of a citrus empire, whom Merle Armitage (another Zeitlin intimate) eventually debuted at New York City's Metropolitan Opera House (Starr, *Material Dreams,* 305–13.) See also Zeitlin, *Books,* 1:1–63, 84.

8. The other two Zeitlin clerks were Fuqua (as noted extensively in Lehman, *Paul Landacre*) and Karl Zamboni (as listed on Altivo Way in The Club, *The Club: A List of the Members* [Los Angeles: Ward Ritchie Press, 1940], 9); Zeitlin described his own home on Landa Street, in Zeitlin, *Books,* 1:36. On the wider variety of artists, see Nancy Dustin Wall Moure and Lyn Wall Smith, *Dictionary of Art and Artists in Southern California before 1930* (Los Angeles: privately printed, 1975). On book enthusiasts, see Zeitlin, *Books,* 1:132–33: steady Edendale clients included Gordon Raye Young, who lived there with his wife; Oscar and Sadye Moss; and Maurice Seta. On architects, see David Gebhard and Robert Winter, *Los Angeles: An Architectural Guide* (Salt Lake City: Gibbs-Smith, 1994); Thomas Hines, *Richard Neutra and the Search for Modern Architecture: A Biography and History* (New York: Oxford University Press, 1982). On music, see Peter Yates, *Evenings on the Roof, 1939–1954: Peter Yates,* interviewed by Adelaide G. Tusler (OHP, 1972). One local historian also noted that by the late 1920s, art festivals regularly graced the banks of Echo Park Lake (Joe Kennelley, *Sunset Boulevard: America's Dream Street* [Burbank, CA: Darwin, 1981], 39–40).

9. Starr, *Material Dreams,* 329; Lionel Rolfe, "L.A. Arts & Letters: From A to Zeitlin," *Los Angeles Reader,* 31 August 1982, 9.

10. Rolfe, "L.A. Arts," 9. On Edendale demographics, see Klein, *History of Forgetting,* 125–26. On Greenwich Village immigrants and artists, see Stansell, *American Moderns,* chaps. 2–5.

11. My argument in favor of viewing the city as containing not just one arts center, but many, challenges the ubiquitous critiques of Los Angeles as lacking any center, artistic or otherwise. This familiar critique consistently has marked Los Angeles as always broken, always fractured, always isolating. See, for example, Robert Fogelson, *The Fragmented Metropolis: Los Angeles, 1850–1930* (Berkeley and Los Angeles: University of California Press, 1993); Allen Scott and Edward Soja, eds., *The City: Los Angeles and Urban Theory at the End of the Twentieth Century* (Berkeley and Los Angeles: University of California Press, 1996).

This broad critique has been echoed by artists and art historians. Historian Richard Cándida Smith cited a litany of mid-twentieth-century artists like Edward Kienholz and Billy Al Bergston who declared that the city was "virgin as far as art was concerned," or that "there was nothing going on in Los Angeles. Simply nothing" (Edward Kienholz, *Los Angeles Art Community: Group Portrait—Edward Kienholz,* interviewed by Lawrence Weschler [OHP, 1976], 86; Bergston in "California Stories," *Paintbox Stories,* television program, Southern California Community Television, 1987; both cited in Smith, *Utopia and Dissent,* 29). Similarly, painter Lorser Feitelson arrived from New York in 1927 and complained that if you wanted the company or insight of other artists, you "had to take two or three days—one lives out here, another one very far in the opposite direction. Very few even knew of each other, or if they did, they never saw each other." Even Feitelson undercut his own claim, however, explaining later that there were "many, many circles here that are not aware of each other, little in-groups, where they sort of feed each other with the same ideal" (Feitelson, *Los Angeles Art Community: Group Portrait—Lorser Feitelson,* interviewed by Fiedl Danieli [OHP, 1982], 3, 8).

12. Arthur Millier, "Laguna's Art Nabobs Do It Again," *LAT,* 8 May 1938. Sixteen-year-old Millard Sheets was invited down to Laguna by artist Clarence Hinkle in the early 1920s and saw that visit as "one of the most important moments of my life. I knew that there was *no* question about what I was going to do all the rest of my life. . . . The kind of lives they lived and the way they thought about what they were doing was so real" (Sheets, interviewed by Paul Karlstrom, 28 October 1986, 6–7, AAA).

13. Millard Sheets, *Los Angeles Art Community: Group Portrait—Millard Sheets,* interviewed by George M. Goodwin (OHP, 1977), 362–64. On Macdonald-Wright, see Paul Karlstrom and Susan Ehrlich, *Turning the Tide: Early Los Angeles Modernists 1920–1956* (Santa Barbara: Santa Barbara Museum of Art, 1990), 89–91; Nancy Dustin Wall Moure, *Painting and Sculpture in Los Angeles, 1900–1945* (Los Angeles: Los Angeles County Museum of Art, 1980), 31.

14. Sheets, *Los Angeles Art Community,* 33–34.

15. Lehman, *Paul Landacre,* 40.

16. Margaret McCreery [Landacre], "The Woodcut Prints of Paul Landacre," *The Print Connoisseur* 12 (1932), 121–22, file "Margaret's Writings," box 12, PLP.

17. Suzanne Keller, *The Urban Neighborhood: A Sociological Perspective* (New York: Random House, 1968), chap. 2; Stansell, *American Moderns,* especially chaps. 6–8.

18. Landacre, "Roof," 3.

19. Ibid., 7–8; Lehman, *Paul Landacre,* 40. This camaraderie was also documented in a guest book that the Landacres used sporadically over thirty-odd years for their various parties: see the Visitors' Book, 1930–1962, item 14, box 14, PLP.

20. Lehman, *Paul Landacre,* 59.

21. Landacre, "Roof," 4.

22. Lehman, *Paul Landacre,* 43, 47, 49. Additionally, the foreword to *California Hills* was written by Arthur Millier, the art critic for the *Los Angeles Times,* who was in the Zeitlin circle and had raved about Landacre's work when he had seen it in Zeitlin's shop the year before (Paul Landacre, *California Hills and Other Wood-Engravings* [Los Angeles: B. McCallister, 1931]).

23. Smith, *Utopia and Dissent,* xviii; McCreery [Landacre], "Woodcut Prints," 121–22.

24. On the Rounce & Coffin Club's history, see Zeitlin, *Books,* 1:109–12; "Proposed Draft of By-Laws for the Rounce and Coffin Club," file "Rounce & Coffin Club Ephemera," box 12, PLP; and Ward Ritchie, *Years Touched with*

Memories (Clifton, NJ: AB Bookman, 1992). On Saul Marks's shop, see Ed Robbin, *Woody Guthrie and Me: An Intimate Reminiscence* (Berkeley: Lancaster-Miller, 1979), 53. The original UCLA library, now the undergraduate library on campus, is named after Lawrence Powell.

25. "Proposed Draft of By-Laws"; Zeitlin, *Books,* 1:112.

26. Lawrence Powell, cited in Ritchie, *Years,* 80; Ritchie, *Years,* 100; Zeitlin, *Books,* 1:101; Lehman, *Paul Landacre,* 42. The 1933 volume, *A Gil Blas in California,* was a translation of an 1852 Alexander Dumas travelogue of California.

27. Ward Ritchie, *Printing and Publishing in Southern California: Ward Ritchie,* interviewed by Elizabeth Dixon (OHP, 1969), 14, 34.

28. Ritchie, *Years,* 91–93. Canfield's daughter married Antonio Moreno, another silent-film star, and was still living in a mansion on top of the hill when Ritchie moved in. Moreno had developed a large part of the area as "Moreno Highlands." See Hart's autobiography, William S. Hart, *My Life East and West* (New York: Houghton Mifflin, 1929).

29. Lawrence Powell, *Looking Back at Sixty: Recollections of Lawrence Clark Powell, Librarian, Teacher, and Writer,* interviewed by James V. Mink (OHP, 1973), 147; Ritchie, *Years,* 93–94; David Revill, *The Roaring Silence: John Cage, A Life* (London: Bloomsbury, 1992), 47–55.

30. Ritchie, *Years,* 94, 96–97. Only one issue of *The Mousetrap* was produced, due to the loud objections of Walt Disney; a copy of it is in the Ward Ritchie Press Collection at the William Andrews Clark Memorial Library. Stuart returned to fame in the 1990s when she portrayed a survivor of the Titanic in the eponymous film.

31. *The Club,* 1; Ward Ritchie, *Some Books with Illustrations by Paul Landacre* (Los Angeles: Santa Susana Press, 1978), 20.

32. Ritchie, *Some Books,* ix, 20–21.

33. *The Club,* cover.

34. Invitation, file 31, box 1, JZP.

35. Ritchie, *Printing,* 471; Ward Ritchie, "Rare Edition," *Westways,* May 1980, file "Landacre, Paul—'Rare Edition,'" box 250, JZP. See also Lehman, *Paul Landacre,* 87–89; and *The Club.*

36. Ward Ritchie, *Paul Landacre* (Los Angeles: Book Club of California, 1982), 39–41. See Phipps and Landacre correspondence in box 5, PLP. See several twenty-five-dollar purchases by Dr. Alonzo Cass throughout 1944 in Account Book Two, as well as purchases from various Club members—and the Club in general—during 1938 in Account Book One (item 1, box 14, PLP). As for the twenty-five-dollar print, it is likely that many of the artists could not afford the purchase, since Ritchie pointed out that Delmer Daves frequently covered many of the other members' two-dollar dues.

37. Separate from Landacre's economic life, the hills of Edendale also provided clients and investors for Zeitlin and his shops (Zeitlin, *Books,* 1:148–49).

38. Daves cited in Lehman, *Paul Landacre,* 84–85. Daves graduated from Stanford in 1926 and went to work as a prop handler at MGM in 1928. He soon appeared in *Duke Steps Out* with Joan Crawford and then began moving around, writing or directing for *The Petrified Forest, Destination Tokyo, Hollywood Canteen, Demetrius and the Gladiator, 3:10 to Yuma,* and *Kings Go Forth.*

39. "The Paul Landacre Association," 1, item 4, file 1, box 250, JZP.

40. "Landacre Association," 6. Belt, with Zeitlin, developed a renowned collection of Leonardo da Vinci, now housed at UCLA (Powell, *Looking Back,* 479). On Crotty, see Zeitlin, *Books,* 149, 470–71; *LAE,* 18 January 1931, 6 April 1950, 9 May 1961. Ritchie referred to Mrs. Doheny as "Countess Estelle" (Ritchie, *Paul Landacre,* 43). Doheny also sponsored Zeitlin when he was short for a down payment (Zeitlin, *Books,* 149, 470–71). See also Ward Ritchie, *The Dohenys of Los Angeles: A Talk before the Zamorano Club on December 1, 1971* (Los Angeles: Dawson's Book Shop, 1974), 30–35. On Borzage, see *Who Was Who in America, 1961–1968* (Chicago: Marquis–Who's Who, 1968), 4:103. On Struss, see Barbara McCandless, Bonnie Yochelson, and Richard Koszarski, *New York to Hollywood: The Photography of Karl Struss* (Albuquerque: University of New Mexico Press, 1995).

41. See various Association membership lists in file 20, box 3, PLP. Maitland was later described by Millard Sheets as "a remarkable woman, the kind of woman you'd dream about for really supporting the purpose of art—not just support financially. She had not only marvelous resources, but she had a wonderful vision." She purchased Sheets's acclaimed painting *Angel's Flight* and donated it to the County Museum (Sheets, interviewed by Paul Karlstrom, 14 July 1988, 117, AAA). On Millar, see *Who Was Who in America, 1989–1993* (New Providence, NJ: Reed Reference, 1993), 10:246. On distant members, see correspondence between Landacre and John Halliday in New York and Fred Hall in Boston, file 20, box 2, PLP.

42. Richard Cándida Smith, "The Elusive Quest of the Moderns," in *On the Edge of America: California Modernist Art, 1900–1950,* ed. Paul Karlstrom (Berkeley and Los Angeles: University of California Press, 1996), 23. Victoria Dailey, "Art: Naturally Modern," in Victoria Dailey, Natalie Shivers, and Michael Dawson, *LA's Early Moderns: Art / Architecture / Photography* (Los Angeles: Balcony Press, 2003), 33.

43. Richard Pine, *The Dandy and the Herald: Manners, Mind and Morals from Brummell to Durrell* (New York: St. Martin's Press, 1988), 13. See also James Adams, *Dandies and Desert Saints: Styles of Victorian Masculinity* (Ithaca, NY: Cornell University Press, 1995); Rhonda Garelick, *Rising Star: Dandyism, Gender, and Performance in the Fin de Siècle* (Princeton: Princeton University Press, 1998).

44. Pine, *Dandy,* 12. The historic relation between dandyism and heraldry was hardly so schematic or teleological. Indeed, Pine described the emergence

of the "heraldic dandy," who simultaneously focused on the self and attempted to speak to society (Pine, *Dandy,* 13).

45. While modernism in Europe is often dated to the late nineteenth century, according to local art historian Nancy Moure, modernist art arrived in Southern California in the 1910s, but was not encouraged there until the 1920s. Moure, *Painting and Sculpture,* 28–30.

46. Feitelson to Millier, June 1950, roll 1103, FLP (italics added). See also Sheets, Karlstrom interview, 28 October 1986, 82–92; Paul Karlstrom, "Introduction," in *On the Edge,* ed. Karlstrom, 4.

47. Karlstrom and Ehrlich, *Turning the Tide,* 53–54.

48. Grace Clements, *—but is it ART?* unpublished memoir [1968?], 15–16, 18–19, in David W. Forsberg Papers, Reel 4048, AAA (emphasis in original).

49. Stanton Macdonald-Wright, *A Treatise on Color* (Los Angeles, 1924), 27–28, in *The Art of Stanton Macdonald-Wright* (Washington, DC: National Collection of Fine Arts, Smithsonian Institution, 1967), as cited in Karlstrom and Ehrlich, *Turning the Tide,* 93. Mabel Alvarez cited in Smith, *Utopia and Dissent,* 6–7. Francis O'Connor to Lorser Feitelson, 1 June 1964; Feitelson to O'Connor, 3 June 1964, both in Roll 1103, FLP.

50. Karlstrom and Ehrlich, *Turning the Tide,* 57–62, 84–88. See also Susan Anderson, "Journey into the Sun: California Artists and Surrealism," in *On the Edge,* ed. Karlstrom, 183–91.

51. *Americans 1942: 18 Artists from 9 States* (New York: Museum of Modern Art, 1942), 93, as cited in Karlstrom and Ehrlich, *Turning the Tide,* 84. Lorser Feitelson, "What Is Postsurrealism?" *Spanish Village Art Quarterly,* Spring 1941; Harry Muir Kurtzworth, "Art Comment," *Saturday Night,* 2 January 1937; Images from Elizabeth Mills, "Catastrophic Division," reprinted in "The Post Surrealists Are at It Again," *Los Angeles Evening Herald and Express,* 22 Jan. 1938; all in roll 1103, FLP. See also Smith, *Utopia and Dissent,* 9–13.

52. Bram Dijkstra, "Early Modernism in Southern California: Provincialism or Eccentricity?" in *Edge of America,* ed. Karlstrom, 161. For some of the breadth of California abstraction, see Susan Landauer, "Painting under the Shadow: California Modernism and the Second World War," in the same volume.

53. Robert Brophy, "Robinson Jeffers," in *Dictionary of Literary Biography,* 2d ser., vol. 212, *Twentieth-Century American Western Writers,* ed. Richard Cracroft (Detroit: Gale Group, 1999), 144; William Van Wyck, *Robinson Jeffers* (Los Angeles: Ward Ritchie Press, 1938), 9.

54. Ward Ritchie, *I Remember Robinson Jeffers* (Los Angeles: Zamorano Club, 1978), 2, 4–6; Lawrence Powell, "Homage to the Big Sur," in *Books West Southwest: Essays on Writers, Their Books, and Their Land* (Los Angeles: Ward Ritchie Press, 1957), 95; Robinson Jeffers, "First Book," *The Colophon: A Book Collectors' Quarterly* (Part Ten), 1932; Louis Adamic, *Robinson Jeffers: A Portrait*

(Seattle: University of Washington Bookstore, 1929); Van Wyck, *Robinson Jeffers.*

55. Powell, *Looking Back,* 95.

56. Dailey, "Art," 39. Sheets, Karlstrom interview, 28 October 1986, 27–29. On California painting generally, see Moure, *Painting and Sculpture;* Patricia Trenton and William Gerdts, *California Light, 1900–1930* (Laguna Beach, CA: Laguna Art Museum, 1990); Susan Landauer, Donald Keyes, and Jean Stern, *California Impressionists* (Atlanta: Georgia Museum of Art and University of Georgia Press, 1996); and Jean Stern, Bolton Colburn, and Susan Anderson, *Impressions of California: Early Currents in Art, 1850–1930* (Irvine, CA: Irvine Museum, 1996).

57. Sheets, Karlstrom interview, 28 October 1986, 27–29, 52.

58. Dailey, "Art," 40; Karlstrom and Ehrlich, *Turning the Tide,* 29; Cox, *Art-as-Politics,* 20–21. See Sheets's *Angel's Flight* (1931) or *Tenement Flats* (1934).

59. Thurman Wilkins, "At the Sign of the Petrel," *VO Magazine* 4 (March 1936), 38–39, file 16, box 12, PLP.

60. Clements, *—but is it ART?* 23; Stanton Macdonald-Wright, "Art," *Rob Wagner's Script,* 21 October 1944, in Roll 1103, FLP. See Edwyn Hunt, "Sanity in Art," *California Arts and Architecture,* November 1939.

61. Cox, *Art-as-Politics,* 7, 19.

62. Clements, *—but is it ART?* 30, 31, 41, 43, 55, 57. On the history of the John Reed Clubs, and the League of American Writers, to whom Clements gave her speech, see Harvey Klehr, *The Heyday of American Communism: The Depression Decade* (New York: Basic Books, 1984), 72–77, 350–57; Alan Wald, *Exiles from a Future Time: The Forging of the Mid-Twentieth-Century Literary Left* (Chapel Hill: University of North Carolina Press, 2002); Daniel Aron, *Writers on the Left: Episodes in American Literary Communism* (New York: Columbia University Press, 1992).

63. Bella Lewitzky, "Los Angeles in the '40s," lecture, San Francisco, 29 March 1985, tape recording, AAA.

64. Lewitzky, "Los Angeles."

65. Peter Krasnow, "Writings on Art, 1937–1938," 95–96, Peter Krasnow Papers, AAA.

66. Margarita Nieto, "Mexican Art and Los Angeles, 1920–1940," in *On the Edge,* ed. Karlstrom, 120–35; Shifra Goldman, "Siqueiros and Three Early Murals in Los Angeles," in *Dimensions of the Americans: Art and Social Change in Latin America and the United States* (Chicago: University of Chicago Press, 1994), 87–100; Fletcher Martin, interviewed by Joseph Trovato, 5 November 1964, 3, roll 3949, AAA.

67. Goldman, "Siqueiros"; Laurance Hurlburt, *The Mexican Muralists in the United States* (Albuquerque: University of New Mexico, 1989), 206–13. Hurl-

burt titled the Chouinard mural *Workers' Meeting*. See also Arthur Millier, interviewed by Betty Hoag, 4 May 1965, 2:20–21, 3:1–2, AAA.

68. Nieto, "Mexican Art," 134. Herman Cherry, *Interview with Herman Cherry*, interviewed by Judd Tully, 8 May 1989, 98, AAA; Hurlburt, *Mexican Muralists*, 216.

69. Siqueiros also worked with a group called the "Block of Painters" that made portable murals about American antiblack racism. Martin, Trovato interview, 4; Millier, Hoag interview, 3:5; Clements, —*but is it ART?;* Dorr Bothwell, interviewed by Mary Fuller McChesney, 27 February 1965, AAA, 17.

70. Barbara Melosh, *Engendering Culture: Manhood and Womanhood in New Deal Public Art and Theater* (Washington, DC: Smithsonian Institution Press, 1991), 4–5; Andrew Hemingway, *Artists on the Left: American Artists and the Communist Movement, 1926–1956* (New Haven: Yale University Press, 2002), 75–79.

71. Letterheads, Ben Messick Papers, Roll LA9, AAA; Sheets, Karlstrom interview, 28 October 1986, 88–90; Merle Armitage, *Merle Armitage Oral History*, interviewed by Sylvia Loomis, 6 February 1964, 6, AAA.

72. Letterheads, Messick Papers; Macdonald-Wright to King, 18 April 1938, Roll LA6, AAA; "List of People Present at the Meeting Held on Oct. 27, 1937," Roll LA6, AAA; "Federal Art Project," brochure, Albert King Papers, Roll LA5, AAA. Buckley MacGurrin, also an Edendale resident, was hired through the FAP to do murals for the offices of the county supervisors and became an FAP supervisor (Buckley MacGurrin Papers, Roll LA2, AAA).

73. Conrad Buff, interviewed by Betty Hoag, 21 May 1965, 2:6, AAA; Bothwell, McChesney interview, 10–11.

74. "Data on the World's Largest Texturalized Mosaic," Roll LA6, AAA. The FAP regularly used Gladding, McBean (King memo, 12 March 1937; invoice, 24 April 1937; Gladding, McBean to FAP, 7 February 1938, Roll LA6, AAA).

75. Millier, Hoag interview, 2:5–16, AAA. Sheets remembered ninety on the PWAP, while Armitage said 125 (Sheets, Karlstrom interview, 28 October 1986, 88; Armitage, *Merle Armitage,* 6).

76. Dorothy Jeakins, interviewed by Betty Hoag, 19 June 1964, 2, 13, AAA; Anton Blazek, interviewed by Betty Hoag, 13 April 1965, 2:12, AAA; David Rose, interviewed by Betty Hoag, Los Angeles, 28 March 1965, 21–22, AAA.

77. Lorser Feitelson, interviewed by Betty Hoag, 9 May 1964, A:17, B:6, roll 3419, AAA.

78. Cherry also met his first wife, Denny Winters, on the FAP. Cherry, *Interview;* Herman Cherry, interviewed by Harlan Phillips, September 1965, 12, 22, Roll 3949, AAA. On different reactions to FAP, see Bothwell, McChesney interview, 11–12; Nick Brigante, interviewed by Betty Hoag, 25 May 1964, 15, AAA.

79. Sheets, Karlstrom interview, 28 October 1986, 88–90; Ames, Hoag interview, 1:22.

80. Sueo Serisawa to Paul Landacre, 1944; Sueo Serisawa to Landacres [1944], both in file 5, box 6, PLP.

81. Ritchie, "Rare Edition," 16–17. Note that while the essay as a whole was published in 1980, Ritchie quotes within it from an essay he had started years earlier but never completed. This passage is from that section.

3. 1930S CONTAINMENT

I am grateful to the *Journal of Urban History*, which published an earlier version of this chapter.

1. "The WPA Federal Art Project, a Summary of Activities and Accomplishments," as quoted in Dailey, "Art," 40; Cherry, Philips interview, 5–8. See also Arthur and Jean Goodwin Ames, interviewed by Betty Hoag, 9 June 1965, 2:3, AAA.

2. Sheets, Karlstrom interview, 28 October 1986, 90; Armitage, *Merle Armitage*, 13–15.

3. "Furor Stirred by Noted Artist's Paintings at School Depicting War and Greed," *LAT*, 24 July 1935; "Art Out of Place," *LAT*, 27 July 1935; Clements to *Art Front*, February 1936, quoted in Clements, *—but is it ART?* 37–38; Arthur Millier, "Brush Strokes," *LAT*, 25 August 1935, and "Mural Row Due to Artists' Failure to Understand Job," *LAT*, 25 August 1935. See also Arthur Millier, "Murals and Monuments Multiply with Federal Aid," *LAT*, 1 April 1934, and "Current Year Notable for Important Mural Paintings," *LAT*, 8 July 1934.

4. Historians disagree about the experience of Los Angeles during the Great Depression. For the argument that the city numbered among the most depressed in the nation, see Kevin Starr, *Dream Endures: California Enters the 1940s* (New York: Oxford University Press, 2002), 165; William H. Mullins, *The Depression and the Urban West Coast, 1929–1933: Los Angeles, San Francisco, Seattle and Portland* (Bloomington: University of Indiana Press, 1991), 5. For the counterargument, see Leonard Joseph Leader, "Los Angeles and the Great Depression" (Ph.D. diss., University of California, Los Angeles, 1972), x; Greg Hise, "Industry and Imaginative Geographers," in *Metropolis in the Making*, ed. Sitton and Deverell, 21, 36.

5. While state hostility to homosexuality is a familiar theme in gay historiography, it has rarely been treated as significant in broader or more traditional political histories. The gay historiography that deals with state hostility is broad, ranging from Bérubé, *Coming Out*, to Chauncey, *Gay New York;* Jonathan Ned Katz, *Gay American History: Lesbians and Gay Men in the U.S.A.,* 2nd ed. (New York: Meridian, 1992); Kennedy and Davis, *Boots of Leather;* and Stein, *City of Sisterly and Brotherly Loves.*

6. Chauncey, *Gay New York*, 320–21, 353.

7. "Night Club Reviews: La Boheme," *Variety*, 4 October 1932, 52.

8. "Night Club Reviews: Club New Yorker," *Variety,* 4 October 1932, 52–53.

9. "Night Club Reviews: B.B.B.'s Cellar," *Variety,* 4 October 1932, 53. B.B.B. was Bobby Burns Berman, who was the emcee. See "Coast Raid on Panze Joints," *Variety,* 4 October 1932, 52.

10. Hamilton, "I'm the Queen," 116. These notions of the erotics of drag performances are explored more fully in Elizabeth Drorbaugh, "Sliding Scales: Notes on Storme DeLarverie and the Jewel Box Revue, the Cross-Dressed Woman on the Contemporary Stage, and the Invert," in *Crossing the Stage,* ed. Ferris, 36–37; Steven Schacht, "Beyond the Boundaries of the Classroom: Teaching about Gender and Sexuality at a Drag Show," in "The Drag Queen Anthology: The Absolutely Fabulous but Flawlessly Customary World of Female Impersonators," ed. Steven Schacht and Lisa Underwood, special issue, *Journal of Homosexuality* 46, nos. 3–4 (2004): 231–36; Laurence Senelick, *The Changing Room: Sex, Drag and Theatre* (New York: Routledge, 2000), 12; Boyd, *Wide-Open Town,* 30–38.

11. Chauncey, *Gay New York,* 327, 328. The pornographic film *The Surprise of a Knight* opens on a young woman with long white gloves adjusting a sleeveless gown, fixing stockings, and fussing with her hair before a mirror. Eventually a young man in a suit and tie arrives for a date. They sit on the sofa, drink wine, and proceed to kiss and fondle each other. Soon enough they are engaged in oral sex and then penetrative sex. At the end of the film, after the young man leaves, the woman looks ecstatic and dances around, raising her skirt, until suddenly her penis drops free from where it had been restrained with a ribbon. A title card appears, saying "Surprise." Another film, entitled *Three Comrades,* dates from the late 1920s and shows three naked men simply having sex with each other. There is no plot line or story imposed. Clearly this suggests that there was an audience for straightforward homosexual sex, as distinguished from those interested in fairy sex. (Both films in Film Collections, KI.) See also Waugh, *Hard to Imagine,* 312–22.

12. Russo, *Celluloid Closet,* 41; "Banned from Bathroom by Hays Office, Pictures Hop into Pansy Stuff," *Variety,* 2 February 1932, 6, as quoted in Thomas Doherty, *Pre-Code Hollywood: Sex, Immorality, and Insurrection in American Cinema, 1930–1934* (New York: Columbia University Press, 1999), 121. Nonetheless, according to the *Los Angeles Examiner,* one impersonator show was so hostilely received that a waiter at the Santa Monica club felt it necessary to face down the jeering audience with a gun in order to defend the performers ("One Shot in 'Free-for-All' When Crowd Jeers Actors," *LAE,* 8 August 1933).

13. "Liquor Charges Made by Guests," 4 October 1932; "Officers Again Raid B.B.B. in Hollywood," 14 October 1932; "U.S. Acts to Padlock Jimmie's Back Yard," 27 November 1932; "Potato Chips with Beer?" 8 August 1933; " 'Back Yard' Raided Again; 5 Arrested," 22 November 1933; "Five Arrested in Raid on Café Plead Not Guilty," 23 November 1933; "Indecent Show Trial Closing," 14

December 1933; "Manager of Café Gets Jail Term," 19 December 1933; " 'Back-yard' Hostess Gets 90-Day Term," 27 December 1933; all in *LAE*.

14. "Suspect Seized: 'She' Is a Man," *LAE,* 20 August 1928; "Masquerade as Woman Gets Man $25 Fine," *Los Angeles Express,* 24 August 1928; "She Poses 8 Years as Man," 9 January 1930, "Woman Guilty in Masquerade," 12 February 1930, "Posing as Women Gets 3 Men Terms," 26 May 1933, all in *LAE. Variety* suggested that similar raids were occurring on Main Street burlesque houses, as a campaign boost for the mayor. The pansy club raids may have been a part of that ("Chi and L.A. Authorities Mop Up Shows; Minskys Lose in N.Y. Court," *Variety,* 4 October 1932, 40).

15. Boyd, *Wide-Open Town,* 47–52; Johnson, "Kids," 112; "Five Men Held as Vagrants in Hollywood Raids," 21 May 1933, "Posing as Women Gets 3 Men Terms," 26 May 1933, both in *LAE.*

16. "Four Arrested in Hollywood Resort Raids," 27 May 1933, "Fists, Knife, Clubs Fly in Resort Raid," 19 September 1932, "Impersonators Banned by Police," 6 September 1933, "Permit Denied Dancing Café," 16 August 1933, all in *LAE.*

17. "Coast Raid on Panze Joints," *Variety,* 4 October 1932, 52.

18. For a recent engaging account of the recall in historical perspective, see Tom Sitton, *Los Angeles Transformed: Fletcher Bowron's Urban Reform Revival, 1938–1953* (Albuquerque: University of New Mexico Press, 2005).

19. The account that follows is culled from Ernest R. Chamberlain, "The Civic Committee of Los Angles: Its background, activities and accomplish-ments," Pasadena, 1941, a nearly one-hundred-page manuscript in an epony-mous file, box 1, CCP; Jerry Saul Caplan, "The CIVIC Committee in the Re-call of Mayor Frank Shaw" (M.A. thesis, University of California, Los Angeles, 1947); Fred W. Viehe, "The Recall of Mayor Frank L. Shaw: A Revision," *Cali-fornia History* 59 (Winter 1980–81); and Thomas Sitton, "Urban Politics and Re-form in New Deal Los Angeles: The Recall of Mayor Frank L. Shaw" (Ph.D. diss., University of California, Riverside, 1983).

In Los Angeles, the recall was instituted in 1903 and used the following year to recall a member of the city council; then in 1909 the threat of a recall con-vinced the mayor to resign. Sitton, *Los Angeles Transformed,* 4.

20. Clinton's biographical synopsis comes from Chamberlain, "Civic Com-mittee"; Caplan, "CIVIC Committee"; Viehe, "Recall"; and Sitton, "Urban Pol-itics." Similar accounts appear in Starr, *Dream Endures,* 164–70; Michael Wood-iwiss, *Crime, Crusades, and Corruption: Prohibitions in the United States, 1900–1987* (London: Pinter, 1988); and Guy Finney, *Angel City in Turmoil: A Story of the Minute Men of Los Angeles in their War on Civic Corruption, Graft and Priv-ilege* (Los Angeles: Amer Press, 1945).

21. Caplan, "CIVIC Committee," 8, 9, 20–23. According to Mullins, when Shaw was a county supervisor in 1931, he fought for the removal of the then head of the hospital (Mullins, *Depression and Urban West,* 67–68).

22. Caplan, "CIVIC Committee," 1–3, 10–16, 25–31, 33. Sitton also argued that Clinton and Ford in fact lobbied Bowron to name him to the grand jury. Sitton, "Urban Politics," 166–67. Anti-gambling efforts were also under way in New York City, and the FBI's battles with the likes of Al Capone were memorialized by Hollywood throughout the decade. See Roger Sharpe, *Pinball!* (New York: Dutton, 1977), 43–54; John Springhall, "Censoring Hollywood: Youth, Moral Panic and Crime/Gangster Movies of the 1930s," *Journal of Popular Culture* 32 (1998): 135–55.

23. Caplan, "CIVIC Committee," 34–44, 58–60. According to the chair of the recall committee, when people were approached to sign the recall petition prior to the conviction of Earl Kynette, head of the suspect detective squad, 60 percent of them refused; afterward, 90 percent signed. See "Minutes of Committee of 25," 7 July 1938, item 110, box 134, DHP.

24. Historians have disagreed over whether Clinton or Shaw rightfully deserved to carry the day in the recall. For views of Clinton as the heroic reformer, see Caplan, "CIVIC Committee"; Finney, *Angel City,* 40–173; Starr, *Dream Endures,* 166–70. For accounts of Shaw as unfairly condemned by corrupt culprits, see Viehe, "Recall," 290; Woodiwiss, *Crime, Crusades,* 82–88.

25. Challenging mayors and police chiefs with accusations of vice was not new for Los Angeles, though the way sexual perversion came to operate in these campaigns was new. Gerald Wood explained that between 1915 and 1933, five Los Angeles mayors and a dozen police chiefs left office under a dark cloud of accusations (Wood, "A Penchant for Probity: California Progressives and the Disreputable Pleasures," in *California Progressivism Revisited,* ed. William Deverell and Tom Sitton [Berkeley and Los Angeles: University of California Press, 1994], 109). See also Tom Sitton, "Did the Ruling Class Rule at City Hall in 1920s Los Angeles?" in *Metropolis in the Making,* ed. Sitton and Deverell.

26. Mason, author interview; Hay, author interview; "Los Angeles . . . 'America's Wickedest City' . . . Cleans Up Its Gambling, Graft and Girls Rackets," *Look,* 26 September 1939, 29, 30; *Hollywood Citizen-News,* 10 July 1937, reprint, WMC.

27. Photos in file 13, box 1, CCP. On figures, see CIVIC leaflet, file 12, box 1, CCP. Clifford Clinton, "The Truth Can Set You Free If Expressed in Votes," *Shopping News,* 7 August 1937, and Clinton, "The Truth Can Set You Free If Expressed in Votes," *Shopping News,* 28 August 1937, both in scrapbook 1, pp. 44, 45, box 11, CCP.

28. Dyer to Clinton, n.d., and Thompson to Clinton, n.d., both in file 30, "Shaw Recall—Letters Offering Help in Recall," box 3, CCP. Clinton to Bostwick, hand-written draft, on Bostwick to Clinton, 29 August 1938, file "Letters of Appreciation, Recall Election," box 24, CCP.

29. Croxall to Clinton, 19 September 1938, file "Letters of Appreciation, Recall Election," box 24, CCP.

30. Anonymous to Clinton, 14 October 1937; "A buddie" to Clinton, 13 September 1938, both in file "CLINTON:—Letters of abuse, criticism, advice, apology 1938–9," box 25, CCP. Among the various charges about Clinton's morality, one spreadsheet, the *Herald of Decency*, in the spring of 1938 went so far as to claim that Clinton in fact showed his "great contempt for American womanhood" by arguing against abolishing vice and protecting it instead in a red light district ("Clinton Gives Statement," *Herald of Decency*, 4 April 1938, 1, file "Mayor Shaw Clippings," box 134, DHP). According to the recall organizers, Mayor Shaw also asserted that the recall campaign was funded by gambling interests. (See "Minutes of Committee of 25," 29 March 1938, item 89, box 134, DHP, and "Minutes of Committee of 25," 22 June 1938, item 103, box 134, DHP.)

31. During the summer of 1938, Shaw supporters published a bilingual English-Yiddish brochure demanding, "BOYCOTT Traitors [that is, Bowron] Who would take Nazi, Fascist and Ku-Klux Klan Money!" scrapbook 12, p. 9, CCP. Similarly, the election-week headline of a paper that alleged to speak for the black community charged, "Bowron's Backers Exposed: Does Bowron Offer Us 'Clean' Government—or—KLeAN Government?" *Los Angeles Club Reporter*, 15 September 1938, scrapbook 12, p. 12, CCP.

32. Leader, "Los Angeles," 178, 141. See also Upton Sinclair, *I, Candidate for Governor and How I Got Licked* (Los Angeles: End Poverty League, 1935); Paul Greenstein, Nigey Lennon, and Lionel Rolfe, *Bread & Hyacinths: The Rise and Fall of Utopian Los Angeles* (Los Angeles: California Classic Books, 1992).

33. Dwight McKinney and Fred Allhoff, "The Lid off Los Angeles, Part Three: The Spy Squad That Floored Uncle Sam," *Liberty*, 25 November 1939, 24, file 7, box 2, CCP. Fainer quoted in, "Fainer Flays 'Brother Joe' in Bomb Case," and "Intelligence Squad Scored," both n.p., 9 June 1938, scrapbook 8, p. 9, box 13, CCP.

34. Anonymous to Clinton, n.d.; Lewis to Clinton, 5 May 1938; Z. Alexander to Clinton, 5 May 1938; Bennett to Clinton, 10 August 1938; all in file "CLINTON:—Letters of Abuse, Criticism, Advice, Apology 1938–9," box 25, CCP. S. M. Doyle, "Stalin and Clinton over Los Angeles," speech, 19 July 1940, delivered at Patriotic Hall, in Rev. Folder 1–1, WMC. For Bowron charges, see "Reiterates Charge Bowron Supported by Communists," *Southwest News*, scrapbook 11, p. 25, box 14, CCP; and "Reaction versus Liberalism," *Allied Democrat*, scrapbook 11, p. 6, box 14, CCP.

35. Files 14 and 15, box 3, CCP; Chamberlain, "Civic Committee," 63.

36. Leaflet, scrapbook 8, p. 43, CCP.

37. Clifford Clinton, "On Communist Charge," 1938, box 26, CCP. Paul Cline, executive secretary for the county Communist Party, also got on the radio to deny that the Party endorsed Judge Bowron or was "affiliated with the Federation for Civic Betterment, and we had no voice in the selection of Judge

Bowron." Paul Cline, radio address, in Communist Party of Los Angeles brochure, scrapbook 11, p. 48, CCP.

38. Shuler to Wilkinson, 12 February 1938, file 9 "CIVIC—internal affairs," box 1, CCP.

39. Shuler to Wilkinson, 12 February 1938; Wilkinson to Shuler, 14 February 1938, both in file 9, box 1, CCP.

40. *The Equalizer,* September 1937, 4, folder 1-7, WMC. The paper was published in Los Angeles and its subhead read, "Hypocrites Are Those Who Do Not Fear God, But Do Fear Printer's Ink." Single issues also appear in the Shaw and Clinton papers.

41. Lee, "Everybody's Baby Estelle"; Milmar, author interview.

42. "170 Arrested in L.A. War on Vagrants," *LAE,* 10 February 1936.

43. Press releases, 20 July 1937, 26 July 1937, 30 August 1937, file "Campaign PR," box 8, JSP.

44. J. Edgar Hoover, "War on the Sex Criminal!" *LAT,* 26 September 1937. Some academics decried the argument that there was a sex crime wave underway: see "Degeneration Wave Denied," *LAT,* 11 April 1937. For the broader historical claims, see Estelle Freedman, "'Uncontrolled Desires': The Response to the Sexual Psychopath, 1920–1960," *Journal of American History* 74 (1987): 83–106; George Chauncey, "The Post-war Sex Crime Panic," in *True Stories from the American Past,* ed. William Graebner (New York: McGraw-Hill, 1993), 160–78; Stephen Robertson, "Separating the Men from the Boys: Masculinity, Psychosexual Development, and Sex Crime in the United States, 1930s–1960s," *Journal of the History of Medicine and Allied Sciences* 56 (2001): 3–35.

45. Freedman argued that the psychopath fever involved containing Depression-era single men not tied to jobs or family. Such men were also targeted by the Los Angeles police under Shaw. See H. Mark Wild, "If You Ain't Got That Do-Re-Mi: The Los Angeles Border Patrol and White Migration in Depression-Era California," *Southern California Quarterly* 83 (Fall 2001): 317–34, 324. Municipal concerns about sexual degeneracy had been appearing increasingly since the 1910s in cities as varied as Portland, Los Angeles, and New York. See Peter Boag, "Sex & Politics in Progressive-Era Portland & Eugene: The 1912 Same-Sex Vice Scandal," *Oregon Historical Quarterly* 100 (Summer 1999): 158–81; Ullman, *Sex Seen,* chap. 3; Leslie Taylor, "'I Made Up My Mind to Get It': The American Trial of *The Well of Loneliness,* New York City, 1928–1929," *Journal of the History of Sexuality* 10 (2001): 250–86; Andrea Friedman, "'The Habitats of Sex-Crazed Perverts': Campaigns against Burlesque in Depression-Era New York City," *Journal of the History of Sexuality* 7 (1996): 203–38; Chauncey, *Gay New York,* chap. 12.

46. "Officials Pledge Aid to Sex Bureau Plan," 29 August 1937; "Law Agencies Will Discuss Sex Bureau," 1 September 1937; "Official Bureau," 3 September 1937 (italics added); all in *LAE.*

47. "Mayor Shaw Urges Police Sex Bureau," 16 October 1937; "Action on Sex Bureau," 1 September 1938, both in *LAE*. Freedman also argues that the overlapping use of terms like "sex criminal," "pervert," "psychopath," and "homosexual" indicated that they mostly were used to mean "homosexual." See Freedman, " 'Uncontrolled Desires,' " 103.

48. "Psychiatrist, Sex, Bombing Case Engage Council," n.p., n.d. [April 1938?], scrapbook 6, p. 56, CCP.

49. Ibid.

50. Kevin Murphy, "The Manly World of Urban Reform: Political Manhood and the New Politics of Progressivism in New York City, 1877–1916" (Ph.D. diss., New York University, 2001), chaps. 1, 6.

51. Beverly Hills "housewife" to Clinton, 4 January 1938, file "CLINTON:— Letters of Abuse, Criticism, Advice, Apology 1938–9," box 25, CCP. On the growth of psychoanalytic thinking and practice in Los Angeles, which began with an informal study group in 1927, see Nathan G. Hale Jr., "New Heads for Freud's Hydras: Psychoanalysis in Los Angeles," *Journal of the History of the Behavioral Sciences* 37 (Spring 2001): 111–22. On 1930s masculinity, see Freedman, " 'Uncontrolled Desires,' " 88–90; Joseph Pleck, "The Theory of Male Sex Role Identity: Its Rise and Fall, 1936 to the Present," in *In the Shadow of the Past: Psychology Portrays the Sexes,* ed. Miriam Lewin (New York, 1983): 205–25; Peter Filene, *Him/Her/Self: Gender Identities in Modern America,* 3rd ed. (Baltimore: Johns Hopkins University Press, 1998).

52. *Highland Park Post Dispatch,* 9 September 1937, scrapbook 11, p. 45, box 4, CCP.

53. Nielsen-Lange to Clinton, 1 August 1938, file "Letters of Appreciation, Recall Election," box 24, CCP.

54. "Black Reaction + Red Communism = Loathsome Fascism," *Allied Democrat,* 7 September 1938, 2, scrapbook 11, p. 47, box 14, CCP. Presumably a similar analysis could be made of a 13 September cartoon that appeared in the *Times* under the title "Strange Bedfellows!": it shows a racketeer, professional politician, radical, and CIO member all in a bed labeled "Shaw Recall Support," while a reformer sits on the floor claiming the bed is his own.

55. "Minutes of Committee of 25," 7 July 1938, item 110, box 134, DHP.

56. "Sex Crimes Clinic Opens," *LAT,* 30 July 1938; "Police Form Sex Offense Bureau Here," 30 July 1938, *LAE*. The *Examiner* pushed steadily, as well, for the city to register all "perverts," even those merely under advice or treatment from physicians. See "Menace to Society: Registration of Perverts Vital," 20 September 1940, *LAE*. On de River, see "Police Force's Psychiatrist to Be Investigated," *LAT,* 9 March 1949; "Dr. de River Held Needed by Police," *LAT,* 26 March 1949.

57. "Disturbing Figures," *LAT,* 22 April 1939; "Police Organize Sex Crime Unit," *LAT,* 28 April 1939; Ordinance 1380, Sec. 5238, Los Angeles City Council Minutes, vol. 287: p 412; "Sex Criminal Registration Plan Up Today," *LAE,*

23 September 1940; "Sex Offenders Must Register," *LAT,* 24 September 1940. "Megan's Law Calling Up Old, Minor Offenses," *LAT,* February 24, 1997; Lamberson and Doyle to Los Angeles City Council, 10 April 1940, and Hohmann to Board of Police Commissioners, 22 April 1940, both in City Council File 1380 (1940).

58. For a rare instance of oral sex involving a woman, see *People v. Katherine Rayol,* Crim. No. 3803, 65 Cal. App. 2d 462.

59. On institutionalization, see Freedman, "'Uncontrolled Desires,'"; Chauncey, "Post-war Sex Crime," and Robertson, "Men from the Boys."

60. "Reporter's Transcript on Appeal," and "Respondent's Brief," *The People, Respondent v. Edward Jones et al., Defendants; Fred Cabaney, Appellant,* Crim. 3048, 25 Cal. App. 2d 517.

61. "Reporter's Transcript," 279, 281–303, 135, 137, 138, 144, filed for *The People, Respondent v. Edward Jordan et al., Appellants,* Crim. 351, Court of Appeal of California, 4th Appellate Dist., 24 Cal. App. 2d 39; 74 P.2d 519; 1937 Cal. App. LEXIS 20, in California State Archives, Sacramento.

62. Ibid., 370, 371–81, 385, 400, 404, 406, 407, 415, 423, 424, 426, 486, 1355.

63. Ibid., 137, 148–49, 150, 157, 385, 426, 432, 457, 461, 465, 483, 612. See also Verdict Document, *People v. Edward Jordan et al.,* Riverside County Superior Court, Riverside, CA.

64. "Reporter's Transcript," 129, 130–31, *People, Respondent v. Jordan, Appellants.*

65. Ibid., 1342, 1344, 1385.

66. Ibid., 1343.

67. Sentencing Document, *People v. Jordan,* Riverside Superior Court records.

68. Olga Martin, *Hollywood's Movie Commandments: A Handbook for Motion Picture Writers and Reviewers* (New York: H. W. Wilson, 1937), 180, as quoted in Anthony Slide, "The Silent Closet," 31. Martin was the former secretary of Joseph Breen, head of the Production Code Administration.

69. The decision was accompanied by bans on indecent songs or acts and the requirement that no performer come within four feet of a patron. "L.A. Cops Make It Tough for Swishes," *Variety,* 17 January 1940, 1.

70. "Eltinge Can't Wear Dresses for Café Act," *Los Angeles Herald,* 17 January 1940; "That Stuff Won't Go Here, Julian," *Los Angeles Daily News,* 17 January 1940; both in Eltinge clipping file at Margaret Herrick Library, Academy of Motion Picture Arts and Sciences, Beverly Hills, CA. Cohen, author interview. See also Minutes of Board of Police Commissioners, City of Los Angeles, 16 January 1940, in Los Angeles City Archives.

71. Cohen, author interview. Also see Lester Strong and David Hanna, "Hollywood Watering Holes, 30's Style," *Harvard Gay & Lesbian Review* (Summer 1996): 31.

72. "Eltinge Can't Wear Dresses"; "That Stuff." Gladys Bentley, the great lesbian drag star of Harlem, had her performances equally condemned and closed by the new Los Angeles code. She, unlike Eltinge, re-emerged in the 1950s, but then she played the public role of heterosexual housewife. See Minutes of Board of Police Commissioners, City of Los Angeles, 20 February 1940 and 26 March 1940, in Los Angeles City Archives. Also see Eric Garber, "Gladys Bentley: The Bulldagger Who Sang the Blues," *Outlook* 1 (1988): 52–61.

4. LEFT OF EDENDALE

1. "Biographical Introduction," MBS; "Comrades at Brooks' Memorial Donate $52 to Movement," *Western Worker,* 31 January 1935; Letter from Bessie Brooks and Daughters, *Daily Worker,* 23 January 1935. On Boyle Heights, see John Laslett, "Historical Perspectives: Immigration and the Rise of a Distinctive Urban Region, 1900–1970," in *Ethnic Los Angeles,* ed. Roger Waldinger and Medhi Bozorgmehr (New York: Russell Sage, 1996), 41.

2. Kevin Starr, *Endangered Dreams: The Great Depression in California* (New York: Oxford University Press, 1996), 131–55.

3. Greenstein, *Bread and Hyacinths;* California Communist Party, *Two Decades of Progress: Communist Party, Los Angeles County, 1919–1939* (Los Angeles: Communist Party, Los Angeles County, Sept. 1939), 5; Mark Wild, *Street Meetings: Multiethnic Neighborhoods in Early Twentieth-Century Los Angeles* (Berkeley and Los Angeles: University of California Press, 2005), chap. 7.

4. Gerald Horne, *Class Struggle in Hollywood, 1930–1950: Moguls, Mobsters, Stars, Reds, and Trade Unionists* (Austin: University of Texas Press, 2001), 20, 69.

5. Michael Denning, *The Cultural Front: The Laboring of American Culture in the Twentieth Century* (New York: Verso, 1997), xviii.

6. According to Paul Lyons, Communists placed a "damper . . . on any serious consideration of the ways in which personal life relates to political efficacy." Lyons, *Philadelphia Communists, 1936–1956* (Philadelphia: Temple University Press, 1982), 17, 106. That damper has been repeated by scholars who argued that examining the personal elements that bound people to the Party would be like "making them into psychopathological case studies. We will avoid such a dead end, such an act of bad faith. . . . What distinguished Communists was their commitment to Marxism-Leninism, their conviction that industrial capitalism as such was for them the root cause of the injustice"—not, presumably, the intricate and intimate ways they lived their lives (Albert Fried, "Summary and Overview," in *Communism in America: A History in Documents,* ed. Albert Fried [New York: Columbia University Press, 1997], 4). Variations on this view can also be seen in Theodore Draper, *The Roots of American Communism* (New York: Viking, 1957); Klehr, *Heyday of American Communism;* and even Robbie Lieberman, *"My Song Is My Weapon": People's Songs, American Communism, and the Pol-*

itics of Culture, 1930–1950 (Urbana: University of Illinois Press, 1989), which looks at the interactive elements of political culture, but does not push at the interpersonal experience of that cultural activity.

Fried fits into a broad historiographical tradition that downplayed individual volition among Party members and instead emphasized organizational leadership, their points of conviction, and the ties between the American Party and the Soviet Union. That tradition includes Draper, *Roots of American;* Irving Howe and Lewis Coser, *The American Communist Party: A Critical History,* 2d ed. (New York: Frederik Praeger, 1962); Joseph Starobin, *American Communism in Crisis, 1943–1957,* 2d ed. (Los Angeles: University of California Press, 1975); Guenter Lewy, *The Cause That Failed: Communism in American Political Life* (New York: Oxford University Press, 1990); Fraser Ottanelli, *The Communist Party of the United States: From the Depression to World War II* (New Brunswick: Rutgers University Press, 1991); Harvey Klehr and John Earl Haynes, *The American Communist Movement: Storming Heaven Itself* (New York: Twayne, 1992); and John Earl Haynes, *Red Scare or Red Menace? American Communism and Anticommunism in the Cold War Era* (Chicago: Ivan R. Dee, 1996). While Klehr in his own volume (*Heyday of American Communism*) devotes a pair of chapters to the social life of the party, by and large his work falls into this same category.

7. Vivian Gornick, *The Romance of American Communism* (New York: Basic Books, 1977), 9. Many details of the lived social experience of Party members have come through memoirs, autobiographies, and occasional biographies. See, for instance, Al Richmond, *A Long View from the Left: Memoirs of an American Revolutionary* (Boston: Houghton Mifflin, 1973); Jessica Mitford, *A Fine Old Conflict* (New York: Knopf, 1977); Dennis, *Autobiography;* Steve Nelson, James R. Barrett, and Rob Ruck, *Steve Nelson: American Radical* (Pittsburgh: University of Pittsburgh Press, 1981); Dorothy Ray Healey and Maurice Isserman, *California Red: A Life in the American Communist Party* (Urbana: University of Illinois Press, 1990). Broader studies such as Paul Lyons's account of Communists in Philadelphia and Aileen Kraditor's analytic portrait of the Party rank-and-file supplement the narrowness of biography. See Lyons, *Philadelphia Communists;* Aileen Kraditor, *"Jimmy Higgins": The Mental World of the American Rank-and-File Communist, 1930–1958* (New York: Greenwood Press, 1988). That work has been further expanded by studies that liberated the American Party from Soviet control and attended more to the specifics of the American experience, such as Maurice Isserman, *Which Side Were You On? The American Communist Party during the Second World War* (Middletown, CT: Wesleyan University Press, 1982); Mark Naison, *Communists in Harlem during the Depression* (Urbana: University of Illinois Press, 1983); Robin Kelley, *Hammer and Hoe: Alabama Communists during the Great Depression* (Chapel Hill: University of North Carolina Press, 1990); Mark I. Solomon, *The Cry Was Unity: Communists and African Americans, 1917–36* (Jackson: University Press of Mississippi, 1998); and Paul Mishler, *Rais-*

ing Reds: The Young Pioneers, Radical Summer Camps, and Communist Political Culture in the United States (New York: Columbia University Press, 1999).

8. Michael Furmanovsky, "Let's Free California Too: A Social and Political History of the Los Angeles California Communist Party," Ph.D. diss. draft, University of California, Los Angeles, 1986, chap. 1, p. 1. I am grateful for the opportunity to learn from Professor Furmanovsky's work. By contrast see Wild, *Street Meetings,* chap. 7; and Horne, *Class Struggle.*

9. Furmanovsky, "Let's Free California," chap. 1, 3–7.

10. Dennis, *Autobiography,* 19–26. For a broad history of Communist youth activities, see Mishler, *Raising Reds.*

11. On Red Squad activity, see Escobar, *Race, Police,* 80–101; Pitt and Pitt, *Los Angeles,* 427; Gerald Woods, *The Police in Los Angeles: Reform and Professionalization* (New York: Garland, 1992); Furmanovsky, "Let's Free California," chaps. 1–3; Senate Committee on Labor and Public Welfare, *Documents Relating to Intelligence Bureau or Red Squad of Los Angeles Police Department* (1940; reprint, New York: Arno Press and New York Times, 1971); Karl Yoneda, *Ganbatte: Sixty-Year Struggle of a Kibei Worker* (Los Angeles: University of California, Los Angeles, Asian American Studies Center, 1983); Abu-Lughod, *New York, Chicago,* 243; Healey and Isserman, *California Red;* Dorothy Healey, interview with author, Washington, DC, 20 October 2000; Sherman, author interview. Steve Nelson was sent to Los Angeles in the late 1930s to find the infiltrators (Nelson, Barrett, and Ruck, *Steve Nelson,* chap. 8).

12. George Kirchwey, *A Survey of the Workings of the Criminal Syndicalism Law of California* (Los Angeles: California Committee, American Civil Liberties Union, 1926); Furmanovsky, "Let's Free California," chap. 1, 17–23; Dennis, *Autobiography,* 34–35; Yoneda, *Ganbatte,* 18.

13. Furmanovsky, "Let's Free California," chap. 2, 1–6; Dennis, *Autobiography,* 42–46; Dorothy Healey and Maurice Isserman, *Dorothy Healey Remembers: A Life in the American Communist Party* (New York: Oxford University Press, 1990), 44–45; Denning, *Cultural Front,* xiv.

14. Furmanovsky, "Let's Free California," chap. 2, 6–12; Wild, *Street Meeting,* 187–88; Dennis, *Autobiography,* 46–49; Sherman, author interview.

15. Vivian McGuckin Raineri, *The Red Angel: The Life and Times of Elaine Black Yoneda, 1906–1988* (New York: International, 1991), 29, 38–39; Horne, *Class Struggle,* 42–43, 62–63.

16. Raineri, *Red Angel,* 1–26; Furmanovsky, "Let's Free California," chap. 2, 6–10, and chap. 3; Dennis, *Autobiography,* 46–49.

17. Mark Wild, "A Rumored Congregation: Cross-Cultural Interaction in the Immigrant Neighborhoods of Early Twentieth Century Los Angeles" (Ph.D. diss., University of California, San Diego, 2000), 394 n. 67.

18. Miriam Brooks Sherman, *Diary from Albany, NY to Los Angeles, Calif.,* folder "Miriam's Diary, Albany to LA, 1927," MBS.

19. Max Hilberman, interview with author, Malibu, 7 July 2005; Barbara Kaplan, interview with author, Los Angeles, 28 November 2002; Stanley Schneider, interview with author, Los Angeles, 3 March 2000. Samuel Reisbord, an architect, was hired to work on the Moscow subway and then to build an automobile factory. Jeannette Reisbord was a writer and reporter. The Micheltorrena friends were schoolteachers, a profession that Jeannette Reisbord said was well represented in the neighborhood (Jeannette Reisbord, interview with author, Los Angeles, 21 March 2000).

20. Hay, author interview. Miriam Sherman and her first husband moved back to the neighborhood in the late 1930s, in part to rejoin her family there and in part for cheap rent. Nevertheless, for several years Sherman and her family moved around the neighborhood without leaving it (Sherman, author interview).

21. Luba Perlin, interview with author, Los Angeles, March 1997. Max Hilberman, interview with author, 7 July 2005; Kaplan, author interview; Timmons, *Trouble*, 115. Jared Perlin was later blacklisted and worked on the film *The Salt of the Earth*. David Hilberman, who tried to organize the animators at Disney, was later named by Walt Disney as a Communist to the House Un-American Activities Committee. See Karl Cohen, *Forbidden Animation: Censored Cartoons and Blacklisted Animators in America* (Jefferson, NC: McFarland, 1997), chap. 5.

22. Timmons, *Trouble*, 115; Hay, author interview; Kaplan, author interview.

23. Isserman, *Which Side*, 36. Alice Greenfield McGrath, *The Education of Alice McGrath*, interviewed by Michael Balter (OHP, 1987), 84–85 (italics added); Dorothy Healey used the name "Red Gulch" to describe the neighborhood (Healey, author interview); "Mt. Moscow" from Hay, author interview; Morris Markoff recalled the phrase "Lenin's Hills" (Morris and Betty Markoff, interview with author, Los Angeles, 27 November 2002); Reisbord, author interview.

24. Sophia Lewis, interview with author, Los Angeles, March 1997.

25. McGrath, *Education*, 50–52.

26. George Charney, for instance, noted that a key reason for belonging to the Party "was the fact that I was in the company of my dearest friends." Jessica Mitford wrote about "the instant friendship based on mutual loyalties and shared dangers that one developed with fellow Communists, the total welcome and acceptance by complete strangers once one had established one's comradely credentials" (George Charney, *A Long Journey* [Chicago: Quadrangle Books, 1968], 29; Jessica Mitford, *A Fine Old Conflict* [New York: Knopf, 1977], 236, both cited in Lyons, *Philadelphia Communists*, 67).

27. Eleanor Grossman (pseudonym), unpublished interview, details withheld at interviewee's request.

28. Sherman, author interview.

29. Klehr and Haynes, *American Communist,* 64–73, 81–84; Klehr, *Heyday,* 270–73; Denning, *Cultural Front,* 77–83. Isserman noted that the percentage of Jewish membership in the Party grew from 15 percent in the 1920s to 50 percent in the 1930s and '40s (Isserman, *Which Side,* 10).

30. Donald Christopher Gantner, "Regional Imagination and Radical Conscience: Carey McWilliams in the West" (Ph.D. diss., University of California, Los Angeles, 2001), 157, 263–66. On heyday, see Klehr and Haynes, *American Communist,* 84–92, 99; their chapter is titled "The Heyday: The 1930s," and the name of Klehr's own volume on the decade is *The Heyday of American Communism.* On the excitement of the Mooney pardon, see Richmond, *A Long View,* 269; Kevin Starr, *Embattled Dreams: California in War and Peace, 1940–1950* (New York: Oxford University Press, 2002), 23. Note that in the second half of the 1930s, the Party, long dominated by immigrants, shifted to a majority membership that was native-born and pushed to present itself as representative of traditional America (Klehr, *Heyday,* 381).

31. Sherman, author interview; "County to Vote on Aspirants in 30 Legislative Districts," *LAT,* 25 August 1940.

32. Lyons, *Philadelphia Communists,* 61–64.

33. Sherman, author interview; Furmanovsky, "Let's Free California," chap. 2, 14–17. Sherman and her classmate Lillian Carlson were granted their high school diplomas only in 1990.

34. Sherman, author interview; Miriam Brooks Sherman, notebook, November 1932, folder "Miriam's Notebook on Trip to World Youth Conference in Moscow, November 1932," MBS; Furmanovsky, "Let's Free California," chap. 3, 36–37; Raineri, *Red Angel,* 37. For an analysis of the Ada Wright international speaking tour and the global movement on behalf of the Scottsboro Boys, see James Miller, Susan Pennybacker, and Eve Rosenhaft, "Mother Ada Wright and the International Campaign to Free the Scottsboro Boys," *American Historical Review* (April 2001): 387–431.

35. Gerber, author interview; Dennis, *Autobiography,* 60–62; Raineri, *Red Angel,* 43.

36. Eggan to Brooks, 3 September 1938; Eggan to Brooks, n.d., both in folder "Jack Eggan letters to Miriam Brooks from Spain, 1938," MBS; Sherman, author interview. When Morris Markoff moved to Echo Park from New York in 1936, three friends moved with him; one of them also died fighting in Spain (Markoffs, author interview).

37. Gerber, author interview.

38. Michael Webb, *Modernism Reborn: Mid-Century American Houses* (New York: Universe, 2001), 188; Robert Harmon, *The Search for Low-Cost Housing in the Architectural Work of Gregory Ain: A Selected Bibliography,* Architecture Se-

ries, Bibliography no. A542 (Monticello, IL: Vance Bibliographies, 1981), 2, 3; "Avenel Housing Associates: Los Angeles, California," *Progressive Architecture,* February 1951, 62–63.

39. Gerber, author interview.

40. Ibid.

41. Esther Asimow, interview with author, Los Angeles, 3 July 2005; Gerber, author interview. Reisbord, author interview (Jeanette and Sam Reisbord were later residents of the complex); Gebhard and Winter, *Architectural Guide,* 180. I am indebted to Raphael Simon, who opened up the world of Avenel to me and introduced me to the many people who lived there.

42. Before they moved into the Avenel co-op in the 1950s, Betty and Morris Markoff bought and shared a duplex in the neighborhood with another family, with whom they became intensely close (Markoffs, author interview).

43. Hilberman, author interview; Hay, author interview; "Echo Nursery School Seeks Fixed Site," *LAT,* 14 August 1945.

44. Asimow, author interview; Markoffs, author interview; "Lakeview Nursery School Notes Second Anniversary," *LAT,* 30 April 1948.

45. People's Educational Center, *Fall Term 1946 Catalogue* (Los Angeles: People's Educational Center, 1946), 1, 4, 6, 10, 14, 19, folder "People's Educational Center, 1940s," box 20, Organizational Papers Collection, SCL (the enrollment figure is handwritten in the catalogue of Sidney Davison, PEC director); Denning, *Cultural Front,* 70. Biberman was later jailed as one of the Hollywood Ten; his brother Edward, a painter, lived around the block from the Hays (Hay, author interview).

46. Sherman, author interview.

47. Markoffs, author interview.

48. East Hollywood CRC, "Everybody Loves Saturday Nite!" 22 August 1953, folder 20, box 12, CRC. East Hollywood CRC, "3 Good Reasons . . . ," 10 May 1952; "1st Thanks-giving Birthday Party," 22 November 1952; "1952 Jamboree," 12 January 1952; all in folder 19, box 12, CRC.

49. Sherman, author interview.

50. Denning, *Cultural Front,* xv, 208–9. Eleanor Brooks to Esther, 4 February 1935; Eleanor Brooks, 20 February 1936, both in folder "Eleanor's Letters, 1932–1939," MBS.

51. House Committee on Un-American Activities, *Communist Infiltration of the Hollywood Motion-Picture Industry—Part 9,* 82d Cong., 2d sess., 1952, 4255, 4274. For the broader debates, see Howe and Coser, *American Communist Party,* chap. 7; Klehr, *Heyday;* Klehr and Haynes, *American Communist;* Draper, *Roots.* More interesting analyses appear in Daniel Aaron, *Writers on the Left: Episodes in American Literary Communism* (New York: Harcourt, Brace & World, 1961); Denning, *Cultural Front;* Hemingway, *Artists on the Left.*

52. Sherman, author interview; Healey, author interview.

53. Ed Cray, *Ramblin' Man: The Life and Times of Woody Guthrie* (New York: W. W. Norton, 2004), 101–40; Denning, *Cultural Front*, 264–69.

54. Ed Robbin, *Woody Guthrie and Me: An Intimate Reminiscence* (Berkeley: Lancaster-Miller, 1979), 31, as cited in Cray, *Ramblin' Man*, 140.

55. Robbin, *Woody Guthrie*, 32–33, 53, 59–61, 74, 101; Joe Klein, *Woody Guthrie: A Life* (New York: Knopf, 1980), 87–135. Nelson, Barrett, and Ruck, *Steve Nelson*, 246–47.

56. Woody Guthrie, "People's Songs," *Sunday Worker*, 13 March 1946, 7, cited in R. Serge Desinoff, *Great Day Coming: Folk Music and the American Left* (Urbana: University of Illinois Press, 1971), 109. See also Cray, *Ramblin' Man*, 293–334.

57. Irwin Silber, *Hootenanny at Carnegie Hall*, Folkways Records, FN 2512 (Notes), 2–3, cited in Desinoff, *Great Day*, 114; Desinoff, *Great Day*, 110–15; Lieberman, *"My Song Is My Weapon,"* xix.

58. Lieberman, *"My Song Is My Weapon,"* 22–23; Timmons, *Trouble*, 127–30; Wolff to Goldstein, 7 August 1948, folder "People's Song—Finances—Late 1940s," William Wolff Collection, SCL; Card Catalogue, box 3, William Wolff Collection, SCL. Dorothy Healy kept a small songbook among her personal papers, *America Sings . . .* , that emphasized the same easy singing of the card catalogue (item 2, box 65, DHP).

59. Timmons, *Trouble*, 127–30; Hay, author interview.

60. Lieberman, *"My Song Is My Weapon,"* 76, 81.

61. Healey, author interview; Mario Casetta, interviewed by Robbie Lieberman, 5 January 1983, cited in Lieberman, *"My Song Is My Weapon,"* 117–18.

62. Peggy Dennis, "Memories from the '20's," in *Red Diapers: Growing Up in the Communist Left*, ed. Judy Kaplan and Linn Shapiro (Chicago: University of Illinois Press, 1998), 18.

63. Lillian Carlson, "A California Girlhood," in *Red Diapers*, ed. Kaplan and Shapiro, 21.

64. As Jeff Goodwin, James Jasper, and Francesca Polletta write, "If emotions are intimately involved in the processes by which people come to join social movements, they are even more obvious in the on-going activities of the movements. The richer a movement's culture—with more rituals, songs, folktales, heroes, denunciation of enemies, and so on—the greater those pleasures." Goodwin, Jasper, and Polletta, "Why Emotions Matter," in *Passionate Politics: Emotions and Social Movements*, ed. Jeff Goodwin, James Jasper, and Francesca Polletta (Chicago: University of Chicago Press, 2001), 18.

65. Ibid., 8; Hay, author interview.

66. Isidor Brooks to Bessie Brooks, 21 August 1927, folder 1, MBS.

67. "Comrades at Brooks' Memorial Donate $52 to Movement," *Western Worker*, 31 January 1935; Bessie Brooks and Daughters, letter, *Daily Worker*, 23 January 1935, both in folder 3, MBS.

68. Gornick, *Romance,* 213; Sherman, author interview. See also comments from Anthony Ehrenpreis in Gornick, *Romance,* 237.

69. Gornick, *Romance,* 65.

70. Ibid., 178, 180, 181–82.

71. Gerber, author interview.

72. Dennis, *Autobiography,* 17.

73. Gornick, *Romance,* 57, 58, 59.

74. Healy, author interview; Sherman, author interview; Timmons, *Trouble,* 100.

75. Kaplan, author interview; Sherman, author interview.

76. Sherman, author interview; Raineri, *Red Angel,* 40; Dennis, *Autobiography,* 90–91; Healey and Isserman, *Dorothy Healey Remembers,* 89.

77. Sherman reported that the local party took up the question of "male chauvinism" early on, telling husbands they needed to contribute to maintaining their homes (Sherman, author interview). In Philadelphia, Lyons also found that most Party members either married other radicals or converted them to the Party after marriage; Lyons described similar strains in their marriages too (Lyons, *Philadelphia Communists,* 88, 90–91).

78. Sherman, author interview.

79. Kaplan, author interview; Healey and Isserman, *Dorothy Healey Remembers,* 88; Dennis, *Autobiography,* 42.

80. Kaplan, author interview; Gornick, *Romance,* 247–48. Dorothy Healey similarly commented that "there was no such thing as a division between your personal and your political life. Again, we didn't use terms like 'lifestyle' " (Dorothy Healey, *Tradition's Chains Have Bound Us: Dorothy Healey,* interviewed by Joel Gardner [OHP, 1982], I: 53).

5. THE UNITED NATIONS IN A CITY

1. Sherman, author interview; Healey, author interview; Healey and Isserman, *California Red.* Healey's and Sherman's attitudes echoed those in Philadelphia, where racism was also a magnetic issue. "A number of Jewish Communists [the majority in that study] speak of race relations as a primary cause of their radicalization and of the Party's antiracism as one of its primary attractions" (Lyons, *Philadelphia Communists,* 77).

2. Carey McWilliams, "What We Did about Racial Minorities," in *While You Were Gone: A Report on Wartime Life in the United States,* ed. Jack Goodman (New York: Simon & Schuster, 1946), 89, 99, as quoted in Kevin Allen Leonard, "Years of Hope, Days of Fear: The Impact of World War II on Race Relations in Los Angeles" (Ph.D. diss., University of California, Davis, 1992), 12. Portions of my argument in this chapter echo Leonard's claims both in his dissertation and article " 'In the Interest of All Races': African Americans and Inter-racial Coopera-

tion in Los Angeles during and after World War II," in *Seeking El Dorado: African Americans in California, 1769–1999,* ed. Lawrence B. de Graaf, Quintard Taylor, and Kevin Mulroy (Seattle: University of Washington Press, 2001), 309–40.

3. Recent contributions to the racial history of Los Angeles include Douglas Monroy, *Rebirth: Mexican Los Angeles from the Great Migration to the Great Depression* (Berkeley and Los Angeles: University of California Press, 1999); Escobar, *Race, Police;* William Deverell, *Whitewashed Adobe: The Rise of Los Angeles and the Remaking of its Mexican Past* (Berkeley and Los Angeles: University of California Press, 2002); Lon Kurashige, *Japanese American Celebration and Conflict: A History of Ethnic Identity and Festival in Los Angeles, 1934–1990* (Berkeley and Los Angeles: University of California Press, 2002); Josh Sides, *L.A. City Limits: African American Los Angeles from the Great Depression to the Present* (Berkeley and Los Angeles: University of California Press, 2003); Eric Avila, *Popular Culture in the Age of White Flight: Fear and Fantasy in Suburban Los Angeles* (Berkeley and Los Angeles: University of California Press, 2004); Douglas Flamming, *Bound for Freedom: Black Los Angeles in Jim Crow America* (Berkeley and Los Angeles: University of California Press, 2005); and Wild, *Street Meeting.*

4. Michael Omi and Howard Winant, *Racial Formation in the United States: From the 1960s to the 1990s,* 2d ed. (New York: Routledge, 1994), 4. Note that this emphasis on elites echoes Deverell's approach in *Whitewashed Adobe.*

5. Wild, *Street Meeting,* 38; Avila, *Popular Culture,* 20–21; Deverell, *Whitewashed Adobe,* 4.

6. Laslett, "Historical Perspectives," 55; Sides, *L.A. City Limits,* 43.

7. Flamming, 90–110, 117; Sides, *L.A. City Limits,* 8, 34.

8. Donald Teruo Hata Jr. and Nadine Ishitani Hata, "Asian-Pacific Angelinos: Model Minorities and Indispensable Scapegoats," in *20th Century Los Angeles: Power, Promotion, and Social Conflict,* ed. Norman Klein and Martin Schiesl (Claremont, CA: Regina Books, 1990), 71; Pitt and Pitt, *Los Angeles,* 229; David Yoo, *Growing Up Nisei: Race, Generation, and Culture among Japanese Americans of California, 1924–49* (Urbana: University of Illinois Press, 2000), 2; John Modell, *The Economics and Politics of Racial Accommodation: The Japanese of Los Angeles, 1900–1942* (Urbana: University of Illinois Press, 1977), 2. According to Lon Kurashige, Los Angeles had the largest urban concentration in the country (Kurashige, *Japanese American,* xvi).

9. Escobar, *Race, Police,* 166. Escobar pointed out that the census for 1940 gave an official figure of 133,000, as compared to 97,000 in 1930. Chicano scholars, however, estimated that the 1930 figure should have been closer to 190,000, and thus the 1940 figure would have been much larger than that. Starr, *Embattled Dreams,* 97; Carlos Navarro and Rodolfo Acuña, "In Search of Community: A Comparative Essay on Mexicans in Los Angeles and San Antonio," in *20th Century Los Angeles,* ed. Klein and Schiesl, 200. On indifference as an act of violent forgetting, see Deverell, *Whitewashed Adobe,* and Monroy, *Rebirth.*

10. Solomon, *Cry Was Unity,* 7, chaps. 1, 5. Mark Naison framed the tension in Party positions as "nationalism" versus "integration" (Naison, *Communists in Harlem during the Depression* [New York: Grove Press, 1983], xviii). The shifting terrain of Party thinking can be seen in Party publications like C. A. Hathaway, "Who Are the Friends of the Negro People?" (New York: Workers Library Publishers, July 1932), 8–9; Harry Haywood, *The Road to Negro Liberation* (New York: Workers Library Publishers, 1934); George W. Crockett Jr., *Freedom Is Everybody's Job! The Crime of the Government against the Negro People* (New York: National Non-Partisan Committee [1949?]); "The Fight for the Freedom of the Negro People: Material for Club Discussions in Connection with the Anniversaries of Lincoln and Douglass and also in relation to the Communist Position on the Negro Question," issued by State Education Committee, Communist Party of California, San Francisco, 12 February 1946, box 69c, DHP; "Study Outline Negro Liberation," L.A. County Communist Party Educational Dept., January 1950, box 69d, DHP; and "The Struggle against White Chauvinism: Outline for Discussion and Study Guide for Schools, Classes, Study Groups," issued by National Education Department, Communist Party, New York, September 1949, box 69d, DHP. These developments are more broadly discussed in Klehr, *Heyday,* 343; Kelley, *Hammer and Hoe;* Naison, *Communists in Harlem;* and Wilson Record, *The Negro and the Communist Party* (1951; reprint, Westport, CT: Greenwood Press, 1980).

11. On the breadth of the Scottsboro campaign, see Miller, Pennybacker, and Rosenhaft, "Mother Ada Wright"; Klehr and Haynes, *American Communist,* 75–77; Klehr, *Heyday,* 324–43; Sherman, author interview.

12. C. A. Hathaway, "Who Are the Friends"; titles listed on back of J. S. Allen, "Smash the Scottsboro Lynch Verdict" (New York: Workers Library Publishers, April 1933), box 68a, DHP.

13. Sides, *L.A. City Limits,* 32; Healey, author interview.

14. Keith Collins, *Black Los Angeles: The Maturing of the Ghetto, 1940–1950* (Saratoga, CA: Century Twenty One, 1980), 18–19; Sides, *L.A. City Limits,* 44.

15. Hollywood Anti-Nazi League to Ford, 24 December 1936, file 1936, folder B III 11 d, box 46, JAF. On racism in wartime propaganda, see John Dower, "Race, Language, and War in Two Cultures: World War II in Asia," in *The War in American Culture: Society and Consciousness during World War II,* ed. Lewis Erenberg and Susan Hirsch (Chicago: University of Chicago Press, 1996).

16. Leonard, "Years of Hope," 26; Gerald Nash, *The American West Transformed: The Impact of the Second World War* (Bloomington: Indiana University Press, 1985), 88, as quoted in Leonard, "Years of Hope," 19.

Peggy Pascoe uses the term "racialism" to encompass all intellectual systems that maintain that "race, understood as an indivisible essence that included not only biology but also culture, morality, and intelligence, was a compellingly significant factor in history and society." Racism, thus, was a form of racialism. "Inter-racialism" was, in fact, a more contemporary term, though it did not emerge until 1943. It called for acceptance of racial difference and a peaceful co-existence in interrace relations. Harvard Sitkoff later disparagingly defined inter-racialism as a philosophy "which all too easily accepted the appearance of racial peace for the reality of racial justice" (Peggy Pascoe, "Miscegenation Law, Court Cases, and Ideologies of 'Race' in Twentieth-Century America," *Journal of American History* 83 [June 1996], 48; Harvard Sitkoff, "Racial Militancy and Inter-racial Violence in the Second World War," *Journal of American History* 58 [1971]: 662).

Gary Gerstle has also argued that the war years shifted the nation's attention away from "democratizing relations between capital and labor" and onto a "pluralist creed focused instead on eliminating racial and religious bigotry from American life." He explained that the war served to fold ethnicity into whiteness even as it elevated racial difference. (Gary Gerstle, *Working-Class Americanism: The Politics of Labor in a Textile City, 1914–1960* [New York: Cambridge University Press, 1989], 5).

17. Pitt and Pitt, *Los Angeles,* 204–5.

18. "Young Voters Paid Tribute," *LAT,* 13 June 1939. By 1941 FDR had joined Mayor Bowron and the leaders of three hundred other cities in setting aside a day for such an American declaration. See Neal to Ford, 8 February 1941, file 1941; Bowron proclamation, 31 March 1941, file 1941; and Ford to Governor Culbert Olson, 7 June 1939, file 1939; all in folder B IV 4 C, "I Am an American," box 71, JAF.

19. Bowron to Easter, 30 January 1939, file "Mayor's Personal, 1939, Jan–Feb," box 5, FBP.

20. Radio broadcast, *Jewish-International Broadcasting Hour,* 12 June 1939, file "Speeches," box 36, FBP; Pascoe, "Miscegenation Law," 48. Bowron made similar declarations about Japanese Americans, one of which was used by the Japanese American Citizens League in a brochure (Statement issued to JACL, 1 March 1939, file "Mayor's personal, 1939, March," box 5, FBP).

21. Ford to Yamato, 5 September 1935, file 1934, folder B IV 5 I bb, box 74, JAF; Ford to editors of *DOHO: A Progressive Japanese Bi-Monthly for Equality, Peace and Progress,* 19 August 1938, file 1938, folder B IV 5 I bb, box 74, JAF; Ford to Mellinkoff, 5 July 1940, file 1940, folder B IV 5 I cc, file 1940, box 75, JAF. See also two Ford autobiographies: John Anson Ford, *Thirty Explosive Years in Los Angeles County* (San Marino, CA: Huntington Library, 1961); and John Anson Ford, *Honest Politics My Theme: The Story of a Veteran Public Official's Troubles and Triumphs: An Autobiography* (New York: Vantage Press, 1978).

22. John Anson Ford, "Superficial Democracy," 24 June 1941; John Anson Ford, "Racial Discrimination and War," 6 October 1942, both in file 1, folder A VI, box 2, JAF.

23. Arthur C. Verge, *Paradise Transformed: Los Angeles during the Second World War* (Dubuque, IA: Kendall/Hunt, 1993), 22–27, 32.

24. Starr, *Embattled Dreams,* 63–64.

25. Escobar, *Race, Police,* 157; Verge, *Paradise Transformed,* 28, 33; Sides, *L.A. City Limits,* 37; Starr, *Embattled Dreams,* 68–69.

26. Sitton, *Los Angeles Transformed,* 65.

27. Mary Serisawa to Landacres, 4 May 1944; Mary Serisawa to Landacres, 16 July 1944; Sueo Serisawa to Landacres [1944]; all in file 5, box 6, PLP. See also "Sueo Serisawa: Exhibition, April 12 to May 8," brochure (Los Angeles: Dalzell Hatfield Galleries [1948]), file 5, box 6, PLP; Sueo Serisawa, interview with author, 17 May 2000; Lehman, *Paul Landacre,* 103.

28. Minutes of JACL, Southern District Council, Anti-Axis Committee Meeting, 8 December 1941, file 1941, folder B IV 5 I bb, box 74, JAF. Ford drafted a parallel resolution, calling on the superintendent of schools to protect Japanese children (Resolution, 9 December 1941, file 1941, folder B IV 5 I bb, box 74, JAF). Kurashige pointed out that international tensions during the late 1930s led the JACL to work ever harder to emphasize the Americanism of Japanese Americans (Kurashige, *Japanese American,* 43). See also Patricia Limerick, *The Legacy of Conquest: The Unbroken Past of the American West* (New York: W. W. Norton, 1988), 274, on JACL; and Lon Kurashige, "The Problem of Biculturalism: Japanese American Identity and Festival before World War II," *Journal of American History* 86 (March 2000), 1634, 1653, on Nisei.

29. Bowron address, 5 February 1942, cited in Modell, *Economics and Politics,* 184, and in Verge, *Paradise Transformed,* 41; Verge, *Paradise Transformed,* 39–40; statement from Clifford N. Amsden, Secretary of the Los Angeles County Civil Service Commission, 28 January 1942, file 1942, folder B IV 5 I bb, box 74, JAF; Sitton, *Los Angeles Transformed,* 64.

30. Starr, *Embattled Dreams,* 36, chap. 2. Also see Modell, *Economics and Politics,* 14, 32–39; Tomas Almaguer, *Racial Faultlines: The Historical Origins of White Supremacy in California* (Berkeley and Los Angeles: University of California Press, 1994); Ichiro Mike Murasi, *Little Tokyo: One Hundred Years in Pictures* (Los Angeles: Visual Communications/Asian American Studies Central, 1983); Alexander Saxton, *The Indispensable Enemy: Labor and the Anti-Chinese Movement in California* (Berkeley and Los Angeles: University of California Press, 1971).

31. Modell, *Economics and Politics,* 6–7; Verge, *Paradise Transformed,* 40–41. For an analysis of how first-generation Japanese were tied to Japan, see Yuji Ichioka, "Japanese Immigrant Nationalism: The Issei and the Sino-Japanese War, 1937–1941," *California History* 69 (Fall 1990).

32. Gantner, "Regional Imagination," 231; Starr, *Embattled Dreams,* 92; Denning, *Cultural Front,* 450.

33. Sherman, author interview. On the history of ethnic Japanese labor and left activism, see Yoneda, *Ganbatte;* Wild, *Street Meeting,* chap. 7.

34. Tayama to Ford, 8 May 1942, file 1942, folder B IV 5 I bb, box 74, JAF. Roger Daniels pointed out that within seven months of writing Ford, Tayama was attacked by a group of Japan-identified Kibei, Nisei who had been sent to Japan for education. His attack and the subsequent arrests provoked the Manzanar riot of 6 December 1942, "the most serious outbreak of violence in the entire evacuation" (Roger Daniels, "The Incarceration of Japanese Americans during World War II," excerpts of *Concentration Camps, North America: Japanese in the United States and Canada during World War II,* in *Peoples of Color in the American West,* ed. Sucheng Chen [Lexington, MA: D. C. Heath, 1994], 470–80).

35. Sugahara to Ford, 20 May 1942, file 1942, folder B IV 5 I bb, box 74, JAF. On Sugahara, also see Kurashige, "Problem of Biculturalism," 1637.

36. Mexicans' and Mexican Americans' status in the country had long been framed as an international issue, as immigrants were alternately sought out as agricultural workers or deported as welfare burdens across the first half of the twentieth century. See Camille Guerrin Gonzalez, *Mexican Workers and American Dreams: Immigration, Repatriation, and California Farm Labor, 1900–1939* (New Brunswick, NJ: Rutgers University Press, 1994); and Escobar, *Race, Police,* 84–90. See also Los Angeles County Supervisor Harry Baine (Ford's predecessor) to Jensen, 14 November 1933, file 1933; W. W. Brown, Assistant to Commissioner of INS to Ford, 4 March 1935, file 1935, both in folder B IV 5 I dd, box 75, JAF; folder B IV 5 I dd, box 75, JAF.

For a race analysis of the riots, see Escobar, *Race, Police,* and Mauricio Mazón, *The Zoot-Suit Riots: The Psychology of Symbolic Annihilation* (Austin: University of Texas, 1984.)

37. Escobar, *Race, Police,* 178; Stuart Cosgrove, "The Zoot-Suit and Style Warfare," *Radical America* 18 (1984), 39–50.

38. Escobar, *Race, Police,* 200, 208; Verge, *Paradise Transformed,* 56. Pitt and Pitt, *Los Angeles,* 472.

39. Ayres quoted in Escobar, *Race, Police,* 212; Carey McWilliams, "Testimony of Carey McWilliams," and Harry Hoijer, "The Problem of Crime among the Mexican Youth of Los Angeles," in "Meeting of Special Mexican Relations Committee of Los Angeles County Grand Jury," 8 October 1942, p. 22, file 1942, folder B IV 5 I dd, box 75, JAF. Verge, *Paradise Transformed,* 56; Escobar, *Race, Police,* 215–17.

40. *Los Angeles Daily News,* 11 November 1942; *LAT,* 20 April 1943; *LAE,* 30 April 1943; *LAT,* 25 May 1943; all cited in Escobar, *Race, Police,* 201. Pitt and Pitt, *Los Angeles,* 571; Escobar, *Race, Police,* 234–43; Starr, *Embattled Dreams,* 104–11.

41. Tenney cited in Cosgrove, "Zoot-Suit," 47; Sanchez cited in Escobar, *Race, Police,* 238; Bowron to Davis, 28 June 1943, file "Extra Copies of Letters—

1943—Jan–June," box 1, FBP; Pitt and Pitt, *Los Angeles,* 571; Starr, *Embattled Dreams,* 98, 111. Ford was also troubled by the international implications. Writing to Nelson Rockefeller, then coordinator for inter-American affairs, he suggested that "the situation does present serious aspects, primarily because of its psychological effect upon our Latin American neighbors" (Ford to Nelson Rockefeller, 9 June 1943, file 1943, folder B IV 5 I dd, box 75, JAF).

42. Bowron to Davis, 18 June 1943.

43. Ibid. On Cranston, see Escobar, *Race, Police,* 249.

44. "Fight for the Freedom"; "Session Seven: The Negro Nation," in "Study Outline Negro Liberation," 1–4.

45. Leonard, "Years of Hope," 141, 152, 168, 276, 314–47. While there was clear leadership concerning the Party's interpretation of the "Negro Question"—at least from the Comintern—the subject of Mexican oppression was the focus of long debates. At issue, according to Healey, was whether the Mexicans constituted an "oppressed national minority" or simply an "oppressed minority." As a nation, they would have been treated to the same accord African Americans received in the formulation of the Black Belt question, and particularly an allocation of special funds. The work on Mexican discrimination and particularly the Sleepy Lagoon case went forward as if Mexicans were an oppressed nation, separate from this theoretical debate (Healey, author interview).

46. Home Owners Loan Corporation, Los Angeles City Survey Files, Area Description Reports, 378, 379–82, Record Group 195, Records of the Federal Home Loan Bank Board, National Archives, Washington, DC. (I am grateful to Becky Nicolaides for providing me with this material.) The findings are supported as well by author's sample of manuscript data from U.S. Bureau of the Census, *Thirteenth Census of the United States: 1910—Population; Fourteenth Census of the United States: 1920—Population;* and *Fifteenth Census of the United States: 1930—Population Schedule,* in conjunction with published statistics in *Sixteenth Census of the U.S.: 1940—Population,* vol. 3, *Characteristics of the Population,* part 1 (Washington, DC: GPO, 1943), and U.S. Bureau of the Census, *United States Census of Population: 1950—Census Tract Statistics: Los Angeles, California, and Adjacent Area,* Bulletin P-D28 (Washington, DC: GPO, 1952). On HOLC, see Becky Nicolaides, *My Blue Heaven: Life and Politics in the Working-Class Suburbs of Los Angeles, 1920–1965* (Chicago: University of Chicago Press, 2002), 179–81.

47. Sherman, author interview; Lyons, *Philadelphia Communists,* 70–71; Isserman, *Which Side,* 10. Horne pointed out as well that the Party in California was, in terms of percentages, "probably more racially and ethnically diverse than any other party in California at that time" (Horne, *Class Struggle,* 66).

48. Susan Martin, interview with author, Los Angeles, 29 February 2000. Martin said of the male couple, "The impression I got was to leave them alone, don't make a big deal about this. I was sort of told to stay away, more for their

privacy. 'Don't be curious.' My impression was they may have wanted it that way."

49. Schneider, author interview.

50. Ibid.; Markoffs, author interview.

51. Sherman, author interview. She and Hay worked together on the Bimini Baths, and an open letter from Pettis Perry, a local and national Party leader, noted their efforts in spring 1946 (Perry to All Club Executive Committees and Sections, 7 May 1946, folder "Los Angeles Communist Party," Pamphlets Collection, SCL). Leonard noted a campaign at Bimini led by the local chapter of the Congress of Racial Equality (CORE) in 1948 (Leonard, "Years of Hope," 292–94).

52. Denning, *Cultural Front,* 18; Escobar, *Race, Police,* 200, 208; Verge, *Paradise Transformed,* 56; Pitt and Pitt, *Los Angeles,* 472; Sleepy Lagoon Defense Committee, *The Sleepy Lagoon Case* (Los Angeles: Sleepy Lagoon Defense Committee, 1943), 24–25, folder "Sleepy Lagoon Case Pamphlets," Alice McGrath Collection, SCL.

53. Alice McGrath, "Sleepy Lagoon Chronology," author's collection. Alice McGrath, telephone interview with author, Ventura, CA, 3 November 2005.

54. Sleepy Lagoon Defense Committee, *Sleepy Lagoon,* 15, 13–17, 18, 6, 8–11.

55. Escobar, *Race, Police,* 273, 276, 281.

56. Fletcher Bowron, remarks at Declaration of INTERdependence celebration, 4 July 1945, file "Remarks July–Dec 1945," box 34, FBP.

57. Frank Murphy, remarks, 4 July 1945, file 1945, folder B IV 5 J, box 76, JAF. On the high court, Murphy issued a famous dissent in the internment case *Korematsu v. United States.*

58. John Anson Ford, "For Us the Living: A Ten-Point Program for California and the Nation," 2d printing (Los Angeles, 1943), 18–19, file 1942, folder A V 1, box 2, JAF.

59. Escobar, *Race, Police,* 285. Note that Escobar did not use the internationalist framework. Instead he, in part, explained the forums as indicative of community-based, volitional developments by Mexican Americans themselves— their "growing political maturity, sophistication, and power." (Escobar, *Race, Police,* 254–55.)

60. Kurashige, *Japanese American,* 125; Leonard, "Years of Hope," 255, 304; Ronald Takaki, *Strangers from a Different Shore: A History of Asian Americans* (Boston: Little, Brown, 1989), cited in Kurashige, *Japanese American,* 120.

61. Sides, *L.A. City Limits,* 52–54.

62. Ibid., 131, 132; Ford to Edwards, 10 May 1944, folder B IV 5 J, file 1944, box 76, JAF.

63. Ford to Herrick, 20 August 1946, file 1946, folder B IV 5 J, box 76, JAF. The actions came in the wake of arrests of Mr. and Mrs. Henry Laws and their daughter for violating covenants and were part of a continuing legal battle that

only slowly affected intransigent geographic segregation. See Catholic Inter-
racial Council of Los Angeles to Ford, 15 January 1946, file 1946, folder B IV 5 J,
box 76, JAF; Clement Vose, *Caucasians Only: The Supreme Court, the NAACP, and
the Restrictive Covenant Cases* (Los Angeles: University of California Press, 1959).

64. Sitton, *Los Angeles Transformed,* 82–88; Mobilization for Democracy, *Los
Angeles against Gerald L. K. Smith: How a City Organized to Combat Native Fascism!* (Los Angeles: Mobilization for Democracy, [1945?]); Sherman, author interview. See also Glen Jeansonne, *Gerald L. K. Smith: Minister of Hate* (New
Haven, CT: Yale University Press, 1988).

65. *Los Angeles Committees of Correspondence Action Letter,* ed. Annette Cim-
ring and Susan Wright, 16 July 1945 and 1 January 1947, SCL. At an October
1945 speech at a local high school, some fifteen thousand to twenty thousand
protesters appeared (Mobilization for Democracy, *Los Angeles against Smith;*
Gerald L. K. Smith, *Hollywood High School Speech: Exposing Reds and Their
Dupes in the Film Colony* [St. Louis: Christian Nationalist Crusade (1948?)], 2).
Anita Platky, Harry Hay's wife, and Hay himself to a lesser degree were involved
in organizing protests against Smith, including a dramatic march out of one of
Smith's local lectures (Hay, D'Emilio interview, 16 October 1976, tape 00402,
IGIC). On Roden, see "McClanahan Will Face Recall Election Tuesday,"
17 March 1946; "Voters Recall Councilman McClanahan," 20 March 1946;
"The McClanahan Recall," 21 March 1946; all in *LAT.*

66. Gerald Horne, *Communist Front? The Civil Rights Congress, 1946–1956*
(Madison, WI: Fairleigh Dickinson University Press, 1988), 22, 29–41, 47;
Healey, author interview. Not surprisingly, like other Communist-inspired or-
ganizations, the CRC developed its own culture of activities, including picnics,
parties, concerts, barbecues, and songs. There were "CRC Folk Singers" in
Southern California, and a Detroit chapter even went so far as to organize a
"Miss Civil Rights" pageant in 1948.

67. The list of cases is drawn from folder 22 "Case Files . . . Case Histories,
1948," box 1, CRC. See "Historical Sketch," CRC; and Horne, *Communist
Front?* 45, 59, 320–37. Horne deemed the Los Angeles lawyers panel "probably
the best in the organization" (331).

68. Leaflet for meeting 22 January 1952, folder 19, box 12, CRC. See various
telegrams, 18 January 1952, folder 22, box 12, CRC. Also see Leonard, "'In the
Interest of All Races,'" on how the notion of equivalent racial status gained
ground among Mexican American, Japanese American, and African American
leaders during the war.

69. East Hollywood CRC, "Bomb Terror in L.A.!" leaflet, folder 19, box 12,
CRC; Sides, *L.A. City Limits,* 102–3.

70. CRC, "Bomb Terror in L.A.!" The leaflet totaled five racial bombings in
the prior eight months.

71. East Hollywood CRC, "A Call to Protest by the Emergency Committee against the Dunsmuir Bombings," meeting for 28 March 1952, folder 19, box 12, CRC; Sherman, author interview. Raphael Lemkin, the key lobbyist for the United Nations Genocide Convention, published the term "genocide" in 1944: see Barbara Crossette, "Salute to a Rights Campaigner Who Gave Genocide Its Name," *NYT,* 13 June 2001.

72. "Conference Minutes," June 1952, folder 20, box 20, CRC.

73. Ibid., 1–2.

74. Ibid., 7.

75. They also determined that "unless we have social relationships, we cannot have successful political relationships" between races (Ibid., 4–6).

76. Horne, *Communist Front?* 55, 333. Josh Sides pointed out as well that blacks were drawn to the CRC and the Party after the war because it was effective and successful. A small group of African Americans were attracted "to the party's rhetorical commitment to racial equality and its aggressive protest tactics." Sides, *L.A. City Limits,* 141–42.

77. Campbell to Ford, 2 November 1943, file 1943, folder B IV 5 I cc, box 75, JAF.

78. Fletcher Bowron, remarks for testimonial, 3 November 1946, as reported in *Los Angeles Japanese Daily News,* 21 December 1946; Fletcher Bowron, remarks to the Los Angeles Kiwanis, 23 September 1946, both in file "Addresses—Remarks 1946," box 35, FBP.

79. Bowron to Foreman, Los Angeles County Grand Jury, 13 September 1946; and Bowron to DeWitt Wallace, 13 September 1946, both in file "Extra Copies July–Dec—1946," box 2, FBP.

80. Sitton, *Los Angeles Transformed,* 100–101, 108–17; Transcript of City Council meeting, 25 March 1947, file 1947, folder B III 11 d, box 46, JAF; Horne, *Class Struggle,* 56–57.

81. For an extended discussion of the housing battle, see Don Parson, "Los Angeles' 'Headline-Happy Public Housing War,'" *Southern California Quarterly* 65 (Fall 1983), 251–85, and *Making a Better World: Public Housing, the Red Scare, and the Direction of Modern Los Angeles* (Minneapolis: University of Minnesota Press, 2005).

82. "Librarian at UCLA Admits Red Sign-Up," 28 November 1951; "Ouster Asked for 2 More Teachers," 10 April 1953; "Ousted Teachers Begin Court Move," 22 April 1953; "KTTV Newsreel Admitted as Evidence in Teacher Firing," 20 November 1953; "Teacher Ouster Suits Being Studied by Judge," 26 November 1953; all in *LAT.* Gerber, author interview.

83. Sherman remembered that her younger daughter used to encourage her parents to take Sunday drives in order to see if they could get the FBI to follow them and then try to lose them (Sherman, author interview).

84. "UCLA Told of Woman's Repeated Red Registry; Still Employs Her," *LAE,* 28 March 1950; "UCLA Pianist Fired in Loyalty Dispute," *LAT,* 21 April 1950; "Bare Commie Record of UCLA Pianist," *Los Angeles Evening Herald and Express,* 27 March 1930. On the University of California more generally, see "UC Regents Vote Ban on Communists," *LAT,* 25 June 1949; on the Harvard experience, see James Hershberg, *James B. Conant: Harvard to Hiroshima and the Making of the Nuclear Age* (New York: Knopf, 1993).

85. "UCLA Red Charge," *Los Angeles Evening Herald and Express,* 29 March 1950; "UCLA Employee Defies Tenney Ban," *Daily People's World,* 31 March 1950; "Pianist Defies UCLA on Job," *LAE,* 30 March 1950; "UCLA Woman Involved in Loyalty Row Fired," *LAT,* 21 April 1950; "Registered Red Finally Fired off UCLA Staff," *Los Angeles Evening Herald and Express,* 21 April 1950; "Thrice-Registered Red Fired at UCLA Due to 'Nepotism,'" *LAE,* 21 April 1950.

86. Looking back on his life from the 1970s, Edendale liberal Carey McWilliams argued that wartime was transformative for thinking about race in the United States and particularly in California. "The fact is—and it deserves emphasis—that the civil-rights movement of a later period is to be understood only in terms of what happened from 1941 to 1945. . . . [C]atastrophe initiates social change; it was the war that set the racial revolution in motion" (Carey McWilliams, *The Education of Carey McWilliams,* as quoted in Denning, *Cultural Front,* 451).

6. GETTING SOME IDENTITY

1. "Information Bulletin 1," addressed "To the People/Echo Park Community," file 5, box 2, CRC. The incident is also noted in John D'Emilio, "Out of the Shadows: The Gay Emancipation Movement in the United States, 1940–1970" (Ph.D. diss., Columbia University, 1982), 146 n. 30, and dated January 27, 1952.

2. Bérubé, *Coming Out.*

3. Kinsey reported that while 50 percent of American men were exclusively heterosexual, 37 percent had post-adolescent homosexual experiences to orgasm and 10 percent had been more or less exclusively homosexual for three years (Alfred Kinsey, *Sexual Behavior in the Human Male* [Philadelphia: W. B. Saunders, 1949), 623, 650–51; Terry, *American Obsession,* 300).

4. Between 1 January 1947 and 1 November 1950, 574 civilian federal employees were investigated for "sex perversion"; 420 resigned (Terry, *American Obsession,* 335–42; Randolph Baxter, " 'Eradicating This Menace': Homophobia and Anti-Communism in Congress, 1947–1954" [Ph.D. diss., University of California, Irvine, 1999]). See also Robert Dean, *Imperial Brotherhood: Gender and the Making of Cold War Foreign Policy* (Amherst: University of Massachusetts Press, 2003); David Johnson, *Lavender Scare: The Cold War Persecution of Gays*

and Lesbians in the Federal Government (Chicago: University of Chicago Press, 2004); John D'Emilio, "The Homosexual Menace: The Politics of Sexuality in Cold War America," in *Passion and Power: Sexuality in History*, ed. Kathy Peiss and Christina Simmons (Philadelphia: Temple University Press, 1989); Senate Committee on Expenditures in the Executive Departments, *Employment of Homosexuals and Other Sex Perverts in Government*, 81st Cong., 2d sess., 1950, in *Government versus Homosexuals* (New York: Arno Press, 1975).

5. Bérubé, *Coming Out*, 114, as quoted in Starr, *Embattled Dreams*, 85. See also Kepner, *Loves of a Long-Time Activist;* de Leigh, "1930s Bars"; Frisbie, "Talk."

6. "The Service Man's Guide to Los Angeles," ts., 23 January 1942, file 1924, box 150, FWP; Zsa Zsa Gershick, *Gay Old Girls* (Los Angeles: Alyson Books, 1998), 36–73; Kenney, *Mapping*, 37–38.

7. Gard, interview; Carol Gwen, *The History of the Sunset Strip*, ch. 4, www .sunsetstrip.com/history/4.html. Marlene Dietrich attended the club's opening ("Notables Attend Café Opening," *LAT*, 28 September 1941).

8. Tom Gibbons and Bob Clark, interview with author, Los Angeles, 5 April & 17 April 2000.

9. "Entrapment Letter (Los Angeles)," Correspondence Collection, Archival Collections, KI.

10. Ibid. As corroborating cases, see, for example, *People v. Paul Perciful Bentley*, 102 Cal. App. 2d 97, 30 January 1951; *People v. Russell L. Sellers*, 103 Cal. App. 2d 830, 27 April 1951; *People v. Milton Guthrie et al.*, 113 Cal. App. 2d 720, 17 October 1952; *People v. Alfred John Mason et al.*, 130 Cal. App. 2d 533, 1 February 1955. Propositioning corroborated by Gard, author interview.

11. "Special Session to Deal with Sex Cases Urged," 22 November 1949; "Four Official Groups Move on Problem of Sex Offender," 30 November, 1949; "Governor Calls State Parley to Tackle Sex Crime Problem," 2 December 1949; "Death Penalty Urged for Child Molesters," 8 December 1949; "State Plans More Aid to Psychopaths," 10 December 1949; "Five Sex Crime Bills Get Warren Signature," 7 January 1950; "Study of Sex Crimes Ordered," 27 April 1950, all in *LAT*.

12. Kaplan, author interview. Jim Kepner was active in the Party in New York in the late 1940s and had several intense interviews about his sex life before being expelled as "an enemy of the people" (Ernie Potvin, "Kepner Remembered," *ONE-IGLA Bulletin* [Summer 1998]).

13. This idea that sexual identity formation worked in tandem with racial formation echoes the scholarship of Siobhan Somerville, *Queering the Color Line: Race and the Invention of Homosexuality in American Culture* (Chapel Hill, NC: Duke University Press, 2000); Lisa Duggan, *Sapphic Slashers: Sex, Violence, and American Modernity* (Chapel Hill, NC: Duke University Press, 2000); and Boyd, *Wide-Open Town*.

14. Hay, D'Emilio interview, 16 October 1976, tape 00425. I am indebted in this chapter to John D'Emilio, whose early interviews with the Mattachine

members proved a research treasure trove for me; unable to meet most of these men in person, I met them through D'Emilio's thoughtful and engaging interviews from his graduate student days. That work culminated in D'Emilio, *Sexual Politics.* I've also relied on the diligent scholarship of Stuart Timmons, who captured Hay's life story in Timmons, *Trouble.*

15. Hay, D'Emilio interview, tape 00419.

16. Asked by D'Emilio what "gay life" was like at Stanford, Hay responded, "It was just sex, dear. But the point was it was pretty good. There was no such thing as gay life. Everybody was the same as everybody else, except you were different" (Hay, D'Emilio interview, tape 00403). Importantly, later in his life, Hay returned to a gendered view, ultimately that homosexuals existed as a kind of true third sex. See Timmons, *Trouble.*

17. Hay, D'Emilio interview, tape 00419; Timmons, *Trouble,* 36, 43. Interestingly, the Chicago group was started by a German émigré, Henry Gerber, who brought German cultural ideas of sexuality and politics with him to the states. In Germany notions of a sexual identity were much more elaborated at that time than here; see Jonathan Ned Katz, *Gay American History: Lesbians and Gay Men in the U.S.A.,* 2d ed. (New York: Meridian, 1992), 385–97.

18. The closest term they had to "gay"—and apparently the essential term Hay came to learn in the 1930s—was of being "temperamental." And having a certain temperament, even a permanent one, was far from having an inherent identity. Hay also heard "sophisticated" and being "that way." Champ account in Hay, D'Emilio interview, tape 00419; Timmons, *Trouble,* chap. 3. For D'Emilio's interrogation of "gayness," see Hay, D'Emilio interview, tape 00425. On "temperamental," see Hay, D'Emilio interview, tape 00419, and Timmons, *Trouble,* 43.

19. Timmons, *Trouble,* 56–77.

20. Hay, D'Emilio interview, tape 00404.

21. Ibid.

22. Ibid.

23. Anita Hay to Harry Hay, summer 1938, cited in Timmons, *Trouble,* 100; Hay, D'Emilio, tape 00404. At the time of their final separation, in the fall of 1951, Platky told Hay, "You know, I finally realized. You never married me, you married the Communist Party." Hay added later, "Which was probably true" (Hay, D'Emilio interview, tape 00427).

24. Ted Rolfs, interviewed by Len Evans, 1983, 37, in Gay, Lesbian, Bisexual, Transgender Historical Society, San Francisco.

25. James Kepner, interviewed by John D'Emilio, Los Angeles, 27 September 1976, tape 00438, IGIC.

26. Kepner, author interview.

27. Kepner, D'Emilio interview, tape 00438.

28. Kepner, D'Emilio interview, tapes 00520, 00682.

29. Timmons, *Trouble*, 115; Hay, author interview, San Francisco, 6 April 2001; Hay, D'Emilio interview, tape 00404.

30. Hay, D'Emilio interview, tape 00402.

31. Ibid. Piano comment from Jim Kepner on same tape.

32. Ibid.

33. Ibid.; Will Roscoe, "Mattachine, 1948–1953," in Harry Hay, *Radically Gay: Gay Liberation in the Words of Its Founder*, ed. Will Roscoe (Boston: Beacon Press, 1996), 37–59.

34. Hay, D'Emilio interview, tape 00427; Timmons, *Trouble*, 134–38.

35. Harry Hay, "Preliminary Concepts: International Bachelors' Fraternal Order for Peace & Social Dignity, Sometime Referred to as Bachelors Anonymous," in Hay, *Radically Gay*, 64–67. Note that the citations are to a draft Hay typed in July 1950; no copies of the 1948 version survive.

36. Ibid.

37. Ibid., 67–75.

38. Hay, D'Emilio interview, tape 00402. Not insignificantly, the Wallace campaign marked a new high-water mark for the presence of the Communist Party in presidential electoral politics. Thus, Hay's vision of a place for the Bachelors' society in mainstream politics may also have followed that lead.

39. Hay, "Preliminary Concepts," 70–75. Hay told D'Emilio he imagined the units "like the closed units we'd had in the Party for years, which I was very familiar with because I'd been in them" (Hay, D'Emilio interview, tape 00427).

40. Hay, D'Emilio interview, tape 00427.

41. Ibid. On Horton, see Larry Warren, *Lester Horton: Modern Dance Pioneer* (New York: Marcel Dekker, 1976); Perlin, author interview.

42. Hay, D'Emilio interview, tape 00427.

43. Harry Hay et al., "Mattachine Society Missions and Purposes," April 1951, in Hay, *Radically Gay*, 131–32.

44. Hay et al., "Mattachine Society."

45. Timmons, *Trouble*, 146. On Bernhard, see Marilyn Sanders, "Zeitlin, Weston: Focusing on Film," n.p., n.d., folder 2d, box 144, JZP.

46. Hay, D'Emilio interview, tape 00427.

47. Ibid.; Harry Hay et al., "A Quick Guide to Conducting Discussion Groups," n.d., in Hay, *Radically Gay*, 133; Gerard Brissette, interviewed by John D'Emilio, El Cerrito, CA, 17 November 1976, tape 00429, IGIC.

48. Dorr Legg, interviewed by John D'Emilio, Los Angeles, 6 October 1976, tape 00418, IGIC; James Gruber, interviewed by John D'Emilio, Los Angeles, 29 December 1976, tape 00398, IGIC.

49. Kepner, D'Emilio interview, tape 00395; Hay to Will Roscoe, cited in Hay, *Radically Gay*, 77; Gruber, D'Emilio interview, tape 00398. There were also recruitment meetings. As the various meetings became more public, one would occasionally be announced as a discussion of the Kinsey report on male sexual-

ity. The discussion was steered toward Kinsey's analysis of homosexuality, and these evenings were used to recruit future members. Avid listeners or talkers were spoken to by a guild member who might then invite them to a less public meeting (Hay, author interview).

50. Hay, D'Emilio interview, tape 00427; Gruber, D'Emilio interview, tapes 00428, 00398.

51. Kennedy and Davis, *Boots of Leather,* 65; Boyd, *Wide-Open Town,* 10; Stein, *City of Sisterly and Brotherly Loves,* 93; D'Emilio, "Out of the Shadows," 67.

52. Kenneth Burns, interviewed by John D'Emilio, 10 January 1977, tape 00401, IGIC; Kennedy and Davis, *Boots of Leather,* 378.

53. Hay, D'Emilio interview, tape 00420.

54. Harry Hay, "Slogan 'Children and Fools Speak the Truth': Les Mattachines (The Society of Fools)," November 1950, in Hay, *Radically Gay,* 79; Eann MacDonald [pseudonym for Harry Hay], "A Speculation on the Dialectics of Homosexual Social Directions," 18 September 1951, 1, 6, 8, 11, file "Mattachine Society—Early 1950s," ONE. Another formulation of his position appeared in Hay's discussion group notes for the fall of 1951, entitled "Social Directions of the Homosexual." There he insisted that "homosexuals are 'lone wolves' through fear. In society as it now stands, they congratulate themselves for not being caught as have their less fortunate brothers, and understandably retreat more within themselves." Rather than remaining isolated, though, Hay looked forward to the day when research demonstrated that "homosexuals, as a group, have much in common and that they are unique cases. Should we be considered individuals or be considered a group? We are essentially a group of individuals which have been forced together by society." And while he acknowledged there were a handful of "individualists" who found the status quo manageable, "the fact remains, however, that the majority of homosexuals are inept at adjusting without an acceptable atmosphere and an adequate pattern" (Harry Hay, "Social Directions of the Homosexual," 4 October 1951, 1–2, file "Mattachine Society—Early 1950s," ONE).

55. Hay, D'Emilio interview, tape 00420; Timmons, *Trouble,* 151; Konrad Stevens, interviewed by John D'Emilio, Los Angeles, 5 January 1977, tape 00405, IGIC.

56. Gruber, D'Emilio interview, tape 00398; Legg, D'Emilio interview, tape 00418.

57. Stevens, D'Emilio interview, tape 00463.

58. Ibid.

59. Hay, D'Emilio interview, tape 00420. Jim Kepner recalled a similar division in San Francisco homosexual circles. His first lover, John, whom he described as "butch-looking, but old auntie in manner," was also homophobic about "queens." Kepner said that in his experience, if you were not "openly ef-

feminate," you had a small circle of friends and didn't go to bars (Kepner, D'Emilio interview, tape 00438).

60. D'Emilio, *Sexual Politics,* 68–69; Hay, D'Emilio interview, tape 00405.

61. Brissette, D'Emilio interview, tape 00429.

62. Stevens, D'Emilio interview, tape 00463; Kepner, D'Emilio interview, tape 00395.

63. Hay, D'Emilio interview, tape 00420. On Mexican American identity, see Escobar, *Race, Police.*

64. "Information Bulletin 1."

65. "Joseph Harrison" to Myers, 28 April 1952, file 5, box 2, CRC; Hay, D'Emilio interview, tape 00420.

66. Citizens' Committee to Outlaw Entrapment, "An Anonymous Call to Arms," open letter [1952], file 5, box 2, CRC; "Harrison" to Myers, 28 April 1952. See also Citizens' Committee to Outlaw Entrapment, "Now Is the Time to Fight," leaflet [April–May 1952?], file 5, box 2, CRC.

67. Hay, D'Emilio interview, tape 00405; Timmons, *Trouble,* 165; "Harry Hay Remembers Jim Kepner," *ONE-IGLA Bulletin* (Summer 1998).

68. Citizens' Committee, "Anonymous Call."

69. Jennings, "To Be Accused Is to Be Guilty," *ONE Magazine* (January 1953): 10–12.

70. Timmons, *Trouble,* 167; D'Emilio, *Sexual Politics,* 71.

71. Hay, D'Emilio interview, tape 00406.

72. Paul Coates, "Well, Medium and Rare," *Los Angeles Mirror,* 12 March 1953, file "Mattachine Society: Early 1950s," ONE.

73. Stevens, D'Emilio interview, tape 00463; Coates, "Well, Medium and Rare."

74. D'Emilio, *Sexual Politics,* 89, 115.

CONCLUSION

1. James Reston, *NYT,* 18 May 1954, as cited in Jack Balkin, "*Brown* as Icon," in *What* Brown v. Board *Should Have Said: The Nation's Top Legal Experts Rewrite America's Landmark Civil Rights Decision,* ed. Jack Balkin (New York: New York University Press, 2001), 4. For a scathing critique of the "psychologistic" framing of the decision, see Donald Howie, "The Image of Black People in *Brown v. Board of Education,*" *Journal of Black Studies* 3 (1973), 371–84.

2. Kenneth Clark, "The *Brown* Decision: Racism, Education, and Human Values," *Journal of Negro Education* 57 (1988), 128.

3. Richard King, *Civil Rights and the Idea of Freedom* (Athens: University of Georgia Press, 1992), 4–5. See George Levesque, "A Reappraisal of Historical Consensus," *Journal of the Early Republic* 1 (1981), 269–87; William Van Deburg, *New Day in Babylon: The Black Power Movement and American Culture, 1965–*

1975 (Chicago: University of Chicago Press, 1992), chap. 2. On the difference between early philosophies and later ones, and the limitations of early ideology, see Kevin Gaines, *Uplifting the Race: Black Leadership, Politics, and Culture in the Twentieth Century* (Chapel Hill: University of North Carolina Press, 1996).

4. Carlos Cooks, "Speech on the 'Buy Black' Campaign," 85–92; Malcolm X, "Basic Unity Program," 108–18; Frantz Fanon, "Concerning Violence," 128–32; all in *Modern Black Nationalism: From Marcus Garvey to Louis Farrakhan,* ed. William Van Deburg (New York: New York University Press, 1997). On education, see, for instance, Sonia Jarvis, "*Brown* and the Afrocentric Curriculum," *Yale Law Journal* 101 (April 1992), 1285–1304.

5. Phelan, *Identity Politics,* 43, 58.

6. Jenny Bourne, "Homelands of the Mind: Jewish Feminism and Identity Politics," *Race and Class* 29 (1987): 1, as cited in Liz Bondi, "Locating Identity Politics," in *Place and the Politics of Identity,* ed. Michael Keith and Steve Pile (New York: Routledge, 1993), 84; Eli Zaretsky, "Identity Theory, Identity Politics: Psychoanalysis, Marxism, Post-Structuralism," in *Social Theory,* ed. Calhoun, 201, 202; Phelan, *Identity Politics,* 135–36.

7. Elizabeth Armstrong, *Forging Gay Identities: Organizing Sexuality in San Francisco, 1950–1994* (Chicago: University of Chicago Press, 2002).

8. Hay, D'Emilio interview, tape 00405.

9. Stevens, D'Emilio interview, tape 00463; Hal Call, interviewed by John D'Emilio, San Francisco, 16 November 1976, tape 00443, IGIC.

10. D'Emilio, *Sexual Politics,* 77–84; Timmons, *Trouble,* 177–80.

11. D'Emilio, *Sexual Politics,* 77; Kepner, D'Emilio interview, tape 00395; Hal Call, D'Emilio interview, cited in John D'Emilio, "Sexual Politics, Sexual Communities," unpublished ts., 12 March 1981, chap. 3, p. 14, in IGIC.

12. Marilyn Rieger, "Delegates of the Convention . . . ," 23 May 1953, in file "Mattachine of L.A., Inc.," ONE.

13. Rieger, "Delegates of the Convention."

14. Hay to Rowland, n.d. [March 1953], cited in D'Emilio, "Sexual Politics," ts., chap. 3, p. 4.

15. Call, D'Emilio interview, tape 00443.

16. Southern Area Council meeting minutes, 5 October 1953, 2, in file, "Mattachine 1953–54," ONE; "The Mattachine Society Today—An Information Digest," 1954, Appendix II, 1, in file "Mattachine," ONE.

17. Timmons, *Trouble,* 157–60, 180; Hay, author interview; D'Emilio, *Sexual Politics,* 81. D'Emilio deemed Mattachine's rejection of Hay and the new leadership a tragic turn and a "retreat to respectability." Martin Meeker challenged this assessment, arguing for the efficacy of later Mattachine efforts, in "Behind the Mask of Respectability: Reconsidering the Mattachine Society and Male Homophile Practice, 1950s and 1960s," *Journal of the History of Sexuality* 10 (January 2001): 79.

18. Timmons, *Trouble,* 219–20; Jennings, author interview.

19. Manning Marable, *Race, Reform, and Rebellion: The Second Reconstruction in Black America, 1945–1990* (Jackson: University Press of Mississippi, 1991), esp. chaps. 3–6.

20. As Moira Kenney pointed out in 2001, Silver Lake, "by all accounts the second-largest (or densest) center of gay and lesbian culture in Los Angeles, reveals few traces of the community, apart from a half dozen bars and clubs" that hardly advertise their presence. It never took on the appearance or narrowly circumscribed commercial life of West Hollywood, Los Angeles' more typical "gay ghetto" (Kenney, *Mapping,* 195).

21. Skrentny, *Minority Rights Revolution.*

22. Zaretsky, *Capitalism, Family, Personal Life,* 9–10, 30, 76, chap. 4.

ACKNOWLEDGMENTS

THIS BOOK TOOK MANY YEARS to come into being, starting first as a dissertation and then slowly transforming into a book. As a result it is very much the product of the encouragement, prodding, support, and insights of many other people whom I am pleased to thank.

First and foremost are the men and women who sat with me and my poorly operated tape recorder to tell me about their lives. Their patience with my questions and their willingness to share their stories allowed me to glimpse the world as they had known it. They include Esther Asimow, Jeb Brighouse, Harold Burton, Bob Clark, Flo Fleischman, Jack Gard, Serril Gerber, Tom Gibbons, Don Greenfield, Harry Hay, Dorothy Healey, Max Hilberman, Dale Jennings, Barbara Kaplan, Jim Kepner, Morris Kight, Sophia Lewis, Betty and Morris Markoff, Susan Martin, William Mason, Alice McGrath, Estelle Milmar, Luba Perlin, Jeannette Reisbord, Stan Schneider, Miriam Sherman, Sueo Serisawa, and William Taube. Not all of them lived to see this book in print, but I am hopeful that some portion of their memories continue in these pages. I was certainly honored to hear their stories.

The tales they told me were enriched by the wonderful letters, books, pamphlets, and interviews I found at multiple archives through the assistance of many fine people. Much of the research for this project began in the Special Collections of the Young Research Library at UCLA, where I was continually aided by Dan Luckenbill, Octavio Olivero, and Jeff Rankin. At the Clark Library, I was able to pore over countless volumes of beautiful printing and craftsmanship and benefited from the enthusiasm and diligence of Jennifer Schaffner, Suzanne Tatian, and Scott Jacobs. At the San Marino offices for the Smithsonian's Archives of American Art, I was steadily encouraged by Paul Karlstrom, Barbara Bishop, and Marian Kovinick. I benefited as well from the collections at the Gay, Lesbian, Bisexual, and Transgender History Library and Archives; the Kinsey Institute for Research in Sex, Gender, and Reproduction; the Los Angeles City Archives; the Los Angeles County Hall of Records; the Los Angeles Public Library; the New York Public Library for the Performing Arts; the ONE National Gay and Lesbian Archives; the Regional History Center at the University of Southern California; the Sacramento Archives and Museum Collection; the Southern California Library for Social Studies and Research; and Special Collections at the University Library, California State University, Long Beach. Finally, at the Henry Huntington Library, I basked in the warm kindness of Susie Krasnoo and Mona Noureldin.

As a graduate student at UCLA, my thinking and ideas were informed and influenced by a dynamic cohort of faculty members: Jan Reiff, who encouraged me to think big thoughts and had faith in what I came up with; David Sabean, who modeled for me an ideal combination of discipline and creativity; Eric Monkkonen, who supported my very first efforts exploring this topic; Joe Bristow, who insisted on the value of difficult theoretical ideas; Ellen Dubois, who never relented in insisting that I could do better; Susan Johnson, who made history a human discipline for me; Joyce Appleby, who set a terrific standard for articulateness and thoughtfulness; and Steve Aron, who was a model of teacherly commitment. In multiple ways, I learned from them all, and I appreciate the degree to which they have continued to support me in the subsequent years.

During graduate school, through various classes and writing groups, multiple friends and colleagues read my work and helped me to improve it, including Shana Bernstein, Mike Bottoms, Anastasia Christman, Clark Davis, Bill Deverell, Jim Green, Ben Johnson, Lisa Materson, Michelle Nickerson, Moshe Sluhovsky, Amy Sueyoshi, and Mark Wild. Through them, I came to appreciate the value of a vital intellectual community. That ideal was demonstrated for me so clearly by the warm heart and thoughtful mind of Clark Davis, whose example remains steadily present for me. Raphael Simon introduced me to many early Edendale residents, and for that I am very grateful. Many other wonderful friends, including Xan Horowitz, Stephen Gutwillig, Rebecca Spivack, Jeanne Ward, Nina Schwalbe, Dawn Logsdon, Lucie Faulknor, Anastasia Pappas, and the Luna family, reminded me of life's pleasures beyond history. Most especially during this project, my focus and spirits were maintained by my compatriots at Dissgo, Laura Lee and Alexandra Garbarini, who patiently kept me on topic, on schedule, writing in some version of English, and happy.

At Tulane University, I was lucky to work with Mark Baer, Marline Otte, Steven Pierce, Linda Pollock, and Justin Wolfe, who all gave me feedback on my ideas and kept me pointed toward the shore.

Additionally, several institutions provided generous financial support that helped me continue my work. A dissertation grant from the Sexuality Research Fellows Program at the Social Science Research Council (funded by the Ford Foundation) not only afforded me an unfettered year of research and writing but also introduced me into the dynamic network of sexuality scholars. That year was complemented by a wonderful year I spent at Columbia University's Program for the Study of Sexuality, Gender, Health, and Human Rights (funded by the Rockefeller Foundation), where I engaged in exciting conversations and enjoyed the warmth and intellect of Carole Vance and Ali Miller. The Huntington Library, UCLA, and Tulane University, through its Faculty Senate and Lurcy funds, also provided vital support for which I remain grateful.

I am thankful, as well, for the assistance of multiple editors and readers. Both Monica McCormick at UC Press and Doug Mitchell at the University of Chicago Press encouraged me regularly when this book was just a few shakily conceived dissertation chapters. Niels Hooper shared his enthusiasm for my final vision. Several anonymous readers, as well as Marc Stein and Nan Boyd, provided valuable comments to help strengthen my ideas. And Laura Harger and Steven Baker have been painstaking in their efforts to make the manuscript publishable. All of them have made my work better.

Studying and writing about Los Angeles allowed me the opportunity to nourish and expand my relationships with my parents and siblings and their families. I benefited happily from their good company and generosity, doled out in delicious meals, better clothes, beautiful art, sage advice, and even, for a time, an old station wagon. I know that my passion for history is a product of both my parents' enthusiasm for ideas, stories, and self-expression. I treasure the gifts of theirs that I carry, not least of all the sense of family they instilled in all of us.

Here in New York, I have been embraced by my second family, replete with extra siblings, cousins, nephews, and parents. Their love, concern, and encouragement have been a source of joy for me.

Finally, I have been steadily sustained by the love of my own family. Maggie reminded me to get dirty and live fully. Hermalinda continues to soothe my soul. And Michael is a blessing every day: I cherish the life we have made together and continue to make. And I cannot wait for our next adventure to begin.

INDEX

Page numbers in italics indicate illustrations or material contained in their captions.

Cass, Alonzo, 304n36
Catalina Channel, 199
CCOE. *See* Citizens' Committee to Outlaw Entrapment
censorship, 113; anti-homosexual, 146–49; political, 115–16
Central Avenue, 194
Central Labor Council, 129
Central Park. *See* Pershing Square
Chamberlain, Ernest R., 311n19
Champ (Hay's first lover), 238, 240
Chaplin, Charlie, 26, 39
Charney, George, 320n26
Chauncey, George, 36–37, 60, 118, 120, 132
Cherry, Denny Winters, 308n78
Cherry, Herman, 108, 111, 115, 308n78
Chicago, 58, 121, 336n17; Mattachine in, 264
Chicago Tribune, 31
China, 124, 233
Chodorow, Nancy, 271
Chouinard, Nelbert, 109
Chouinard School, 10, 84, 99, 107
Chronicle (dance piece; Horton), 106. *See also* Horton, Lester
Citizens' Committee to Outlaw Entrapment (CCOE), 231–32, 259–61. *See also* Mattachine Society
CIVIC (Citizens Independent Vice Investigating Committee), 124–25; Intelligence Department of, 126; moralism of, as Communism, 127; moralism of, as effeminate, 134–35; police anti-vice campaign and, 126–27, 132–33
Civic News Forum (radio program), 114–15
civil defense programs, 199
Civil Liberties Union. *See* Southern California Civil Liberties Union
Civil Rights Congress (CRC): African American involvement in, 220–22, 333n76; anti-racist campaigns of, 218, 220–23, 231; Communist influence on, 219; founding of, 218–19; Hay influenced by, 247, 248, 255–56; homosexuality and, 231–32, 261; on police entrapment, 259; social/cultural events held by, 173–74, 332n66

civil rights movement. *See* African Americans, civil rights movement
the Clan, 86–87, 96, 281
Clark, Bob, 235
Clark, Kenneth, 270
Clark Library (UCLA), 88
Clements, Grace: aesthetics of, 98–100; cultural significance of, 281–82; in Los Angeles John Reed Club, 174–75; New Deal art projects of, 110; and politicization of art, 104, 105, 108, 115, 116, 186. See also *—but is it ART?;* Edendale arts community
Clifton's Cafeterias, 123–24
Cline, Paul, 136, *137,* 313–14n37. *See also* Los Angeles Communist Party
Clinton, Clifford E., *114,* 313n30; background of, 123–24; moralism of, as Communism, 127–31; moralism of, as effeminate, 134–35, 136, *137;* police anti-vice campaign and, *115,* 126–27; Shaw recall and, 123, 136, 138, 312n22. *See also* CIVIC
closet, as political metaphor, 242
the Club, 89, *90, 91*–94, 95–96, 304n36. *See also* artistic organizations
Club New Yorker (nightclub), 118
Coates, Paul, 263–64, 273
Cold War: Communists persecuted during, 123, 225–27; homosexuality persecuted during, 123, 232–33, 334–35n4; identity politics during, 227–28; inter-racialism and, 217; racial conflicts during, 16–17
Colophon (journal), 102
Comintern, 193, 330n45
Committee on Home Front Unity, 216
Communism: American, 153; homosexuality and, 117; moralism and, 127–31, 136, *137;* politics emotionalized in, 10–11, 154–55, 195–96; race-nationhood and, 206–8; racism and, 192–93; sexual perversion politically linked to, 123, 135–38, *137,* 152
Communist Party, American: activism of, 163–64; Brooks family and, 151–52; Cold War persecution of, 123, 228;

CRC and, 218–19; Hay joins, 241; heyday of, 10; homosexuals as security threat to, 276, 330–31n48, 335n12; internal cultural debates of, 175–76; in Los Angeles, 155–59; marriages in, 324nn77, 80, 336n23; Mattachine and, 17, 242–43, 248, 255–64, 273; peak membership of, 163; personal/political connections in, 10–11, 16, 149, 154–55, 165, 166, 180–82, 317–18n6, 320n26; presidential election (1932), 193, 337n38; racial/ethnic diversity in, 321nn29–30, 330n47; racism and, 193–94, 324n1, 326n10; secret cell system of, 248. *See also* Edendale Communist community; Los Angeles Communist Party

Congress of Industrial Organizations (CIO), 129, 136, 163–64

Congress of Racial Equality (CORE), 331n51

Connell, Will, 301n7

Connelly, Phil, 163–64

Cooperative Building (Boyle Heights), 155

cooperatives, 168–71, *170,* 225, 245. *See also* Avenel co-op; nursery schools

Cove Avenue, 208–9, *230,* 244, 249

Cox, Annette, 105

Craig, Tom, 81, 93, 102

Cranston, Alan, 206

CRC. *See* Civil Rights Congress

Criley, Theodore, 93

The Crinoline Girl (musical comedy), 26–27, 33, 75

Cronyn, Hume, 172

crossdressing, *143. See also* fairies; female impersonators; masquerading

Crotty, Homer, 94

Crown Hill, 125

Crown Jewel (bar), 55

Croxall, E. Zacariah, 126–27

cruising. *See* homosexual cruising

Crystal Baths (bathhouse), 54

Cubism, 97

The Culture of Narcissism (Lasch), 271

Culver City, 42, 294n3

Czechoslovakia, 233

Dahlstrom, Grant, 79, 88, 93

Dailey, Victoria, 97, 102

Daily Worker, 180

Dalton, William. *See* Eltinge, Julian

Dalzell Hatfield Gallery, 84

dance. *See* Lester Horton Dance Group

dandyism, 97, 305–6n44

Daniels, Roger, 329n34

Danz, Louis, 109

Daughters of Bilitis, 264. *See also* homophile movement

Daves, Delmer, 79, 92–93, 95, 304n36, 305n38

Davis, James, 122, 125, 140

Davis, Madeline D., 57–58, 253–54, 288n14

Dean, Robert, 232

Defense Committee of Southern California, 198–99

degenerate/desire identity paradigm: defined, 71–72; Eltinge and, 148; Hay and, 238; legal acceptance of, 145–46; Los Angeles police crackdowns and, 117, 131; in Solovich/Irby case, 68–71. *See also* homosexuality; sexual identity

D'Emilio, John: on capitalism and homosexuality, 9, 287n13; Hay interviewed by, 240, 242, 255, 336n16; on hypermasculinity and anti-Communism, 232–33; on Mattachine ideological shift, 340n17; on Mattachine internal debates, 251; Mattachine interviews of, 335–36n14; on World War II and homosexuality, 16

DeMille, Cecil B., 109

Democratic Party, 153

Denning, Michael, 154, 174, 211

Dennis, Eugene, 157, 167, 182, 184

Dennis, Peggy: as Communist activist, 153, 157, 182; Edendale Communist community and, 156, 185; marriage of, 182, 184; move to Edendale, 21–22; singing and, 179

Depression, Great, 152–53; Communist activism during, 157; impact on Edendale arts community, 15, 79–80, 105–6; impact on Los Angeles, 116–17, 309n4 desegregation, 208–10, 216, 220, 245, 331n51

Detroit, 332n66; Mattachine in, 264

Díaz, José, *188,* 203–4. *See also* Sleepy Lagoon case

Dictator (dance piece; Horton), 175

Dietrich, Marlene, 335n7

Dijkstra, Bram, 100

Dike, Phil, 84, 107, 109

Disney, Walt, 304n30

Disney Company, 10, 91, 320n21

Doheny, Carrie Estelle (Mrs. E. L.), 95, 305n40

Doheny, E. L., 83, 95

"Do Re Mi" (song; Guthrie), 176, 179

Dorff, Stephen, 291n25

Doyle, S. M. ("Larry"), 129

drag queens, 27, 34, 258, 300n70. *See also* female impersonators

Dust Bowl refugees, 106

Dyer, Irene, 126

Earl, Edwin T., 65

East Hollywood, 219–20

Echo Park, 278; cooperative nursery school at, 171; CRC chapter in neighborhood, 219–20, 221; homosexual activity at, 52, 297n23; Mexican gangs in, 209; police entrapment at, 259–60. *See also* Edendale

Edel, Boris, 185

Edendale: anti-Communist persecution in, 225–27; as artistic mecca, 10, 12, 81–83; as bohemia, 13; as Communist and leftist mecca, 10, 12, 153–54, 159–63; cultural transformation of, 4–5, 10, 12, 74–75; Eltinge home in, 1–2, 42–43; film industry in, 23–26, *25,* 39, 42, 79; as gay mecca, 277–78, 341n20; geography of, 12–13, 85, 112–13; identity construction in, 13–14; inter-racial harmony in, 208–10, *210;* location of, *24;* Mattachine as product of, 13–14; modern, *268;* neighborhood attractions of, 83

Edendale arts community: aesthetics of, 97–104, 301n6; censorship of, 113; Communist community and, 154–55,

161; as community, 77, 78–79, 80, 92–94, 96, 111–13; cultural transformation and, 12; economic support of, 94–96, 304nn36–37; emergence of, 10; impact of Depression on, 15, 79–80, 105–6; internal debates of, 11, 74–75, 79–81, 96–97, 104–5; Mattachine influenced by, 113, 232, 250–51, 264–65, 279; members of, 79, 81–83, 93, 301n7; New Deal art projects of, 108–12, 265; nostalgia for, 112–13; personal connections among, 85–87, 303n19; politicization of, 104–8; quest for essence, 79–81, 81, 96–104; World War II Japanese internment and, 200. *See also* artistic organizations; *specific persons*

Edendale Communist community: antiracist activism of, 189–90, 194, 204, 208; artists among, 160–61; arts community and, 154–55, 161; Avenel co-op of, 168–71, *170,* 225, 245; Cold War persecution of, 225–27, 320n21; as community, 154–55, 161–63, 169–72; CRC and, 223; cultural transformation and, 12; emergence of, 153, 159–63; Hay and, 244–46; homosexuals as security threat to, 236; influence of, 155, 186–87; international connections of, 165–68; inter-racialism and, 208–10, *210,* 227–28; marriages among, 184–85; Mattachine influenced by, 232, 250–51, 255–64, 265–66, 279; neighborhood organizations of, 164–65, 171–72; nicknames for, 320n23; participatory culture in, 175–76, 178–79; politicized emotion in, 153, 179–85; politicized identity of, 153–55, 185–87, 250; Sleepy Lagoon defense and, 211–13, *212;* social/cultural events held by, 165, 172–79, *173;* World War II Japanese internment and, 202. See also *specific persons*

Edward VII (king of England), 27

effeminacy, male: criticized by homosexuals, 73–74, 244; criticized by Mattachine members, 257–58; Eltinge and, 27, 31–33; fairies and, 36–38; as heterosexual quality, 36; as homosexual trait, 130, 133–38, 146–49, 293n36; masculine anxiety and, 35; moralism as, 134–35; Progressive-Era views of, 66; as sign of sexuality, 34–39, 60–61, 68–70, 71. *See also* fairies; fairy/gender identity paradigm; female impersonators; gender; masculinity

Eggan, Jack, 167, 168

808 Night Club, 56, 118, 125, 131–32

Ellis, Havelock, 72, 285n6

Eltinge, Julian, *29;* critical reviews of, 31–32, *32;* death of, 148; as female impersonator, 14, 15, 27–33, *28,* 292n27; film career of, 26, 36, 39, 75, 292n27; Hay compared to, 4, 8, 269–70; home of, 1–2, *40, 42*–43, 294n4; homosexual activity of, 4, 8, 34, 292n29; masculinity of, 34–38; police censorship of, 147–48; popular forgetting of, 3–4; press coverage of, 41–43, 291nn22–23, 294n4; relocation to Edendale, 26, 39, 74; scholarship on, 285n3; sexual identity of, 34–38, 43, 70, 73, 97, 258, 293n38, 293–94n40; success of, 27–31, 291n25; vaudeville career of, 2–3, 26–33, 35–36, 38

Eltinge Theater (NY), 2

emotion: aestheticized in Edendale arts community, 79–80, 96–100, 102–4; communal exploration of, 85–87; politicized by state, 149, 153; politicized in Edendale Communist community, 153, 179–85. *See also* essence

Epperson, Walter, 145

The Equalizer (tabloid), 131, 133, 136, 314n40

Equal Rights Amendment, 277

Erlanger, Catherine d', 234. *See also* Café Gala

Erwin, John, 295n17

Escobar, Edward, 213, 215, 325n9, 331n59

Essanay Films, 24

essence (emotional self), 43–44; artistic, 79–81, 81, 96–104; female impersonation and, 43–44; homosexuality as indication of, 59–66; identity politics and, 264–66; inverted, gender inversion as, 15–16, 148–49; politicized in

Edendale Communist community, 146–47, 149, 153–55, 185–87; selfhood and, 5, 280–81; sexuality and, 74–75, 81. *See also* authenticity; emotion; identity; self

"Evenings on the Roof" chamber music series, 82–83

The Exclusive Sailor (pornographic film; 1920s), 72–73, 300n69

Exodus from the Land (dance piece; Horton), 106

expressionism, 80

Factories in the Field (McWilliams), 164

Fainer, Joseph, 128

fairies: Eltinge and, 36–39, 293n37; gender inversion as code, 36–38; moralists as, 136–38; police crackdowns on, 117, 121–22, 131; political linkage to radicalism, 149, 152; press coverage of, *46;* public fascination with, 59, 117, 118–22, *119;* queers vs., 60; sexual identity of, 293nn36–37, 293n39, 293–94n40; as sexual perverts, 133. *See also* female impersonators; homosexuality; sexual identity

fairy/gender identity paradigm: decline of, and state repression, 117, 148; defined, 71–72; homosexuality and, 73–74; in Solovich/Irby case, 66, 67–71. *See also* homosexuality; sexual identity

Fanon, Frantz, 270

"Fantastic Art, Dada, and Surrealism" (exhibition), 100

The Fascinating Widow (musical comedy), 2, 26–27, *32,* 33, 35–36

fascism, 168, 175, 194–95, 246

Federal Art Project (FAP): community ties of, 110–11; Edendale arts community and, 15, 79, 80, 93, 108–12, 265, 308n78; political controversy in, 115–16; PWAP vs., 109; significance of, 111–12

Federal Bureau of Investigation (FBI), 152, 225, 312n22

Federal Theater Project, 160, 174

Federation for Civic Betterment, 130, 313–14n37. *See also* CIVIC

nity and, 169; impact of Cold War anti-Communism on, 225–26, 227; marriage of, 182, 184; move to Edendale, 23; political significance of, 281

Germany, sexual identity in, 336n17

Gernreich, Rudi, *230,* 249, 256. *See also* Mattachine Society

Gerstle, Gary, 327n16

Gibbons, Tom, 235

Gilligan, Carole, 271

Gladding, McBean and Company, 110

Goldman, Emma, 85

Goldstein, Cesar, 178

Goodwin, Jeff, 323n64

Gornick, Vivian, 154, 180–82, 185

Grable, Betty, 118

Great Depression. *See* Depression, Great

Green Book, 291n22

Greenfield, Don, 48–49, 54, 58

Greenwich Village (NY), 85–86

Grey, Elmer, 43

Griffith Park, 24

Grossman, Aubrey, 219

Grossman, Eleanor (pseudonym), 162–63, 184

Gruber, Jim, *230,* 251, 252, 253, 256, 259. *See also* Mattachine Society

Guston, Philip, 107

Guthrie, Woody, 173, 176–77, 179

Hahn, G. A., *143*

Hamilton, Marybeth, 120

Hanna, Phil, 89, 102

Harlem (NY), 120

Harline, Leigh, 93

Harold's (bar), 55

Harrigan, Lawrence, 67

Harriman, Job, 153

Harrison, R. B., 54

Harstein family, 220

Hart, William S., 90

Hatfield, Dalzell, 109

Hay, Anita: as Communist activist, 332n66; divorce of, 276, 336n23; Edendale Communist community and, 171, *173;* marriage of, 183, 184, 242; move to Edendale, 244–45

Hay, Harry: antiracist activism of, 331n57; Bachelors Anonymous idea of, 246–48, 337n38; background of, 237–40; as Communist activist, 153, 161, 180, 186, *239,* 241–42, 332n66; cooperative nursery school set up by, 171; divorce of, 276, 336n23; Edendale Communist community and, *173,* 244–46; on Eltinge, 27; Eltinge compared to, 4, 8, 269–70; later years of, 280; on gayness, early terms for, 336n18; homosexual activity of, 4, 8; on homosexual meeting spots, 50, 54, 56–57, 297n23; identity politics of, 9, 74, 255–64, 269–70, 274–76, 336n16, 338n54; marriage of, 183, 184, 242; as Mattachine founder, 3, *230,* 274; on Mattachine political divisions, 273; on Mattachine solidarity, 253, 255; migration to California, 22, 50, 160, 244–45; People's Song and, 178; political significance of, 272–73, 277–79, 281–82; resignation from Mattachine, 276–77, 340n17; theatrical career of, *239,* 240–41. *See also* Mattachine Society

Hay, Mrs. Henry, 263

Hayman, William, *142*

Healey, Don, 129, 136, *137,* 164

Healey, Dorothy, 185; antiracist activism of, 189, 194; as Communist activist, 245; on Communist Party marriages, 183, 324n80; Edendale Communist community and, *173,* 175–76, 178–79, 320n23; later years of, 280; impact of Cold War anti-Communism on, 226; on Mexican American minority status, 330n45; political significance of, 281–82

Herald of Decency (newspaper), 313n30

heraldry, dandyism and, 305–6n44

Herman, Paul, 295n10

Herron, Jason, 109, 110

Higgins, Ross, 58

Highland Park Post Dispatch, 135

Hilberman, David, 160, 171, 320n21

Hilberman, Max, 160, 171

Hilberman, Molly, 171

Hill Street, 49

queers, 60

race: identity politics and, 6–7, 189–91, 195–96, 199–200, 203; Shaw recall and, 313n31; World War II and social change, 334n86

race-nationhood, 206–7; African Americans and, 207, 257, 330n45; Communist view of, 206–8; CRC and, 219; homosexual oppressed minority framework and, 257; identity politics and, 17; inter-racialism and, 216–17, 227–28; Japanese and, 206, 214, 228; Mattachine and, 250–51; Mexicans and, 207, 214, 228, 329n34, 330n45. *See also* racial identity politics

racial identity politics, 6–7, 203, 270, 277, 335n13; Americanism rallies and, 196–97; CRC and, 217–23; Edendale Communist community and, 189–90; empathic analogies and, 221–23; group identity and, 227–28; inter-racialism and, 213–17, 223–28; Japanese internment and, 200–3; in Los Angeles, 191–96; Los Angeles Communists and, 192–96; as model for Mattachine, 248, 250, 257–63, 274–77; politicization of identity and, 195–96; pre–World War II, 191–92, 196–98; Sleepy Lagoon case and, 16, 203–4, 210–13, *212;* during World War II, 194–96, 198–203; World War II racial conflicts and, 189–91; Zoot Suit Riots and, 190–91, 203, 205, 207. *See also* inter-racialism; race-nationhood

racialism, 326–27n16

racism: anti-black, 191–92, 220–22, 308n69; anti-Japanese, 190–91, 199–203; anti-Mexican, *188,* 203–13, 221–22; bombings, 220–21, 332n70; Communist activism against, 164, 189–90, 192–95, 221–23, 245, 324n1; in housing covenants, 209–10, 216, 224–25, 245, 331–32n63; minority status and, 190; Nazism and, 194–95, 197–98, 214; as racialism, 326–27n16

radicalism, *137,* 149, 152, 154

radio, *114–15,* 129, 138, 197

Raymond, Harry, 124–25, 128, 134, 138

Reader's Digest, 55, 224

recalls, 123, 311n19, 312n25. *See also* Shaw, Frank, recall campaign against

Red Cross, 206

Red Hill, 161. *See also* Edendale Communist community

Red Scare, 232–33

red-smear campaigns, 128–31, 152. *See also* anti-Communism

Red Song Book, 179

Red Squad: anti-Communist persecution by, 156, 157–59, 180; disbanding of, 164; leftist art destroyed by, 108; recall petition against, 312n23. *See also* Hynes, William; police brutality

Reed, John, 85. *See also* John Reed Club

reformers, as effeminate, 134–35

re-generate identity paradigm, 71, 72–73

Reisbord, Jeannette, 160, 161, 320n19

Reisbord, Samuel, 160, 320n19

Reisbord, Susan. *See* Martin, Susan

rent strikes, 153

Rhetta, Virgil, 167–68

Rhodes, Erik, 293n36

Richards, The Great, 35, 37. *See also* female impersonators

Rieger, Marilyn, 274–76, 277. *See also* Mattachine Society

riots: Manzanar riot (1942), 329n34; Zoot Suit Riots, 190–91, 204–205, 207

Ritchie, Janet Smith, 91

Ritchie, Ward: aesthetics of, 102; background of, 89–91, 116; on Club dues, 304n36; cultural significance of, 281–82; Edendale arts community and, 79, 80, 81, 82; on Landacre home, 112–13, 309n81; literary influences on, 102; professional organizations, 88, 89, *90,* 91–93. *See also* Edendale arts community

Ritchie's Roadhouse, *90,* 91

River, J. Paul de, 138

Rivera, Diego, 106

Riverside (CA), 144

Robbin, Ed, 176–77

municipal concerns about, 314n45; political linkage to Communism, 123, 135–38, *137*, 152; politicization of, 117; public curiosity about, 120; recall campaigns and, 312n25; sentences for, 146. *See also* homosexuality

sexual psychopath laws, 132, 141

Shaw, Frank: LAPD under, 314n45; political background, 123; recall campaign against, 123–27, 135–38, *137*, 153, 241, 312nn22–24, 313n30; Sex Bureau and, 132–33

Shaw, Joseph, 123, 125

Sheets, Millard: aesthetics of, 102–3; Edendale arts community and, 10, 81, 98; on federal art projects, 111; on Los Angeles arts centers, 84, 303n12; on Maitland, 305n41; paintings of, 10, 305n41; PWAP and, 109, 115–16; Siqueiros and, 107

Sherman, Miriam Brooks, *150*, 276; antiracist activism of, 189, 193, 194, 210, 331n57; as Communist activist, 10, 151–52, 153, 163, 165–67, *166*, 180, 181, 221; Communist Party social/cultural events and, 172–73, 174; impact of Cold War anti-Communism on, 225, 226–27, 321n33; later years of, 281; marriages of, 184; move to Edendale, 22, 151, 159–60, 320n20; on personal/political responsibilities, 183–84; political significance of, 281–82. *See also* Edendale Communist community

Shibley, George, 261

Shuler, Robert, 130, 136, *137*

Sides, Josh, 192, 194, 216, 333n76

Silver, Herman, 23

Silver Lake, 23, 278, 341n20

Silver Lake Boulevard, 12

Silver Lake Film Festival, 2

Simon, Raphael, 322n41

Sinclair, Upton, 128, 152–53, 164, 241

Siqueiros, David, 106–8, 175, 308n69

sissies, 36–38, 135–38, 146. *See also* effeminacy, male

Sitkoff, Harvard, 327n16

606 Club, 63

Sixth Street, 78, 109

Skrentny, John, 279

Sleepy Lagoon case, 16, 203–4, 210–13, *212*

Sleepy Lagoon Defense Committee (SLDC), 211–13, *212*

Slide, Anthony, 75

Smith, Gerald L. K., 16, 217, *218*, 220, 224, 332n66. *See also* Mobilization for Democracy

Smith, Janet, 91

Smith, Paul Jordan, 82, 91

Smith, Sarah Bixby, 82, 91

social Darwinism, 62

social movements, culture of, 323n64

sodomy laws, 44, 139, *140*, 144, 236. *See also* anal sex; oral sex; sex crimes

Soja, Edward, 12–13

Solomon, Mark, 192–93

Solovich, Don, 66–71, 148, 300n61

Somerville, Siobhan, 335n13

Southern California Civil Liberties Union, 157, 159. *See also* American Civil Liberties Union

Soviet Union, 128, 160, 167, 225, 233

Spanish Civil War, 167–68, 321n36

speakeasies. *See* bars/speakeasies

Sproul, Robert, 227

Stalin, Joseph, 136

Stanford University, Hay at, 238

Stanley, George, 93

Stansell, Christine, 85–86

Starr, Kevin, 83, 201, 301n7

Stein, Marc, 253

Stelzriede, John A. W., 300n61

Stendahl, Earl, 107

Stendahl Galleries, 99

Sternberg, Josef von, 107

Stevens, Konrad, 251, 256, 257, 259, 264. *See also* Mattachine Society

Stravinsky, Igor, 83

Street Meeting (mural; Siqueiros), 107

strikebreaking, 157–58

strikes, 153, 157

Struss, Karl, 95

Stuart, Gloria, 91, 304n30

student movement, 7

Subway Terminal Building, 49, 58

Sugahara, Keiichi ("Kay"), 203

Sunset Strip, 234
The Surprise of a Knight (pornographic film), 310n11
Surrealism, 97
Symbolism, 97
Synchronism, 97, 104

Takaki, Ronald, 215
Tarrow, Sidney, 13, 288–89n21
Tayama, Fred, 202–3, 329n34
Taylor, Charles, 5, 285–86n9
te-dansant parties, 57
temperamental, 336n18
Tenney, Jack, 205, 227
Terry, Jennifer, 292n30
Tess (nightclub owner), 234
thirdspaces, 13
Thomas Starr King Junior High School baseball team, *210*
Thompson, T. Matthew, 126
Three Comrades (pornographic film), 310n11
Tibbett, Lawrence, 301n7
Timmons, Stuart, 238, 336n14
Toledo Blade, 32, 291n22
Toll, Robert, 32–33
Townsend, Francis, 152
Trade Union Unity League, 163
Tropical America (mural; Siqueiros), 107
Truman, Harry S., 220
Tuttle, Frank, 172

Ullman, Sharon, 45, 47–48, 64, 65–66, 293–94n40
Ulrichs, Karl Heinrich, 292n30. *See also* sexology
Unemployed Councils, 153
unemployment, 157
United Front, 163
U.S. Congress, 201, 202
U.S. Employment Service, 216
U.S. Marines, 157–58
U.S. Office of War Information, 206
U.S. State Department, 246
U.S. Supreme Court, 201, 270, 278, 331n57
U.S. War Department, 200
University of California, 226–27

"Unofficial Map of Booklovers' Lane & Environs" (print; P. Landacre), *76*
Urban League, 207
urban subculture, 9

vagrancy, arrests for, 139, 140 ·
Vale, Joan, 34, 292n29, 293n38
Valentino, Rudolph, 26
Variety, 35, 75, 118–21, 122, 311n14
vaudeville: Eltinge in, 2–3, 26–33, 35–36, 38; female impersonators in, 3, 26, 32–33; stars recruited by film industry, 26
V Club (bar), 234
Venice Beach, 46–47
Verge, Arthur, 199
"vice dens," 124
vice police, 55, 121–22
Villa Capistrano (Los Angeles), 1–2, *40,* 42–43, 148, 294n4. *See also* Eltinge, Julian
Vitagraph (film company), 24

wage-labor system, 9
Waiting for Lefty (Odets), 240
Walcott Way, 78, 85
Waldorf (bar), 55, 298n33
Wallace, Henry, 245–46, 337n38
Walsh, Johnny, 234. *See also* Café Gala
war industry, race and, 194–95
War Manpower Commission, 205
"War on the Sex Criminal!" (Hoover), 132
Warren, Earl, 7, 202, 236
Warren, W. H., 63
Washington, DC, 264
Waugh, Thomas, 73
Webb, Michael, 168
Weber, Kem, 301n7
Weeks, Jeffrey, 5, 285n6, 287n13
West Adams, 220
West Coaster (magazine), 82
West Hollywood, 341n20
Westlake Park: art schools in, 10, 84; federal arts project offices in, 108–9, 110; homosexual activity in, 52, 132; sodomy arrests in, 142

Weston, Edward: aesthetics of, 102; Edendale arts community and, 81, 83, 87; in FAP, 109; on "the Run," 52–53
Wetzsteon, Ross, 13
white chauvinism, 221–23. *See also* Edendale Communist community, antiracist activism of
white supremacists, 221
Wild, Mark, 153
Wilde, Oscar, 65, 97
Wilkinson, A. M., 130
Wilshire district, 125
Winant, Howard, 191
Winters, Denny, 308n78
Wintner, Lee, 172
Witt, Stan, *230*
women: identity politics of, 271; minority status of, 260
Women Consumers' Educational League, 155
women's movement. *See* feminism
Wood, Gerald, 312n25
Workers Library, 194
Workers' Meeting (mural; Siqueiros), 107
Workers' School, 177
Works Progress Administration (WPA), 93, 108, 164. *See also* Federal Art Project; New Deal
World War II: African Americans' experience during, 215–16; Edendale arts community and, 91, 301n6; homosexuality as perceived during, 232; identity politics during, 227–28, 286n11; Japanese/Japanese Americans' experience during, 200–3, 215; Los Angeles

mobilization, 198–99; Mexicans/Mexican Americans' experience during, *188*, 203–6, 215; pluralism during, 327n16; post-war race relations, 16–17, 213–17; pre-war race relations, 196–98; racial conflicts during, 16, 186–87, 214, 265; racism and, 194–95, 334n86
Wright, Ada, 166
Wright, Lloyd, 301n7

Yankwich, Leon, 301n7
Yates, Peter, 82
Yoneda, Karl, 158, 202
Young Communist League, 151, 165, 173, 181
Young People's Socialist League, 83
Young Pioneers, 151, 165, 179, 181

Zamboni, Karl, 93, 302n8
Zamorano Club, 88
Zaretsky, Eli, 281
Zeitlin, Jake: aesthetics of, 102; background of, 22, 81; on bohemianism, 83; community generated by, 77, 87, 301n7, 303n22; cultural significance of, 281–82; economic support of, 304n37, 305n40; Edendale arts community and, 10, 79, 80, 82, 91; press label started by, 89; professional organizations, 88, 93, 94–95; rare book shop of, *76, 77*–78, 81, 302n8. *See also* Edendale arts community
Zoot Suit Riots, 190–91, 204–5, 207
Zornes, Milfred, 81, 102

Text:	11.25/13.5 Adobe Garamond
Display:	Adobe Garamond
Cartographer:	Bill Nelson
Compositor, printer, and binder:	Sheridan Book & Journal Services